Undisciplined Women
Tradition and Culture in Canada

DISCARD
RETIRÉ

Undisciplined Women, an interdisciplinary collection of twenty essays dealing with women and culture in Canada, explores a neglected area in folklore scholarship. Covering a range of subjects from female sailors to women preachers, contributors examine how women have been involved in identifying, collecting, and interpreting women's folklore, how various images of women have been created, used, and resisted, and how women transform their own – and others' – lives and culture.

Contributors demonstrate that informal traditional and popular expressive cultural forms continue to be central to Canadians' gender constructions and clearly display the creation and re-creation of women's often subordinate position in society. They not only explore positive and negative images of women – the witch, the Icelandic Mountain Woman, and the Hollywood "killer dyke," but also examine how women – taxi drivers, quilters, spiritual healers, and storytellers – negotiate and remake these images in their lives and work. Contributors also propose models for facilitating feminist dialogue on traditional and popular culture in Canada.

Drawing on perspectives from women's studies, folklore, anthropology, sociology, art history, literature, and religious studies, *Undisciplined Women* is an insightful exploration of the multiplicity of women's experiences and the importance of reclaiming women's cultures and traditions.

PAULINE GREENHILL is professor of women's studies and anthropology, University of Winnipeg.

DIANE TYE is assistant professor of folklore, Memorial University of Newfoundland.

Undisciplined Women

Tradition and Culture in Canada

EDITED BY
PAULINE GREENHILL
AND DIANE TYE

McGill-Queen's University Press
Montreal & Kingston · London · Buffalo

© McGill-Queen's University Press 1997
ISBN 0-7735-1614-x (cloth)
ISBN 0-7735-1615-8 (paper)

Legal deposit fourth quarter 1997
Bibliothèque nationale du Québec

Printed in Canada on acid-free paper

This book has been published with the help of a grant
from the Humanities and Social Sciences Federation of
Canada, using funds provided by the Social Sciences
and Humanities Research Council of Canada.

McGill-Queen's University Press acknowledges the
support received for its publishing program from the
Canada Council's Block Grants program.

Canadian Cataloguing in Publication Data

Main entry under title:
    Undisciplined women : tradition and culture in Canada
    Includes bibliographical references and index.
    Includes some text in French.
    ISBN 0-7735-1614-x (bound) –
    ISBN 0-7735-1615-8 (pbk.)
    1. Women – Canada – Folklore. 2. Folklore – Canada.
    3. Women – Canada – Social life and customs.
    I. Greenhill, Pauline, 1955–   II. Tye, Diane, 1957–
    HQ1453.U53 1997   398'.082'0971   C97-900460-8

Typeset in Palatino 10/12
by Caractéra inc., Quebec City

Contents

Editors' Preface and
Acknowledgments

This book was conceived in a cafe in Tatamagouche, Nova Scotia, in June 1990. We (the book's organizers and editors, Diane Tye and Pauline Greenhill) were on our way to Prince Edward Island for a holiday, after attending the annual meeting of the Folklore Studies Association of Canada/Association canadienne d'ethnologie et de folklore (FSAC/ACEF) in Moncton, New Brunswick. We are both trained as folklorists – which means that we view folklore as the material itself (popular as well as traditional culture) and as a scholarly study – and at the time we were both working in Canadian studies programs, Diane at Mount Allison University in Sackville, New Brunswick; Pauline at the University of Waterloo in Ontario. But intellectually we had begun to locate ourselves outside our discipline and were finding ourselves in women's studies, drawing increasingly upon feminist perspectives in our own work. Feminism, we were discovering, offered a voice we had not heard from in Canadian studies or in folklore.

Folklorists, unlike scholars in other disciplines, are very rarely surrounded by departments full of like-minded, similarly trained individuals. Most who are lucky enough to have academic jobs are the only folklorists in their universities, and many others work in similar isolation in museums, art galleries, government agencies, and the private sector. So even though the two of us were on holiday, we seized the opportunity to talk about our common academic concerns. As we considered the standard works in Canadian folklore studies, we began to notice the gaps in awareness of the discipline's history

and theoretical perspectives, the omission of women, and the androcentrism that have characterised the field. More and more keenly, we
felt that Canadian folklore studies had both neglected women's traditions and ignored feminist perspectives. We wished to redress this
situation, not only for the benefit of students of traditional and popular culture but also for those interested in Canadian society and
women. We began to envision a book that would highlight female
experiences of traditional culture from feminist viewpoints and
would be a resource for women's studies, Canadian studies, and
folklore.[1] The voice offered by feminism was one we wanted to use
to say the kinds of things we felt.

We first thought that we would simply gather and publish a collection of those few articles that featured Canadian women performers and presenters of traditional culture. In an introduction, we
would point out their implicit focus on women's folklore and draw
attention to the need for more study. However, we quickly realized
that such an anthology would be problematic. While reissue would
make early studies more readily available, their ideological and geographical biases would neither represent contemporary or feminist
perspectives nor adequately reflect the diversity of women and their
sociocultural traditions in Canada.

After meeting six months later to discuss the project in more detail,
we sent out a call for papers to be given at the October 1991 joint
meetings of FSAC/ACEF and the American Folklore Society in St
John's, Newfoundland, on the subject of women and traditional culture in Canada. We also organized a forum to consider the possibilities for a book. This volume was born from the resulting four panels
and discussion. At the latter, in fact, the book's godmother, American
folklorist Elaine K. Miller, proposed its name. Many of those attending – some of whom are contributors to the book – had commented
on the discipline of folklore and its lack of recognition of women's
culture, women collectors' contributions, and feminist perspectives.
Elaine suggested that we should call the book "Undisciplined
Women," both to recognize this exclusion of women and feminism
and to mark our resistance to it.[2] Reaction was generally – if not
unanimously – positive, and the book was named.

Subsequently, we tried to address lacunae in the core material. To
supplement papers presented at the 1991 meeting, we solicited the
involvement of various scholars. Some people wrote to us, asking to
be part of the collective. Several presented their work to the group
at later meetings of FSAC/ACEF in 1992 and 1993. Throughout the
preparation of this collection, women in various Canadian locations
met periodically to discuss the book, the individual papers, and the

issues of their own "undisciplined" locations – marginalization, joblessness, trivialization, and so on. Gathering at academic meetings – including the Learned Societies in Charlottetown in 1992 and in Ottawa in 1993 – as well as in homes and around restaurant and cafeteria tables, the "Undisciplined Women Collective" became a contingently organized group intent on critically redefining folklore, Canadian studies, and women's studies while linking the three. In order to ensure that the book we produced was truly collective, the Undisciplined Women not only met face to face at every opportunity but we also circulated the entire collection to each contributor after the initial round of gathering material. The resulting commentaries further changed the directions of individual papers and of the book as a whole. The book began to take shape around three foci: women folklorists, images of women, and women's traditions.

The contributors felt strongly that in order to show the complexity of the issues involved it was necessary to consider a broad variety of women's contributions to traditional and popular culture. To exclude a consideration of women's roles in collecting would not only obscure some of the historic biases in Canadian folklore but also ignore some possible alternative theories and methodologies. Ideas about women as scholars and writers, the subject of the first section, led to looking at the variety of other cultural constructions that pertain to gender, from dancing, to rituals, to stories, in the second section. And both suggested the third section's concern with resistance and alternatives.

Each area developed as we read, discussed, and commented upon each others' work. Initially, Diane and Pauline had thought of women folklorists in professional academic terms. But as contributors began to talk about the exclusions this implied, the collective turned to rethinking and re-evaluating not only those women who had been marginalized within university contexts, like Edith Fowke and Catherine Jolicœur, but also those who worked outside academic locations entirely, like Jean Heffernan, who wrote community interest columns for her local weekly newspaper. Our first section's act of indiscipline, then, is to include as significant and valid collectors and (re)presenters of traditional and popular culture not only those women associated with the academy but also those who have never been near it. And our writers in that section – as well as in the others – are also variously placed in and around the academy and the discipline.

The images section began as a collection of negative portrayals of women, with the women's traditions section as their more positive counterpart. However, the collaborative process made it clear that such simple dichotomies would not work, and the oppositions between these sections, though useful starting points, became less significant than their overlaps and interrelationships. Canadian society provides an extremely wide variety of conceptions of women, changing through time and across regions and ethnic groups. The judgement that any one image – the witch, the *fjallkona*, the killer dyke, and so on – is univocally bad indicates a lack of understanding of how these images have developed, and how they have been deployed. The indiscipline of the second section, then, is to open our exploration of cultural constructions and perceptions of women to a range of possibilities and of valences.

Similarly, in their own traditions, women's resistance has as often – perhaps even more often – been co-opted or used to maintain the status quo as it has enabled substantive change in women's material and social conditions. Resistance's effectiveness cannot always be judged immediately or univocally. Our indiscipline is to offer these possibilities, unrestricted by justifications. Women's actions can be resistant even without, for example, the formation of effective legal challenges (in the face of sexual harassment), the production of efficacious healing (somatically speaking), the creation of beautiful quilts (by fine art standards), and so on. The writers in this section take a longer view, one which takes a variety of potentialities and prospects into account. Finally, the collective's work made it obvious that the very acts of gathering, representing, and theorizing culture are linked to particular images of women and their roles, and that resistance to constraint is as evident in women folklorists' and collectors' research activities as it is in the materials they collect and how they analyse them.

As is appropriate in feminist work, these intellectual reflections led to re-examinations of the experiences of the contributors. In what has been one of the most exciting, empowering and, we hope, lasting aspects of this collaboration, almost all of the writers represented here have discovered a new pride in women's undisciplined traditions – which present alternatives to the mainstream – and appreciation for their own status as undisciplined scholars – too often positioned outside academe. Collaboration on *Undisciplined Women* has strengthened the Undisciplined Women Collective's commitment to profoundly changing the paradigms of conventional academic folklore in this country as well as to developing concepts of traditional and popular culture in women's studies and Canadian studies.

Though *Undisciplined Women* speaks with a variety of voices that reflect multiple disciplinary and interdisciplinary perspectives, each presents a new contribution to the understanding of Canadian traditional and popular culture. Contributors represent sociology, social psychology, literature, art history, anthropology, and history as well as folklore, Canadian studies, and women's studies. They are professors, students, museum workers, librarians, and private scholars. Some describe themselves as committed feminists; others find the term and its connotations problematic. We did not try to edit this collection so as to discipline this chorus and disguise or subvert the contributors' collective pluralism. Such divergent approaches and opposing views will help develop Canadian folklore studies as a lively (inter)discipline, rather than the moribund imposition of functionalist consensus by the powerful which currently characterizes too much work in the area. As this can only be a prelude to Canadian women's folklore studies and feminist folkloristics in Canada, our intention is to foster discussion that will undoubtedly provide useful, meaningful, and plural models.

We are proud of the range of ethnic groups, regions, and sexual orientations presented by *Undisciplined Women*'s contributors and their subjects. We are proud that the contributors have spoken out, many for the first time in public, on issues of personal and social concern. We are proud that many have chosen to represent themselves and their works in modes that are experimental or unconventional. We think this is a much better book for its variety of perspectives and range of topics, although we wish we had succeeded in locating and eliciting even more diverse material. We had hoped, for example, to include work by aboriginal women, women of colour, and minority ethnic women who study their own culture. We wanted examples exploring a broader range of lesbian women's traditions. We envisioned the collection reflecting Canada's regional and cultural diversity more accurately: we would have liked more French language material and also more from western and northern areas.

These omissions result from a variety of forces, including but not limited to the domination of academic work by whiteness and the power/knowledge base that it implies; the literal as well as figurative lack of understanding between anglophone and francophone scholars, and too frequent unidirectional discussion in which francophones are forced to speak English in order to be heard; and, until recently, a scholarly silence on issues of sexual orientation. But we sincerely hope this won't be the last word and that scholars will take up this collection's explicit and collective challenges by attending more thoroughly to the issues of gender, sexuality, ethnicity, and so on raised here.

We have reason to believe that the indisciplining of Canadian folklore will prove fruitful. Since we began this collection, feminist folklorists in the United States have produced several works that we feel share many of our aims (as well as our collective format), including Radner's *Feminist Messages* (1993), Young's *Bodylore* (1993) and Hollis, Pershing, and Young's *Feminist Theory and the Study of Folklore* (1994). Diane, Pauline, and several of our undisciplined contributors have also participated in a special issue of *Canadian Folklore canadien* on "Femmes et traditions/Women and Traditions," edited by Jocelyne Mathieu. These works not only include women folklorists and women subjects in the mainstream of folklore – rather than as special topics or theoretical alternatives – but also take into account the political implications of folklorists' positions and practices, as we want to do here. By showing the (inter)(un)disciplined alternatives we see as imperative, we are asking for the dismantling of the functionalist, anti-Canadian, exclusive, hegemonic role of the discipline in English Canada. But however tempting it may be to suggest that English Canadian folklore has been a substantive and theoretical disappointment, we don't wish to dismantle it entirely. Instead we offer what we hope are intellectual challenges to the status quo that will be so valuable as to prove their own justification and will be incorporated into how folklore is done here.

One of the readers of this manuscript for the Publications of the American Folklore Society[3] challenged us to be even more unruly, unconventional, and insurrectionist. The context of folklore in the U.S. is quite different: feminist readings and feminist practice are now part of the American folklore scene. Alas, this is not the case in Canada. Initially, our collaborators were unruly, unconventional, and insurrectionist simply by gathering as women doing women-centred or feminist work. While Diane and Pauline are glad to be encouraged to take more risks with our work, the results will not resemble those of our American predecessors. No Ellen Stekert has yet come forward to challenge the sexism of our Richard Dorsons (see Stekert 1988), though Laurel Doucette has challenged the immorality and political vacuousness of folklore's disciplinary conventions. No international range of topics will address our concerns: internationalism – as ignorance of local and national contexts – is one of the Canadian disciplinary conventions we plan to flout. Of course, there is a great deal more to be done, but our small acts of rebellion here will, we hope, inspire a later revolution.

Diane and Pauline thank all the contributors to this volume for their hard work, perseverance, and patience with a lengthy process of discussion, revision, and collective critique. We hope they agree that while feminist methodology is not without its problems, true collaboration is rewarding in the end. Laurel Doucette deserves special recognition for keeping this project on track and in continuous engagement with the most important issues. We've drawn extensively on her experience and knowledge, and benefitted immeasurably from it. The anonymous readers for PAFS and the Aid to Scholarly Publications Program gave us the kind of critique that improves a work, being both challenging and enthusiastic. We appreciate the sensitive and careful copyediting of Sarah Wight (English essays) and Helen Paré (French essays). Rita Campbell composed the index. And we thank Elaine K. Miller for naming the book.

The Secretary of State's Intercultural/Interregional Exchange Program of the Association for Canadian Studies funded two of our visits to develop the project. Our research was in part supported by Diane's postdoctoral fellowship and Pauline's research grant, both from the Social Science and Humanities Research Council of Canada. We gratefully acknowledge their backing.

NOTES

1 Two earlier publications (Greenhill and Tye 1993 and 1994) similarly addressed feminist folkloristics and folklore of women in Canada.
2 Throughout the book we use "discipline" to mean academic discipline. While we recognize an academic disciplining of practice as discipline in Foucault's sense, this is not at all an exploration of Foucault's idea of discipline per se. Rather, it is an exploration of Canadian folklore as a discipline.
3 Now, alas, defunct.

Undisciplined Women

Introduction

This book locates the intersection of three all too often marginalized areas of academic inquiry – folklore, women, and Canada. These areas of theoretical and substantive concern are made peripheral by assumptions that "real" culture (fine arts, mainstream materials, and even mass culture), men (their persons and productions), and the international are somehow more significant, more universal, more valuable. *Undisciplined Women* counters these tendencies by attending to and celebrating the traditional and popular, the female, and the local. It also addresses lacunae within those marginalized (inter)disciplines which were themselves formed to deal with these absences: folklore, women's studies, and Canadian studies. Canadian studies, for example, has looked primarily at master narratives, women's studies has too often constructed feminist monoliths (as opposed to pluralities), and folklore has almost completely ignored Canadian women.

The solution we present here is multidisciplinary – drawing upon a series of academic disciplines to approach common territory – as well as interdisciplinary – critiquing disciplinary perspectives and creating alternatives. Although individual contributors draw upon their own disciplines' ideas, theories, and constructs, they also link their analysis with other perspectives. The introductory essays not only focus on the parallels between these specialists' works but also locate a field of collective study – Canadian women's traditions – and question the notion of disciplinarity itself.

THE CONCEPT OF FOLKLORE

For many Canadians the terms "traditional culture" and "folklore" – which can be considered interchangeable – carry connotations of antiquated thinking. Readers might ask why this "old stuff" is relevant given the important battles women continually wage to gain control over their own bodies, to earn a living free from sexual harassment, and to locate adequate day care for their children, to give only a few examples. Yet such political, economic, and social issues cannot be separated from the conventional attitudes that engender and support them. These attitudes are pervasively expressed in folklore.

Traditional culture also offers women opportunities to resist oppression. Women's experiences of confronting domestic violence, for example, show both that what has remained (publicly) unspoken and unnoticed is very powerful, and that speaking out, which often involves the traditional activity of telling one's own story, is usually the first step toward action. As Cynthia Boyd indicates, women's stories of sexual harassment on the job have multiple uses, though action – political, legal, and so on – is still necessary to redress the situation itself. And Laurel Doucette's paper is an object lesson in the insight that telling and doing can be interwoven in academic practice.

In *Undisciplined Women* contributors break many kinds of silences – originating in or emanating from language difference, coercion, complicity, and stubbornness, among others – as we strive to raise awareness of what is usually unconscious and to articulate what often goes unvoiced. Informal traditional and popular expressive cultural forms – folklore – have been and continue to be central in Canadians' gender construction and clearly display the creation and recreation of women's often subordinate position. Folklore also offers Canadian women opportunities to express solidarity with each other, and with some men, as in Vivian Labrie's paper, to ensure their social and psychological stability, as in Diane Tye's paper, as well as to resist patriarchy and introduce change, as in Kay Stone's paper.[1]

Folklore is shared communication and expression within sociocultural groups. Describing it as "the way in which you and I are creative, clever, and artistic in our everyday lives" (Taft 1983:12) conveys a sense of its broad range. Everyone knows about and participates in a variety of rituals, skills, and creative expressions. Folklore happens whenever people gather to celebrate, as in the mock weddings discussed by Michael Taft, to practice their religion, as in Gail Grant's paper on charismatic healing and Pamela Klassen's on a woman preacher, to dance, as in Barbara LeBlanc's work on Acadia, or just to talk, as discussed by Cynthia Boyd on cab drivers and Marie-Annick Desplanques on Newfoundland women's gatherings. Folklore also happens when people are expressing their ethnicity, like the Icelandic-Canadians discussed by Anne Brydon, or doing conventionally "folky" stuff such as quilting, discussed by Susan Shantz, or singing old ballads, discussed by Pauline Greenhill.

As a form of cultural expression folklore may be frustratingly hard to pin down, but enumerative definitions are too limiting. One list cannot include everything. Because not all traditional and popular culture is old, folklore studies must constantly expand to accommodate new materials as diverse as the bureaucratic culture commented on by Vivian Labrie or the Inuit written autobiographies discussed by Robin McGrath. As American folklorist Elliott Oring says, "the field is still being mapped and any hard and fast definition is likely to prove partial, idiosyncratic, or inconsistent. What is necessary is an orientation ... based upon those concepts that seem to regularly inform the perspectives of folklorists in their research" (1986:17). He continues: "Folklorists seem to pursue reflections of the *communal* (a group or collective), the *common* (the everyday rather than the extraordinary), the *informal* (in relation to the formal and institutional), the *marginal* (in relation to the centres of power and privilege), the *personal* (communication face-to-face), the *traditional* (stable over time), the *aesthetic* (artistic expressions), and the *ideological* (expressions of belief and systems of knowledge)" (Ibid., 17–18). The undisciplined women contributors to this collection, like other folklore scholars, also attend at times to the individual, the uncommon, the formal, the impersonal, and the an/unaesthetic, but often so as to problematize them. Clearly folklore has been a theoretically flexible area of study.[2]

WOMEN'S STUDIES, CANADIAN STUDIES, AND INTERDISCIPLINARITY

Canadian studies has predominantly been conceptualized in terms of its relatively closed subject of study – Canada. Its practitioners have focused primarily upon examinations of literature, politics, and history. While some have devoted their attention to regionalism (Matthews 1983), and others to national identity and character (Atwood 1972), few beyond such notables as Northrop Frye, Harold Adams Innis, and Marshall McLuhan have burst the boundaries of their disciplines and ventured into synthesis. Canadian studies has remained essentially multidisciplinary.

Interdisciplinary areas such as women's studies tend to occupy the margins of academic discourse and practice. When success in teaching and research is evaluated within the conventional paradigm of discipline-based "normal science" (Kuhn 1970), interdisciplinary perspectives are often presumed to be insignificant, incomprehensible, or both. But being marginal can have advantages. When unfettered by disciplinary hegemony, interdisciplinary scholars can choose theoretical perspectives and subject matter independent of disciplinary histories or worldviews and thus present unique intellectual contributions as well as challenge disciplinary boundaries. In fact, anthropologist Clifford Geertz asserts that current tendencies toward the "refiguration of social thought" (1980:165) have blurred the disciplinary distinctions between humanistic studies and social sciences. He cites (among others): "baroque fantasies presented as deadpan empirical observations (Borges, Barthelme), histories that consist of equation and tables or law court testimony (Fogel and Engerman, Le Roi Ladurie), documentaries that read like true confessions (Mailer), parables posing as ethnographies (Castaneda), theoretical treatises set out as travelogues (Lévi-Strauss), [and] ideological arguments cast as historical inquiries (Edward Said)" (Ibid., 165–6). Interdisciplinarity, then, exists as a critique of and alternative to traditional disciplines' approaches. Several of the studies in *Undisciplined Women* use notions from folklore studies to critique other disciplines. For example, Susan Shantz's work criticizes fine arts notions of aesthetics, and Pamela Klassen's analysis redresses the lack of focus upon women's spirituality in religious studies.

Though some advocates for interdisciplinarity may try to fight for inclusion in the existing hierarchy, others do not attempt to appropriate power but instead present innovative, radical, and sometimes startling alternatives. Rather than seeking a place in the hegemonic sun, they find their own sources of light. Feminist scholar Trinh Minh-Ha comments:

Interdisciplinarity is … not just a question of putting several fields together, so that individuals can share their specialised knowledge and converse with one another within their expertise. It is to create in sharing a field that belongs to no one, not even to those who create it. What is at stake, therefore, in this inter-creation is the very notion of *specialisation* and of *expertise*, of *discipline* and *professionalism*. To identify oneself with a position of specialised knowledge, to see oneself as an expert or as an authority on certain matters … is to give up all attempts at understanding relations in the game of power. To survive, to live with heterogeneity, [is to be] necessarily polyvalent in … skills, … function, … role. (Trinh 1991:108)

The very marginalization of women's studies has been its source of strength. Since its adherents have not had to pretend rhetorical allegiance to academic convention, they have developed distinctive perspectives (including those from communities outside universities) and yet remained critically engaged with conventional disciplines. As feminist scholars have pointed out, academics have too often simply researched men and assumed that their results applied equally well to women. Feminist theorists have shown the intrinsic value of considering women's experiences and have established a discursive centre for women as scholars as well as subjects of study, both of which roles are addressed here.

THE LINKAGES: CANADIAN WOMEN'S FOLKLORE

Canadian folklore scholarship has generally overlooked women's traditions or underestimated their significance. A few important studies (e.g., Pocius 1976; Kirshenblatt-Gimblett 1975) have included considerations of women performers and their gendered roles (see Greenhill and Tye 1994), but a first task for Canadian folklore studies will be to recover women's traditions – simply to describe those forms and processes that have been ignored, as Jocelyne Mathieu does in showing how wardrobe traditions have developed in changing social circumstances. Other essential aspects of feminist scholarship include critique of patriarchal scholarship (Barbara Rieti shows a variety of possible meanings for Newfoundland witches); reassessment of women's scholarly work (Ronald Labelle describes the life's work of Catherine Jolicœur, and Christine St. Peter reconsiders the controversies surrounding Anne Cameron's *Daughters of Copper Woman*); and gynocriticism, creating new, feminist scholarship (Kay Stone discusses storytellers' conscious rebellions against interpretation, in counterpart with her own).[3] While there may appear to be a hierarchical and chronological relationship between these scholarly processes, each element implies at least one other – gynocriticism depends upon critique and reassessment, recovery leads to critique, and so on.

Clearly, talking about, analysing, and recovering women's traditional and popular culture – filling the lacunae where women's communication and expression have been ignored – are necessary steps. In the opening section, Edith Fowke's account of her life as a collector and disseminator of folklore, Ronald Labelle's consideration of Catherine Jolicœur's œuvre, and Diane Tye's examination of Jean Heffernan begin the work of recovering and reassessing women's contributions to the study of traditional and popular culture. Recovery is also an issue elsewhere in this volume, for example when Janice Ristock shows the value of looking at all women's stories of domestic abuse, or Jocelyne Mathieu considers women's dress as an indicator of tradition.

However, as Laurel Doucette's opening chapter argues, analysts of cultural processes must go beyond recovering and describing the folklore of women and begin developing and using a model of feminist folklore studies. Diane Tye's evaluation of the feminist aspects of Jean Heffernan's work and Christine St. Peter's consideration of the inclusion and exclusion of aboriginal and non-aboriginal women in the communication of aboriginal culture suggest possible directions. They exemplify ideas, alternatives, and concepts which will be of particular interest to feminist folklorists seeking alternatives to the academic status quo.

A "folklore of women" approach can be seen in Barbara LeBlanc's contribution, which primarily describes distinctions between heterosexual women's and men's cultures, showing that many similarities – and differences – between the sexes can't simply be assumed. Pauline Greenhill and Michael Taft similarly recover and describe representations implicating a variety of sexual orientations. But the work of Anne Brydon, Barbara Rieti, Janice Ristock, and Vivian Labrie is implicitly and sometimes unequivocally direction-setting for feminist folkloristics in its juxtaposition of a variety of genres, perspectives, and types of materials. Each relates some aspect of traditional and popular culture – the figure of the *fjallkona*, stories about witches, narratives of women in abusive lesbian relationships, and traditional folktales – to a profoundly different aspect – the sexuality/sexualization of nationalism and ethnicity, (male) abuse of women, popular films and popular understandings of lesbian lives, and bureaucratic office culture. Rather than focusing primarily on one aspect of women's folklore, or on the representation of women in folklore, these works exemplify feminist principles in arguing the interconnections of patriarchy and women's experience. Clearly, these papers, like those of the first section, demonstrate that both folklore of women and feminist folklore are necessary, and perhaps even mutually dependent.

All the writers included in the final section open with a recovery of women's own traditions. Contributors present the extradisciplinary and the undisciplined: quilting, making clothing, healing, negotiating work roles, preaching, talking, and storytelling. They also show how women use these forms to assert themselves, undermining patriarchy and validating themselves through creative practices and communication. Thus, each article presents a polemically feminist reading of folklore.

Women rely on traditional culture for a variety of purposes, such as to express group solidarity (Marie-Annick Desplanques), to make individual statements (Robin McGrath), or even to produce somatic effects (Gail Grant). Women's folklore is not just a passive reflection of sociocultural norms but can be an active agent for social change, as when the woman described by Pamela Klassen counters stereotypes by preaching publicly in church. Social change is also implicit in the gender-bending of mock weddings (Taft) or cross-dressing ballads (Greenhill), or when women like Edith Fowke overcome obstacles to find a niche in an academic field like folklore studies.

FEMINIST FOLKLORISTICS AS INTERDISCIPLINARITY

The notion of interdisciplinarity is part of what makes this book, its contributors, and its subjects "undisciplined." They present undisciplinarity/interdisciplinarity as intellectual alternatives to the disciplines and as bases for theoretical and methodological innovation. They see a need to diverge from current directions of research on folklore and on Canada and add further depth to studies of women. The academic options, as well as the national political options, are to follow diversity to fragmentation – whether it involves women vs men, French vs English, or some other division – or to use it to develop pluralism. Contributors to *Undisciplined Women* prefer the latter. Thus the articles here explore power issues as they pertain to theorists and collectors – academics, students, interested and committed community workers – as well as to the people they work with – (re)creators and owners of traditional culture. For example the appropriation by academics and other European-origin peoples of the heritage of First Nations is an issue folklorists must address (see St. Peter), while at the same time academics must value the marginalised traditions of marginalised peoples (see McGrath). Or the place of traditional culture in enabling or perpetrating violence against and harassment of women (see Rieti and Boyd) must be juxtaposed with folkloric texts which refuse stereotypes (see Greenhill) or show their complex valences (see Stone).

As much as *Undisciplined Women*'s contributors seek alternatives to disciplinarity, they also seek alternatives to being disciplined. Much work here is experimental (as in Shantz's dialogues), unorthodox, quirky, or blurred (as in Labrie's conflation of folktale and film plots), perverse (as in Greenhill's queer reading of cross-dressing ballads), advocates the violation of canons of theory (Doucette), method (Tye), or material (Ristock), or is otherwise inspired by the wonderful, the dreadful, the daunting, the irritating paraphernalia of feminist discourse. Writers represented here have personalized their analysis, positioning themselves individually and historically with respect to their research, often in terms of a critical relationship to structures of authority, including their disciplines. In a way, *Undisciplined Women* is planting a *níðstöng* – a pole into which an insult or defamation is carved (see Brydon) – to folklore studies in Canada. But its contributors are also suggesting alternatives.

Folklore needs to discover new theory in description and methodology by considering such neglected questions as how Canadian women's gender is constructed in and through folkloric communication (see for example Doucette, Tye, Brydon, LeBlanc, Desplanques, and Mathieu). Perspectives must include the plurality of women's experience and the fact that traditional symbolic constructions can celebrate the distinctiveness of women's culture (see Shantz and Taft) or allow women to appropriate other symbolic domains, including men's (see McGrath and Klassen).

The contributors hope this book responds to the challenges we see in studies of Canadian traditional and popular culture. We want to suggest models for recovering women's traditions and also for facilitating feminist dialogue on traditional culture in Canada. Focusing on traditions encourages feminist scholars to pay more attention to the multiplicity of women's everyday experiences and to value their individual and collective creativity. Folklorists can contribute to this process because historically they have been alert to the intrinsic worth of traditional and popular cultural expressions and to the necessity of understanding these materials' origins, structures, meanings, and contexts. As well, those who study traditional culture are accustomed to listening to voices that are too often excluded from central, public discourses. Since folklorists frequently work in rural, ethnic, and other enclaves, their subjects of study tend to be dominated peoples and discourses. Thus, whatever their previous neglect of this area, folklorists are primed to be sensitive to women and their sociocultural position.

Canadian studies, too, can benefit from an increased understanding of marginalized forms of culture as well as of the sociocultural creations of more than half the population. In examining not only women's traditions but also women's scholarship, Canadian studies may locate distinctive theoretical models. Women's everyday lives and their creative expressions are linked in traditional and popular culture. We are convinced that "old wives' tales" and other forms of women's folklore are telling, reasonable, and significant interpretations of women's experiences. They are central to an understanding of women's culture, as well as to a demystification of women's and men's places in the world.

Ultimately, the contributors hope to show more than simply how women have contributed to the collection and (re)presentation of traditional and popular culture (the first group of essays), how women are depicted in folklore (the second group of essays), and how women have created distinctive traditional and popular culture (the third group of essays). They concern themselves not only with the Canadian feminist constitution of folklore but with the Canadian folklore constitution of feminism and the folklore feminist constitution of Canada. *Undisciplined Women* (re)invents women, folklorists, Canadians, and the linkages between the three.

NOTES

1 For other examples of alternative readings of women's folklore, see Radner (1993).
2 Laurel Doucette in this volume reviews some of the most influential theories for folkloristics. For a discussion of folklore's relationship to postmodernism, see Workman (1989) and Warshaver (1991).
3 For more extensive discussion of these processes, see Finn (1993) and Sachs (1993). See also Gilbert and Gubar (1985).

PART ONE

Identifying, Collecting, and Interpreting Women's Folklore

Many Canadians can identify women who influenced their knowledge of traditional culture. Popularly known folklorists, like Helen Creighton and Edith Fowke, who have published books on the subject, may come to mind immediately. But many might also think of lesser-known community collectors who have written local histories or weekly newspaper columns, or of family members – mothers, grandmothers, aunts, or sisters – who preserved family photograph albums or stories about ancestors. All these women developed and shared their knowledge in ways that helped to shape others' identities. Yet their contributions have been underestimated by too many of those engaged in the academic study of folklore in Canada.

The lack of recognition of women's work as collectors and disseminators of traditional and popular culture may not be surprising in the context of the history of other academic disciplines where women's voices were muted as well, but it is particularly ironic in a country where popular understanding of folklore draws on the well-known publications and recordings compiled by women such as Creighton and Fowke. Thus this book opens with a section that explores the place of women collectors and interpreters within Canadian folkloristics. Working toward a better understanding and appreciation of their efforts, it locates them in the context of the discipline's inclusions and exclusions of gender, politics, colonialism, and other areas of possible consideration. As the other sections demonstrate, the gender of collectors can influence both what they find and how they interpret it.

Within the Canadian context there has been a clear discursive struggle played out between folklore as academic study – a largely male-dominated activity – and as non-academic collection – generally a female domain – that dates at least from the establishment of folklore archives and/or departments at Laval University in 1944 and Memorial University of Newfoundland (MUN) in 1968. Centres for folklore study in English Canada have not yet provided sustained support for women's collecting efforts, appreciation for women's contributions, or jobs for the multitude of Canadian female Ph.D. graduates they have produced. Notwithstanding large numbers of female graduate students, academic departments of folklore in Canada remain predominantly male. Elli-Kaija Kongas-Maranda (1932–1982), the first woman to be given a regular faculty position in a Canadian folklore program, began teaching at Laval only in 1976. A full ten years later, the Folklore Department at Memorial University of Newfoundland hired its first female member (now tenured) in their ten-person faculty.[1]

This situation has meant that most women have collected without permanent institutional affiliation and with few funding possibilities. Some early fieldworkers were able to take advantage of National Museum funding, administered by its director, Marius Barbeau.[2] For example, several contracts from the museum and from the Library of Congress in Washington, D.C., beginning in 1942, assisted Helen Creighton in amassing her impressive collection of Maritime traditional culture. However, once the Canadian Centre for Folk Culture Studies (CCFCS) was established in the 1970s at the museum (now the Canadian Museum of Civilization), non-academic Canadians, many of them women like Creighton, who had been collecting folklore for little or no financial reward, were largely replaced by visiting American funded academics, usually male.[3] The practice reflected the growing value placed on academic education and preference for outsiders' credentials to compile Canadian collections, trends Laurel Doucette documents in her article in this section.

Some academic folklorists have found the work of the popularly known Canadian folklore researchers problematic. The situation was not unlike that in the United States, where from the 1960s until very recently academics tried to confirm their professionalization by separating themselves from "popularizers" (see Dorson 1976). Too often (usually male) academics dismissed (usually female) non-academics' work as lacking seriousness. They saw it as atheoretical, as evidence that these collectors failed to understand what folklore really is. Retrospective consideration recognizes these academic judgements as flawed. Such notions of "what is theory" and "what is folklore" are linked with gender bias. As feminist theorist Chris Weedon suggests: "It is no coincidence that ... theorists are all men; this is a consequence of the gender relations which have structured women's absence from the active production of most theory within a whole range of discourses over the last 300 years. It is also a mark of the particular conditions under which prestigious and powerful bodies of knowledge were and are produced. This is manifest in the professional institutions of science, social science, medicine and the humanities which exclude alternative forms of knowledge, in particular those produced by women under different social conditions of knowledge production" (1987:13). But as Doucette's paper argues, in Canada cultural colonialism is equally implicated in ideas of folklore and theory.

In this opening section, writers identify ways in which a patriarchal, anti-Canadian academic system alternatively appropriated the work of women academic and community collectors and dismissed or undervalued it.[4] Contributors also assert that Canadian folkloristics as practised by women enthusiasts and collectors is not only ideological, but also fundamentally – if implicitly – theoretical. These observations on folklore research done by women in Canada shed light on the nature of folklore studies and other theoretical discourses in this country.

The women whose labours are highlighted here – Edith Fowke, Catherine Jolicœur, Jean Heffernan, and Anne Cameron – are just four of the many who collected folklore in Canada. The ways they wove their complex understandings of traditional culture into family and community educational, religious, and artistic life provide inspiration for researchers who want to explore the significance of women's contributions to scholarship. This group and their works suggest that the recovery and reassessment process must include women whose fieldwork was subsumed at times by other activities, as well as those for whom collecting was absolutely central to their lives. Both Laurel Doucette and Christine St. Peter also point out that the act of collecting traditional and popular culture is not an apolitical or unproblematic task.

The section begins with a pioneering critique of current directions in mainstream Canadian folklore studies by Doucette, a doctoral graduate of the MUN folklore department. Her examination of Canadian women's exclusion from and/or marginalization in folklore studies offers alternatives that draw on feminist theory, analysis, and methodology. Following this critical overview we are privileged to include the late Edith Fowke's first-hand account of her history as a woman who has been integral to the collection and dissemination of

Canadian folklore. She and colleagues like Creighton (1899–1990) were among Canada's most productive fieldworkers and are certainly the best known nationally and internationally. Her opinions on traditional culture might not be shared by most contributors to *Undisciplined Women*, but Fowke was herself, as her comments show, a quintessential undisciplined woman. Ronald Labelle's article on Catherine Jolicœur offers an account of her life and life's work. Trained at Laval, Jolicœur compiled an extensive collection of Acadian legend traditions. Labelle, a doctoral student in history at the University of New Brunswick and folklore MA from Laval, who worked extensively with Jolicœur in his capacity as Director of the Centre d'études acadiennes explores her unique and significant contributions to Canadian traditional culture studies.[5]

With or without institutional support, women usually fit collecting around other responsibilities, in Jolicœur's case as a member of a religious order. Many women meshed their interest in traditional culture with research in local history, or employment as a newspaper correspondent, like Jean Heffernan, whose work is discussed and evaluated by Diane Tye, currently a tenure-track faculty member in the MUN folklore program. Moving Jean Heffernan and the multitude of other community collectors (e.g., Frances Fraser [1990], Marion Robertson [1991], Rona Rustige [1988]) from the margins to the centre foregrounds their insights into Canadian traditional and popular culture and provides a foundation for continuing discussion of the nature and treatment of the country's folklore. Such women fieldworkers developed particular skills because they were less removed from their communities of study than academically trained, foreign-born folklorists who often visited only briefly. Thus their wide-ranging portrayals of traditional and popular culture often deserve recognition for thorough and sensitive documentation.

Though this introduction sets up dichotomies between known and unknown collectors, academics and non-academics, it is their structural similarities and commonalities, contributors argue, that are most significant. All four women collectors discussed in this section demonstrated an interest in traditional culture that is motivated by a sense of the intrinsic as well as the national/regional/ethnic values of the material they gathered and (re)presented. All were in some sense marginalized by the academy, though Fowke and Jolicœur had associations with universities. Only Jolicœur had academic folklore training, though by focusing on typology she chose, like many other women academics, to work in an unconventional area of research.[6] Each worked with proximate culture: Fowke and Cameron in the provinces where they lived, Heffernan in her native Maritime community, and Jolicœur in French Canada. In a world where folklorists were by definition outsiders, these insider folklorists' very presence was alternative. Yet some of their collections are also uncommonly useful for current folklorists precisely because they well reflect regional repertoires, rather than being restricted by the now outdated academic ideologies of their times.

Moreover, much of the work by female community collectors foreshadows recent theoretical concepts. Reflexive/critical anthropological perspectives (e.g., Clifford and Marcus 1986) are prefigured by their active presences as both Selves – full members of the groups they studied – and Others – collectors who distanced themselves to engage in scholarly, popular, or journalistic discourse. As folklorists trained in contemporary techniques and with modern theoretical orientations begin the task of uncovering women's folklore, such researchers' work can provide models for understanding how people use their traditional culture, where and why it is performed, what it means, and the forms it takes.

We do not want to suggest that these women's works provide flawless sources, or that their research would fit current standards: rarely did they include information now considered vital – names, dates, places, and contexts of performance, among others. Especially as time separates us from the work, it is possible to identify biases that shaped interpretation. And the very processes of collection and publication themselves can be controversial. Thus this section ends with a critical assessment of writer Anne Cameron. From her perspective as a professor of women's studies, Christine St. Peter discusses the controversies surrounding Cameron's literary representation of aboriginal women's narratives.

Women folklore collectors' work cannot be incorporated uncritically into current scholarship; the contributors do not advocate an uncritical approach to the work of *any* scholar. Nor do we wish to diminish or overlook the work of male folklorists like Marius Barbeau, Luc Lacourcière, Herbert Halpert, and W. Roy Mackenzie.[7] But we do not think women's discourse should be summarily dismissed or repudiated. Instead we seek to emulate its open, diverse, and creative qualities. As this section's authors review the contributions of women to folklore collecting in Canada, we recognize the value of hearing many voices.[8] The re-evaluation and rehabilitation of folklore research done in the past by women are central to the theoretical refiguration that must take place within the academic study of folklore in Canada.

NOTES

1 The recent hiring of Diane Tye in that department may change its dynamics somewhat.

2 Not all early collectors were successful in tapping this funding source. For example, Louise Manny, who collected folksongs in New Brunswick, was never able to receive support from the National Museum (see Carmen Roy's letters to Helen Creighton 18 September 1958 and 5 April 1960, Public Archives of Nova Scotia MG1 vol 2817 #86). Manny's research was minimally funded by Lord Beaverbrook whose personal interest in native compositions only confined her collecting.

3 Now-established American folklorists who once did studies for CCFCS include Michael Owen Jones (1972) and Jan Harold Brunvand (1974). Hungarian-American Linda Dégh (1975) was the only woman contracted by CCFCS whose work was published in its Mercury Series in its first five years.

4 One of the most blatant examples of academic study appropriating women's work is found in those women who collected folklore with their husbands or partners. Like so much of women's work, their involvement usually goes unrecognized and instead is absorbed with little or no credit into the men's projects. W. Roy Mackenzie (1883–1957) is considered a pioneer in the collection of North American folksong. Reading his account of collecting along Nova Scotia's north shore in the early years of this century, one learns that his wife, Ethel Mackenzie (1884–1972), visited traditional singers with him and helped to take down the songs by hand as they were being performed – a task he found very difficult. Roy Mackenzie acknowledged that his wife's enthusiasm ensured that he finished the project (Mackenzie 1919:xi). Helen Creighton credited Ethel Mackenzie with first recognizing the richness of the repertoire and drawing her husband's attention to it (Creighton 1967:15). Yet Ethel Mackenzie's name is absent from the publications resulting from the fieldwork (Mackenzie 1919; 1928) and she does not share her husband's reputation as a pioneer of folklore research.

Similarly in Western Canada, James Teit (1864–1922), who collaborated with the famous anthropologist Franz Boas in studies of interior British Columbia Salish culture, had a unique perspective on and entrée into local women's culture through his Salish wife, Lucy Antko (c1865–1899). As a result, his portrayal of aboriginal women as "strong, independent, and fully-participating members of their community" (Wickwire 1993), as well as his attention to aspects of the culture which concerned women, from pictography to ethnobotany to basketry, is unique for his time. While Lucy Antko's help is seldom acknowledged,

James Teit is praised for his extensive knowledge of the Salish and his significant contributions to the understanding of native cultures.

These women's efforts are part of a larger pattern in which women's editorial, intellectual, and other academic work is appropriated by their husbands or partners. "Through the centuries and across the creative spectrum, there have been countless cases of men claiming the credit for women's contributions" (Spender 1981:141). This appropriation keeps women from finding out about their culture, by making their own labours invisible. As well, these women's experiences offer revealing parallels with the larger relationship of academic and non-academic collectors.

5 Although not the focus of articles here, other Francophone women joined Jolicœur in documenting and interpreting folklore. For example Carmen Roy worked from the 1950s with Marius Barbeau at the National Museum. As first chief of ccfcs, she not only built up a large staff of researchers and collections managers, she also set the centre's direction. She felt strongly that ccfcs should examine multiculturalism, contrary to earlier notions that saw folklore as pertaining only to Native people and French Canadians. She further ensured that all folk culture, rather than folklore – oral tradition exclusively – should come under the centre's purview. Her own collections, from St Pierre and Miquelon to Vancouver, cover not only the songs and tales that were the focus of researchers at Laval University but also life histories, foodways, and fishing culture.

6 As Aisenberg and Harrington (1988) suggest, many women academics similarly choose research/study areas which personally interest them rather than ones which are currently popular or important. We suggest that this often makes their work seem ahead of its time and often valuably separates it from academic trendiness.

7 Like Ethel and Roy Mackenzie, Herbert Halpert and his wife Violetta M. Halpert worked together.

8 Carole Carpenter's historical study of folklore activities in Canada is so named (1979).

Reclaiming the Study of Our Cultural Lives

LAUREL DOUCETTE

The study of cultural traditions has a long and complex history in Canada involving major public figures and reflecting central concerns of sociopolitical life (Carpenter 1979; Inglis 1982; McFeat 1980; Trigger 1988). The field has been shared by self-trained researchers – such as Jean Heffernan and Anne Cameron (see respectively Tye and St. Peter, this volume) – and by university- and museum-based scholars – such as Edith Fowke and Catherine Jolicœur (see respectively Fowke and Labelle) – who have been grounded in various fields, chiefly history, anthropology, and folklore. While anthropology and history are firmly established as disciplines in Canadian academe, folklore, at least in anglophone Canada, remains marginal.[1]

This fact has frequently been the subject of comment and complaint, particularly within the Folklore Studies Association of Canada/Association canadienne d'ethnologie et de folklore (FSAC/ACEF), but has not been the subject of extended and probing analysis. It is a fortuitous irony that the *Undisciplined Women* project, designed to redress the marginalization of female traditional culture and its study, has prompted a deeper examination of the marginalization of folklore studies itself within the Canadian academic milieu.

The study of folklore, if it is known at all in Canada, tends to be seen as a quaint and trivial occupation, and certainly not as one meriting employment at the university level. The question of whether or not this perception is justified highlights a major concern: the lack of intellectual rigour which has characterized folklore studies here, especially rigour of a theoretical nature. As early as 1973, Carole

Henderson Carpenter described Canadian work in the field as "theoretically limited" (Henderson 1973:97). However, too much of what has been presented at FSAC/ACEF annual meetings since its 1975 founding, and too much of what has been published over the fourteen year history of the FSAC/ACEF journal, *Canadian Folklore canadien*, has been as descriptive and intellectually unsophisticated as the scholarship Carpenter critiqued twenty years ago.

As I have argued elsewhere,[2] this situation has continued in English language scholarship because the activity of studying Canadian cultural traditions has been burdened by ideological approaches, frequently unrecognized by those adopting them, which have left the field of folklore studies theoretically underdeveloped despite its long history of research activity. Moreover, these ideologies, though generally not overtly evoked in contemporary scholarship, persist as undercurrents which shape relationships within the field, and as such need to be recognized in order to be surmounted.

First among these intellectual frameworks is modernization theory, a perspective which imposes a dichotomizing tendency on examinations of cultural manifestations: the old vs the new, the traditional vs the modern, the folk vs the non-folk. Critical scholarship on modernization as a theoretical construct now abounds, especially in the field of anthropology.[3] But there are still scholars who, consciously or unconsciously, trace all cultural change from a mythical baseline of supposedly authentic tradition: a timeless golden age before Canada became multicultural, before Confederation, before the Conquest, before the Expulsion, before Columbus, and so on.

This approach effectively denies history to some segments of the Canadian population, while simultaneously privileging the history of others. It is clearly exemplified in the longstanding compartmentalization of research activities at the Canadian Museum of Civilization (formerly the National Museum of Man) into separate administrative divisions: History for the British and French populations, Ethnology for First Nations, and Folk Culture for everyone else.[4] In conceptualizing particular groups as victims of social and cultural change, unfortunates whose natural and genuine milieu should be a timeless world of tradition, researchers relegate them to the status of passive observers of their own sociocultural experience, and limit themselves to scholarly interpretations of cultural transformation based exclusively upon principles of retention or loss.[5]

Modernization theory is both a product of and an attempted justification for colonial domination; it alleges that superior "modern" people have the right – even the responsibility – to direct the lives of those who are less socioculturally advanced than themselves. Much scholarly attention has been given to colonialism as the single major factor in the creation of anthropology (see for example Lewis 1973; McGrane 1989; Pandian 1985; Willis 1972), but relationships between colonial attitudes and folklore scholarship also merit close attention.

Carpenter, in her history of folklore scholarship in Canada, noted the early and continued presence of foreign scholars, many of whom exhibited an interest based on a view of the country as isolated, slow to industrialize, and therefore a source of "pure" folk tradition (Carpenter 1979:159). This is a perspective which unfortunately has been maintained through selective hiring within the folklore department at Memorial University of Newfoundland (MUN) in St John's, the only degree program in folklore studies available within the country to anglophone students.[6]

Other fields in Canada have already faced the fact that departments made up chiefly of scholars with personal and professional ties elsewhere, who perceive the centres of intellectual activity to be elsewhere, and who utilize theoretical paradigms developed elsewhere, are unlikely to develop intellectual approaches which reflect local realities, experiences, and knowledge. Instead, such a situation assures the continued separation of the people studied from the people doing the studying, and the constant translation of one group of Canadians to another through the medium of a foreign voice.[7]

Continuing intellectual colonialism in the field of folklore studies means that students seeking academic training in the field have been forced to study their own culture from the perspective of the "other." It is, then, no wonder that it has been difficult to develop approaches informed by the sensibilities of Canadian people and places, and that, as a result, the area has remained theoretically underdeveloped.

In many ways, the study of cultural traditions in Canada has not succeeded in moving beyond the "founding paradigm" (Fox 1987) of nineteenth-century folklore studies, romantic nationalism, an ethnocentric, anti-intellectual, uncritical approach which results in the celebration of culture, but seldom in a worthwhile analysis of it. As a persistent social phenomenon, romantic nationalism deserves analytical attention, particularly in relation to collecting activities which are in themselves cultural statements about regional and national identity.[8] But as a conceptual model, romantic nationalism, with its view of culture as the "heritage" of a specific regional or ethnic group, must be recognized as a structure of domination (Stocking 1989; Whisnant 1983). Because it suppresses any hint of social stratification or diversity of opinion among the "folk," it is deeply conservative, acting to maintain the position of the elite while purporting – often with an attitude of paternalism – to preserve the culture of the less advantaged.

Like romantic nationalism, the theoretical model of structural functionalism exhibits inherent power dimensions. The structural functionalist paradigm suggests that if a custom has persisted over time, it must benefit the society, providing stability, continuity, social integration, and so on. Under this model, the research questions are limited and the answers are predictable. There is no consideration of the fact that societies are not homogeneous, that what provides stability and security for one group may oppress another, nor of the fact that the structures of a society may be "internally rational yet unjust" (MacKinnon 1982:2). Once the dominant anthropological/sociological paradigm, structural functionalism has long since been rejected by most scholars in those fields as positivistic and mechanistic, a model inherently supportive of the patriarchal, sexist, and racist status quo of many societies.[9] It persists, however, in studies of traditional culture; Peter Narváez has termed functionalism the "predominant interpretive method in the social study of folklore" (1992:24).

The cluster of conceptual orientations just mentioned, combined with the general androcentrism of all academic disciplines, and the specific androcentrism of the MUN folklore department where many Canadian scholars of cultural traditions received training, have worked to stifle appropriate and intellectually stimulating theoretical analysis. The feeling that available theory is divorced from daily life and cultural experience has been particularly common among Canadian women folklorists and ethnologists, who have been doubly oppressed by the dominant intellectual models which marginalize both their nationality and their gender. Modernization theory, romantic nationalism, and structural functionalism all exalt a supposedly "golden" age of oral tradition. It was, in fact, an age when women had few legal and political rights, and frequently lived lives of drudgery and physical victimization. Intellectual colonialism preserves cognitive models and maintains power structures which have precluded an examination of the reality of that past, or indeed the reality of the present, for women.

It seems that increasingly many women folklorists and ethnologists, although trained in folklore, have been drifting towards women's studies, not because we want to concentrate our research and teaching efforts exclusively on gender issues, but because we feel reinforced there, in terms of both professional respect and personal valuation. To many of us, the dominant voice in Canadian folklore studies has for too long been a foreign male voice, a voice which has cast the field of study in its own image and rendered us silent and invisible.

However, feminist thought, which has provided a framework for a critique of problems embedded in the practice of folklore studies, can also provide direction in setting a course for reclaiming the field. In order to accomplish this, a paradigm shift is required. With it must come the creation of a new intellectual and attitudinal framework, based on feminist principles (including interdisciplinarity and indiscipline), within which to pursue individual research goals.

Such a framework must, first of all, operate out of a recognition that all scholarly work is culture-based. Methodologies, theories of interpretation, and ethnographic texts alike are not objective, unbiased products of neutral research (as we have been told), but are culturally influenced products of specific economic, social and political ideologies and circumstances, and serve to validate those ideologies (romantic nationalism, colonialism, capitalism, and so on).[10] Ignorance of this fact may have led to the intellectual and often very real victimization of the people whose cultures have served as topics of study. This domination can be true of Canadian folklorists and ethnologists now, working here in our own country with our fellow-citizens, as surely as it was true in the past of many scholars working in some outpost of a colonial empire.[11]

Secondly, the adoption of feminist approaches implies a rejection of positivism. Folklorists must follow other scholars in abandoning the hope of establishing general laws of social behaviour, except perhaps in very limited circumstances, and accept that much past generalizing was Eurocentric and androcentric. It is also necessary to recognize that there can be more than one valid view of a social/cultural event, including the view (or views) of insiders to the culture – members of the community or group being studied.

Thirdly, a feminist approach to cultural studies will be grounded always in experience – our own and that of the subjects of our study. Because of the effects of colonialism and romantic nationalism, Canadian understandings of traditional culture have not been integrated into the life of contemporary society. In this country, English-language folklore scholars are concentrated in the Atlantic region. Yet many folklorists have been ignoring the distressing economic facts of daily life for thousands of Atlantic citizens while we analyse their culture.[12] Canadian scholars of folklore have yet to find a way to incorporate economic knowledge and cultural knowledge into one description that will have validity and serve some useful purpose for the community.

This will happen only when folklorists follow the lead of other Canadian scholars in insisting that, contrary to intellectual colonialism, the centre for the study of the cultural traditions of this society must lie inside this society, not in the scholarly practices of other nations.[13] To bring this about, we need to do what academically trained Canadian folklorists have tended not to do – avail ourselves of the advanced scholarship of established national disciplines, and ground research on traditional culture firmly in the Canadian scholarly milieu.

The study of social and cultural behaviour must be made as broadly inclusive as possible. Folklore scholars, who have long maintained a unitary view of particular societies, must accept the fact of social divisions, not only on bases we have been willing to recognize (such as ethnicity, region, and religion), but also along axes we have been prone to ignore (such as gender, class, and sexual orientation). In particular, we must be cognizant of the political economy of daily life, facing up to the fact that much of what we study is the culture of the disadvantaged, although we neglect to name it as such. No longer pretending to remain the disinterested observer (a culturally impossible feat, in any event), we must locate our commitment in the groups we study, not as *we* define their interests, but as *they* do, and pledge ourselves to the betterment of their lives, on their terms.

Such an approach demands a commitment to ideals which are shared by feminists: a commitment to social change which brings about equality and justice; a cooperative, empowering, non-hierarchical approach in all that we do; and a spirit of inclusiveness, on the level of both theory and practice. This means that rather than splitting human cultural experience into conceptual bits, one bit for native populations (anthropology), one bit for the elite (history), one bit for the "folk" (folklore), we should aim towards a holistic approach. In our ethnographic practice, we should be active in promoting the incorporation of all groups in Canadian society into our scholarly projects, not just as subjects of study but as co-workers. We must work to make bilingualism the asset it could be in terms of collaborative work and the cross-fertilization of ideas. And regional sensibilities, rather than factionalizing us, must be turned into tools for the better comprehension of cultural dimensions of common experiences.

For women this means following the lead of anthropology in going beyond the "folklore of women" approach to establish a feminist model of folklore studies;[14] and it may ultimately mean abandoning the term "folklore" entirely in favour of one less loaded with socioeconomic and ideological connotations. The challenge is to create *our* paradigm for the study of our culture, in all its rich and perplexing diversity, and with all its historical tensions and emergent conflicts; and to do this not in a sense of narrow nationalism but because the culture of this country is the reality we share.[15]

Concepts and categories previously taken for granted must be dismantled and reconstituted from new perspectives, their often biased underpinnings examined, their meanings clarified, their heuristic usefulness and their relevance to Canadian society critically evaluated.[16] And as understandings of our increasingly pluralistic society become more sophisticated, so must the scholarly models become more complex (Farnham 1987:7).

The endeavour of renewing the intellectual framework for the study of traditional culture in Canada presents a challenge, not due to any lack of scholars who operate from a feminist perspective, but due to a lack of such scholars who enjoy the security of continuous employment. Situating folklore studies firmly within Canadian academic life as a multidisciplinary and interdisciplinary research activity presents the best hope for halting the continued stagnation of the field. It is through projects like *Undisciplined Women* that we will direct our energies in ways that are at once socially useful and intellectually fulfilling.

NOTES

1 In Canada, there is only one English-language degree program in Folklore, offered by the Department of Folklore at Memorial University of Newfoundland. The offerings at other institutions are limited to individual courses in the subject area within various other departments and programs, such as English, Canadian studies, History, or Anthropology.

2 For a more detailed examination of the ideas presented in summary form in this essay, see Doucette (1993).

3 An early discussion of modernization as a hypothetical explanation of historic change is found in Tipps (1973). Wolf (1982) presents a comprehensive examination of the weaknesses of the modernization paradigm.

4 McFeat (1980) presents an intriguing explanation of how these social distinctions came to be applied to separate museum research units.

5 For more detailed examinations of the workings of modernization theory in the field of cultural studies, see Doucette (1985:50–66), and Pocius (1991:272–99).

6 At the time of writing, nine of the ten permanent faculty members in Folklore at Memorial University were of British or American origin,

the most recent hiring (before Diane Tye in 1995) having occurred in
1990. There is one woman represented among this total.

7 For a critique and alternative to this perspective, see Tye's discussion
(this volume) of local ethnographer Jean Heffernan. See also St. Peter's
examination (this volume) of the controversy surrounding Anne Cameron's *Daughters of Copper Woman*.

8 Links between romantic nationalism and folklore studies in Canada
have been traced by Carpenter (1979) and McNaughton (1982; 1985).

9 For a series of articles placing the functionalist paradigm in historical
perspective, see Stocking (1984).

10 This is a point which Carpenter recognized in relation to folklore scholarship in Canada where research was "considerably divorced from
major international or theoretical paradigms" (Henderson 1973:100).
She did not, however, consider to what extent international trends in
scholarship were themselves the products of social, political and economic factors.

11 See Whisnant (1983) for a telling description of the cultural exploitation of rural Americans by urban Americans.

12 Folklore students currently at Memorial have provided a notable and
admirable exception to this tendency by organizing a series of forums
to address the East Coast fishery crisis.

13 See Carroll, Christiansen-Ruffman, Currie, and Harrison (1992) for a
detailed study of controversies surrounding the Canadianization of
sociology and anthropology.

14 The distinction between the anthropology of women and feminist
anthropology is drawn by Moore (1988:1–11; 186–98).

15 The challenge of developing a paradigm to define that reality in a situation of close proximity to the world's most economically and culturally influential power is daunting. The Canadian dilemma is
encapsulated in the request made by one of the anonymous PAFS
reviewers of this article for "some slight expansion of the distinctive
character of (the Canadian) instance." The pressure for self-definition
for the benefit of the "other" rather than for "self" represents a frustration commonly experienced by Canadian academics, especially those
who labour in a field too small to constitute an economically viable
readership within the Canadian population. It is, however, a frustration not confined to the world of scholarship. Consider the following
joke in current circulation: What is the difference between an American and a Canadian? The Canadian is the one who knows there *is* a
difference.

16 On the development of new feminist models of scholarship, see Boxer
(1982) and Lamphere (1987); in relation to folklore studies see Babcock
(1987).

La grande œuvre inachevée de sœur Catherine Jolicœur

RONALD LABELLE

Dans le domaine de l'étude du folklore au Canada français, plusieurs femmes se sont distinguées pendant la période qui suivit la fondation des Archives de folklore de l'Université Laval, en 1944.[1] La plupart de ces femmes ont réalisé des thèses sous la direction de Luc Lacourcière. Certaines, comme Hélène Bernier, Margaret Low, et Nancy Schmitz, se sont consacrées à l'étude des contes. D'autres ont plutôt exploré de nouveaux champs de recherche. Pensons à l'œuvre immense de Madeleine Doyon-Ferland, dans le domaine des mœurs et coutumes, et à celle de Simone Voyer en danse traditionnelle. En Acadie, sœur Jeanne-d'Arc Daigle a rédigé une thèse basée sur sa collecte de comptines enfantines, alors que Lauraine Léger a eu l'audace de mener une enquête approfondie sur les sanctions populaires au Nouveau-Brunswick. Toutes ces folkloristes ont en commun la ténacité avec laquelle elles ont mené leurs collectes sur le terrain et le dévouement dont elles ont fait preuve en accomplissant leurs recherches. On pourrait mentionner aussi sœur Marie-Ursule, qui a publié une étude extrêmement détaillée sur la vie traditionnelle dans un village québécois (Marie-Ursule 1951), Carmen Roy, dont les enquêtes ont été particulièrement abondantes en Gaspésie, de même que Geneviève Massignon qui a parcouru l'Acadie et l'ouest de la France pour y étudier la langue et la littérature orale.

Parmi toutes les femmes qui ont étudié le folklore du Canada français, Catherine Jolicœur a été une des plus persévérantes et elle a sans doute été la plus ambitieuse. Après avoir accompli pendant des années une longue série d'enquêtes en prévision de sa thèse de doctorat sur la légende du vaisseau fantôme (1965), elle s'est lancée dans le projet grandiose de recueillir toutes les légendes connues chez les Acadiens du Nouveau-Brunswick. En 1975, même si elle atteignait la soixantaine, elle avait conservé l'enthousiasme d'une jeune chercheuse avide de recueillir des documents originaux. Ce qui est encore plus surprenant, c'est qu'elle réalisait en même temps des expériences originales dans le domaine de l'enseignement du folklore. Pendant les dernières années de sa vie active, en plus d'enseigner elle-même au niveau universitaire, elle a visité des salles de classe dans les écoles primaires et secondaires, partout au Nouveau-Brunswick, et elle a préparé des ateliers pédagogiques pour apprendre aux enseignants à intégrer le folklore à leurs programmes. Tout en contribuant au développement de la discipline au niveau universitaire, elle partageait son amour du folklore avec tous les gens qu'elle côtoyait et elle saisissait toutes les occasions pour faire connaître l'importance de la tradition orale. C'est ce qui a fait d'elle une figure bien connue au Nouveau-Brunswick.

Née à Nouvelle, en Gaspésie (Québec), en 1915, Catherine Jolicœur était la fille d'un cheminot nommé Wilfrid Jolicœur et d'une mère de descendance irlandaise, Hélène Parker. Elle passa la plupart de son enfance avec sa famille, dans le nord du Nouveau-Brunswick. Elle s'est intéressée très jeune à la lecture, s'occupant d'une petite bibliothèque publique que le curé de sa paroisse avait aménagée dans la sacristie. À l'âge de dix-neuf ans, ses études secondaires terminées, elle devint institutrice. Deux ans plus tard, au grand chagrin de ses parents, elle entra dans la congrégation des Filles de Marie de l'Assomption.[2] Cette congrégation, dont la maison-mère est située à Campbellton (Nouveau-Brunswick), se consacre surtout à l'enseignement. Catherine Jolicœur, devenue sœur Marie-Sainte-Hélène, obtint donc un brevet et enseigna pendant plusieurs années au Nouveau-Brunswick, en Nouvelle-Écosse et en Gaspésie.

Tout au long de sa carrière, Catherine Jolicœur ressentait un besoin de liberté. Le fait d'appartenir à une congrégation religieuse lui donnait la possibilité d'accéder à une carrière d'enseignante; en revanche, elle devait se plier à la discipline de la vie en communauté. Pendant ses premières années dans l'enseignement, elle acceptait difficilement les règles qui lui étaient imposées comme institutrice. Elle me confia un jour que sa méthode d'enseignement n'était pas bien acceptée, car, plutôt que de suivre les normes d'une façon rigide, elle tentait de créer chez les élèves une disposition propice à l'étude en leur proposant, par exemple, de faire des exercices physiques au début des cours, pour dépenser de l'énergie. On l'a donc retirée de l'enseignement et, pendant trois ans, elle a été affectée à des tâches domestiques à la maison-mère de la congrégation. Catherine trouva ces années particulièrement pénibles et me dit que seule sa foi religieuse lui avait permis d'accepter l'humiliation d'être assignée à l'entretien du poulailler, alors qu'elle rêvait de poursuivre ses études.[3]

Bien que la vocation des Filles de Marie de l'Assomption ait été l'enseignement au niveau primaire et secondaire, il arrivait que des membres de la congrégation poursuivent des études avancées. Catherine Jolicœur dut patienter pendant plusieurs années, mais elle eut par la suite la possibilité de retourner aux études, se rendant d'abord à l'Université du Sacré-Cœur, à Bathurst, puis à l'Université Saint-Louis, à Edmundston, avant de s'inscrire à l'Université Laval. Voyant son grand potentiel intellectuel, sa congrégation lui fournit l'appui dont elle avait besoin pour aller au bout de son projet. C'est en suivant un programme de maîtrise à la Faculté des lettres de l'Université Laval que Catherine Jolicœur s'initia à l'étude du folklore. Au départ, elle n'était pas particulièrement attirée par la tradition populaire, mais, comme dans le cas de plusieurs autres Acadiens étudiant à la Faculté des lettres de l'Université Laval, le contact avec le professeur Luc Lacourcière l'orienta vers ce domaine. Elle obtint sa maîtrise ès arts en 1959 et commença aussitôt à recueillir des traditions orales, s'intéressant entre autres aux chansons et aux comptines enfantines. Elle entreprit ensuite son projet de doctorat et choisit comme sujet de thèse la légende du vaisseau fantôme. En 1965, elle déposa sa thèse, intitulée *Le Vaisseau fantôme : Légende étiologique*.[4] Il s'agit d'une étude comparative des légendes de bateaux fantômes retrouvées à travers le monde, qui comporte de nombreuses versions recueillies par Catherine Jolicœur sur les côtes du golfe du Saint-Laurent. Pendant les vingt-cinq dernières années de sa vie active, ce sont les légendes acadiennes qui ont retenu son attention, bien qu'elle ait continué à s'intéresser au folklore enfantin.

De 1971 à 1974, elle travailla à la classification des légendes de l'Amérique française dans le cadre du projet Killam, à l'Université Laval. Au goût déjà acquis de l'enquête sur le terrain s'ajouta alors un intérêt pour la classification. De retour au Nouveau-Brunswick en 1975, elle se lança dans un projet de catalogue de légendes acadiennes, avec l'encouragement du père Anselme Chiasson, directeur du Centre d'études acadiennes. Le projet était ambitieux, car il fallait d'abord parcourir l'Acadie pour recueillir des milliers de récits légendaires. Elle décida de se limiter aux régions francophones du Nouveau-Brunswick et réussit à obtenir, en 1976, une bourse du Conseil des Arts du Canada, qui lui permit d'enregistrer des centaines d'informateurs dans le sud-est du Nouveau-Brunswick. L'année suivante, une autre bourse lui permit d'étendre son enquête au comté de Restigouche, en bordure de la Gaspésie.

Les années 1976, 1977 et 1978 furent une période de recherche intensive pour Catherine Jolicœur. Elle accumula alors 482 heures d'enregistrements de faits de folklore et recueillit ainsi la grande majorité des légendes de sa collection. Le respect dont jouissent les congrégations religieuses au sein de la population acadienne a sans doute facilité sa prise de contact avec les informateurs. Il lui a cependant fallu gagner la confiance des gens afin qu'ils lui confient leurs récits de croyances populaires. C'est ce qu'elle réussit à faire grâce à son approche accueillante et à son ouverture d'esprit.

À partir de 1977, Catherine a été professeure invitée au Centre universitaire Saint-Louis-Maillet, à Edmundston, où elle donna des cours de folklore jusqu'à sa retraite en 1984. Grâce à une subvention du Conseil de recherches en sciences humaines du Canada, en 1979, elle embaucha des équipes d'étudiants madawaskayens pour recueillir des légendes dans le nord-ouest de la province et dans les villages francophones du nord de l'État du Maine. Sa grande déception fut cependant d'être atteinte par la maladie avant d'avoir pu compléter son enquête dans une région particulièrement riche en légendes, le nord-est du Nouveau-Brunswick.

Ce fut pendant ses années d'enseignement à Edmundston, entre 1977 et 1982, que Catherine Jolicœur s'épanouit vraiment au point de vue professionnel. Sa production à cette époque fut phénoménale. Tout en poursuivant son enseignement et sa recherche au Centre universitaire Saint-Louis-Maillet, elle participa à plusieurs ateliers pédagogiques organisés par le ministère de l'Éducation du Nouveau-Brunswick. Elle visita aussi des écoles primaires (1re à 6e années) et intermédiaires (7e à 9e années) partout dans la province, menant des expériences tout à fait originales, où elle racontait des contes aux enfants et les incitait ensuite à faire usage de leur créativité pour écrire, dessiner, jouer, mimer et même réinventer ces contes (Jolicœur 1979). Pour Catherine Jolicœur, qui avait eu de la difficulté à faire accepter des méthodes pédagogiques peu orthodoxes au cours de sa carrière d'enseignante, ce fut une joie d'être invitée à mettre en pratique ses idées auprès de centaines d'écoliers et même à partager ses techniques avec d'autres enseignantes et enseignants.

À la même époque, elle devint active dans la nouvelle Association canadienne pour les études du folklore (ACEF), faisant partie de l'exécutif pendant trois ans et occupant le poste de présidente en 1981–1982. En plus d'assister à chaque réunion annuelle de l'ACEF, elle participa à de nombreuses conférences, tant au Canada qu'à l'étranger. Mentionnons par exemple le Colloque international de l'Acadie, tenu à Moncton en 1978, la conférence sur le thème «Creatures of Legendry», à Omaha (Nebraska) en 1978, la conférence quinquennale de l'International Society for Folk Narrative Research, à Edimbourg (Écosse) en 1979, la conférence sur le thème «Médecine populaire et religion traditionnelle», au Musée national de l'homme, à Ottawa en 1980, et le colloque de l'Association d'histoire orale en Atlantique, à Saint-Jean (Terre-Neuve) en 1982. De plus, en 1981, elle a été invitée à passer deux mois aux archives acadiennes et créoles de l'University of Southwestern Louisiana, à Lafayette (Louisiane), où elle a mené une série intensive d'enquêtes sur le terrain.

Pendant cette même période, entre 1977 et 1982, Catherine Jolicœur publia 22 articles, de même que son étude intitulée Les plus belles légendes acadiennes (Jolicœur 1981). Elle considérait cet ouvrage comme le premier volume d'une anthologie des légendes acadiennes du Nouveau-Brunswick, dont les quatre autres n'ont pas été publiés, bien que leur préparation ait été entamée.

Malgré toutes ses autres tâches, Catherine Jolicœur ne négligeait pas la question de la conservation de sa collection de légendes. À chacune de ses visites à Moncton, elle se rendait au Centre d'études acadiennes, les bras chargés de boîtes contenant ses derniers enregistrements accompagnés de transcriptions intégrales, souvent en copies multiples. C'était avec une fierté légitime qu'elle parlait de sa collection de 20 000 légendes. Mais son projet de développer une méthode de classification pour les légendes acadiennes ralentit beaucoup à partir de 1982, alors qu'elle commençait à souffrir de la maladie d'Alzheimer.

L'année 1983–1984 fut extrêmement pénible pour Catherine, qui essayait de poursuivre le traitement de sa collection alors que son état de santé se détériorait. Vers la fin de 1984, elle dut être hospitalisée de façon permanente à l'infirmerie de sa congrégation, à Campbellton.

En 1985, les Filles de Marie de l'Assomption ont décidé de déposer la collection de folklore de Catherine Jolicœur, ainsi que son fonds documentaire, au Centre d'études acadiennes. Au cours des quatre années suivantes, la collection a été inventoriée en entier et un index des titres a été réalisé selon le catalogue des faits de folklore du Centre d'études acadiennes. Étant donné que la collection était déjà presque entièrement transcrite au moment où elle fut déposée au CEA, elle est donc très accessible.

La méthode de classification de légendes envisagée par Catherine Jolicœur n'a malheureusement jamais été mise au point et il est donc impossible à d'autres chercheurs de compléter l'œuvre qu'elle avait entreprise. Elle avait étudié en profondeur les différents systèmes de classification de légendes existant dans le monde, en collaboration avec le professeur Wayland Hand, du Center for the Study of Comparative Folklore and Mythology (University of California at Los Angeles). En 1980, elle a d'ailleurs suivi un stage de recherche auprès de Wayland Hand, qui était devenu le principal conseiller de recherche de Catherine Jolicœur au cours des dernières années de sa carrière.

L'élaboration d'une méthode de classification des légendes acadiennes s'est avérée très lente, en raison des nombreux problèmes taxonomiques[5] rencontrés par Catherine et que l'on peut résumer ainsi : les récits légendaires sont peu structurés, les personnages qu'ils contiennent ont des fonctions variables et les thèmes légendaires sont toujours en transformation. Catherine Jolicœur n'a pas trouvé de solutions à ces difficultés, mais elle a quand même accompli l'étape préliminaire du catalogue de légendes. Elle a identifié environ quatre-vingts thèmes légendaires propres au folklore acadien, pour ensuite regrouper toutes les versions se rapportant à chaque thème. Dans beaucoup de cas, elle a complété les résumés de chaque version, pour ensuite faire ressortir les sous-thèmes. Dans le cas des thèmes légendaires comportant un nombre limité d'éléments variables, elle a aussi tenté de placer les éléments à l'intérieur d'une structure narrative de base. Pour tester cette approche, elle a proposé aux membres de l'ACEF un schéma de la légende de la charrette fantôme, selon lequel elle situe d'abord la légende dans l'espace et le temps, pour ensuite énumérer les manifestations de la charrette; en troisième lieu viennent les interventions provoquées par l'apparition, après quoi sont présentés les résultats des interventions et, finalement, les interprétations du phénomène (Jolicœur 1978).

Une structure semblable peut s'appliquer à plusieurs thèmes légendaires. La situation de la légende dans l'espace et le temps constitue l'introduction à la narration, la présentation des manifestations surnaturelles constitue le cœur du récit et les interprétations concluent la narration. Les deux autres étapes, les interventions et leurs résultats, se retrouvent dans les récits où l'on a recours à de l'aide pour vaincre un adversaire ou affronter un danger. C'est le cas, par exemple, lorsque les interventions d'un prêtre font suite aux actions d'un sorcier.

En structurant ainsi les récits, Catherine Jolicœur a créé un cadre pour ordonner l'énumération de leurs éléments. Elle n'est cependant pas arrivée à faire la décomposition des légendes les plus répandues en Acadie, car le nombre de variantes s'avérait tellement grand qu'une représentation schématique n'aurait pas été pratique. Elle n'est pas non plus parvenue à déterminer la forme précise que prendrait

le catalogue des légendes. Le catalogue qu'elle commençait à conce-
voir aurait groupé les textes par catégories selon leur thématique,
alors qu'à un second niveau les variantes de chaque thème légendaire auraient été décomposées selon un schéma structurel s'appli-
quant à l'ensemble du corpus.

Catherine Jolicœur penchait vers un système de classification basé
sur les thèmes légendaires – c'est ce qu'elle trouvait le plus pratique
– mais elle ne s'est jamais prononcée définitivement là-dessus et elle
n'est pas arrivée à mettre au point la méthode de décomposition de
l'ensemble des variantes légendaires qui aurait permis de dégager
chaque élément. Elle était très consciente de l'universalité de la
légende et visait à identifier des motifs pouvant être associés à plus
d'un thème et pouvant être comparés aux motifs existant dans les
légendes d'autres cultures. Même s'il n'était pas fixe, le corpus légendaire acadien constituait un ensemble relativement facile à circons-
crire, composé essentiellement de récits issus des croyances populaires
reliées à la religion catholique. Mais les difficultés survenaient
lorsqu'il fallait aller au-delà des catégories et des thèmes, pour analyser en détail la structure des récits.

Pendant les années où Catherine Jolicœur a travaillé à la classification des légendes, elle me semblait débordée par la masse de documentation qu'elle avait recueillie. Sa vie active de professeure, de
conférencière et d'animatrice pédagogique l'empêchait aussi de se
consacrer entièrement à son projet. Mais je soupçonnais aussi qu'elle
ne voyait pas clairement où ses efforts allaient aboutir. Elle œuvrait
à une époque où peu de gens étaient intéressés aux questions taxonomiques. La plupart des modèles de classification à sa disposition
dataient des années 1950 ou 1960 et seul le professeur Wayland Hand
lui fournissait l'appui qui lui était important. Wayland Hand lui-
même me confiait en 1984 qu'il avait surtout essayé d'offrir à Catherine Jolicœur de l'encouragement, car il constatait qu'elle travaillait
d'une façon isolée.[6] Pendant les décennies de 1970 et de 1980, l'ethnologie au Canada français était dominée par l'étude de questions
reliées à la société québécoise, les chercheurs de l'Université Laval
ayant concentré leur champ d'intérêt sur le Québec. Ailleurs au
Canada français, les ethnologues continuaient à orienter leurs efforts
vers la collecte des faits de folklore des communautés francophones
minoritaires. Ne s'inscrivant pas dans le champ de l'ethnologie québécoise, le projet de classification de légendes acadiennes se situait
donc à l'écart de ce milieu scientifique. Catherine Jolicœur travaillait
effectivement dans l'isolement, mis à part ses contacts avec le Centre
d'études acadiennes et avec le professeur Wayland Hand, de UCLA.

Dans son état actuel, la collection Catherine Jolicœur comprend
deux volets. D'une part, il y a le fonds manuscrit déposé dans les

archives privées au Centre d'études acadiennes. On y trouve, outre les documents personnels de la donatrice, de nombreuses boîtes contenant des copies de transcriptions de légendes regroupées par thèmes avec des notes de recherche, des résumés et, parfois, des listes d'éléments légendaires. D'autre part, il y a les enregistrements sonores ainsi que deux copies de chaque transcription, déposés dans les archives de folklore du CEA.

Étant donné que le projet de classification de Catherine Jolicœur n'a pas abouti à des résultats concrets, il faudra, pour toute analyse de thèmes légendaires entreprise à l'avenir, retourner aux transcriptions elles-mêmes, afin d'examiner les variantes des légendes. Les nombreux résumés préparés par Catherine Jolicœur ont aussi une utilité, car ils nous fournissent un aperçu de l'ensemble des variantes rattachées à chaque thème.

Afin de fournir un exemple de la richesse que représente la collection Catherine Jolicœur pour l'étude de la mentalité populaire, il suffira de présenter ici un des thèmes légendaires répandus en Acadie. Puisque la question autochtone suscite beaucoup d'intérêt aujourd'hui,[7] mon choix s'est arrêté sur le thème des Amérindiens dans la légende acadienne. Cet exemple démontre que l'étude des légendes peut nous apprendre beaucoup sur les relations entre Amérindiens et Blancs.

Dans l'ensemble de la collection Catherine Jolicœur, il y a environ 400 variantes de légendes ayant rapport aux Amérindiens, ce qui représente 2 % du total. Lorsque l'on examine le contenu de ces variantes, on se rend compte que la grande majorité d'entre elles, soit 350, associent les Amérindiens avec la sorcellerie. La plupart des autres constituent des anecdotes sur des mendiants amérindiens. L'image des Amérindiens présentée dans presque toutes les légendes est celle de mendiants aux pouvoirs mystérieux qui jettent des sorts maléfiques si on leur refuse la charité.

Si l'on veut interpréter les légendes se rapportant aux Amérindiens, il faut d'abord les placer dans l'ensemble des récits concernant la sorcellerie en Acadie. La collection Catherine Jolicœur contient un peu plus de mille légendes de sorcellerie. Dans un tiers des récits, les sorciers sont des Amérindiens, alors que dans les autres, ce sont en général des marginaux. On y trouve beaucoup de mendiants nomades que l'on croit souvent être des Gitans. Il y a aussi les « Arabies », colporteurs originaires du Moyen-Orient. Enfin, il y a des sorciers qui demeurent dans la communauté tout en vivant en marge de la société locale. Ce sont souvent des gens originaires d'autres pays, comme la France, par exemple, qui vivent seuls et n'ont aucune pratique religieuse ou sont de confession autre que catholique. Une des caractéristiques des légendes de sorcellerie amérindienne, c'est que l'on parle plus souvent de sorcières, que l'on nomme « taoueilles », alors que dans le folklore acadien en général, la plupart des sorciers sont des hommes.[8]

Les sorciers avaient tous en commun de ne pas être intégrés à la société acadienne rurale. La méfiance que l'on ressentait dans les villages, envers tout ce qui était étranger, expliquerait en partie les cas de supposés ensorcellements. Dans ce contexte culturel, les Amérindiens nomades devenaient des marginaux, au même titre que les Gitans et les apostats, et le comportement des sorciers amérindiens était, à tout point de vue, pareil à celui des autres sorciers. Pour les Acadiens, la sorcellerie n'était donc pas associée à la culture amérindienne d'une façon spécifique. Ce qui ressort de la lecture des multiples variantes est tout simplement que les Acadiens avaient une grande peur des Amérindiens, ce qui les poussait à s'en méfier d'une façon excessive. Un récit recueilli par Catherine Jolicœur rapporte que quand une « taoueille » donnait naissance à un enfant, la première prière qu'elle lui apprenait était le secret du « sorcelage ». C'était une façon de dire que toutes les Amérindiennes étaient des sorcières. Bien sûr, cette croyance n'était pas partagée par tous. Catherine Jolicœur a d'ailleurs recueilli une quinzaine de récits de « bons sauvages », où les Amérindiens sont présentés comme des gens honnêtes qui accomplissent leurs devoirs religieux avec piété.

En Acadie, l'histoire orale nous apprend qu'il fut un temps où les Micmacs des Maritimes ont aidé les Acadiens à survivre. Mais il a toujours existé une distance entre Acadiens et Amérindiens et il semble que le fossé entre ces deux peuples se soit agrandi tout au long du dix-neuvième siècle, pour aboutir enfin à un dédain et à une méfiance irraisonnée des Acadiens à l'égard de leurs voisins micmacs.

Lorsque Catherine Jolicœur compila sa collection de légendes recueillies dans le comté de Westmorland, pour publier le volume intitulé *Les plus belles légendes acadiennes*, elle évita d'y inclure des récits de sorcellerie amérindienne. Dans sa collection de légendes du comté de Kent, qui est restée inédite,[9] il n'y a pas non plus de textes concernant les Amérindiens, bien qu'on y trouve des histoires de sorcellerie. Je crois qu'elle hésitait à publier des légendes concernant les Amérindiens, tellement on y véhiculait une image négative des autochtones, image qui tend à se modifier aujourd'hui, alors que les relations entre les deux groupes s'améliorent.

Catherine Jolicœur définissait la légende comme étant le reflet de l'âme d'un peuple. Or, des sentiments de peur et de méfiance peuvent avoir leur place dans l'âme populaire, à côté de sentiments plus nobles. Il ne faut donc pas avoir honte de faire ressortir des aspects peu flatteurs de la culture populaire. Catherine hésitait cependant à publier certaines légendes, parce qu'elle destinait ses écrits au grand public aussi bien qu'aux spécialistes de la littérature orale et elle était sensible aux réactions de la population.[10] À l'autocensure qu'exerçaient sans doute de nombreux informateurs en racontant leurs récits à une religieuse s'ajoutait alors une attitude prudente de la part de l'auteure, très consciente du rôle qu'elle jouait en mettant les légendes entre les mains du public.

Malgré les précautions prises par Catherine Jolicœur dans le choix de son matériel, le volume *Les plus belles légendes acadiennes* a quand même fait l'objet d'une censure au Nouveau-Brunswick, à cause de l'inclusion de légendes sur le Juif errant.[11] La publication de légendes de sorcellerie amérindienne aurait probablement aussi provoqué une réaction négative. Tout au long de sa carrière de folkloriste, Catherine a poursuivi le double but de faire avancer la science et de faire partager au public son intérêt pour la littérature orale. Elle a conservé une simplicité qui lui a permis de demeurer près des gens et d'en être très appréciée. C'est précisément ce contact privilégié qui la rendait plus vulnérable aux critiques que ne le sont les chercheurs qui s'adressent essentiellement à une population universitaire et publient uniquement dans des revues scientifiques.[12]

Catherine Jolicœur a reconnu la richesse que représentait la tradition légendaire en Acadie et elle a consacré des efforts presque surhumains à la poursuite de son but, soit la cueillette, l'analyse, et la mise en valeur de ce patrimoine. Malheureusement, ce n'est que tard dans sa vie qu'elle a eu l'occasion de mettre en œuvre ses idées et d'apporter une contribution originale à la science. Comme pour bien d'autres femmes professionnelles, le chemin qui l'a menée à l'accomplissement de sa carrière a été long et tortueux. Dans son cas, une carrière de chercheuse universitaire est venue s'ajouter à sa première vocation de religieuse enseignante. À cause de tous les défis qu'elle a dû relever, Catherine Jolicœur n'a pas été en mesure de mener à terme son plus grand projet, mais elle nous a laissé une œuvre extrêmement riche et unique.

Le 17 mars 1997, jour de la saint Patrice, Sœur Catherine Jolicœur est décédée à la maison mère de la congrégation des Filles de Marie-de-l'Assomption, située à Campbellton, Nouveau-Brunswick. Elle y avait passé les dernières années de sa vie auprès des membres de sa famille religieuse. Au Nouveau-Brunswick, ainsi que dans sa Gaspésie natale, on se souviendra longtemps de Sœur Catherine Jolicœur à cause du rôle qu'elle a joué comme enseignante, chercheure et auteure, mais surtout à cause de sa vivacité, son enthousiasme et l'amour du folklore qu'elle transmettait aux personnes qui l'entouraient. Enfin, sa contribution à l'Université de Moncton est mainte-

nant reconnue de façon permanente par la présence au Centre
d'études acadiennes de la «Salle Catherine-Jolicœur».

NOTES

1 L'auteur remercie Lauraine Léger qui a lu et commenté l'ébauche de
cet article.
2 Une brève biographie est contenue dans Lemieux et Caron (1981).
3 Voir aussi le magazine *Châtelaine* (août, 1983).
4 Cette thèse fut ensuite publiée par les Presses de l'Université Laval
(Jolicœur 1970).
5 Voir CEA, fonds Catherine Jolicœur 63–067, p. 91–3.
6 Ce sentiment d'isolement n'est certainement pas particulier à Catherine Jolicœur. Tel que suggéré par Doucette et Tye, ainsi que par Edith
Fowke dans ses mémoires, la marginalisation est le sort commun de
bien des femmes ethnographes.
7 Voir, par exemple, les textes de St. Peter et de McGrath dans le présent
ouvrage.
8 Le texte de Rieti, dans ce même volume, présente des exemples de sorcières, situées dans leurs contextes.
9 Voir CEA, fonds Catherine Jolicœur, 63.54.
10 Dans ses écrits, Jean Heffernan exprime un désir semblable de com-
prendre les réactions possibles que peuvent provoquer la publication
d'éléments de culture traditionnelle.
11 À la suite de plaintes adressées au ministère de l'Éducation du
Nouveau-Brunswick, le volume a été retiré des bibliothèques des
écoles publiques de la province.
12 De la même façon, l'écrivaine Anne Cameron a été sévèrement criti-
quée, autant par les érudits que par les peuples aborigènes parmi les-
quels elle a travaillé. Ses difficultés provenaient, au moins en partie,
de son désir de rejoindre par ses publications un auditoire populaire
en dehors de sa région (voir St. Peter dans le présent ouvrage).

A Personal Odyssey and Personal Prejudices

EDITH FOWKE

This is the story of one Canadian woman's odyssey. Born Edith Fulton, I grew up in a small town, Lumsden, Saskatchewan, which then had a population of about five hundred. I went to the local public and high schools, scrounged all the books I could find from neighbours – Lumsden had no public library – and was considered odd because I liked to read in a town where the main recreations were hockey and bridge.

I took a BA Honours degree in English and History at the University of Saskatchewan, where my exposure to folklore was minimal. I did learn something about ballads and I wrote an essay on the mystery and miracle plays for a medieval English course. When I graduated at the depth of the depression, I taught for a year in a two-room country school – all the subjects for all the high-school grades – and now I can't imagine how I did it. The area was in the drought belt and everyone was on relief. My salary was supposed to be $400; I actually got $200 plus board. My best memories of that year are of the square dances held in the school.

The next year I went back to Saskatoon, took my master's in English, and began working for the Western Extension College which provided teaching aids to rural teachers. Then I married Frank Fowke and moved to Toronto where my engineer husband had managed to find work. Soon I became involved in political and pacifist activities. For a dozen years – which I call my political period – I spent most of my time working for the Cooperative Commonwealth Federation (CCF; forerunner of the New Democratic Party), the Fellowship of Reconciliation, the Women's International League for Peace and Freedom, the Co-operative Committee for Japanese Canadians, the *Canadian Forum*, and the Woodsworth Memorial Foundation (an educational socialist organization).

I was a feminist before there was such a term. I remember writing a skit in the form of a radio broadcast, pointing out all the inequalities women faced, and staging it at Woodsworth House. As a member of the CCF Women's Committee, I helped to draft the first Ontario equal-pay law. Agnes MacPhail introduced it in the Ontario legislature, and though it wasn't passed, it prompted the government to introduce their own inferior bill a little later.

In the early 1950s a bitter struggle developed between the CCF establishment and the Woodsworth Foundation, between those who wanted the Foundation to be an adjunct of the CCF and those who wanted it to be educational. The Steelworkers, led by David Lewis, packed our meeting and voted out most of those who had been running the programs. I fought them for a year, managing to get myself elected to the CCF Provincial Council, and then decided I could find better things to do. I'm proud of the fact that David Lewis told our Foundation president that I was a dangerous woman; that is, I was managing to resist his domination.[1] However, I now feel that I owe little David a great debt of gratitude. If he hadn't driven me out of the CCF, I might still be wasting my time in politics. I'd already become interested in folksongs, and so I switched to folklore which has proved much more satisfying.[2]

Growing up in Saskatchewan, I had little contact with folksongs, but in Toronto, Frank and I belonged to an informal group of English, Austrian, and Canadian friends who met occasionally to sing. The sociologist Martin Lipset, who spent a couple of years in Toronto, played us some Library of Congress folksong records and I was hooked. We'd been buying all kinds of records, from pop to classical, including some early Burl Ives, Josh White, and Richard Dyer-Bennett, and I soon found I was getting more folksong records than anything else.

Then I decided the CBC should have a folksong program so I suggested it to Harry Boyle, the radio program director, and he agreed to let me try. I started *Folk Song Time*, a weekly documentary that used records with linking narrative. I got help from John Robins, a University of Toronto professor interested in folklore who also helped Helen Creighton with her early books. Soon after I started the program, Frank and I drove down to the Maritimes one summer and met Helen Creighton. She took us to visit some of her singers – my first contact with traditional singing.

"Folk Song Time" proved popular and continued off and on through the 1950s. We supplied record lists to listeners on request, and whenever I played Canadian songs – usually sung by Alan Mills or Ed McCurdy – I'd get letters asking where to find them. Realizing that there was no general collection to which I could refer people, I teamed up with Richard Johnston, a University of Toronto music professor, and we put together *Folk Songs of Canada* (Fowke and Johnston 1954) – an anthology that drew upon the collections of Marius Barbeau, Creighton, Ernest Gagnon, Elizabeth Greenleaf, Maud Karpeles, and Roy Mackenzie. We followed this with *Folk Songs of Quebec* (Fowke and Johnston 1957), for which I provided singable translations, hoping to make some fine French-Canadian songs available to English Canadians.

Meanwhile I'd been preparing various programs for national CBC radio, some illustrated with records and others with live singers – Alan Mills, Charles Jordan, Joyce Sullivan, and Merrick Jarrett. We did series on sea songs, lumbering songs, cowboy songs, Australian songs, and love songs. One thirteen-week series with Alan Mills, "Canada's Story in Song," led to a two-record Folkways album (Fowke and Mills 1960a), and a book that we hoped would be used to enliven the teaching of Canadian history (Fowke and Mills 1960b).

But these were not my only radio ventures. For CBC's *Matinee*, I prepared series based on Burl Ives' *The Wayfaring Stranger* (1948) and Jean Ritchie's *The Singing Family of the Cumberlands* (1955), with condensed texts read by actors and illustrated with songs from their recordings. By that time I had got to know Burl and Jean, who were pleased to have me adapt their stories. I also scripted some programs presenting folktales, and a long series on "Folklore and Folksongs," which was later to provide a basis for some of the classes I taught at York University. I even wrote a few radio plays; one I remember was based on "The Cowboy's Lament."

Record companies would give me records to use on my programs. But in preparing the scripts I found I was spending a lot of time going back and forth to the reference library, so I began buying folk-song books. I used to drive down to New York every summer to collect records and books, and on these trips I met many singers and folklorists. The first time I met Kenneth Goldstein was in the Stinson record shop shortly after *Folk Songs of Canada* came out. I was surprised to find that he had a copy, and he invited me to his home that evening – the start of a friendship that's lasted nearly forty years and been a constant pleasure and source of inspiration.

In preparing *Folk Songs of Canada* I realized that practically no Canadian songs had been reported from west of Quebec, so I decided to see what I could find in Ontario. I wasn't too hopeful. I assumed that it was too late to find traditional singers in Canada's most industrialized province, but Roy Mackenzie, our pioneer song collector, had thought they were dying out in Nova Scotia back in 1908. I was very lucky. In 1959 I made my first rather hesitant collecting trip to Peterborough – which was originally settled by Irish colonists – and it proved one of the richest areas in the province. This was before the days of Canada Council largesse, so I did my collecting on weekends, with my husband going along to carry the tape recorder – my first, a Revere, was too heavy for me. I was delighted to find good singers with many interesting songs.

A television show on which I talked about the singers I was finding around Peterborough brought a letter from an Ottawa woman saying that her father knew some old songs, and from a list she sent me I realized he had a great repertoire. He was then 85 so I wasn't hopeful about his singing ability. However, on our summer holidays Frank and I drove up to Hull to record O.J. Abbott. Imagine my delight when he began to sing in his fine clear voice, and produced song after song with hardly a pause, even though, as he often said, "I haven't sung that song for sixty years." Later collecting uncovered more fine informants like C.H.J. Snider, an authority on Great Lakes ships who knew and sang many sea songs; Mrs Grace Fraser of Glengarry County, from whom I got Scottish songs; Tom Brandon, one of my younger informants; and LaRena Clark who turned out to be an unusually interesting singer with a remarkable repertoire.

By this time Marius Barbeau had founded the Canadian Folk Music Society and enlisted me as one of the directors. He arranged for the International Folk Music Council to meet in Quebec City in 1961, and I took three singers – O.J. Abbott, Mary Towns, and Tom Brandon – to sing there. I also arranged for them and some of the other Ontario singers to appear at several early Mariposa Folk Festivals.[3]

The results of my collection included *Traditional Singers and Songs of Ontario* (1965), which introduced six fine singers with some of their songs, largely of British origin; and *Lumbering Songs from the Northern Woods* (1970a), which looked at the main native Ontario folksongs. But I've always felt that the best way to present folksongs is through records. Even the best transcriber can't represent the melody exactly as it was sung, so whenever I give song references I always include records. I wanted to make it possible for people to hear the Ontario singers. I'd met Moe Asch early in my New York visits and had already written notes for several Folkways albums, so I persuaded him to issue four records of traditional singers – *Folk Songs of Ontario*

(1950), *Lumbering Songs from the Ontario Shanties* (1961), *Songs of the Great Lakes* (1964a), and *Irish and British Songs from the Ottawa Valley* (Abbott 1951). Ken Goldstein brought out an Ontario record (Fowke 1962); Sandy Paton issued one (Brandon 1963); and one of LaRena Clark was issued in England (Clark 1965).

I was delighted to find that some of the songs I collected are circulating in Britain.[4] When Tom Gilfellon of the High Level Ranters recorded Mr Abbott's "The Plains of Waterloo," a music magazine named it the best folksong record of that year, and it's since been recorded by half a dozen other singers. Two British singers made records called "By the Hush" – after Mr Abbott's Irish ballad "By the Hush Me B'ys." And in a tiny club down in South Devon I heard someone sing "The Banks of Ero" – a version of "Rare Willie Drowned in Yarrow" that Sara Grey had learned from my tapes and carried to England. Some songs have been picked up on this continent too. James Reaney used Mr Abbott's "The Barley Grain for Me" as a theme in his play, *The Donnellys*. Pete Seeger sings that song, and Canadians have recorded "The Poor Little Girls of Ontario," "The Jolly Raftsman O," "Rattle on the Stovepipe," and others.

By this time too I'd started going to the American Folklore Society (AFS) meetings, in the days when, to quote D.K. Wilgus, we could have met in a telephone booth. For years I was the only Canadian attending. Then everyone knew everyone else and there were single sessions – a far cry from the current crowded and overlapping programs. D.K. Wilgus became particularly important to me because of his research in Irish songs. As I showed (1988a), the Irish influence is dominant in Anglo-Canadian songs, not only in Newfoundland but throughout the country.

Some of my articles revised certain beliefs. In one about "The Red River Valley," (1964b), I claimed the song was from the Red River in Manitoba, not the one in Texas, as previously supposed. In another (1979a), I emphasized that Paul Bunyan tales were in oral tradition before they were commercialized and mistakenly termed fakelore by Richard Dorson. I think I was the first to present "filk songs" (sung by science fiction fans) as modern folksongs (1989). One article (1966) brought me in touch with Gershon Legman who claimed a brief article I'd written for a small folksong magazine (1963) was the first on bawdy songs by a woman. He was amazed that I'd found some songs that were new to him – in one letter he joked that I must be writing them myself.

I'd done several radio series on children's lore illustrated with British and American records, so I thought I'd see what I could find in

Canada. Children's rhymes proved very easy to collect and I began putting together the book that became *Sally Go Round the Sun* (1969), by far the most popular of my books, partly because of the attractive illustrations by Carlos Marchiori and the record (1970b) that accompanied it. Later I brought out a sequel with rhymes and songs for slightly older children, *Ring Around the Moon* (1977), and more recently a third on outdoor games, called *Red Rover, Red Rover* (1988b), named for what is perhaps the most popular game in Canada.

The way my books came about reminds me of Alan Dundes' formula for North American aboriginal tales: lack leading to lack liquidated (1964). I produced *The Penguin Book of Canadian Folk Songs* (1973; see also recording 1975) because Canadian songs were practically unknown in Britain and the United States and I hoped to spread them beyond our borders. When I noted that no general collection was available, I began working on *Folklore of Canada* (1976). Choosing representative items and annotating them gave me a pretty thorough knowledge of what folklore had been collected in this country. While working at that I began teaching at York University, and learning more about folklore areas I hadn't researched.[5] I've been delighted that some of my students developed a lasting interest in folklore, going on to study at Memorial University of Newfoundland or the University of Pennsylvania.

Having done half a dozen books of songs, I turned to tales and produced *Folktales of French Canada* (1979b), translations of tales Dr Barbeau collected, and later *Tales Told in Canada* (1986). Two books prepared with Carole Carpenter, *A Bibliography of Canadian Folklore in English* (Fowke and Carpenter 1981) and *Explorations in Canadian Folklore* (Fowke and Carpenter 1985) – a collection of articles – were attempts to fill needs we saw as folklore professors.

Two books I edited are unusual. Alice Kane, one of Canada's best storytellers, was born in Belfast, and every time I saw her she'd come out with a rhyme or song she knew. I kept telling her to write them down, and finally one year she gave me a Christmas present: the story of her first twelve years in Belfast. It was loaded with folkloric materials – songs, sayings, games, customs, recipes – so I felt it had to be published. It became *Songs and Sayings of an Ulster Childhood* (Kane 1983).

Another unusual book resulted from my reading Thomas Raddall's story "Blind MacNair" which featured a singing match. Noticing that the ballads quoted in it were not from printed texts, I wrote to Mr Raddall asking about his sources. He told me of two manuscripts: one of ballads in a sea captain's notebook, and one of sea shanties from a Nova Scotia sailor. With his permission, I published them as *Sea Songs and Ballads from Nineteenth-Century Nova Scotia* (1981). The ballad notebook, written before 1883, is the earliest body of Anglo-Canadian songs to come to light.

My most recent books are *A Family Heritage: The Story and Songs of LaRena Clark* (1994a) and *Legends Told in Canada* (1994b) which is illustrated with artifacts from the Royal Ontario Museum collection. On my computer I have manuscripts of a couple of slight books: *Sing for Your Supper: A Folksong Cookbook*, and *Black Cats and Shooting Stars: Canadian Superstitions and Folk Beliefs*, for children. So far they haven't found publishers. And I'm currently working on two books: one with Ken Goldstein of bawdy songs from Newfoundland and Ontario, and one of Canadian women's songs with Beverlie Robertson – as I noted, I was a feminist before there was such a term.

Having recounted my personal odyssey, I now want to mention some of my personal prejudices. I object to the tendency of certain academics to distinguish sharply between what they term professionals and amateurs on the basis of their training.[6] I don't have a Ph.D. in folklore, a lack I share with Roy Mackenzie, Helen Creighton, and some of the pioneer Americans who became excellent folklorists before any folklore departments existed. I think folklorists should be judged strictly on the basis of their work. If it's good, they're professionals. I firmly believe the old saying that you learn by doing; I learned more about Canadian history in researching our historical songs than when I studied history at university. Academic courses can speed up the learning process; they can tell you where to find information and point you in the right direction. But basically it's what you do – collecting, researching, annotating, or analysing – that teaches you about folklore.

I also object to the assumption that academic and popular treatments of folklore are necessarily opposed. I've always believed that one of the objects of collecting folklore is to make it available to people, not to bury it in archives and academic journals.[7] I deplore as strongly as anyone the bastardization of folk materials for commercial profit, and I object to rewritten tales being called folklore – although some of them have merit in their own right. However, I maintain that it's possible – and desirable – to present genuine folk materials in forms that can be appreciated and used by the general public. My attempts to do this led some folklorists to consider me a popularizer – which is apparently a very bad thing to be – while folkniks consider me a purist – also a bad thing. Nevertheless I believe it's possible to serve both the people and the scholars. I believe genuine folklore can be presented so that non-academics can read and enjoy it, yet with sufficient background information to make it of value to folklorists.

I believe that one purpose of folksong collecting should be to bring songs back into use – to make them available to those who want to sing them – and hence I see nothing wrong with singing books. In them, the songs should be altered as little as possible, and readers should be told where the original versions can be found. But some academics are critical when songs are slightly modified to make them easier to sing. Such necessary changes are different from the arbitrary changes sometimes made so that songs can be copyrighted. The free style of traditional singers, who adapt the melody to the words, has to be regularized for non-traditional singers, and when there is instrumental accompaniment, the words must conform to a metrical pattern.

Another of my complaints is that in Canada research on the folklore of a great variety of ethnic groups has been emphasized at the expense of Anglo-Canadians, who still form our largest single group. Our Canadian Centre for Folk Culture Studies archive contains material from over seventy groups, of which some fifty together make up about five percent of our population. I don't object to the folklore of recent immigrants being collected, but it shouldn't be emphasized over that of people of British or Irish ancestry. Also, I don't think folklore from immigrants should be considered Canadian until it has survived here for at least one generation.

I also have a strong prejudice against the tendency of some folklorists to write in jargon. I'm an English professor, and I deplore the practice of concealing meaning by using supposedly scientific terms. Of course this fault is widespread – authorities in most academic disciplines tend to develop jargon, claiming that their ideas are too complex to express simply. But high-falutin' overblown language seems particularly unfortunate in a discipline whose subject is the folk.

Supplementary to my prejudice against inflated language is a distrust of supposedly scientific definitions. The desire to turn folklore into a science[8] has led to attempts to coin technical terms and definitions. Folklore genres are very difficult to pin down, and some apparently exact definitions sound more precise than they are. For example, Alan Dundes defined superstitions as "traditional expressions of one or more conditions and one or more results with some of the conditions signs and others causes" (1961). That may hold for most superstitions – although some aren't traditional expressions at all, they're beliefs – but it also covers many traditional expressions that aren't superstitions. For example: "All work and no play makes

Jack a dull boy": all work and no play the cause, a dull boy the result; or in little Miss Muffet, the spider is the cause, a frightened Miss Muffet the result; and so on.

Recently the tendency is to downgrade the content of folklore in favour of the process. Because my approach is literary and began with an interest in songs, I naturally think that texts are of some importance. I applauded D.K. Wilgus when he proclaimed, "The text is the thing," (1973) and I was glad to hear Herbert Halpert's comment that context without text is as bad or even worse than text without context.

I've always thought that studying folklore should lead to greater tolerance; that it should help us to understand and hence to accept differences in cultures and beliefs; that it should counteract racial and other prejudices. It should also, I feel, help us to be more tolerant of fellow folklorists whose approach to our subject differs from our own. I don't object to any particular theory or method. I ask only that folklorists don't assume that everyone who doesn't follow their pattern is automatically wrong.[9] So I implore all of you not to be dogmatic in your attitude toward those who take a somewhat different approach, who do not adhere to the gospel as set forth by the currently anointed prophets. Variety is the lifeblood of folklore. It should also be the lifeblood of folkloristics.

Enough of complaints. To sum up, from what began as a casual interest in folksong records, my personal odyssey has led me through radio programs, singing books, field collecting, records, scholarly books, children's lore, and teaching: to "a life in folklore," to borrow Helen Creighton's phrase. It's also brought me many rewards – honorary degrees, the Order of Canada, becoming a Fellow of the AFS and of the Royal Society of Canada, honorary life memberships in the Canadian Folk Music Society, the AFS Children's Folklore Section, and the Writers' Union of Canada. Best of all, it has brought me many dear friends, many priceless experiences, and many fond memories. May it do the same for all of you.

NOTES

This is a revised and shortened version of the Elli Kongas-Maranda Lecture given at the American Folklore Society meeting, St John's, Newfoundland, October 1991.

1 [Editors' note] Although Dr Fowke was one who objected to our calling the collection *Undisciplined Women*, it is clear that just as she was a

feminist before the term was popular, she was an undisciplined woman before this book was ever thought of!

2 A postscript to my political days was *Songs of Work and Freedom* (Fowke and Glazer 1965). Although I'd lost my enthusiasm for big unions, I was still sympathetic to the ones fighting to improve conditions for oppressed workers. I'd been thinking of doing a book of labour songs when I met Joe Glazer, the American labour singer and songwriter, so we did it together.

3 Later, in 1971, I started the *Canadian Folk Music Journal* to give Canadian folklorists an outlet for articles.

4 I've been going to Britain almost every summer for the last fifteen years, to visit folk clubs and festivals. I found their festivals, which emphasized traditional songs, much more to my taste than those on this continent. Lately many of the English ones have become more commercial, but on my recent trips I have vastly enjoyed the Sidmouth, Auchtermuchty, and Whitby festivals. Auchtermuchty, a tiny Scottish town, presents only traditional singers, dancers, storytellers, and musicians. Hamish Henderson's "Freedom Come All Ye," my favourite of all modern songs, seems to have become their anthem.

5 My course was for English literature students so I dealt with folklore as oral literature and stressed its similarities, differences, and links with written literature.

6 Note also Tye's concerns about this dichotomy, this volume.

7 Tye (this volume) also notes that local ethnographers share my concern.

8 Doucette (this volume) also critiques this tendency.

9 This of course isn't new. For over a century theories have risen, had their day, and been replaced by new ones, which in their turn have been supplanted.

Lessons from "Undisciplined" Ethnography: The Case of Jean D. Heffernan[1]

DIANE TYE

> Folklore fulfils the important but often overlooked function of maintaining conformity to the accepted patterns of behavior.   (Bascom 1965:294)

> Some rather odd things happened in the Rows [neighbourhood of mining company housing]. One time a small child died and a neighbour's calf strayed over and ate the flowers off the door. Those neighbours never spoke to each other again in all the years they lived within speaking distance.   (Springhill Heritage Group 1993:133–4)

These quotations, the first from an American academic and the second from a Canadian local ethnographer, reflect divergent approaches to folklore. So widely separated are their perspectives that they seem to have little to say to one another. Local ethnographers[2] and their constituencies are relatively uninterested in outsiders' generalizations, and academically based folklorists have disregarded "popular," local ethnography as atheoretical and sullied by commodification.[3] Ironically in light of these dismissals, the body of largely unexplored work produced by undisciplined collectors – often women who have worked, usually without recognition, financial support, or institutional affiliation, to collect, assemble, disseminate and interpret traditional culture – can contribute both theoretical and methodological innovation to academic perspectives. Photograph albums, scrapbooks, exhibits for local museums, published and unpublished histories, and community newspaper columns provide essential building blocks of individual, family, and community identity. Local ethnography's suggestions about the role of folklore and in its incorporation of the collector sometimes reveal more radical subtexts than academic folklorists have previously recognized.

Since the publication of William Bascom's pioneering essay "Four Functions of Folklore" (quoted above), university-based folklorists have read traditional culture primarily as a way of maintaining conformity. Historian Ian McKay's analysis of antimodernism in Nova Scotia (1994) claims that folklorists, most specifically Helen Creighton, were not just reporters of traditional culture; instead they were instrumental in creating and selling the concept of a provincial "folk" type that continues to characterize regional identity and divert local and national attention from regional underdevelopment. Through their selection and explanation of folklore materials, folklorists often helped to perpetuate the status quo, creating a kind of self-fulfilling interpretation. Conversely function has often been unimportant to local ethnographers for whom the primacy of folklore in everyday life was self-evident. Less influenced by passing ideological fashions, they collected and wrote about traditional culture for purposes other than those that motivated academics, including self-expression and self sufficiency, invocation of community, and initiation of concepts of social change.

The work of local ethnographer Jean Heffernan, who collected and disseminated folklore in Nova Scotia during the 1950s, foreshadows several current concerns and approaches. Specifically these are her rejection of antimodernism, the intellectual construct that framed much writing about Nova Scotian culture during her lifetime; her sometimes coded uses of folklore to refashion her town's past and to ensure that her view of community and women's place in it be heard; and her depiction of self as ethnographer, a configuration that defies the scientific model of objectivity. Thus her method is relevant to future inquiries into the nature and development of Canadian cultural studies and the place of women in those studies.

The following consideration of Jean Heffernan's ethnographic record draws largely on Joan N. Radner and Susan S. Lanser's interpretative concept of "coding." While Radner and Lanser identify stategies of coding with much of women's folk culture, they indicate one possible criticism: intentionality is inferable only from performance in context and does not depend on the performer's interpretation (Radner and Lanser 1993:7). Some then may ask, How can we know that coding has actually taken place? While the answer may never be definitive, here I supplement an analysis of Heffernan's writing with interviews with her nephew and several of her friends. As well, members of the local historical society read an earlier version of the article and shared their comments. This community input acted as a check on the interpretive methodology and validated my reading of Heffernan's coded messages.

ANTI-INNOCENCE

Innocence emerged in the period from 1920 to 1950 as a kind of mythomoteur, a set of fused and elaborated myths that provided Nova Scotians with an overall framework of meaning, a new way of imagining their community, a new core of a hegemonic liberal common sense. Innocence discerned the essence of the society. The province was essentially innocent of the complications and anxieties of twentieth-century modernity. Nova Scotia's heart, its true essence, resided in the primitive, the rustic, the unspoiled, the picturesque, the quaint, the unchanging; in all those pre-modern things and traditions that seemed outside the rapid flow of change in the twentieth century.   (McKay 1994:30)

The existence of the town depends upon the mines because there is noth-ing else to work at here. All through the years there have been strikes, bumps, and depressions, runaways and accidents, falls of coal and stone and, despite all these, the mines are here and the men work in them.
                    (Springhill Heritage Group 1993:93)

Jean Dryden Heffernan recorded stories of Springhill, Nova Scotia,[4] the town where she was born in 1900 and where she lived for most of her life. For several years beginning in 1952,[5] Heffernan was the town's representative for *The Amherst Daily News*, published in the county seat located fifteen miles away. As such she was responsible both for the paper's distribution within Springhill and for filling the one page devoted to town news. Her articles describe local events, including weddings, anniversaries, and town council meetings, but most significantly for this analysis, approximately 120 concern Springhill's folklore and history.

Heffernan documented aspects of life in Springhill from her posi-tion as a member of its middle class.[6] Her columns, which reflect both an extensive knowledge of Springhill and an exceptional story-telling ability, paint a vivid and often humorous picture of Springhill life, touching on politics, sports, early tourism, professional and com-mercial life, education, religion, child and adult pastimes, and cus-tom.[7] Articles include topics that many would overlook and still more would never consider viable as newspaper story material: washday, hunting, insurance sellers, and the countless practical uses of both books and salt herring (Ibid., 127, 279, 134, 46, 47).[8]

Heffernan wrote frankly about the physical drabness, the hard work, and the lack of child labour laws during the early days of mining, and of occasional disagreements among residents. As she documented the meagre day-to-day existence of mining families, she talked of hardship, poverty, and conflicts but also of the town's resources, primarily its people. She considered as integral not only town leaders but also local characters[9] and ordinary residents who treated each other with generosity. From the vantage point of remem-bered youth, she conveyed the egalitarian vision of a child who was

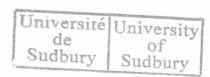

as fascinated by a neighbourhood woman who made and sold yeast from her home (Ibid., 128) as by men's tall silk hats (Ibid., 342) or women's "hookings" and "quiltings" (Ibid., 343).[10]

Heffernan's descriptions of community life challenged the antimodernist framework of folklore that Ian McKay argues informed the work of "professional" folklore collectors since the 1920s. Starting with W. Roy Mackenzie's collecting in 1902, Nova Scotians had looked backwards in time for their folklore. Mackenzie chose to document ballad singing, a tradition he felt was coming to a close (Mackenzie 1919:18). Helen Creighton's collecting also focused on ballads when she began thirty years later. She echoed Mackenzie's conviction that the tradition was dying and that she was recording its vestiges (Creighton 1967).

Although many of Heffernan's stories were rooted in past experiences and happenings, she placed their meaning and resonances firmly in the present, not in outmoded practices relevant only to older residents and ancestors. While some of the customs she described, like yeast making, were no longer practised, their memory was still significant to contemporary Springhillers. She also showed how some contemporary practices, such as spring cleaning, had long histories. Her columns presented the past as more than nostalgia; instead it was an integral part of the present. In her accounts of housekeeping – "The methods of housekeeping have changed with the times but there is just as much of it" (Springhill Heritage Group 1993:130) – she demonstrated that technological change obliterates neither the task nor the commonly held aesthetics for its evaluation. More generally, her work reminded readers that changing forms do not signal the end of a community.

McKay contends that in part through the work of folklorists like Creighton, a "local variant of antimodernism" arose which he refers to as Innocence (McKay 1994:30). He sees five perceptual and practical changes that accompanied an embrace of Innocence: "The new doctrine that the province was essentially Scottish was fortified with invented traditions and emblems; the province's history was seen anew as a collection of static artifacts testifying to the lost splendours of a vanished golden age; the symbolic landscapes of the province became those which emphasized insularity, rockbound coasts, and an omnipresent sea; and representations of the archetypical Nova Scotia came to emphasize muscle-bound masculinity and prowess. Finally … Nova Scotia came to be seen, at least on the level of its myths and symbols, as *essentially* a 'Folk society'" (McKay 1994:31–2). Stalwart, ballad-singing fishermen emerged as a provincial folk type even though few people living in Nova Scotia at the time knew the ballads, many men earned their livelihoods from the land – agriculture, lumbering, and mining – and from manufacturing, and many singers were women. Heffernan's writing fell outside this view of provincial history and character. Certainly Springhill, located inland and held tightly in the grip of the coal mines that employed the majority of its male work force, was not sought out by folklore collectors. W. Roy Mackenzie, Helen Creighton, and William Doerflinger focused on coastal communities and avoided grimy industrial settings.[11] From most published regional collections readers might suspect that industrial workers lacked folklore equal to that of the fisherfolk, and thus local histories and columns such as Heffernan's are important sources for developing an understanding of such traditions.

Certainly Heffernan's view of community was less narrowly defined than the one McKay critiqued. She spent her youth surrounded by her father's family, who were of Irish Catholic descent. Thus her columns documented Irish family traditions, as well as Irish-based community celebrations of Saint Patrick's Day and the Orange Lodge. Introducing a column based on her grandmother Heffernan's Scottish grandfather, she satirised the provincial embrace of Scottish invented traditions: "Now that Nova Scotia has had a piper and Highland dancers, in full regatta [sic], at the border and St. Andrew's Day is being celebrated in Amherst with haggis and the heather ... most of the Irish think it is time to take to the tall timbers" (Springhill Heritage Group 1993:345). In place of the sacred Scottish mythomoteur that McKay describes as characterizing provincial folklore, Heffernan often irreverently discussed realities of an ethnically diverse community whose members failed to conform to a stereotypical conceptualization of "the folk." Overall, Heffernan's work provided an alternative to "innocence" through acceptance of change, recognition of the value of industrialized workers' traditional culture, and acknowledgment of ethnic plurality. Free from the academic restraints of the days that would have directed her toward the collection of only a few genres, such as ballad, Heffernan was not hampered by some of the biases that mark contemporaneous scholarly publication. Her columns often centred on aspects of life that folklorists of her day never considered.

CODING AND COMMUNITY

The surface meanings of innocuous everyday discourse conceal the existence of coded behavior.   (Radner and Lanser 1993:5)

The Fullers played an important part in church and social affairs. And they could always be depended upon to stir up a little excitement ... And so it goes. The history of a town and its people, as written for those who can read between the lines on stones in an old cemetery.

(Springhill Heritage Group 1993:285)[12]

Jean Heffernan sometimes challenged structures of power openly. Reviewing the mines' history, she wrote critically of J.R. Cowans, the general manager in the 1890s who was in charge of operations during a twenty-two-month strike. She satirized the opulence of his house, to which an invitation was like "a royal command," and stated that "he never understood the working men and they never understood him" (Ibid., 91). More frequently, however, her critiques were subtle, clothed in humour and coded in language only Springhillers fully understood. Throughout her writing Heffernan relied heavily on what Joan N. Radner and Susan S. Lanser term "complicit" as well as "implicit" coding.

According to Radner and Lanser, a complicit "code has been collectively determined ahead of time and therefore can be adopted by an entire community" (Radner and Lanser 1993:5). Heffernan's apparently accessible narratives held references full of hidden connotation which functioned like passwords or code names. Presumably everyone in the community who knew the Fullers referred to above would understand Heffernan's meaning. However, such knowledge is not easily accessible to outsiders, or perhaps even to many current Springhillers.

Radner and Lanser suggest that "a context for implicit coding exists when there is a situation of oppression, dominance, or risk for a particular individual or identifiable group; when there is some kind of opposition to this situation that cannot safely be made explicit; and when there is a community of potential 'listeners' from which one would want to protect oneself" (Ibid., 9). Both gender and class would provide such contexts in Springhill. For example, in critiquing the mine boss, Heffernan followed her derogatory comments on the historical person with a reference to the superintendent, who, she said, displayed none of these negative characteristics. Read as a coded message, this might be termed juxtaposition, distraction, or indirection (Ibid., 13–19). The first, faultfinding part of the message is publicly obviated by the second; yet the message enables a criticism.

Gendered coding is often evident in articles about male members of the community. Heffernan's breezy style was in itself a kind of code disguising "feminist messages," for, as Radner and Lanser explain, women's "attitudes and understandings cannot always be openly acknowledged because of their social, economic, and emotional dependence on the goodwill of men" (1993:2). Heffernan's columns, chatty glimpses of community life on the surface, challenged the exclusivity of the male perspective. For example, a comment addressed to women readers accustomed to being ridiculed by men can be read as a singular public expression of women's resistance: "I wonder if, in the good old days, the men growled about the price of ladies' hats. Well, one thing, a woman always buys a hat; but a man usually invests in one. And, I suppose, since they wear them so long, men's hats really are an investment although some I have seen looked as if they had stopped paying dividends a long time ago" (Springhill Heritage Group 1993:6). Humour allowed her to minimize male experience and turn patriarchy on its head by silencing – if only momentarily – those who usually silenced women.

Whereas Mackenzie and Creighton emphasized the "maleness" of the folk, or at best relied on the male model as gender neutral, Jean Heffernan's version of history and culture was woman-centred. She sometimes presented female experience as gender neutral: "In Springhill, where nearly everyone burns coal, people talk house-cleaning practically the whole year. They are usually finished with the spring cleaning when the subject of fall cleaning comes up for discussion" (Ibid., 125). The articles, as an extension of the published accounts of women's visiting patterns commonly found in small town newspapers (see also Greenhill 1989b), would have held special significance for women, who were probably her largest readership. From domestic work routines (Springhill Heritage Group 1993:125) to fashion (Ibid., 5)[13] she described women's domains and considered women's participation in every subject she tackled. Men's experiences were presented from a female point of view. One article, for example, exposed the contradiction between men's passion for hunting – which she described as sleeping on a hard bed in a cold shack and eating out of a tin – and their demands for domestic comfort at home (Ibid., 279).

Some of her gendered commentary was relatively uncoded and explicit in its aims, asserting positive, though not always conventional, images of women's activities. In one article she described how her grandmother, a respected elder of the community, often sat on the kitchen floor and made kites for neighborhood children (Ibid., 221).[14] In another she lauded the first women in Springhill to enter the wage labour market (Ibid., 125). Much of her writing conveyed the sentiment expressed by her comment on Mrs Parks, one of Springhill's early settlers who reportedly discovered coal: "They always say never underestimate the power of a woman" (Ibid., 90).

Heffernan also relied on complicit coding to speak to fellow residents. Just as she suggested that the history of a town and its people was represented in an old cemetery, so it was found in her columns. Her articles produced a map of Springhill that revealed much about the ways residents read their physical and social landscape, drawing not only on visual memories but also on those that were olfactory – the smell of yeast and brown bread – and auditory – the sound of the school bell. Through narratives about residents, landmarks, events, and experiences, Heffernan drew on commonalities – the threads that wove together community. Her descriptions and references operated in the same way as esoteric traditional expressions (see Small 1975); they solidified group memberships through shared knowledge and separated insiders from outsiders. Heffernan never broke the complicity; for example, she did not elaborate on her statement that the Fuller family could always be depended upon to stir up a little excitement. Only Springhillers who knew them understood fully what this entailed and what constituted "excitement."

Her coded narratives offered residents a picture of themselves not just as employees and dependents of the company – in fact the company received little treatment in her columns – but as individuals with unique personalities. Her articles crossed lines of religion, class, and gender to document contributions of various constituencies to town life and emphasize residents' strength of character. Both in what they described – positive qualities like friendliness, generosity, and resourcefulness – and what they did not – the mine's stranglehold over town economics – her articles offered workers an empowering antidote to the stresses of life under company rule. It is even possible that her writing played a subversive role. Through absenting the company from most of her writing – another coding strategy – Heffernan effectively undermined its control and in this way her work, as well as the oral narratives on which it was based, might be read as expression of working class protest.

As local ethnographer she used folklore as an agent of change. As Laurel Doucette's article in this volume points out, folklorists have not always been aware of the implications of either the materials they collect or of their own positions in promoting change. But Heffernan's example offers an illustration of how individuals can use folklore to ensure that certain voices be heard. For Heffernan, accuracy would have been only one goal of ethnography. Truth would have been more important.[15]

Collecting and disseminating folklore also gave voice to Jean Heffernan herself. In a mining town that accepted patriarchal structures, most people saw women's place to be firmly in the domestic domain.[16] Men may have watched carefully over public forums such as the church and local government, but they apparently had less regard for cultural activities. Perhaps in part because of this inattention, and because Heffernan spoke to a public audience from her secure and approved position in the private sphere, her writings were accepted. Neither her articles, which drew on knowledge of family and town gathered through women's networks, nor her status as community events reporter, overtly threatened patriarchal constructs. The subtexts created by Heffernan, and others like her who wrote out of the oral tradition of their communities, demonstrate what feminists have only recently begun to point out; research has the ability to empower and transform (hooks 1988:49–54). Heffernan relied on folklore to recast both the community and her place within it.

SELF/WOMAN AS
ETHNOGRAPHY/ETHNOGRAPHER

To understand our connection to other people and all other beings and to rejoice in the life that has been given to us.   (Tomm 1992:216)

A friend of mine, who is a native Springhiller now exiled in Toronto, wrote to me a while ago, and said that there is a certain sense of humour prevalent in Nova Scotia which cannot be matched any place else in Canada. In Springhill, where funny things do happen, the stories lose nothing in the telling; and many of the stories come up with a few extra frills after they have been told a few times.   (Springhill Heritage Group 1993:122)

Heffernan's ability to tie community members together through her words and images continued beyond her own lifetime. Current local historian Mary Willa Littler credits Heffernan's writing with sparking her own interest in town history and culture and distributed Heffernan's articles at a town reunion to prompt those attending to remember and share their own stories (Littler 1992). In 1993 the local historical society collected and republished Heffernan's articles.

Most academically trained ethnologists have seen folklore meant to be shared with those whose property it is in the first place as spurious or what Richard Dorson declared "fakelore."[17] But for collectors like Heffernan, her audience was central. Her articles drew on commonalities and they also helped to define community. While acknowledging fault lines, she emphasized qualities that enabled residents to overcome, or at least to live with, divisions. Her writing about community engendered community. Columns described a life characterized by a high degree of mutuality and reciprocity among neighbours. Women's positive competition was expressed through vying for the first line of clothes on wash day or the fullest pantry; their cooperation and collectivity was clear in shared child care and health care. She presented qualities such as friendliness as essential community identity markers.

As an insider, Heffernan wrote about her subjects from a point of view that reflected little separation between self and subject. Often they were one and the same. Academically based folklorists have tended to protect their territory and to emphasise its otherness from their own experience. They have refused to recognize Heffernan and others who did not conform to traditional notions of an ethnographer, whether in status, subject matter, collecting style, or presentation mode. Yet local ethnographers' work is helpful precisely because of those differences. In contrast to the (usually male) research model where an outsider as fieldworker visits a place for a limited period to seek out very specific items – folksongs, tales, and so on – and then separates himself sometimes permanently from the community, Heffernan showed little or no detachment. Unlike W. Roy Mackenzie, who distanced himself sharply from the ballad singers whom he described as "low company" in *The Quest for the Ballad* (Mackenzie 1919:33), or Helen Creighton whom McKay accuses of patronizing "her singers" (McKay 1994:108–9), Heffernan was very much a part of the Springhill she described. She worked throughout her lifetime at keeping in touch with the full meaning of that membership. The respect she communicated for her subjects indicated she saw them not as the removed "other," but as those who shared commonalities with her; writer and subjects are part of a larger self.

In many of her articles, she wrote of friends and neighbours whom she would know and rely on for many years; at other times, she cast herself as both author and subject. Whereas Mackenzie employed the male metaphor of the hunter and Creighton the more passive but still adventurous one of the treasure seeker, Heffernan unwrapped layers of culture to expose the essence of community life and expression. As such, her writing reflected a relationship between ethnographer/writer, subject, and audience that challenges the traditional ethnographic model of tape recorded interviews conducted by a stranger who has little or no personal connection with the community. For Heffernan the constituencies – audience and subjects – were one. In this way, her published writings raise questions about how to judge ethnography.

Many of her columns were based on oral narratives she learned from family and friends. Heffernan's friend Isabel Simpson could trace the genealogy of many stories: some came from grandparents, parents, and other relatives, others were told by a milliner (a close friend of Heffernan's grandmother), and hunting tales were likely generated by her brother and other neighbourhood men.[18] Simpson remembered Heffernan as an inveterate storyteller whose writing was an extension of her role as oral narrator: "she talked the way she wrote, or she wrote the way she talked, either one" (Simpson 1992).[19] She recalled, "Jean Heffernan had an extraordinary sense of humour. She was always telling you something funny ... you know ... a lot of [stories] were experiences and of course she embroidered on them, there's no question about that but that's the way she talked. If you would go in, you'd just be fascinated ... we used to spend hours down there" (Ibid.).

Heffernan's columns and the oral narratives on which they were based tied her to people who comprised her family and community.[20] Collecting and sharing stories brought Heffernan in contact with others and ensured her active membership in a community into which she did not physically venture for the last part of her life.[21] In this way she connected herself not only to her contemporaries but also with Springhill's past incarnations[22] and maintained her sense of belonging in the face of an isolating illness.

Winnie Tomm describes a new paradigm that values women's desire for links with others. Jean Heffernan's writing contains insights for those who challenge the authority of Euro North American rationality, an "intellectual" structure that separates mind from body and privileges "objectivity" (Tomm 1992) as the only "way of knowing" (see Belenky et al. 1986). Rather, as psychologist Mary Field Belenky suggested is the ideal for constructing knowledge, local ethnographers' work depends on connections between intellect and feelings, both within the ethnographers themselves and between them and others (see Tomm 1992:210). Thus Heffernan and her counterparts offer suggestions for those within academe who draw on new frameworks, including feminism, to deconstruct theoretical paradigms and to develop more fair and representative ethnographic models.

Jean Heffernan wrote from the margins; socially and intellectually she came from outside centres of power. Thus positioned, she communicated the richness of small town traditional culture in a manner that accepted the full participation of its female members. Because academic work of Heffernan's time largely overlooked female expression,[23] her columns, and those histories and scrapbooks compiled by countless other women in communities across Canada, can fill gaps in our knowledge of women's folk traditions and women folklore collectors. They sometimes explain ways in which women have relied on folklore to express individuality or solidarity, to bring about social change, or to secure a place for themselves and their communities. Heffernan's ethnographic portrayals of folk culture explored ways in which women and men use traditional culture at once to celebrate the richness and to resist the narrowness that defined small town life. She offered illustrations of tradition as a multifaceted resource that helps individuals resist, survive, and even enjoy lives confined by social expectations and roles.

Heffernan's cultural interpretations are coded and thus are not fully accessible to outsiders. But they clearly extend beyond the construction of "innocence" used to characterize the "folk" of this time period in Nova Scotia. Heffernan's subjects were not ballad-singing fisherfolk clinging to a rocky coastline but pluralistically created and identified human beings exploring custom and narrative within an industrial setting. Through the consideration of local ethnographers like Heffernan, a fresh vision of folklore dynamics emerges.

NOTES

1 I very much appreciate the assistance of staff members of the Public Archives of Nova Scotia, Bill Heffernan, Gwen Layton, Mary Willa Littler, and Isabel Simpson, as well as insights shared by Laurel Doucette and Barbara Rieti. I especially thank Pauline Greenhill who has been particularly generous in her help with this paper.

2 I am using "local ethnography" here to refer to community-based collecting by individuals who are insiders to the culture: journalists, local historians, family archivists, and so on. Often considered amateurs by academics, their work is usually overlooked by that group. For example, Carole Carpenter's history of folklore activities in Canada (1979) does not include any discussion of local ethnographers' work. Allan Dunlop also notes the tendency to ignore local individuals' work in his discussion of nineteenth century Nova Scotian historian and genealogist, George Patterson (Dunlop 1988:139).

3 For a recent discussion of the academic versus popular debate in folklore studies, see Georges (1991). As Christine St. Peter's discussion of Anne Cameron illustrates, the whole concept of commodification must

be reexamined. Condemnation of "popularizers" by academic folklorists denies both academic exploitation of collected materials and the right of community members to represent and profit from their traditional culture. Further, the work of collectors like Jean Heffernan reflects different motivations for the collection and presentation of traditional culture from those guiding academic folklorists.

4 A 1898 gazetteer described as Springhill as a "mining town of importance" (McAlpine 1898:561). According to the directory, in Heffernan's youth the community numbered nearly 5000 and was serviced by five churches, a hotel, thirty stores and three newspaper offices.

5 The exact length of her tenure as reporter is unclear. From 1952–1956 she wrote approximately 120 columns based on elements of Springhill traditional culture and history, but the majority – about 100 – were contributed before her brother Wyndam's death in 1954.

6 She was the third of four children of Margaret Dick and Frank S. Heffernan, an employee of the customs house and later the Cumberland Railway. Her mother's family moved to Springhill in 1873 after the opening of the coal mines where her grandfather worked as a master mechanic. They later returned to their native Pictou County in the northeast of the province. After Margaret's death in 1911, the family drew close to Frank's parents. Many of Jean Heffernan's early memories centred on her eccentric paternal grandfather, William Heffernan, who operated a furniture store and wrote poetry in his spare time. In an unpublished family history, Jean Heffernan described her grandfather as a third generation Halifax furniture maker/seller who moved to Springhill after going bankrupt in Halifax in 1880. This grandfather, whom she described as "a dreamer," was an important influence on her and she wrote of how he read Shakespeare to her as a child (see Heffernan nd). He published one volume of poetry (see Heffernan 1906).

7 See Greenhill (1989a:55–61) for a discussion of local newspapers as a traditional culture context.

8 Originally published by Jean Heffernan as "'Hand power' washer guaranteed to do better job than wash board," *Amherst Daily News* (hereafter *ADN*) 7 Dec. 1953:6; "Hunting season shows oddities in men folk," *ADN* 19 Oct. 1953:6; "Salt herring was favorite fish of Springhiller in good old days," *ADN* 15 Aug. 1953:6; "Book agents did well in Springhill," *ADN* 6 Dec. 1952: 6; and "Insurance agents in Springhill hold peculiar position in town," *ADN* 15 March 1954: 6.

9 Local characters are minor nonconformists who often play a significant role in their communities. Both their "performances" and their treatment by others may reveal much about a community's expectations

for its members. For a discussion of the local character phenomenon, see Tye (1987).

10 Originally published by Jean Heffernan as "Recalls days ... when yeast was 'east' and kids made half-hour errands," ADN 13 July 1953: 6; "Grandpa was in Washington Theatre the night President Lincoln was shot," ADN 19 Sept. 1953: 6; and "Parties, quilting bees were popular and one affair made local history," ADN 1 March 1954: 6.

11 Arthur Huff Fauset (1931) would be an exception to this with his collecting from African Nova Scotians, which drew on both industrial and rural communities.

12 Originally published by Jean Heffernan as "Hillside Cemetery town's headache," ADN 9 Feb. 1954: 6.

13 Originally published by Jean Heffernan as "Housewives in early days of mining town followed ironclad schedules," ADN 5 March 1953:6 and "About ladies' hats then wonder if men growled," ADN 6 Dec. 1952:6.

14 Originally published by Jean Heffernan as "Kites, maple woods, 'glass alleys' bring nostalgic memories of spring," ADN 12 March 1954:6.

15 For a relevant discussion of the distinction between truth and accuracy as illustrated in the writings of Emily Carr, see Adams (1992). Greenhill (1989a:83–92) considers the relationship of history, folklore and truth in her examination of local newspapers.

16 David Frank (1993) has also made this point concerning the coal mining community of Stellarton, Nova Scotia. Ian McKay (McKay and Mannette 1988:92) wrote of the despair women in Springhill felt at being shut out from the coal mines the "pit talk" that engrossed male residents. Patriarchal structures are repeated in some of the best known folklore about Springhill. Rosenberg (1987) noted the contrast of active miners with passive women waiting for news at the pithead in some of the folksongs commemorating the mine disasters of 1956 and 1958.

17 The term "fakelore" refers to items that have been rewritten and are transmitted largely through broadcast, print, or commercial means rather than orally, or have been completely invented by writers.

18 One example of a narrative familiar to Simpson was the story Heffernan told of her grandfather refusing to sell a customer six dining room chairs because he would have to order more (Heffernan nd). Simpson remembered her own mother telling a personal narrative of a time she attempted to purchase a mattress displayed in the furniture store window. W.E. Heffernan would not sell it to her for the same reason (Simpson 1992).

19 Springhill resident Gwen Layton indicated that in preparing a collection of Heffernan's articles, the Springhill Heritage group struggled with

the question of whether or not they should edit some sentences to make them conform to a more conventional written form (Layton 1992).

20 Heffernan relied on her interpretations of traditional culture to financially sustain herself. When Heffernan returned to Springhill after completing her education, she settled into small town life as a single woman. Heffernan's world narrowed further when her father became ill. For the last five years of his life, she provided continuous care, looking after him personally during the day and depleting any financial resources the family had by hiring a night nurse. After her father's death, her activities were restricted because of her own ill health. Perhaps in part from immobility brought on by many years suffering with phlebitis, she developed what seems to have been agoraphobia. For nearly the last 20 years of her life, even after medication controlled the phlebitis, she remained inside her house, going no further than her front doorstep. She supported herself on her meagre salary from the *Amherst Daily News* and on what she earned from what initially started off as a hobby reading friends' and family's tea leaves.

21 Although she lived exclusively within the walls of her own home, her diary recorded a constant stream of people through her door and showed how she wove herself into the community fabric both by marking significant events in neighbours' lives. Bill Heffernan told of the gifts distributed at Christmas and baskets assembled on Remembrance Day. For many years she provided a mental health patient with a monthly allowance. Bill reflected, "if she had a fault it was being too generous" (Heffernan 1992). Isabel Simpson confirmed this, recounting how Heffernan gave willingly to those in greater need than herself. Simpson indicated that she also maintained her end of the reciprocal exchanges that underlie much of community relations in a small town. She used her baking to informally repay goods and services given by Simpson's family (Simpson 1992). As well, she corresponded with many former Springhillers and her nephew Bill reflected that it was nearly a full-time job to read and answer her mail. Bill Heffernan believed his aunt kept a diary throughout her life (Heffernan 1992). Entries he showed me for 1970 reflected the same concerns for community as those evidenced in a scrapbook she complied.

22 She was particularly skilled at (re)creating the Springhill of the past, convincing herself as well as others of its contemporary reality. According to Bill Heffernan, she once commented that living alone in her house, surrounded by items of the family's past, she did not realize she had grown old. The realization hit when she left her house and entered the Victoria General Hospital near the end of her life (Heffernan 1992).

23 For a list of those who did folklore studies in Atlantic Canada, see Tallman (1979:119). Often collectors who included women subjects in their published works did not bring attention to them. As a result, female expression was usually dominated by or subsumed under male expression.

Feminist Afterwords:
Revisiting Copper Woman

CHRISTINE ST. PETER

Early in 1992 Pauline Greenhill contacted me with the request to reprint or excerpt for this collection an article I wrote in 1987 on Anne Cameron's *Daughters of Copper Woman* (1981). I welcomed her request as I had been concerned to add some afterthoughts to my earlier work, published in FS/*Feminist Studies* (St. Peter 1989). In the years since I wrote that article a number of important changes have rendered my earlier work obsolete. The changes occurred in the political situation of First Nations people in Canada, in the growing politicization of Native women writers and in my own developing sense of possibility in the complex interplay among the academic, the artistic, the pedagogical, and the political.[1] What I have to say now is controversial as was the earlier work; moreover it leaves unresolved, as the earlier work did in its way, several considerations important for feminist scholars studying marginalized cultures and writers.[2] The narrative that follows chronicles a process of change, and may speak to the experience of other scholars, like those represented in this volume, addressing the realities of female traditional culture in Canada.

My positions – white, middle-class, Euro-Canadian academic – place me a long way from the lived experiences of Canada's aboriginal women. Yet as a feminist professor of women's studies I, with my colleagues, am determined to build a curriculum that centres the lives and work of the women most marginalized in and by academia.[3] This work ideally reflects both difference and women's struggles about difference. In other words I have a conscious political agenda in my choices, as I wish to provide a place in the classroom for "other/wise"[4] visions of social organization.

I first became acquainted with Cameron's book in 1983 when a student in my introductory women's studies course urged me to include it among our readings. Her reasons were compelling: this book of women's myths and contemporary fictions is set on Vancouver Island, is written by a Vancouver Island writer, and offers exciting intellectual and spiritual visions to University of Victoria feminist students intent on recovering local women's prehistory. More precisely, the book promises a glimpse of a secret society of powerful women in our midst, traces of an ancient women's culture that still exists in attentuated but recoverable form, is healthy for women and the environment and, with the permission of Native elders, is available to women of other races. Cameron explains her sources and her authority for telling Native stories at the beginning of the book: "these women shared their stories with me because they knew I would not use them without their permission ... The summer of 1980 I was told that, if I wanted, I could tell what I knew. The style I have chosen most clearly approached the style in which the stories were given to me" (1981:7).

From a political point of view I found the book valuable because the author, although white, treats the Native traditions and people with deep respect, a respect born of her long association with and attentive study of Native culture. From a pedagogical point of view I liked the book because it demonstrates methods whereby a colonized, exploited group might reclaim their past through revisionist and recuperative thinking, feminist questioning, and sensitive listening to muted voices.

As an experiment I decided to have the class read the book; its celebratory, women-centred knowledge was so successful that I assigned it for two subsequent years as a treat at the end of the course – good news after the often bad or difficult news. Native women, always a small minority in the classes, appeared to relish the book as much as their non-Native colleagues. Did this acceptance reflect my insensitivity to their apparent compliance? Student passivity in the face of professorial decisions? Their own mutedness in a university classroom? An undeveloped awareness of the political issues involved in the appropriation of Native stories by a white author? Whatever the reasons in the 1980s, Native women since the early 1990s have been very clear about their objections to reading this book.

At the time I first assigned the book I also undertook an examination of the extra-textual implications of its use. I met and corresponded with Cameron and remain firmly convinced of her ethical commitment to Native people's welfare.[5] I also made a point of canvassing Native people's and feminist anthropologists' opinions about the book. As both groups had mixed reactions – some supportive, some damning – I set out to examine more closely the responses of Native women writers as well as major ethnographic sources as a way of orienting myself politically and academically in this confused landscape. The more I listened to the growing discussion about the book, the more imperative it became for me, as teacher and scholar, to assess the veracity of the rendering and the ethics of the publication. The need for such orientation became very clear when I gave a lecture on the book in 1987 for the women's studies unit at the University of Copenhagen and discovered how large and enthusiastic was its international audience, and how much these feminist readers wanted to be sure of its accuracy. As one of the anonymous FS/*Feminist Studies* referees stated in her review of my article: "I'd ... like to be able to use the book in a course I teach on Culture and Human Values which emphasizes comparative myth, art, literature. For such a course, I absolutely have to know how authentically Cameron represents especially the 'old' [prehistorical] stories, and where she departs from them, and why. Is there, or isn't there a matriarchal tradition? Is there or isn't there lesbian practice? ... Are Cameron's retellings of the female-matriarchal lineage her own remakings (or those of contemporary Native women), or what?"

These were all questions I set out to study over a two-year period, and I published my discoveries in the FS/*Feminist Studies* article. No small part of my satisfaction in that publication was its acceptance by editor Barbara Christian, an African-American critic whose work I admire as particularly sensitive to questions of racial/cultural imperialism. As she said, "The editors of *Feminist Studies* ... believe [the article] is a significant contribution to the discussion about the appropriation of the texts of an exploited group by a member of the colonizing group and that it raises these issues within a feminist context" (letter to author, 3 June 1988).[6]

As this discussion is available in print, I shall not restate it here; suffice it to say that, with elaborate qualification including the testimony of some Native women writers who praised Cameron's work and the partial approval of the Seattle Women's Anthropology Group,[7] I decided that her use of Native stories was defensible and useful, albeit not without problems of various sorts. Two of the most obvious problems were these: her tendency to homogenize the experiences of women (e.g., "Woman's Truth") in ways that obliterate significant differences among women; and her radical feminist interpretations of stories that did, admittedly, have a defensible "fit" with some ethnographic sources, provided one was willing to ignore other, ambiguous evidence. Put so baldly this sounds obviously unacceptable, yet all ethnography interprets in recording, and Cameron's interpretations did win the approval of some discerning Native people.[8] Only since the publication of my article have I learned how essential is the practice of verbatim recording of elders' words, no matter whether the recorder is Native or non-Native. This stringent ethnographic practice requires as well precise contextualizing – the name and exact words of the storyteller, and the date and conditions of transmission.[9]

But there is another very contentious issue that comes into play here, the result of which is that I no longer teach the book, even though a study of the book and the debates around it might make for a useful exercise in a women's studies classroom. My change of practice here does not signify a diminution of my admiration for Cameron's text; rather it acknowledges that the space she occupies as narrator of Native stories blocks the work of Native women who need to define that space for themselves.

Without referring to Cameron, Canadian Metis writer Maria Campbell points out that Native writers may not be able to sell their own books if they do not interpret Native materials in the way established by white writers (Godard 1985:14). As Okanagan writer Jeannette Armstrong says, "There are a lot of non-Indian people out there speaking on our behalf or pretending to speak on our behalf and I resent that very much; I don't feel that any non-Indian person could represent our point of view adequately (1985:56).

These generalized complaints took a more specific form in 1988 at the third International Feminist Book Fair in Montreal when Native writer Lee Maracle, at the request of other Native women, asked Anne Cameron to "move over." As Maracle explains it, "Anne is occupying the space that has no room for me. So few Canadians want to read about us that there is little room for Native books … If Anne takes up that space there is no room for us at all" (1989:10). According to Maracle, "we asked her to move over, and because she is a great lady, she moved. That is empowering for Anne, for Canadian women and for Native women" (Ibid., 10).

As Maracle explains the situation, one of the reasons why Cameron initially resisted moving over was her "ideological and political" belief that a "writer has a perfect right to write about anything under the heavens. In the larger sense, this is true. But right now it is a bitter pill for me to swallow" (Ibid., 9). This question of an author's freedom of imagination has caused many painful splits among women, as for example in 1988 when this issue of artists' appropriation of exploited groups' experience combined with structural inequities in the workplace resulted in the division of the Women's Press in Toronto.[10] Needless to say, the analogous question about scholars' appropriations is just as challenging.[11] As artists and scholars we invoke freedoms of thought and expression; as feminist artists and scholars we struggle with the realization that this work might be a "bitter pill" for other women struggling to survive not just as writers but as people.

What is interesting about Maracle's discussion is her focus on the ways such disagreements can be empowering: "Does this disagreement separate us? Does it blind my eyes to the beauty, the complexity and honesty of Anne herself? In Anne's own words, 'not fucking likely.' In fact this disagreement makes the talk around our kitchen table the more interesting. Our affection for each other is deepened by our ability to listen carefully to the other" (Ibid., 10).

At the beginning of this paper, I spoke of how unresolved this situation remains. Anne Cameron no longer writes adult books about Native myth, but has not withdrawn *Copper Woman* from publication, nor the very successful *Dreamspeaker* (1978) published under her former name, Cam Hubert.[12] She takes no profits from *Copper Woman*, and all profits, at her request, are used to finance Native projects. The feminist publishers of the book know about the Maracle-Cameron "move over" incident but are not intending to withdraw the book from their list. Instead the Press Gang Publishers have created a current policy of "publishing thoughtful, strong-minded and politically active Native writers, and ... incorporating their views respectfully in [the Collective's] decisions" (letter from Della McCreary to author, 3 August 1992). One of the authors whose works they publish is Lee Maracle.[13]

Removing *Daughters of Copper Woman* from my women's studies course means that my students may not learn, in all their complexity, the reasons why this now famous, quasi-sacred text is not – for political reasons – part of our curriculum. With Canada's most exploited group struggling for survival, and with their authors struggling for publication, those of us who are non-Native cannot use a text that is perceived by some Native women as blocking their road. But there is no longer any need to use the book. Thanks to the efforts of Native publishing firms like Theytus, One Sky, and Pemmican, as well as Canadian presses like NeWest, Press Gang Publishers, Sister Vision: Women of Colour Press, and the Women's Press, the published work of many aboriginal women is now available. An important collection of the writings of fifty-two aboriginal women can be found in *Writing the Circle: Native Women of Western Canada* (Perrault and Vance 1990), but a list of increasingly well-known Native women writers would include the following: Marie Campell, Lee Maracle, Jeannette Armstrong, Beth Brant, Karen Keeshig-Tobias, Lenore Keeshig-Tobias, Beth Cuthand, Ruby Slipperjack, Emma Larocque, Margo Kane, Marie Annharte Baker, Pauline Johnson, Clare E. McNab, Alice Lee, Barbara Higgins, Cindy Bashin, Connie Fife, Joy Asham Fedorick, Shirley Williams, Norma Gladue, Monique Mojica, and Eden Robinson.[14]

The possibility of appropriating the voice of a subordinated group will remain as long as subordination remains. When (if) this is eradicated, the political meaning of using an "other" voice will change. Yet to focus exclusively on this angle is to perpetuate a fatalistic way of looking at Native writing and oppression. As Lee Maracle has stated, "to buy into the notion of 'appropriation of voice' is to request that the paternalism to which it appeals remain intact. Let us get rid of the inequality by increasing the opportunity for First Nations people to publish ... There are endless stories to be told from our side of the colonial bench" (Maracle 1992b:D9).

The task seems clear for those of us who are professional academics (or artists from the dominant group) and in a position to profit professionally from our study of minority women. To appropriate others' stories in the face of centuries of genocidal treatment is simply unethical. Native poet Jeannette Armstrong writes with graphic horror of the social and anthropological encasement of First Nations people as she passes the Royal British Columbia Museum:

There are no Indians here
None
Even in the million dollar museum
that so carefully preserves
their clothing, their cooking utensils
their food
for taxpayers
from all over
to rush their children by

There are some good Indians
hanging around Kings Hotel
and they are dead
preserved in alcohol
It would be neater though
to kill us all at once
Whole clans and tribes
could be dressed and stuffed

Add a fifth floor to the museum
to accommodate them. (from "Death Mummer," Armstrong 1991:31)

To repeat, one cannot appropriate others' stories. But to back guiltily away from them is to allow the hegemonic relations to continue unchecked. As Himani Bannerji, an Indo-Canadian scholar, argues, while the privilege of some women may militate against the rights of other women, we all do share the same social terrain. Racism is not solely a "black" experience, she reminds her readers; people across the terrain will have "different moments and entry points into [racism], since different aspects of the same social relations are visible at different intersections, from different social locations." Therefore, no one is exempt from "the possibility or the responsibility of naming what constitutes the social whole" (Bannerji 1991:85,95).

As feminist scholars we wish not just to name the social whole but to change its configuration. This requires creative thinking about enabling rather than blocking Native women's publishing opportunities. And for those non-Native women who join in this important transformative work – work that may result in erasure from the publishing story – we need to find ways of legitimizing that struggle in professional terms. But finally, we need always to think about our shared terrain as "the colonial bench." Keeping the *consequences* of such divisions firmly in mind will keep us honest. It's not just on the First Nations' side that endless tales remain to be told.

NOTES

1 The political implications of research by folklorists and anthropologists are also discussed by Doucette.

2 Note that McGrath, this volume, also discusses aboriginal women's writing when considering Inuit women's autobiographies.

3 Universities need to devise exceptional strategies to overcome institutional inertia and overt resistance to traditional hiring practices. In 1995 the Women's Studies Department of the University of Victoria was given permission by the B.C. Human Rights Commission to undertake "limited and preferential hiring" of women from minority groups and to advertise the positions as such.

4 The term "other/wise" comes from poet Daphne Marlatt (1992).

5 For example the profits of the book, which were considerable as it has been, in Canadian terms, a runaway bestseller, have been donated by the author to support Native projects.

6 Quoted with permission.

7 My thanks to Pamela Amoss for bringing this discussion to the group at their 12 February 1988 meeting, and for reporting their responses to me.

8 At such a point it is customary to cite one's sources, but I was in fact asked not to name my informants. This reticence is in itself an important indication of the volatility of these issues.

9 I am indebted to Wendy Wickwire and Christine Welsh for their useful comments on my paper, and their more expert knowledge of ethnography.

10 For a discussion of this complex situation, see Gabriel and Scott, 1993.

11 Note that many of the works in this collection are self-studies (e.g. Ristock, Klassen, and LeBlanc), and that Tye's article in this section examines and valorizes the ethnographic value of one woman's representations of her own community.

12 Cameron has published two children's books on Native topics since 1988 with her new publisher, Harbour Publishing of Madeira Park, British Columbia.

13 Press Gang has published a book of Maracle's short stories, *Sojourner's Truth* (1992a), a novel, *Ravensong* (1993), and a revised second edition of her essays, *I Am a Woman: A Native Perspective on Sociology and Feminism* (1996).

14 Some of these have work in a special issue of *Canadian Woman Studies/ Les cahiers de la femme* (special issue 1989). For further orientation in this field see Bowerbank and Wawia (1994).

PART TWO

Images of Women in Canadian Traditional and Popular Culture

The great variety of traditional and popular cultural forms – songs, stories, beliefs, rituals, material culture and so on – gathered by Canadian women collectors and their male counterparts embody various perspectives on women's roles and experiences. Whether these texts depict individuals or represent women in general, the symbolism and imagery they use constructs and reinforces ideas about female gender identity.

Folklore and women's experiences are often intertwined. Familiar, striking images come to mind: the wicked stepmother in "Snow White" or the passive princess in "Sleeping Beauty." Or, as in misogynist jokes (e.g., blonde jokes, as discussed by Greenhill et al. 1993), women are linked with nature, with danger, and with evil. Such depictions reflect how some may see women's real – or ideal, or imagined – place in society; they may be used to reinforce the subordination of women by communicating misogynist frustration, or they may engender dissatisfaction with what little progress women have made. Among the most frightening examples are those that mirror or applaud the abuse women experience on an everyday basis (see Greenhill 1992). Indeed, folklorist Barbara Rieti's paper explores the implications of Newfoundland witchcraft remedies for violence against women. Focusing on recent films, social psychologist and women's studies professor Janice L. Ristock's article shows that instances of violence in Canadian society are not exclusively the individual acts of individual men, but are encouraged and supported by many forms of popular discourse.

While we cannot ignore the misogynist images of women found in much traditional and popular culture, it would be misleading to suggest that all representations are as immediately disturbing. Indeed, Ristock's sensitive evocation of the possible interpretations of killer dykes and female buddies alike indicates the problematic nature of simply assuming that characters are only "good" or "bad," "positive" or "negative." Women's depictions in traditional and popular culture cannot be understood simplistically. As Barbara Rieti points out in her exploration of the witch tradition in Newfoundland, even seemingly negative images cannot be accepted at face value, but may be used to convey a myriad of sometimes conflicting messages.

Those who demand explicit realism from all cultural expressions limit the possibilities for human symbolism. Like the killer dykes, "evil" women characters such as the wicked stepmother can be also interpreted, for example, as models for aggressive resistance, a topic discussed by many writers in the final section. However, it is important that such figures be balanced by ones who can be understood in alternative ways. The problem is not that traditional and popular forms present negative women characters, but instead that all too often they are the only choices made available to popular audiences. The killer dykes, for example, must be balanced by the nurturing lesbian mothers and supportive lesbian friends.

The essays in this section show that images of women are by no means univocal. The suggestion that folklore presents only one view of women is more a reflection of patriarchal ideas about women's images than of how traditional and popular culture might actually construct them, as contributors indicate here. Anthropologist Anne Brydon shows how in Canada the nineteenth century symbol of Icelandic nationalism, the *fjallkona*, becomes a representation of both Icelandic-Canadian nationalism and female propriety. At the Gimli, Manitoba, annual Icelandic Festival, this "Mountain Woman" is portrayed by mature, respected women who use the male-invented symbol to celebrate the centrality of women in strengthening their ethnic community. Similarly folklorist Pauline Greenhill's paper examines songs about women who are by no means confined, literally or symbolically, by the conventional female role, but instead, wearing men's clothes, venture boldly into spaces normally occupied by men.

Several articles, by exploring the constructed, symbolic, even artificial creation of the gender identities "male" and "female," show that popular notions of men's and women's domains and roles are reductive and simplistic. Laval folklore graduate Barbara LeBlanc explores how symbolic representations in dance, on the one hand, and conventional gender identities, on the other, change correspondingly over time within a single ethnic group, the Acadian community in Cape Breton. Exploring parallels between contemporary bureaucratic culture, its depiction in film, and folktale topology, folklorist Vivian Labrie shows how gendered constructs transcend temporal and spatial limitations.

Labrie's study suggests that workplace sexual harassment is part of a complex cultural patterning that links incest, multiple personalities, and traditional narratives. Clearly, women's work experiences intertwine with other aspects of their lives, including their expressive culture. The greater fluidity of women's work roles when compared to men's is considered by folklorist Michael Taft in his consideration of mock weddings. Such events, which involve cross dressing, can also be seen as commentaries upon or even critiques of the establishment and reinforcement of gender roles in a heterosexist society.

Greenhill's paper on cross-dressing ballads supports this interpretation, suggesting that traditional and popular culture may present not only heterosexuality but also same-sex orientation. In fact, she shows that by discussing male and female gendered identities as the only options, folklore research has entrenched heterosexist scholarly attitudes in ways that the material itself does not warrant. Ristock's study makes no such assumptions. She demonstrates that it is not only "killer dyke" films' narrow definition and conceptualization of lesbians but also female buddy films' denial of what she terms lesbian possibility which limit individuals' human potential and may even foster violence.

Much of the folkloric material considered here allows a complex understanding of sex roles, as well as opportunities to counter stereotypes symbolically and in actual practice. Traditional and popular cultural materials are among the building blocks people use to form their own and other people's ideas about humanity. Too many feminist readings of folklore assume that its performers and audience simply accept at face value what a text seems to be saying. Instead, individuals may locate their own understandings and even debate their conceptions with others. It is important that those who study such cultural expressions consider the representations and revisions the essays here suggest, regarding the ways in which women's gender identity is fashioned, as well as how sexual politics is often negotiated.

The negotiation of place is also clear in the ways in which the different writers locate themselves with respect to their subjects. Barbara Rieti's ambivalence to some witch traditions, and her clear horror of the murderous misogyny she sees in them and elsewhere, pervasively motivate her writing. Anne Brydon must find her own position as ethnographer within "a" culture which is by no means univocal on the issues she describes, and her paper is in part a map of her negotiation. Barbara LeBlanc's writing distances herself from the material she discusses, but it is a part of her own heritage; conversely, Michael Taft's different background from the rural Western Canadians he writes about may mask a shared ambivalence about women's and men's roles – and the need to always be a "good sport." Janice Ristock locates her need to look at cultural stereotypes in relation to her research work; Pauline Greenhill traces a personal and intellectual formation that parallels a series of analytical developments. And Vivian Labrie uses a theoretical and analytical system which developed out of her own intellectual history (linking psychology and folklore) and activist stance (linking academic and political knowledge). Even when the "I" is absent, the undisciplined writers' stances are clear, yet contingent.

Indeed, all our efforts to understand folklore must be guided by the fact that there is no intrinsic, essential meaning in any text. Each must be clarified by performers and audiences. The images of women in Canadian folklore reflect the variety of Canadian peoples. Brydon and LeBlanc examine varying representations of women in groups conventionally considered ethnic; Labrie, Taft, and Rieti explore the implications of gendered power relations and challenge conventional notions and images of men and women; and finally, Ristock and Greenhill discover resistant readings as alternatives to patriarchy and heterosexism. Expanding analytical conceptual tools offers a range of meanings, and reveals the complexity of texts and the scope of the messages they can hold. Their complexities and scope also foreshadow some of the expressions of resistance found in the papers in the last section.

Riddling the Witch:
Violence against Women in Newfoundland Witch Tradition

BARBARA RIETI

Question: How is it that, in Newfoundland, respectable family men have freely described – sometimes speaking into the tape recorders of itinerant strangers – how they or their friends injured, disabled, or even killed women in their community?

Answer: They were talking about measures undertaken to break a spell that a witch had put on them.

William Badcock, for example, eighty-two years old when interviewed by Herbert Halpert and John Widdowson in 1964, told about a fishing voyage to Labrador that was plagued with the worst luck he knew in forty years as a schooner master.[1] Although it was not discovered until after the trip that a certain woman had "prayed to God" that the crew would never return because one crew member had killed her rooster, a curse was suspected even during the voyage, for Mr Badcock told his men, "The best way to right it, boys, is mark the bugger out on a piece of paper ... and shoot at it." He was referring to the counterwitchcraft tactic whereby the "bewitched" shoots an image or token of the witch, who at that instant suffers a sudden infirmity. "That's what I did, twelve o'clock at night I shot at her," Mr Badcock said, "Well, she was took there the same time [taken ill], she never lived after, she died after a while. That ended that witch."

Since that recording was made, several hundred accounts of witchcraft have been deposited in the Memorial University of Newfoundland Folklore and Language Archive (MUNFLA), mostly by undergraduate students taking folklore courses, and by me from fieldwork done over the past several years. In 1990 a student wrote about two brothers she knew who decided that an old woman who watched them leave the wharf each morning was responsible for their poor fishing season. They resorted to the common tactic of urinating into a bottle, sealing it, and hiding it away until the witch, unable to urinate, has to remove the spell or "burst." One of the brothers, however, grew impatient and broke the bottle, killing the witch. Also in 1990, a student collector was appalled when her uncle – I'll call him Mr Heywood, and his community Barrenville – said: "The Bible says if you know a witch, take it to another place and destroy it ... shoot it, or something, or drown it." Perhaps linguistically depersonalizing the witch as "it" (as Mr Badcock also did) made the thought of killing her less culpable, although Mr Heywood did not shrink from it. "That's murder!" exclaimed his niece. "Oh yes, it's murder," he said, "but sure, it's in the Bible."

Mr Heywood was probably referring to Exodus 22:18, "Thou shalt not suffer a witch to live," the Scriptural basis for the witchcraft trials in which many thousands of women (and a much smaller number of men) were imprisoned, tortured, and killed at the hands of church and state.[2] Though no longer socially institutionalized, both the idea of witchcraft and the practice of violence against women retain considerable currency. U.S. evangelist Pat Robertson echoed the patriarchal paranoia of his clerical forefathers when he urged the voters of Iowa to reject a proposed equal rights amendment in 1992 because it was part of a "feminist agenda" that "encourages women to leave their husbands, kill their children, practice witchcraft, destroy capitalism and become lesbians" (*Globe and Mail*, Toronto, 26 August: A7). In Canada 1992 marked the third anniversary of the massacre of fourteen women at L'École Polytechnique in Montreal by Marc Lepine, the aftermath of which has included increased awareness of the pandemic of violence against women and a theoretical commitment to its elimination. Given the deep and serpentine roots of violence against women, I suggest that this eradication will entail not only education and sociopolitical change but also analysis of its myriad manifestations across time and cultures, from Biblical injunctions to oral tradition.

Analysis should also include symbolic, narrative, and dramatic forms, which are more widespread than physical aggression itself and pose knotty problems about their relationships to it, as exemplified by debates about television violence, sadistic pornography, or toy guns. Newfoundland witchcraft tradition, compounded of magical thinking and mundane events, presents particularly complex texts about violence in the abstract and violence in the flesh. The ritual actions of persons who think themselves bewitched are often the core of witch narratives, grounding them in physical reality as the only undeniable purposeful behaviour in the witchcraft scenario, the rest being a matter of emotion, imagination, and interpretation. Their graphic violence makes them stark signifiers of their cultural matrix. There can be no doubt, for instance, that these magical attacks on the witch's person depict violence as a successful solution to interpersonal conflict. Moreover, the "solution" is almost always used by men against women, even though both women and men may consider themselves victims of witchcraft, and men may sometimes be witches. At the same time it must be remembered that folk narrative and symbolic processes often contain elements of fantasy and reversal, and that the protagonists act precisely in ways that are prohibited in real life. Careful context-centred readings are thus called for, although the most interesting questions have no certain answers. Did Mr Badcock *really* think he killed someone, and is it reasonable to draw a parallel between his "shooting" the effigy of the "witch" he blamed for the bad voyage and Lepine's shooting of women as representatives of the "feminists" whom he blamed for his problems? Did the two unlucky brothers *really* think that they were responsible for someone's death? (The student collector of the story says yes, and they were glad that she was dead.)

And what about Mr Heywood? Would he really countenance throwing someone out of a boat? "Say, now, if I know a witch – which I don't know, but say if I did know of one – well, I'd take it down Cape somewhere, or down Red Cove, and make away with her." On first reading, his remarks probably arouse in the reader the same dismay felt by his niece, but a closer examination of context mitigates the text. For one thing, killing the witch is for Mr Heywood a hypothetical formulation only; his stories of actual events are innocuous indeed. One is a veritable parable of female domestic tyranny, about a woman who puts a spell on her husband's schooner so that it cannot leave port until he brings her an item he had promised but forgotten. When I interviewed Mr Heywood myself (and a more pleasant, mild-mannered man is hard to imagine) he told me about how his father once affronted a reputed witch by joking that he would not bring her a fish that day, as she asked. When she went away muttering, some of the crew were sure that they would catch nothing the rest of the summer, but Mr Heywood's father insisted that Aunt Sally was "no more a witch than he was a wizard," and as it turned out, that fishing season was one of the best they ever had. This story does not dismiss the idea of witchcraft; Mr Heywood believes that there are witches "in the world, just as in our Saviour's time" – but not as an immediate reality. The anonymous archive text takes on a far less ominous aspect when linked to the genial Mr Heywood in person and to his narrative repertoire. The initial impact (and ultimate interpretation) of Mr Heywood's prescription for witch-killing is also modified by its being the first in twenty-five years of data to propose direct (i.e., nonmagical) murder.

Physical violence, however, is sometimes recommended. To "draw a witch's blood" by cutting, scratching, or hitting her will break her power. There are relatively few accounts of this compared to those of magical attacks, and so far as I know there are no court documents comparable to those in southwestern England (the provenance of Newfoundland witchcraft) where blood-letting attacks on suspected witches occurred well into this century.[3] One Newfoundland narrative is about a woman new to a community who is suspected of being a witch because her arrival coincided with a sudden decline in the fishery, in which she took an unusual interest. On one of her daily visits to the wharf, she leaned across the cutting table and remarked, "Boys, no fish again today," whereupon a man slashed her arm with the splitting knife. She left the community, and the fish returned. Another story was told to me by an informant who said that a woman in her community (Egg Cove, near Barrenville) was stabbed in the finger by a young man who thought that she was spying on courting couples. The informant said this was supposed to have happened when she was a child, over fifty years ago, and that she could not vouch for its truth as she could her own personal experiences with witchcraft. However, when I asked her whether people disapproved of the man's actions, she said that on the contrary, it was "the older people" who had advised him to "bring the blood out of her." A third case, set on the south coast and also said to have happened long ago, is the sole case I found of a woman physically attacking another woman. The attacker, who is white, stabs a Micmac woman with a sewing needle. The pecking order is clear: the white woman attacks the native, who is "lower" than her in status, just as women are the targets of men.

While the blood-letting tactic retains a magical rationale, a few witchcraft narratives move completely to a threat of straightforward unsymbolic violence. Henry Addams of Barrenville told me a story about some fishermen at sea whose boat began pitching about so wildly they could hardly control it. Somehow, one of them found out the cause: a woman at her kitchen table, rocking a bowl of water with a piece of wood in it so that out at sea, the boat rocked as well. "So he went to her house, and he told her: 'Next time that happens,' he said, 'you won't be living no more.' ... A ways back this is, he brought an old musket with him. He said, 'The next time,' he said, 'I got to come to you,' he said, 'I have any trouble, I'm going to blow your brains out.'" A student writing in 1994 recalled that when he lived in Barrenville thirty years ago, his aunt had an illness she thought due to a spell. His uncle went to the suspected woman with a knife, saying, "If she's sick any longer, I'll put that right to the handle."

Did these confrontations and assaults really happen? Maybe, maybe not: it is impossible to say, working retrospectively from legendary materials.[4] Certainly Newfoundland, like everywhere else, has its share of "ordinary" violence and abuse, so there is no reason to rule other varieties out. The possibility that it did happen might explain why there are so few examples in MUNFLA; informants may not choose to convey such potentially discrediting or sensitive information. On the other hand, it would be a mistake to take at face value what might have been the "modern legend" of its day, a widely told, widely believed story of contemporary events (often lurid) that did not happen, or that happened perhaps once out of hundreds of purported instances.[5] Folk narrative is not always factual – even when narrators think it is – and there are good arguments that in real life attacking a witch would have been an unlikely thing to do.

One argument is that the very profusion of symbolic forms (and their prominence in narrative) indicates a taboo against the real thing.[6] That is, if people could *really* do it, they wouldn't need the symbolic forms. A young teacher new to Egg Cove in the 1960s wrote that after a run of minor misfortunes, his fellow teachers suggested that the mother of one of his pupils (a notorious troublemaker) had a spell on him, and urged him to "put up a bottle" to see "if she was a witch or not"; if she was, she would be affected. He declined the procedure, noting that "while people suggested this, they did not take their own advice." The difference between preaching and practice is well to bear in mind in assessing the likelihood of physical violence. If people were reluctant to carry out magical attacks, presumably they would be even more loath to attack the witch in person.

Also counterbalancing the tales of violence is abundant testimony that people went out of their way to oblige – and not to offend – reputed witches. Over and over, one hears that they were given what they asked for, often at considerable expense to the giver. This enforced charity was probably resented, as would be the guilt or fear resulting from a refusal;[7] hence the need for the expression of hostility in safe and secret ways. Bottling and shooting rituals would allow people to focus and discharge anxiety without the risk of personal confrontation. "You'd have to have an awful lot of courage" to go to the witch in person, one Barrenville woman told me, although it has been done by "soft-hearted" people, who wanted to warn the witch before they did something drastic like put up a bottle.

Perhaps the best argument against real violence toward reputed witches is their long and apparently unmolested tenure; most witches (unlike the transient woman who was cut on the arm) were long-time residents of their communities who usually had families and relations there. More importantly, they were often highly respected, if not feared; the image of the witch is not – or was not – always entirely negative. Sometimes they were advisors or prognosticators, consulted before an important venture – especially the fishery – to pronounce on its outcome.[8] Some were even said to control the fishery. "There was one old woman on Indigo Island supposed to have been a witch," wrote one student, "Seamen used to go to her so that she would predict what kind of season they would have; Dad said if they treated her right she would tell them they would have a good season." In the 1960s, an aged informant described his recollection of the community's witch: "It seemed like they put a wonderful dependence on her, they wouldn't do nothing against her, this old Mother Croker in Green Harbour, they wouldn't do a thing against her; oh no, whatever she said'd be the law. There's an old Mother Burton in New Cove, just the same with she down there." It is hard to get a clear picture of these commanding figures in the present day, but the element of propitiation remains. One of my informants would not drive past Sara Colman walking the road between Egg Cove and Barrenville without offering her a ride, lest their car get a flat tire or even overturn.[9] This ended three years ago when Sara entered an old age home, apparently never having been troubled by witch-bashers.

Of course in order to placate the witch one has to know who she is; one complication in the ethnography of Newfoundland witchcraft is that it is not only reputed witches who put spells or "wishes" on others but that almost anyone could, on occasion, be thought to do so. Men are found more frequently among the "occasional" witches than the "established" ones. A witch's identity may be divined through shooting or bottling, whereby whoever is "hit" or suffers is revealed as the witch. In a rare reference to shooting a male effigy, one man told me that if you didn't know whether it was a man or a woman who had a spell on you, you could draw out the figure of each and shoot toward them; whichever you hit would tell the sex of your witch.

Note, though, he did not say this would *affect* the witch. Male witches, it seems, are not subject to bodily harm, as an account from two informants I'll call Dan and Susan illustrates. About twenty years ago, when they were first married, they thought that someone had a spell on them and was trying to break up their marriage. They suspected their neighbour George, whom they think has "power" (you can tell just by looking at him, says Susan, that "anything he wants, in his mind, you know, he could act on it"). One morning a series of bizarre household mishaps – including cracks in their wedding picture and Susan's wedding ring – threw Dan into a rage.

Dan: So I go and gets the bottle. And I pissed into it. I put the cover on good and tight and I turned the oven on and put it in the oven. I said, "You'll bust, you son of a B, you'll bust." And about two hours later I'd say, or three hours, the helicopter was landed on the other side [of the island] to pick up this woman who was gone to the hospital piss-bound blocked solid!
Susan: Yeah, but I don't think she was the one.

Susan still suspected George, but Dan thought the woman may have had something against him too; he says that he was thinking neither of her nor of George as the bottle boiled, but directed his thoughts to "whoever you might be."

Although I heard this myself, I cannot say whether Dan or Susan *truly* thought the bottle *really* sent someone to hospital; Dan stressed the coincidence of it all, and told the story with great laughter among their teenage children, who already knew it well. I am certain that it would not become jocular family folklore if any of Dan's "real" actions harmed another – if, for instance, he had hit someone with a car. Although the interest of the story lies in envisioning "real" results of magical actions, those actions are, after all, only a play with an antique script.

Of course, this process makes them even more suggestive. Whatever it revealed about the witch, Dan's counterspell's "hit" is most telling to me in its bypassing the prime male suspect and landing on a woman, for I see it as paradigmatic of the male-to-female direction of violence in witch stories which mirrors that of "real life." In counterwitch ritual, the witch's body becomes the target of male assailants using weapons of patent male association (guns, knives, and more personal tools).[10] Bewitched women do not "shoot" witches, and even the relatively rare instances in which they "put up bottles" demonstrate the physical vulnerability of the female as opposed to the male, who does not get "bottled" by men *or* women.[11] The witch's envisioned aggression is similarly constructed; bewitched women are typically afflicted in personal health, while men are most commonly affected in economic pursuits like fishing or hunting. Indeed the entire aggression/retaliation relationship is significant in this regard: it is not an eye-for-an-eye or in-kind configuration, but an asymmetrical one in which the witch makes a variety of mischief, but the male response is always an attack on her person. The attack usually "works," and is therefore portrayed as appropriate. The stories may be read as wishful thinking (in the most literal sense), but they take their shapes from fact.

Like a riddle that makes a mundane artefact seem strange through a novel description, Newfoundland witch lore puts the banal reality of violence against women into striking forms which heighten its essential features. There is, however, no sudden solution to resolve the enigma as there is for a riddle, and many questions remain unsettled and unsettling. Part of the puzzle of this particular tradition, and in the larger sphere of violence against women, lies in reconciling the reality of fine and kindly individuals with the apparent viciousness of some of their collective lore. I felt the problem acutely in December 1992 when my son, full of second-grade Christmas carol parodies, sang to the tune of "Jingle Bells":

Barbie Doll, Barbie Doll,
Tried to save her life,
G.I. Joe caught her, though,
And stabbed her with a knife.[12]

Of course Barbie and G.I. Joe are not people, nor is the witch drawn on the stage door; but they are representational forms, and their treatment may be taken as representative as well. Sometimes, instead of a figure, the bewitched man draws and shoots a heart, striking, it seems to me, at the heart of the matter. However symbolic the attacks, and however unthinkable that any particular man would accost a woman in person, the contours of a larger social reality are sketched out along with the witch. That reality is shot through with a murderous misogyny.

NOTES

1 Names of informants, "witches," and communities are pseudonyms; the identification numbers of archival documents have also been omitted in the interest of privacy. (Inquiries may be directed to the Memorial University of Newfoundland Folklore and Language Archive [MUNFLA]). I thank Drs Herbert Halpert and John Widdowson

for permission to quote from their field tapes, and Dr Martin Lovelace, Director of MUNFLA, for permission to use archive materials. I am also grateful to Martin for his contributions to my witchcraft project in general, especially his collaboration in fieldwork. Generous postdoctoral fellowships from the Institute of Social and Economic Research at Memorial University of Newfoundland and from the Social Sciences and Humanities Research Council of Canada enabled me to do this research. A preliminary version of this paper was presented at the 1992 meeting of the California Folklore Society in Sacramento with travel assistance from the Social Sciences and Humanities Research Council of Canada.

2 There is no generally accepted estimate of the number of persons executed as witches in Europe. According to Kors and Peters, few students of witchcraft begin guessing below 50,000, and some double or triple that number ([1972] 1992:13); as Cohn points out, defective records mean that the question will never be fully answered (1975:253). The most recent and careful attempt has been made by Anne Llewellyn Barstow (1994). It should be remembered that besides actual executions, many people died in prison, and even those acquitted were often ruined by the loss of health, property, or livelihood.

3 In 1897, for example, the defendant in a case of "unlawful wounding" in a Somerset police court explained that she had scratched the complainant with a pin in order to draw her blood and thus break a spell that the complainant had put on her (March 1900:11). For sample West Country accounts of murder, abuse, and threatened abuse of suspected witches see Tongue (1963) – she includes an incident from 1962; Bailey (1992); or Karkeek (1882). None of the handful of printed references to Newfoundland witchcraft I have discovered to date concern violence.

4 Storm-raising stories, for instance, are told throughout the island, yet presumably cannot be taken as historical fact. One informant (Dan of this essay) told of a man who, after having trouble landing his boat, "caught" his neighbour waving her hands over a pond and "saying old stuff." (For a key to international analogues see Christiansen 1958, Migratory Legend No. 3035.) Almost all the material in this paper could be similarly annotated from international indexes and collections (for examples of Canadian witchcraft tradition outside Newfoundland, see Creighton 1968, Dupont 1972, Kaplan 1981, Planetta 1981, or Ronald Labelle's discussion in this volume of the work of Jolicœur).

5 See any of Brunvand's collections for examples (e.g. 1986), such as the poodle in the microwave or cats in Chinese restaurant food.

6 However, when women limped or sported bruises, there is always the possibility that a "supernatural" explanation could be concocted to

cover real abuse, as when it is "explained" that Mrs X's arm is broken because some distant person "shot" her in effigy.

7 Thomas (1971) and Macfarlane (1970) see these emotions as key to the rise in witchcraft persecution in England.

8 The one "witch" I have interviewed is widely sought after for fortune-telling, but I do not get the impression of a community-wide consensus on her powers that the archival accounts suggest Mother Croker and her counterparts enjoyed. (That impression may be false; there is a tendency to generalization and overstatement in the description of folk belief, especially that of the past.)

9 Placation is also evident in the past. E.A. Rutherford, a Barrenville physician who kept a diary of a sealing expedition he accompanied in 1904, noted that some sealing captains would take tea and sugar to a certain old woman to ensure that she did not put a spell on their ship as she had on others (1973).

10 I have discussed the possible sexual symbolism of these rituals elsewhere (Rieti 1995).

11 At least they don't in Newfoundland. At the 1993 meeting of the Folklore Studies Association of Canada, Ronald Labelle said that in Acadian witch tradition (as documented in the Centre d'études acadiennes at Université de Moncton), male witches are common and that men put up bottles against other men. In Nova Scotia, Helen Creighton interviewed a woman who said that she killed a man by burning a pig's heart full of pins (1968:25). Comparative material always raises questions – and urges caution – about the interpretation of culture-specific material within a larger contextual framework. Perhaps in this case it weakens my suggestion that the Newfoundland material mirrors the real-life direction of male violence against women, although differences in other places do not necessarily invalidate inferences drawn from a particular corpus.

12 On 9 April 1993, I heard children in Berkeley, California, chanting, "Tic-tac-toe / Three in a row / Mama got shot by G.I. Joe." I wonder if Barrenville mothers have ever been given similar pause by boys pulling snails off rocks and addressing them: "Old woman, old woman, stick out your horns; if you don't, I'll kill your mother, your father, your brother, and your sisters" (FSC89-363/11).

Mother to Her Distant Children: The Icelandic *Fjallkona* in Canada

ANNE BRYDON

In 1989, descendants of Icelandic settlers in North America[1] marked the one-hundredth anniversary of *Íslendingadagurinn*, the Icelandic Festival of Manitoba, held each year in the lakeside town of Gimli. As part of that celebration, President Vigdís Finnbogadóttir of Iceland unveiled a bronze cast bell (Figures 1 and 2). It represents the *Fjallkona*, the Mountain Woman who personifies the Icelandic homeland and "speaks" during every Festival to her farflung "children" in North America.

The bell had been the idea of Linda Sigurdsson Collette. She collaborated with a local sculptor, Richard Osen, to create the figure of a costumed woman suspended at her shoulders between two large, curved metal poles. Both the Festival Board and the Municipality of Gimli granted the necessary approvals for the bell's permanent installation in Gimli Park, without first seeing any preliminary drawings. After the unveiling, some people privately criticized the bell and wondered how its sponsorship could have been allowed.

During the Festival three years later, Elva Simundsson, a vocal and strong-minded woman active in various ethnic organizations, decided to act on her dislike of the bell. She planted in front of it a *níðstöng* – a pole into which a libel or defamation is carved. She got the idea from her niece, who "is into pagan stuff," and who had read about a *níðstöng* planted during medieval times by the saga hero Egill Skallagrímsson, to curse the king and queen of Norway. Elva carved into the pole, in Icelandic, "This is the stupidest thing that we have ever seen," and listed the initials of fifteen people in support of

Figures 1 and 2. The *Fjallkona* Bell, Gimli (photos: Pauline Greenhill)

Figure 3. Artist William Eakin interprets female/male gendering of the bell

the insult.² Egill had used a real horse's head to top the pole; Elva settled for a ceramic one. Knowledge of her gesture did not become widespread, since no one knew its meaning, and the pole itself was pulled down two days after. A few months later, however, rumour of it reached me.

I asked Elva what she thought was the matter with the bell. She argued that it is "grotesque," and that it "makes fun of the *Fjallkona*" who looks like she is "hanging by the neck." She added her husband's complaint, that the bell resembles "a little woman hanging between a man's legs bowed as if standing in front of a urinal" (Figure 3). Elva also criticized the "Icelandicness" of the bell, saying that its symbology had no historical referent. She didn't consider this surprising, since Linda was, in her words, a "born-again Icelander," someone who had discovered her ethnic roots in adulthood, and had not been raised in an Icelandic-speaking household, as had Elva. Thus, by writing the insult in Icelandic so that Linda could not understand it, Elva underscored her insult.

Linda, not surprisingly, disagrees with Elva. She says that her idea for the bell was inspired by a story she heard while visiting Iceland, one she claims is well-known to Icelanders but unknown to *West* Icelanders (North Americans of Icelandic descent). This story, in fact, is a pastiche of events and is not a recognizable historical narrative in Iceland. As she tells it, two bells arrived in Iceland around 1018, one a gift from King Olaf of Norway commemorating Icelanders' acceptance of Christianity, the other from King Harald of England. In 1593, according to her story, these were recast as one bell and used by the *Alþingi* (Parliament). Via a dubious genealogy, that bell is said to be ancestor to the one she calls *Íslandsklukkan*, now rung in Reykjavík on 17 June, Iceland's independence day.[3]

Linda wedded the idea of a nationally important bell to the image of the *Fjallkona*. In 1990, she wrote in a pamphlet, "Not only is the bell ringing for 101 celebrations and for 67 *Fjallkonas*, *Islendingadagurinn*'s most prized possession, it also echoes the roots of both Christianity and Parliamentary procedure in Iceland symbolized by Iceland's most prized possession, *Islandsklukkan*." The bell has deep personal significance for Linda, since her mother became *Fjallkona* in 1991, and the pastor of her church blessed it upon its unveiling.

As an anthropologist interested in identity politics, I have followed with interest various disputes amongst Canadian Icelanders. On its surface, this disagreement over the bell resembles previous clashes between personalities, and between differing definitions and representations of Icelandic-Canadian identity (see Brydon 1990; 1991). However, this intersection of gender and nationalism shows how gender is involved in the construction of national and ethnic identities. The Mountain Woman provides an organizing symbol for the ethnic identity of Icelandic descendants in North America. Her association with notions of nature, blood kinship, history, and motherhood provides grist for the discursive mill generating modern subjectivities. The morality of "proper Icelandicness" mixes indiscriminately with notions of female decorum and propriety.

In this volume, Laurel Doucette discusses the impact of three intellectual models on scholarly practice, and issues a challenge for scholars to overcome their influence on our views of people's lives. Her analysis of romantic nationalism is particularly relevant to my own discussion, since Icelandic nationalism and the *Fjallkona* were in part inspired by the German Johann Gottfried von Herder's influential theories of folklife. But rather than advocating an uncritical celebration of the Mountain Woman's continuing salience amongst North Americans of Icelandic descent, I explore the broader context of this symbol's use and interpretation. This is not a functionalist enterprise; the *Fjallkona* bell may divide members of the community, or even be ignored by them, rather than draw them together into a common identification. Ethnic histories are comprised of such instances, as people continue to define their present in terms of shifting interpretations of the past. It should be obvious that ethnicity is not an essential trait, but rather, as I argue elsewhere (Brydon 1991), a process of identification which arises in social interaction. Not everyone in Canada identifies themself through stories of their ethnic past; for those who do, identity becomes a complex negotiation of meaning amongst individuals sharing that past, however ephemerally.

The following explanation of the production of meaning modifies somewhat the model outlined by Victor Turner in *The Ritual Process* (1969), and gives a symbolic analysis which inquires into its two components. First, a symbol must be explained in terms of its formal or official exegesis and the socio-historical conditions of its invention. Second, since a symbol becomes meaningful when mediating or articulating social interaction, analysis must attend to its uses and contextual interpretations. Examining a symbol whose time and place of origin vary from those of its current usage requires a measure of sensitivity to the intersection of past and present. The past can overshadow current understandings (cf. Boon 1982), and earlier meanings associated with the *Fjallkona* indeed resonate now, although in unexpected and at times ironic ways.

During her efflorescence in nineteenth-century Iceland, the *Fjallkona* fell into that same category of female engenderings of the nation as do Britannia, Germania, Marianne, and the now-forgotten Miss Canada. In each instance, an image of idealized womanhood provides a nativizing female ground as a means of sacralizing what Hobsbawm (1990) terms the *conditional* bond between people, territory, and government. Obviously, nationalisms are not the only domains where men have appropriated women's likenesses to act as representations of their own established order. Nor are these female figures the only symbols of nationhood to have cropped up during the expansionist phase of nineteenth-century Europe. Yet they all furnish provisional identities which link the domains of nature, motherhood, and nurturance to social history and the polity.

Women's association in Euro North American thought with nature ("culture's most precious invention," in Seamus Deane's words [1990:17]) contextualizes these nineteenth-century male imaginings, and suggests elements of contemporaneous metaphors of self and identity. Not only do women with their wombs reproduce the nation, they are said to form its character through their nurturance and discipline. The assumptions of geographical determinism, so popular in early nationalist writings, form an intriguing parallel. Icelandic character was said to be molded by the landscape"s extremes of volcanoes and glaciers, fire and ice. The Icelandic demeanour was consequently said to be both hot and cool, fiery and icy calm. Nature, like woman, is a disciplinary force shaping character; as mother to all Icelanders, the Mountain Woman embodies nature's fecundity while properly raising the children of the nation. Women and the Icelandic land are the organic matter out of which Icelanders emerge; they are also the socializing forces which shape the strong and independent Icelandic character.

Further, the *Fjallkona* summarizes Iceland's history, land, literature, and people. Her presence conveys the enduring spirit of a nation once suppressed by Danish rule. In her original depictions, she is young and beautiful, yet her dignified demeanour suggests the wisdom and nobility of a mature woman. The last century's independence movement was not inflamed by the revolutionary passion of the French Revolution, represented in the half-clad figure of Marianne. Rather, the "battle" was conducted by political elites, Icelandic men educated and residing part-time in Copenhagen. Iceland achieved independence by a series of legislative changes exacted from a Danish government already sympathetic to Icelandic aspirations.

The anthropologist Inga Dóra Björnsdóttir (1992) notes that in Iceland during this time discussion of the *Fjallkona*'s costume (described below) occupied the attention of men engaged in establishing a national culture. No parallel discussion of a male costume ever took place. A man was responsible for the final design of the costume. Later, Eiríkur Magnússon, friend of the British socialist and artist William Morris and himself a scholar at Cambridge University, prevailed upon the German artist Zwecker to compose the first visual image of the *Fjallkona*, which appeared in 1866.

According to the Gimli Festival's official exegesis (cf. Simundsson 1989; Þór 1989), the *Fjallkona* represents Mother Iceland from whom all Icelanders in the world descend, and is recognized by her clothing and bearing. She is a sacred figure, and her representation is framed by reverence. The North American version of her outfit is glossed as the Icelandic landscape itself, as in the account given by Allisen King, 1991 Alberta *Fjallkona*, during her address to those gathered to celebrate the mid-winter feast of *Þorrablót*: "The attire of the *Fjallkona* is a visual reminder of your ancestral homeland. My headdress symbolizes snow capped mountains, nestled in the golden crown radiating sunshine. The green velvet mantle signifies the grassy slopes and valleys, while the white gown portrays purity and integrity."[4] She wears a long, white, bridal-like veil, held in place by a golden circle crown featuring a centre star directly above a rising sun placed against the Icelandic coat of arms. The latter features Iceland's four guardian spirits – a bull, a giant, a vulture, and a dragon. For the *Íslendingadagurinn*, the *Fjallkona* chooses two young female attendants to accompany her; some sources (e.g., Kristjanson

1965) refer to them as "maids of honour," underlining the image of bridal purity.

Although this is not typically acknowledged in commentaries on Icelandic independence, the nationalist movement's history is deeply entwined with the Lutheran Church, religious faith, and morality. During the 1820s and 30s, some higher-ranking pastors, educated in Copenhagen, helped bridge continental political leanings toward romantic nationalism and an Icelandic agenda for economic and social change. In the words of the national anthem, God and nation intertwine; the thousand years of suffering of which every Icelander sings intermingle with the sufferings of Christ, and of life before entrance into the Kingdom of God.

In Canada, the pastor and community leader Jón Bjarnason reminded the newly-immigrated Icelanders of the importance to remember both God and the homeland: "Whoever forgets his *moth-er*land or pretends to have no obligations to preserve that of his ethnic background which is of religious nature for the simple reason he now lives on foreign soil has also forgotten God" (quoted in Þór 1989:8; emphasis added). Whereas in Iceland, church attendance has dropped drastically, and its social power now depends largely on institutionalization by the state, Protestant morality still plays a role amongst many prairie Canadian ethnic groups. The Lutheran and Unitarian churches have had both direct and indirect influence on the definition of Icelandic Canadian identity. As will be shown, this morality has had an impact on the figure of the *Fjallkona*.

Prior to World War I, technical innovations and increased access to world markets led to the expansion of Iceland's fishing industry and provided the economic basis for national independence. Although the nationalist movement gained momentum in the latter half of the nineteenth century, social and economic conditions had not substantially improved for certain regions, particularly the northeast from where many emigrated to North America. In 1875, a volcanic eruption smothered the grass on which the sheep depended, worsening already difficult social conditions, and prompting about 1200 people to join a smaller group of Icelanders recently established in Manitoba. The year previous, about 270 Icelanders had wintered in the Muskoka District of Ontario. They then received from the federal government rights to a block of land, or reserve, on the west shore of Lake Winnipeg. In 1875, they established the "Republic of New Iceland," drafted a constitution, and mapped their own place names onto the bush still used by local Cree as their hunting grounds.

As the second and third generations of West Icelanders grew to adulthood, their sense of ethnic identity shifted from pragmatic to symbolic. That is, Icelandic-Canadian identity arises less and less frequently from within a shared, everyday life, such as working in the Lake Winnipeg fisheries. Rather, making ethnic identity has become the project for organizations and institutions which strive to generate it self-consciously by evoking certain foods, songs, stories, and other nostalgic references to an idealized past. During the post–World War II era, ethnicity became less significant to economic and political behaviour, and the Icelandic enclave in Winnipeg's West End dispersed. Originally separated from other groups by religion, occupation, and language, these categories lost their salience to Western Icelandic cultural distinctiveness. Instead the festival, the Icelandic National League and its chapters in centres across North America, the community-funded Icelandic Department at the University of Manitoba, Icelandic-based church groups operated by women, a weekly newspaper, and a quarterly magazine are the primary institutions through which the Icelandic community reproduces itself. Now, elements of expressive culture, primarily literary-based, mark Icelandic-Canadian identity.

The symbol of the *Fjallkona* was already fading from use in Iceland when Canadians of Icelandic descent introduced her at the 1924 *Íslendingadagurinn*. Organizers of the summertime event wanted to ensure the continuing relevance of what was then a one-day celebration held in Winnipeg. That year, festival ticket holders chose the *Fjallkona* by ballot from a group of young women pre-selected in a combination beauty pageant and popularity contest by the festival's organizing board, comprised entirely of men.[5] The board soon altered this format, and since that time it alone has been responsible for her selection. With rare exceptions (such as in 1919, when one woman served on it), festival boards have been entirely male.[6]

Initially held in Winnipeg, the Icelandic Festival moved in the 1930s to Gimli where it has since remained, celebrated every August. It now lasts three days and includes sports, children's activities, a folk music concert, dances, a parade, and the "traditional programme" held on Monday afternoon. The *Fjallkona* is central to that programme, and being chosen *Fjallkona* is an honour that some women carefully yet surreptitiously attempt to attract. Along with other invited participants who sit on the stage during the afternoon speeches, she rides in the morning parade, waving to the crowds from the back of a convertible. During her "reign," she is treated with special attention, and at the festival she makes a speech in the persona of Mother Iceland to her farflung children in North America.

In English in Canada, the *Fjallkona* is called "Maid of the Mountain," rather than the more accurate "Mountain Woman," a translation which carries the circumspect propriety of the early twentieth century when women were ladies or maids. Until the 1970s, a *Fjallkona* was chosen primarily on the basis of her husband's social standing. Given the conservative, community-based criteria used to determine social position, men did not achieve recognition until later in life. Consequently, their wives, too, were older than the term "maid" might suggest. Although in Icelandic folklore there are frightening female and male mountain beings, ogres and giants, they have nothing to do with the *Fjallkona*, a more bourgeois Enlightenment figure. Her image coincides with the ideal Victorian woman: pure, proper, and virginal. In practice at the festival, she is a grandmotherly figure, assumed to be beyond her sexually active years, and recognized for her service to others.

The theme of motherhood is a more pronounced aspect of the *Fjallkona*'s symbology in Canada than in Iceland, and is more closely aligned with recent North American preoccupations with "family values" than with her original literary associations. If anything, her importance has increased in the last few years. Starting in the 1980s, the Board began to encourage the *Fjallkona*'s family to write brief tributes which were then published in the weekly newspaper *Lögberg-Heimskringla*. These articles detail her community activities, and often present a sentimental portrait of her nurturing, motherly ways. In preparation for the hundredth anniversary celebration of 1989, the festival board of directors sought to define for themselves, as well as for those who attend, what Icelandic identity is, and, in the words of one past president, "how they could capitalize on it." Finding definitive Icelandic symbols has continued to be a problem. Apart from food items such as *vínarterta* (a layered cake) and *pönnukökur* (plain or cream-filled crêpes), and references to Vikings, poetry, and pioneer sufferings, effective public symbols are not a defining feature of the festival. This lack has not affected its success: the move to Gimli has proven fortuitous. The festival coincides with the August holiday long weekend, and currently marks a regularized time for family reunions. Yet in my view the failure to generate effective symbols figures in the factional squabbles surrounding identity issues. The *Fjallkona* bell is just one case in point.

In 1989, the festival board produced a documentary to mark the festival's centenary. The filmmakers, mostly board members, found an organizing metaphor in the figure of the *Fjallkona*. Their film emphasizes the festival's importance as a time of return, of family reunions at summer cottages or parental homes in Gimli. It also records the visit of President Vigdís Finnbogadóttir to a tea given in honour of all previous *Fjallkonas*. The scene then shifts to a reunion of the Arnason family, whose matriarchal head, Rúna – she cele-brated her 101st birthday that year – sits on a lawn chair surrounded by four generations of her offspring. Her squat bulk sitting in the chair rises like a mountain from a sea of squirming children and smiling adults.[7] With this image, the film suggestively links the *Fjallkona* and the festival to notions of an encompassing, nurturing motherhood and to the virtues of familial ties.

The *Fjallkona* has proven to be a flexible symbol tied to the norms and values of patriarchal bourgeois society. Indeed, festival organiz-ers' standards and measures of Western Icelandic success are male, such as the ability to attract big-name politicians to participate in the "traditional" programme. The Icelandic community reflects patterns familiar in Canadian society. For example, in 1962 the festival orga-nizers commissioned a panel of paintings for display behind the *Fjallkona* and other dignitaries during the speeches. The ancient *Alþingi's* image is central, but three scenes represent Iceland's major income-generating resources: agriculture, fishing, and hydro-electric power (Þór 1989). This backdrop reflects the values of modernization-minded community boosters and expresses a decidedly patriarchal take on the Iceland of their ancestry.[8]

Since the 1970s *Fjallkonas* have been chosen on the basis of their own characters and achievements. Speech-making, however, has rarely been a skill these women are accustomed to exercising. For thirty-one years Haraldur Bessason held the Icelandic Chair at the University of Manitoba before his return to Iceland, and during that time he often wrote the *Fjallkona's* speech – until recently given in Icelandic. With a straight face, Haraldur was fond of telling people that he was the true *Fjallkona*.

Despite the *Fjallkona's* earlier selection on the basis of her hus-band's reputation, women's role in the Western Icelandic community has never been limited to that of wife and mother.[9] Around the turn of the century many women formed aid societies associated with local Lutheran and Unitarian churches. For example, in 1895, women in the community of Geysir established a charitable organization, Freyja, with the stated aims of strengthening fellowship amongst local women, promoting the Lutheran faith, and helping the sick and needy. In their early years at least, some of these groups became involved with the feminist politics of the time, then concerned with obtaining women's suffrage. Feminism found receptive supporters amongst Western Icelandic women. Born-in-Iceland Margrét Bene-dictsson, together with her husband Sigfus, published a twenty-page Icelandic language women's newspaper called (again) *Freyja*.[10] The name carries historical referents mobilized during Iceland's romantic revival during the nineteenth century, although it can also refer simply to a woman. Freyja, the beautiful goddess of fertility was, or is, foremost amongst the many goddesses of the old Norse religion. The *Fjallkona* was a representative Icelandic female figure chosen by the all-male festival board. But if their true aim were to celebrate Western Icelandic womanhood, Freyja would seem an ideal figure. The fertility goddess would not only provide a link to the much-venerated saga literature, but she was also the choice of Icelandic women to represent themselves. It is possible that the dubious morality of this pagan goddess lacked the connections to Christian morality which festival organizers find appropriate.

Although the origins of the *Fjallkona* lie in the masculine poetic imagination of nineteenth-century Icelandic nationalists, it would be a mistake to limit our considerations of her possible meanings to male engenderings of the ethnos. Rather, we should hear "the different voices in which [women] fashion and re-fashion themselves" (Babcock 1987:394). To recognize that men have appropriated Woman as the established order's objectified sign does not negate women's active role in re-presenting, in an ennobling and positive light, their lives as mothers, wives, and care-givers.[11] Women have indeed taken the *Fjallkona* as their own, speaking her with their own voices, listening with only half an ear to the speeches made by men on her behalf.

In conversations and interviews with West Icelanders, both men and women emphasize women's importance in maintaining Icelandic culture. The sagas record the exploits of several strong-willed and powerful women. More recently, Icelandic farming relied on women's labour tending sheep and milk cows as well as cutting hay, while men were away on the fishing boats. Björnsdóttir (1992) argues that when nationalist leaders strategically defined Iceland in terms of a woman oppressed by the Danish king, they also opened a space for women to achieve a public voice in the political arena. The recent success of the women's political party *Kvennalistinn* in Iceland demonstrates this, albeit not without prompting some troubling dilemmas.[12] North American Icelandic organisations are increasingly dominated by women. Further, they bear the primary responsibility for fostering the family ties on which ethnic linkages depend (Rice 1971).

The 1989 planting of a *níðstöng* at Gimli deliberately invoked the symbolic power of the Icelandic sagas to denounce what the protester and her supporters saw as a demeaning, undignified image. The criticism was not directed at the idea of the *Fjallkona* herself. Rather, it countered a representation which, they felt, undermined her power to positively symbolize the values of the Icelandic-Canadian community, including kinship, honour, success, and remembering the strengths of Icelandic settlers along the western frontier. For them, the image on the bell was too sentimental and doll-like, too cleansed of women's strength. Thus, while not challenging the male values which underlined the original creation of the virtuous *Fjallkona*, the bell's critics nonetheless sought to assert the values of female strength and independence.

The *Fjallkona* remains a symbol whose attributes and associations articulate the patriarchal values which underlined the nation-state's nineteenth-century ascendancy. As a passive and fecund being, she embodied ideas about the familial bonds of nationhood and the moral values of restraint and propriety. Her official exegesis, supplied by nineteenth-century poets, remains basically unchanged. Nonetheless, her meaning shifts in Canada, where commentators emphasize her linkages to distant volcanic mountains and glaciers by means of an extended trope on ideas of kinship and family, concretized by the popular pastime of tracing genealogies. Further, Icelandic-Canadian writers point out that the *Fjallkona* is "kept alive" here while the symbol has been neglected in Iceland, a view which is only partially true. In this way, they lay claim to her as Canadian, and thus a marker of the differing identities of Icelanders and North Americans of Icelandic descent.

Disagreement over the *Fjallkona* bell occurs in a context where ethnicity is problematic and thus continually being negotiated. Such are the confusions invoked by searching through the past for an authentic and whole modern identity. In North America, the *Fjallkona* addresses the fiction surrounding immigration, and the contradiction of an identity fostered away from the remembered homeland which is said to shape it. The *Fjallkona* bell may well be on its way to being a failed symbol, not unlike the giant Viking who stands on the Lake Winnipeg shore at the south end of Gimli, his horned helmet appallingly referring to the distorted Hollywood images of Vikings and singing Valkyries.[13] Bell or no bell, the *Fjallkona* herself continues to chart a tenuous but meaningful course.

NOTES

1 A detailed account of Icelandic settlement in Canada can be found in Kristjanson (1965).
2 This *níðstöng* planting suggests, as does Reiti's examination of witches in Newfoundland, that stereotypes of actual women as universally

nurturing and unthreatening are inaccurate. Similarly, Elva's bold move is matched by those of the fictional cross-dressed women in Greenhill's work on ballads, and by the prairie women who, as Taft suggests, extensively construct and control mock weddings, even to the extent of sometimes raising issues that are embarrassing or even painful to the honoured couple.

3 Contrary to Linda's assertion, there is no nationally significant bell in Iceland. *Íslandsklukkan* is the name of a novel by Halldór Laxness, Iceland's Nobel prize-winning novelist, not of an actual bell. Although bells have figured in Christian history in Iceland, they do not have the physical descendants Linda creates. In fact, until the invention of the *Fjallkona*, Iceland lacked any national symbols. Shaun Hughes (personal communication) suggests that the best symbol of the nation, used at the beginning of the nineteenth century, would have been three codfish split for drying.

4 *Lögberg-Heimskringla* 22 March 1991, p 2. The three Alberta chapters of the Icelandic National League annually choose a *Fjallkona* from amongst their memberships.

5 The *Fjallkona* also appeared that same year (1924) at the Icelandic celebration in Blaine, Washington. She became a popular figure at local celebrations in smaller Icelandic settlement centres across Western Canada and the United States. She "lent such dignity to these festivals that her appearance has become a permanent feature at Icelandic Day celebrations" (Simundsson 1989).

6 In 1973, one woman served on the Board. In 1988, it had its first woman chairperson, and the centenary board of seventeen had seven women.

7 My thanks to Hulda Karin Daníelsdóttir for pointing this out to me.

8 Women's labour has, of course, been a necessary part of economic success in Iceland, as elsewhere. Feminists are quick to point out, however, that the importance of women has been systematically ignored in accounts of Iceland's modernization, and that the ideology of capitalist development is male-dominated.

9 Michael Taft's paper similarly shows the limitations of the notion of women's work as exclusive to her gender.

10 Margrét Benedictsson travelled widely amongst the scattered Icelandic settlements, lobbying for women's suffrage. She founded several suffrage groups, and actively corresponded with the Toronto-based Canadian Suffrage Association as well as other international groups. Her role in the suffrage movement's success in Manitoba – the first province where women achieved the vote – is overshadowed by the national importance of the Englishwoman, Nellie McClung. Unfortunately, little information has been published about Margrét, and

despite her importance for some Western Icelandic women, she has not been taken up as a symbol of Icelandic fortitude as much as she deserves.

11 Similarly, the undisciplined women discussed in the final section recuperate and re-establish female figures and female genres in their own terms. In this section, Ristock points out that some women, particularly lesbians, have done the same with the "killer dyke" image.

12 Inga Dóra Björnsdóttir (1992) provides a fascinating account of the *Fjallkona* in Iceland in relation to contemporary feminist politics. She examines the dilemmas faced by the Women's List, a political party founded on the principle of women's cultural difference. Emphasizing woman's role as mother has fostered a conservative streak in its political practice. Together with a non-hierarchical, leaderless structure, this strategy has undermined the party's ability to take advantage of its initial popular support.

13 This helmet was another nineteenth-century invented tradition; actually, viking helmets had no horns.

Changing Places: Dance, Society, and Gender in Cheticamp

BARBARA LE BLANC

Dance, like other forms of cultural expression, is embedded within the social world from which it can take and give meaning. Although there are a number of intricate and even contradictory definitions of dance, most ethnologists would agree that dance is a complex social phenomenon and a means of communication which is part of the framework of human culture and society. Dance ethnologists point out that it expresses social institutions, shows the nature of inter-personal relationships (Kealiinohomoku 1972:99–100), and is a par-ticularly good source of information about women's and men's sociocultural roles (Hanna 1988:12).

More than entertainment, and more than just an aesthetic form, dance embodies some aspects of social practice and denies others, exacts restraint upon the dancer's body but also at times frees it, and formalizes movements that skew as well as mirror social forms. These complex manifestations are clear in my own research from the Cheticamp area, Inverness County, Cape Breton Island, Nova Scotia, which shows how dance selectively reflects both the region's social organization and the changing places of women and men through time in the community. My analysis here offers an impressionistic, non-technical overview which I hope will stimulate others to more in depth study of the bodily character of Acadian dance forms.

In Cheticamp, dance forms, gender roles, and social structures alike have been directly influenced by the region's intercultural links with Europe and North America. A large percentage of the area's inhabi-tants are descendants of the first French-speaking settlers of Acadia.[1]

When they arrived in North America, they brought dance forms from their homeland. During the early colonial years in New France and Acadia, cooperation and group cohesion were essential to ensure the survival of the new communities. European settlement in New France occurred at a time in Europe's history when women's roles and places were neither clearly nor rigidly defined (Noel 1991:36). While some division of labour was evident in both the Old World and the New – domestic food preparation, for example, was performed by women – there was also shared work. At peak times in the agricultural season particularly, farm women worked side by side with men in the fields (Prentice 1988; see also Taft, this volume).

The colonial period's dances reflect these social structures: the lack of sharp gendered distinctions as well as the need for cooperation and group cohesion. Dancers, whether in Acadia, New France, or France, formed a circle or line and held hands; all had to move in unison.[2] Information concerning these dances does not always indicate whether the group was same-sex or mixed. In the Cheticamp area, circle and line dances appear to have been indiscriminately ordered as to gender. Participants not only danced together, but in most cases they also sang the songs which provided the musical accompaniment.[3] In some, such as *Les Moutons* (Chiasson and Boudreau 1945, 2:4), a leader emerged for a brief moment to direct the group through a pattern. However, most dances did not encourage individual accomplishment, but instead reinforced adherence to the group and egalitarian social relations among community members, regardless of gender. Enjoyment grew out of participation in a collective activity which was at once musical, poetic, and physical.

Besides cooperation of all participants, another striking characteristic of early dances was the limited degree of body holds used in the dance forms.[4] Though most required participants to hold hands, no other touching was allowed. In some from Europe and New France, participants avoided even that limited contact, linking instead by holding the ends of a handkerchief. Because of religious interdictions, couple dances, which allowed physical contact, were integrated only slowly into Acadian communities.

Such restrictions upon dance gatherings have a long history in Western society. Already in the fourth century, dance was linked with the devil. "Ubi saltatio, ibi diabolis" (where there is dance, there is the devil) affirms St John Chrysostom (Lemieux 1821:25). This idea penetrated not only Roman Catholic attitudes, but also those of all other Christian denominations. Dance was considered an occasion for sin, a sensual expression where passions were unleashed and the soul in danger. Until the mid-twentieth century, religious authorities feared that dance gatherings could be occasions of sins of lust in thought, look, word, and deed – sins against the sixth and ninth commandments.

Throughout the history of the Roman Catholic church, dance has been condemned with greater and lesser fervour depending upon the period and the interpretation of moral law. From the fourth to the mid-twentieth century, a series of councils and edicts expressed Church fathers' and moralists' aim of maintaining a Christian moral and social order. Rarely condemning dance explicitly, these authorities were concerned with the abuses which often accompanied dance gatherings. Dance's circumstances and context of performance were the core of the discussion of moral questions. Pagan tendencies, indecent toilette and clothing, obscene words and gestures, intimacy between the sexes, compromising attitudes, and bad wishes and desires were all considered avenues which led to loss of soul.

From the Church's standpoint, all rules of moral conduct and Christian modesty were forgotten during dance gatherings. Behaviour there, in their opinion, could lead to moral, religious, and social disorder, and a loss of the control mechanisms necessary for a good Christian life. Church officials feared that the devil might take advantage of dance gatherings and of dances themselves, and use women to tempt men. Precautions against such functions and activities, it was hoped, would deter the potential pitfalls that physical contact might elicit (Le Blanc 1986:53–88;161–91).

These attitudes persisted in Europe for centuries and were brought to North America with the transplanted settlers. Quebec City was the ecclesiastical centre of early French-speaking Canada and thus Acadia was under its jurisdiction. Throughout the seventeenth and eighteenth centuries numerous edicts warning against the evils and dangers of dance were sent to all the parishes and missions under the diocese's jurisdiction. An ordinance of 16 February 1691 listed dance as one of eleven abuses which must cease:

Et parce que nous avons été informés qu'il se faisait en divers lieux des assemblés de danse et autres divertissements aux jours de fêtes et de dimanche, et quelque fois même pendant le service divin, ce qui est défendu par les Ordonances du Roi et par les lois de la police séculière, Nous exhortons et conjurons pour l'amour de Notre Seigneur, et pour l'honneur de la Religion tous les Fidèles de notre diocese, de s'abstenir à l'avenir de ces sortes de choses dans les dits jours, et pour ce qui est des danses dangereuses qui se pratiquent entre personnes de différent sexe, comme l'experience fait voir qu'elles sint à la plupart des occasions prochaines d'un grand nombre de péchés considérables, Nous exhortons les curés, confesseurs, et autres qui ont soin des âmes, de les en détourner par toutes les voies les plus efficaces qu'ils pourront trouver. (Chancellerie [1691] 1973:278–9)

All subsequent edicts sent by the Quebec diocese reiterated the 1691 warning. In 1742 a letter was sent to all priests in the Acadian parishes, stating that "evening gatherings with members of the opposite sex were infinitely dangerous" (Chancellerie [1742] 1973:15). It was not until the middle of the twentieth century that such edicts were discontinued. However, despite the strong words against its dangers and evils, most women and men continued to dance.

Although circle and line dances persisted in the seventeenth and eighteenth centuries, rudimentary figures in which dancers changed places, taught by dancing masters, became more prevalent. Dancing masters were "highly educated men, versed in the newly revived classical learning and responsible for the intellectual and social as well as the physical proficiency of their pupils" (Jonas 1992:122). They were sought after not only by the aristocratic class but also by the gentry and middle class who hoped to gain entry into higher rungs of society. The eighteenth-century English and French colonies had their own dancing masters, but to date no documents indicate their presence in Acadia. However, the dances they taught did reach Acadian communities.

Dances of the second half of the seventeenth century reflected a strictly regulated social life. Such factors as appearance, etiquette and clothing were governed by rules of rank. In France, dancing personified the externalization of these rules of behaviour: "Princes et princesses du sang, ducs et duchesses, seigneurs et dames de la cour, sont seuls admis dans l'espace réservé à la danse, chacun assis a la place que son rang lui assigne. Le roi se leve. Toute la cour l'imite. Les danseurs se disposent en cortege. En tete avec la reine, ou, a défaut, la premiere princesse du rang. Puis le dauphin et la dauphine. Puis Monsieur et Madame. Puis les autres couples, dans l'ordre qui impose la différence des naissances et des dignités" (Guilcher 1969:23). This hierarchy penetrated dance gatherings at all social levels. The contradance and the minuet reflected essential though sometimes contradictory traits of eighteenth-century France. The minuet echoed the old system of social and class order in a studied grace; the contradance breathed a new spirit of play, liberty, and capriciousness.

While these dance innovations and changes took place in France, Acadia was in the midst of the Deportation, an event that would mark the Acadians and their sense of identity. In 1755, lieutenant-governor Charles Lawrence decided to deport the Acadians from their homeland, which had been British territory since 1713, because they would not sign an unconditional oath of allegiance to the British King. Some were sent to the English colonies along the Atlantic sea-board; others to England where they were placed in camps in major ports such as Bristol, Falmouth, and Penryn. Still others ended up in France. With the signing of the Treaty of Paris in 1763, Acadians were officially allowed to resettle the British territory of Nova Scotia on the condition that they sign an oath of allegiance and settle in small groups in designated areas. A direct result of the resettlement of Nova Scotia was the establishment the new Acadian community of Cheticamp.[5]

Although a fishing station existed there in 1752, the first families settled the village in 1782. By 1790 there were 26 families in the area, and by 1820 there were 784 residents. During the same period, settlements began in the present day parishes of Saint-Joseph-du-Moine and Saint Michael, Margaree. Information concerning the dances of the period from the initial settlement in the 1780s to the mid-nineteenth century is scarce.

When dance ethnologist Simonne Voyer visited the area in the 1950s, she collected three contradances: the Four-Handed Reel, the Eight-Handed-Reel, and the Long Potato (Voyer 1986). Older residents in the community had seen their parents perform them, or had done so themselves when they were younger. Contradances were popular from the nineteenth to the mid-twentieth centuries. The square set, their descendant, was the most popular dance form at all festive activities from the early to the mid-twentieth century.[6] Besides these forms, residents still performed the early circle dances well into the middle of the twentieth century.

Throughout Acadian society in the nineteenth and early twentieth centuries, the extended family remained important as the nuclear family's role began to expand. However, the community continued to oversee and control the couple. In both the contradances and square sets associated with this period, the couple had a well-defined pattern to follow, with the man directing and guiding his female partner. The two French contradance forms, quadrille and cotillion, as well as their descendant the square set, reflect a society in which group cohesion is still important, yet the couple takes on a central role. Male and female roles are more clearly differentiated than in circle or line dances, with men given control and power over the dance and the dancing woman. Contradances give participants the opportunity to meet other couples and exchange pleasantries

(Guilcher 1969:210), probably showing an intermediary phase between collective dances, such as the circle, and couple dances, such as the waltz (Ibid., 212).

Couple dances became the dances *par excellence* of the nineteenth century in most of Europe and many parts of North America. In the early years of the nineteenth century, when the waltz first became popular in Europe, "men and women fitted their movements to one another in a public display of mutual confidence and teamwork" (Jonas 1992:123–5). In the early waltz, no one led because all dancers followed a pre-established pattern. This curious moment of what appears to be egalitarianism may be due to the values of liberty, equality, and fraternity which followed the French revolution, but further study is needed in this area. By mid-century, steps were simplified and the couple's freedom to move and turn without reference to other dancers led to a need for one partner to become the leader, steering the other around the dance floor safely and without mishap. "The leading role, it goes without saying, fell to the man" (Ibid., 126). It was this second form of the waltz that was eventually adopted by the Acadians. It reflects the society's hierarchical relationships with the nuclear family the central focus of the community, and men guiding and leading women. Couple dances such as the waltz juxtapose solitudes. Each couple is a closed unit unto itself, giving little or no attention to the others on the dance floor (Guilcher 1969:174). Thus, the waltz can be seen as "one of the earliest manifestations of individualism and escape in the dance and its associations with the values of liberty, equality and uncertainty which followed upon the French Revolution. The ... dancers, at first, were the middle clases, soon to be joined by both the upper and lower classes. The Waltz emphasized not uniformity, but individual expression; there are no rules to be studied, save for a few basic steps, the individual is encouraged to introduce his own variations and interpretations" (Katz 1983:524). Of course, this reflection of "individualism" did not extend to allowing women to express their individuality; the female waltzing partner is the mirror of the man, and is controlled by his movements.

Changes in dance forms vibrated throughout Europe and North America, but Cheticamp Acadians adopted the waltz and the foxtrot, both referred to as "round dances," only around 1940. Perhaps the Church's close and watchful eye in the Acadian parishes was one cause of these forms' late introduction and acceptance. Throughout the late nineteenth and early twentieth centuries, ecclesiastic authorities allowed dance only at certain celebrations: parish picnics, weddings, and special feast days such as the *Chandeleur* (Arsenault 1982;

Le Blanc 1954). They frowned upon informal dance gatherings in the home, fearing that such events were likely to be accompanied by other abuses such as alcohol consumption, quarrels, unsupervised interaction between the sexes, and free use of language and gesture. In the latter half of the twentieth century, Church concerns focused more narrowly on spiritual matters. Civil affairs became the responsibility of various organized public services, and the clergy intervened less in both formal and informal social gatherings. As the Church began to slowly loosen its powerful hold over the lives of parishoners, and people began to change their attitudes about the waltz and foxtrot's potential dangers, they became accepted.

Despite the still watchful eye of the Church, various festive activities during winter and summer offered social contexts for dancing. The parish summer picnic developed in the late 1800s. Held to raise money to build or renovate parish facilities, it consisted of games, contests, sporting events, suppers, music, song, and dance. It usually began with mass, followed by a procession to the picnic grounds. These gatherings, also known as bazaars, continue today and include evening dances held in parish halls.

In the second half of the twentieth century, the *Escaouette* festival has to some extent displaced the parish picnic. This week-long summer event offers recreational activities for both residents and tourists, emphasizing history and heritage. Emigrants often return to visit their native communities for this highlight of the summer season. The activities include concerts of traditional music, song, and dance; storytelling; historical skits; reenactments of traditional tasks such as a milling frolic; a parade with historical floats; and choosing the hosts of the festival, Evangeline and Gabriel (Longfellow [1847] 1952), who symbolize the deported Acadians. At times, local business employees wear traditional costumes.

In the nineteenth and early twentieth centuries, weddings took place in winter, a period of reduced work activity. The designated period for weddings was from the feast of Epiphany – le mardi des rois – on January 6 until the beginning of the Lenten season, a forty-day period of fasting and penance. After the marriage ceremony celebrations would begin in the afternoon at the bride's parents' home and continue into the evening at the groom's parents'. Dancing would start after the wedding meal and continue into the early morning and often for several days thereafter.

Towards the mid-twentieth century, summer became the preferred wedding season. Weather conditions were more suitable for friends and relatives travelling to attend the celebration. Pre- and post-wedding festivities provided additional opportunities for celebration:

We had a high old time because we had all kinds of excuses to have dances. First of all we had a dance when Georgie came to *faire la demande,* you know it was the formal asking for the hand in marriage. So everybody was alerted that Georgie was going on a certain night and everyone was prepared. So we all went over and we had a dance. Then I remember the first shower for a bride, say we read about it in a magazine, when we got one ... So we invited the boys too ... we knew darn well we'd have a dance, and so we did ... You had a dance to *enterrer les noces,* to bury the wedding was just another excuse to have a dance ... Perhaps not the night after because everybody was worn out after having danced all afternoon and all night, but maybe a couple of nights after you had a dance to *enterrer les noces.* (Le Blanc and Sadowsky 1985:1319,1)

Perhaps these extended wedding celebrations were a way of getting around the dance restrictions imposed by the priests.

The significance of some celebrations where dance once played an important role has almost completely attenuated. The religious feast day of Candlemas – *Chandeleur* – celebrated on February 2, commemorates the presentation of Christ in the temple and the purification of the Blessed Virgin Mary.[7] In order to prepare for the festivity, a group of men would go from house to house gathering food, an activity called *courir la chandeleur.* A portion of the collected provisions would be given to poorer families in the parishes and the remainder would supply the ingredients for a communal supper at designated homes. Several houses served as the gathering places for an evening of song, music, dance, and card-playing. Although the religious ceremony continues, since 1935 *courir la chandeleur* no longer takes place. But a few years ago Trois Pignons, a cultural centre for Cheticamp area Acadians, revived the celebration by having a supper and dance at a community centre.

Mi-carême – mid-Lent celebration – in contrast, has remained popular. Beginning on the third Thursday of Lent, small costumed groups of Cheticamp-area Acadians go from house to house. In each, the occupants attempt to discover the disguised visitors' identities. Often this leads to informal parties with music, song, and dance. What was once a one-day activity has become a week-long event. Friends and relatives who live outside the province often take their holidays to coincide with *mi-carême* and come back to participate in house parties and public dances held in community halls.

The house party, an evening of merriment which can be either spontaneous or planned, was the main venue for leisure activity in the first half of the twentieth century. Periods of intensive work –

spring, summer, and autumn – left minimal opportunity for amusements and thus winter was the prime period for diversion. House parties were usually held in the kitchen – the largest, warmest, most used room in the house. In the second half of the century, technological changes, better transportation routes, and improvement of social and economic conditions have made summer the season for celebration. Private homes have been replaced by public places such as lounges, clubs, taverns, and parish centres as the preferred festive locations.[8]

After the mid-1960s, Church authorities paid no more attention to dancing as a moral issue. This, along with the changing attitudes of the younger generation of the sixties, is probably why dances such as rock and roll and the twist were so easily integrated into Acadian communities. However, remnants of the question of morality remained. As a teenager in the sixties, and secretary of a girls' Catholic society called the Sodality, I signed a letter which was sent to a local Cape Breton disco television show condemning the immodest go-go dancing it displayed. Later trends such as disco were quickly accepted in the Cheticamp area. The individual dances of the 1960s and 1970s "spoke directly of the social issues of time: if no one leads, no one has to follow" (Jonas 1992:126).

Since the 1960s, in Acadia as in other parts of North America, the traditional nuclear family structure has changed, community cohesion is less evident, and distinctions between the roles of women and men in society are becoming less well-defined. Women as much as men have become leaders or solitary dancers. Contemporary social dances often "isolate the individual in a trance-like self-absorption which virtually disconnects him [sic] from the world and even from his [sic] partner" (Katz 1983:521).

Three trends appeared in North American dance forms in the 1980s and 1990s. The first, "slam dancing," reflects a violence once socially submerged; adolescent and young adult dancers deliberately bang into one another. A second, "line dancing," permits anyone to join into a large linear formation and perform a series of predetermined movements. All ages, women and men alike, can participate, but it is particularly popular among the older generations. Within North American society, statistics indicate that men die at a younger age than women. This dance form offers widows the opportunity to dance without an official or assigned male partner, an acceptable form of interaction in a society which expects the dance floor to be covered with heterosexual couples. By convention and choice, there is no physical contact. Participants are separate entities, controlled by the predetermined movements of the larger structure which glides and flows on the dance space. A final trend is that younger women are forming circles and dancing together. A retired French-Canadian man's informal comment to me that "line dancing is better than seeing two women dance together," suggests that such a formation poses a threat to an established order where the man's role, and heterosexuality, must remain dominant.

Of the three trends, only line dancing seems to have become popular among the Acadians of the Cheticamp area.[9] Slam dancing has not been well received by adolescents, but their young friends from larger urban areas such as Pictou, Sydney, and Halifax perform them when they visit, or tell their Acadian peers about them. Finally, although some women in the Margaree parish will get up and dance together in a group, it is not common practice. But it may only be a matter of time before slam dancing and women's circles will also be part of the dance repertoire in the Cheticamp area.

Cheticamp-area dances reflect changing social, economic, and political patterns as well as the changing places of women and men within society. What began as a society dependant upon a strong sense of group cohesion and extended family structure for survival in a sometimes harsh and difficult environment changed into one that, although still dependent upon a highly structured social organisation, placed more emphasis upon the nuclear family, with a greater role distinction between women and men.[10] Most recently, individualism has become paramount. Concomitantly, dance forms changed from ones in which gender distinctions were relatively unimportant but where the group depended on the harmony of the participants' movements; to contradances and the square set where a strong group social order was felt, but the heterosexual couple began to take a more important role; and finally to individual dances with each dancer a solitary performer.

In the Cheticamp area, as in other parts of North America, remnants of all the earlier dance forms remain and older dances are sometimes revived. These revivals may express the needs of individuals caught up in a world in transition, who search for a dance form corresponding to their own vision of social order and of women's and men's places within society. Perhaps some people feel a need for a dance structure which represents a hierarchical order. Perhaps others feel a certain nostalgia for a time when dancing interactions and society reflected the equal value of women's and men's contributions, if not their equality. These revived dances may represent security in a world moving faster and faster into an unknown and sometimes frightening and violent future. Developments in dance forms show women and men continually changing places socially and sociably.

NOTES

1 The total population of the area (Inverness County – subdivision A – Cheticamp – Margaree), according to Statistics Canada (1981), is 7,170. Of that number, 3,350 claimed to be of French extraction. The Cheticamp area comprises three parishes: Saint-Pierre in Cheticamp; Saint-Joseph-du-Moine in the village of the same name; and Saint Michael in Margaree.

2 These early dances are similar to the rounds in present-day childrens' repertoires of playground games, but were then performed by both children and adults.

3 The *branles* (brawls) described in Arbeau (1967) are dances with instrumental accompaniment; Chiasson and Boudreau (1943–1985) give several examples of dances or rounds with song accompaniment.

4 The introduction of rudimentary figures for two and three dancers in the fifteenth century has been read by some observers as symbolizing love intrigues or flirtations.

5 Information concerning the late nineteenth and early twentieth centuries was obtained during field research between 1983 and 1986. On several field trips I was accompanied by colleague Laura Sadowsky. Together we interviewed Acadians of the area about their history, music, song, and dance repertoire.

6 Informants stated that the square set was introduced into the Cheticamp area in the early twentieth century and remained popular until the mid 1940s. Research with Laura Sadowsky uncovered *Dick's Quadrille Callbook*, which was sold through the Eaton's Catalogue in the early twentieth century (Dick and Fitzgerald Handbook 1878). Several people said that they used it, and it contains the square set which is danced today. The callbook describes it as a quadrille, the *Caledonia Lancers*. Indeed, an interesting feature in Cheticamp region square set is the use of the quadrille numbering system, where the couple facing couple one is designated couple two, rather than couple three as in standard modern day numbering. Few other communities appear to have maintained this older manner of numbering.

   The waltz and the foxtrot, referred to as "round dances," appeared around the 1940s. In the 1950s, a dance evening would alternate between square and round dancing. Square dancing has remained integral to contemporary dance evenings, which usually include two "square sets," each taking approximately twenty minutes.

7 The ritual is so named because it includes the blessing of candles in the local churches.

8 Public and private locations are in this case not gendered, as they are in the Newfoundland women's social gatherings Desplanques

describes, or the male-associated work context of taxi driving discussed by Boyd. As in the papers by Shantz, Grant, and McGrath,
public and private contexts are negotiated by women and men alike.

9 Information concerning trends in the Cheticamp area was obtained
during a telephone interview with several residents in January 1993.

10 Similarly, the enactment of gender roles is seen in Rieti's discussion of
reactions to witches; Greenhill's paper on cross-dressing ballads and
Ristock's on popular films show, in contrast, figures who counter traditional notions of gendered behaviour.

"The Handsome Cabin Boy": Cross-Dressing Ballads, Sexualities, and Gendered Meanings

PAULINE GREENHILL

When I[1] was a young woman, the Mariposa Folk Festival was an experience of freedom and separation, requiring bus and subway travel from my parents' apartment in Don Mills, and then a ferry across the harbour to the Toronto Islands. To spend a summer week-end away from the suburbs, surrounded by trees, water, and music was to be literally and figuratively transported to other historic and symbolic locations. It was probably at Mariposa that I first heard "transvestite," "warrior maiden," "female sailor," or, as I call them here, cross-dressing ballads, likely sung by strong women folksong revival performers like Frankie Armstrong.[2] These songs immediately attracted my attention. They seemed different from others I knew about; although many traditional songs had romantic and adventurous plots, in these the main characters were female, young, and active, and they were men's equals or even their betters. I saw myself as just such a girl as the protagonists, separated – if only too temporarily – from the stifling atmosphere of my parents' home, independent, and venturing boldly into unknown territory.

I did not know then that cross-dressing ballads had been collected in Canada, particularly in the Atlantic provinces, during the first six decades of this century. While versions have also been collected internationally and at other times, those I will draw upon for this paper were collected by Kenneth Peacock in Newfoundland between 1951 and 1961. Peacock's (1965) three volume collection of New-foundland folksongs contains eleven very complete texts of ten cross-dressing ballads: "Jimmy and Nancy on the Sea" sung by Jim

Dalton of Codroy and by William Nash of Branch (Ibid., 202–5; Laws N8);[3] "The 'Lady Leroy'" sung by Harry Curtis of Joe Batt's Arm (208–9; N5); "The Handsome Cabin Boy" sung by Mary Ann Galpin of Codroy, July 1960 (280–1; N13); "Blue Jacket and White Trousers" sung by Charlotte Decker of Codroy, August 1958 (327–8; N12); "Caroline and Her Young Sailor Bold" sung by Chris Cobb of Barred Island, July 1952 (329–30; N17); "The Female Smuggler" sung by Mary Ann Galpin, July 1960 (333–4); "The Golden Glove" sung by Everett Bennett of St Paul's, July 1958 (340–1; N20); "Gold Watch and Chain" sung by Freeman Bennett of St Paul's, July 1958 (342–3; N21); "Polly Oliver" sung by Gordon Willis of St John's, July 1952 (344–5; N14); and "The Soldier Maid" sung by Clara Stevens of Bellburns, August 1959 (346–7).

All the songs in Peacock's collection refer to a range of aspects of human existence, organised as follows: Children's Songs, Comic Ditties, Fishing Songs, Laments, Love Adventures, Love Comedies (which has three cross-dressing ballads), Love Disguises and Other Impersonations (which has seven), Love Eulogies and Other Songs of Praise, Love Ghosts, Love Laments, Love Lyrics, Love Murders, Love Tragedies, Lumbering Ballads, Miscellaneous Songs, Murder Ballads, Pirate Songs, Sailor Songs, Tragic Sea Ballads, and War Songs. Several show women appropriating men's possessions (e.g., "The Maid on the Shore" pp. 296–7; K27) or acting forcefully towards men (e.g., "My Good-Looking Man" pp. 302–3). Those published represent "just over one-half the National Museum's collection of Newfoundland songs made in six short field trips during the decade between 1951 and '61" (Ibid., xx). As a collector, Peacock was apparently uninterested in context. His aim was to find good texts: "I do think collectors should be more ruthless in sifting out poor material at the source" (Ibid., xxii). Thus, these very complete song lyrics may not reflect most Newfoundland singers' versions – Greenleaf and Mansfield's (1933) *Ballads and Sea Songs of Newfoundland*, for example, contains many that are fragmentary, incomplete, and less literary.

A prime example of the cross-dressing ballads in Peacock's collection is "The Soldier Maid." I give this text in its entirety:

Oh what a pretty maiden in my time I have been,
They forced me from my parents, a soldier I became,
They forced me from my parents and certainly I'm undone,
And they learned me to beat upon a drum, a drum, a drum.

With my feather in my hat I will have you all to see,
My officer he taught me a stately man to be,

The soldiers all admired me, my fingers were so small,
And they learned me to beat upon the drum the best of all.

Oh when I went to my quarters the night time for to spend
I was not ashamed for to lie among the men,
And hauling off my small clothes to myself I ofttimes smiled,
A-lying with the soldiers a maid all the while.

Oh many were the battles that I fought upon the field,
And many a brave fellow was forced from me to yield,
I was guarded by my general for fear I would be slain,
And for cruelty they sent me back to old England again.

Then they sent me over to London to take charge of the tower,
I never was discovered until that day and hour,
When a lady fell in love with me I told her I was a maid,
And straight unto my regiment my secrets were betrayed.

Then up steps the officer, he made no more to-do,
He asked me the questions, I answered him quite true.
He laughed at the joke and he smiled as he said:
"It's a pity we should lose such a drummer as a maid."

Here's a health to the Duke, here's a health, sir, unto you,
And here's a health to every British man who keeps his courage true.
And if our King does want more men those Frenchmen to be slain,
I will boldly stand with sword in hand and fight for him again. (346–7)

The names of their authors may be lost, but the texts of these songs have a relatively long history. They were originally composed and circulated as cheaply printed "broadsides" in Britain in the seventeenth, eighteenth, and nineteenth centuries, but when Peacock collected them in the twentieth – in North America – they were disseminated more commonly in oral form. The fact that these songs have been remembered and passed down in family and community repertoire for generations clearly indicates that what they have to say remains relevant and appropriate for their singers and audiences; people do not learn or perform songs to which they are indifferent.

Many folklorists (including for example Ives 1978) have argued that the northeastern North American song tradition is primarily male; certainly much of the "public" singing – that is, in all-male or mixed contexts – was done by men. Yet four of the ten cross-dressing ballads in Peacock's collection are sung by women, and these female singers are well represented elsewhere in his compendium.[4] The primary Atlantic Canadian contexts in which these songs were transmitted may indeed have been "homosocial" – all male – lumbercamps and fishing work locations.[5] Folksong scholarship has traditionally focused upon the meaning of such "original" contexts, avoiding contemporary contexts and meanings – such as folk clubs and folk festivals – (for an exception see Cartwright 1980), as well as those surrounding their collection (for another exception see Kodish 1987). I'm arguing here for an interpretation of songs' meanings based on current as well as possible historical understandings: specifically, that messages they contain about the action and behaviour they depict may not be exclusively heterosexual. This reading is "perverse" (Zimmerman 1993), or undisciplined, in that it willfully goes against the grain of conventional interpretations.[6]

Meanings intended by performers and those understood by audiences need not be congruent; listeners always have latitude in interpreting songs, as singers do in presenting them. Thus whether or not their original or current singers see these songs as pertaining to homosexuality, some audiences, then as now, may so interpret them. Scholars' denials of lesbian and gay readings amount to silencing, ignoring, and suppressing the songs' implications.[7] Other fictional accounts of cross-dressing women abound. And news articles about jazz musician Billy Tipton, for example, indicate that women can cross dress, marry other women, and pass as men. Both fictional and real-life cross dressers' motivations – to gain access to contexts from which they are, as women, excluded – are similar to those of the ballad protagonists. And as historical work and fiction (e.g., Akenson 1990; Durova 1988; Faderman 1991:41–5) begins to explore cases of actual pre-twentieth century cross-dressed Euro-American women, my reading seems less speculative. I'm arguing, then, that since most folklorists assume that other kinds of interpersonal relationships – father to daughter, for example – are intended in ballads to implicate or refer to those same relationships in real life, readers should not assume that woman/woman or man/man relationships are exclusively symbolic. But first, more about the songs.

I prefer to call them "cross-dressing" ballads, based upon their female protagonists who dress in men's clothing. The "female sailor," "female warrior," "female highwayman" designations show sexist assumptions that a woman can/should not be included in the occupations sailor, warrior, or robber. Another alternative, "transvestite ballads," assumes that same sex orientation is primarily the cross dresser's, though this is not the only possibility, or even the most common one.

Folksongs that tell this kind of tale are classified in G. Malcolm Laws' *American Balladry from British Broadsides* (1957) as "Ballads of Lovers' Disguises and Tricks" and are structured, like "The Soldier Maid" (above) around a woman's departure from home; her disguise as a man; her work experiences in that role; discovery of her sex; and finally, a choice about marriage.[8] Notably, the unfolding plots which provide the textual framework for cross dressing differ. These songs do not univocally express same sex orientations. They show considerable variation in the elaboration of their structures and meanings. I will outline some of these below.

It is not clear who is responsible for the "Soldier Maid"'s departure from home. However, leaving is usually the woman's own decision, often as part of a test or trick on her lover, or "to follow a young sailor bold" (329). The cross dresser's motive, when made explicit, is most often to pursue – literally – a heterosexual relationship, sometimes, as in "The 'Lady Leroy,'" against her father's wishes. "The Female Smuggler" is an apparent exception. In search of adventure but sailing with her father, she too ends up marrying the man she chooses. "The Handsome Cabin Boy," who "had a mind to go roving where the foaming billows swell" (280) – not to follow her male lover – ends up "betrayed" by the captain and his wife, and giving birth. The intentions of these cross-dressing women are explicitly adventurous, and implicitly heterosexual; the only lesbian relationship perhaps consummated in these songs is that of the captain's wife and the handsome cabin boy, described as stated above as a "betrayal" – as is the heterosexual relationship which leads to the cabin boy's pregnancy.

The men's clothing and other symbolically male objects the woman appropriates usually pertain specifically to her chosen work or occupation. "Blue jacket and white trousers" does for a sailor, but the female smuggler takes "two loaded pistols," "a glittering sword," and "two daggers" so as to be "well-armed for war" (333). In "Polly Oliver," "With a pair of bright pistols and a broadsword by her side, / On her father's great stallion like a man she did ride" (344). In "The Golden Glove," "Waistcoat and britches this fair girl put on, / And as she went a-hunting with her dog and her gun" (340). And one cross-dressed woman robs "her true love" of his "gold watch and chain" (342). Clearly, men's clothing and their roles are not the only male-associated materials these women appropriate or commandeer.

The cross-dressing ballads represent females doing male work, as well as females wearing male dress, and females appropriating male objects.[9] The work represented – i.e., highway robber, sailor, soldier, and hunter – is selective; they take on roles from which they are, as women, fully and effectively excluded.[10] Often in these songs the woman is more than capable in her chosen work; she excels, as does the "Soldier Maid," in a role normally reserved for men. Caroline "always proved loyal and true" (329), and the woman in "Blue Jacket and White Trousers" was "the bravest sailor there was on board" (327). Even the female smuggler maintains her positive image by challenging the Turkish fleet – never a British ship – during the song's narrative. Lack of success in the adopted role is always mitigated. Though in "The Golden Glove," "Often did she fire but nothing did she kill" (341), it is clear the female protagonist is not hunting game, but the young farmer she is in love with. And the female robber's victory in finding a "true love" is indicated by her relative lack of success in her profession when he refuses to allow her to steal his diamond ring: "'That diamond ring is a pledge of love, / Before I'll deliver it my life I'll lose'" (343). The gendered division of labour is thus presented as arbitrary, not natural.[11]

Usually the cross dresser is eventually discovered to be a woman. Yet while she is disguised, it is common for members of the "wrong" sex to be attracted to her. Both women and men find her alluring, and both are making what could be termed a heterosexual mistake. If a man falls for her, he *thinks* he's falling for another man; if a woman falls for her, she *doesn't think* she's falling for another woman. Both are wrong. What happens to the cross dresser depends in part on who – a woman or a man – discovers or suspects her, and whether that discovery is public or private.

When a man is attracted to her, this does not usually lead immediately to sexual activity; in "Blue Jacket and White Trousers," for example, the captain says: "'Your rosy cheeks and ruby lips they do entice me, / And I do wish with all my heart that you was a maid for me'" (327). When he wishes she was a maid, captain's attraction is to one he thinks is the same sex, and the woman initially treats this comment as an "inappropriate" – that is, non-heterosexual – expression. She supports his impression that she is male, replying:

"Oh leave off talking captain, your talk it's all in vain,
For if the sailors they do know on us they will make game;
And when we reach the southern shores some pretty girls we'll find;
They'll roll us in their arms, to us they will prove kind" (327).

This avoidance of discovery doesn't happen in "The Handsome Cabin Boy." "The captain with his cabin boy would often kiss and toy" (280), and her true sex becomes public when the disguised woman gives birth to a child.

However, if the cross dresser declares her true sex to a male in public, his reaction is invariably to offer marriage or concubinage, suggesting that she exemplifies ideal qualities. That is, the man-associated woman – previously thought to be a woman-associated man – is unusually attractive, perhaps irresistibly so. Thus, in these songs, a male's attraction to a person he thinks is also male is not perceived as negative – in several cases, he is the woman's eventual marriage choice; and clearly having been cross dressed adds to rather than detracts from the woman's desirability.

In "The Soldier Maid," a woman falls in love with the cross-dressed woman, thinking she is a man. The smitten woman, then, perceives herself in heterosexual mode – though the person to whom she is attracted is actually female. Similarly, the cross dresser refuses to pursue the relationship and thus affirms her heterosexuality. The discoverer's reaction to the cross-dresser's "true" sex is to publicize it. There is little social disgrace – even implicit – upon either woman.[12] Interestingly, however, this song ends without any declaration about marriage; the last verse clearly states that the maid's choice would be to return to soldiering. This cross dresser is attractive to women, not to men; her relationship with the male officer is strictly professional. Perhaps uncoincidentally, this woman-identified woman (Radicalesbians 1971:292)[13] ends up the most truly independent of all cross dressers.

Generally, however, once the woman reveals her true sex, she may receive a proposal of marriage or concubinage, or an affirmation of her chosen man's love. The marriage may result in a social elevation for the woman, as when the female smuggler marries "her young commodore," but not always. In "The Golden Glove" the "rich merchant's daughter" marries a farmer; in "Caroline and Her Young Sailor Bold" the woman's "return to old England" leads her previously recalcitrant father to consent to her marriage:

They got married on Caroline's fortune,
With twenty-five thousand in gold,
And now they are living in splendor. (330)

However, the woman may also refuse a proposition in order to continue her search for her true love. The consequences and outcome are completely in the woman's control; it is her decision to marry or not. If she chooses to do so, the husband is also her own choice. The outcomes of these songs are generally positive; the same cannot be said for many other folksongs of similar origins and locations.[14] "The Handsome Cabin Boy" is again an exception. It is unclear whether the consequences of her cross dressing are positive or negative, but the sailors' attitude is obvious: "But if the war should rise again our country to destroy / We'll try and ship some sailors like our handsome cabin boy" (281).

Yet the song is alone in Peacock's Newfoundland material in being apparently explicit about heterosexual and homosexual activities. The captain's wife, like the captain, is pleased with "the handsome cabin boy," and her comment to her husband on the cabin boy's giving birth is "'My dear, I wish you joy, / For 'twas either you or me betrayed our handsome cabin boy'" (281). The "cabin boy" is consistently referred to as "he" after the first verse. Even after "he" has given birth, it's asserted that "he's neither a man nor a maid" (Ibid.).[15] The full text follows:

It's of a pretty fair maid the truth to you I'll tell,
She had a mind to go roving where the foaming billows swell,
She agreed all with our captain his cabin boy to be,
The wind did blow a pleasant gale and we soon put out for sea.

By day the captain worked so hard, at night he took his ease,
The cabin boy he did his best the captain for to please.
The captain's wife she was on board and seemed for to enjoy
For to think the captain had engaged such a handsome cabin boy.

The cabin boy was well-behaved and he did his duty well,
And what next follows after the song itself will tell,
For the captain with his cabin boy would often kiss and toy,
And we soon found out the secret of our handsome cabin boy.

For his cheeks were red like roses and his side-locks they did curl,
The sailors used to smile and say he looked just like a girl,
While eating captain's biscuits his colour did destroy,
And the waist did swell of pretty Phil, our handsome cabin boy.

'Twas across the Bay of Biscay our gallant ship did plow,
One night among the sailors there rose a bloody row,
They all bounded from their hammocks, their rest it did destroy,
For they swore they heard the groaning of their handsome cabin boy.

"Oh doctor, oh doctor," the cabin boy did cry,
The sailors swore by all was good their cabin boy would die.
The doctor ran with all his might, came smiling at the fun,
For to think a sailor lad could have a daughter or a son.

The sailors they were all amazed and at that child did stare,
The child belonged to none of them they solemnly could swear.
Said the captain's wife to her husband: "My dear, I wish you joy,
For 'twas either you or me betrayed our handsome cabin boy."

So we'll all fill up our bumpers and we'll drink success to the trade,
Here's adieu unto our cabin boy for he's neither a man nor a maid,
But if the war would rise again our country to destroy
We'll try and ship some sailors like our handsome cabin boy. (280–1)

Peacock's arch comment on "The Handsome Cabin Boy" is "I feel I am medically incompetent to deal with the psycho-sexual implications of [the captain's wife's] remark to the captain" (281). Avoiding the symbolic issue at hand, he casts her statement in the realm of issues outside ethnomusicology. I see two not necessarily exclusive possibilities: she is telling the captain that she too had a sexual relationship with the "boy," and/or alluding to her lack of (inclination toward) a sexual relationship with him. That both the wife's and the captain's relationship with the "boy" are "betrayals" does not necessarily require that *both* have had a sexual relationship with her. The captain's betrayal could be in making the "boy" pregnant, and the wife's in discovering "his" true sex yet failing to disclose her knowledge.[16]

Though some might suggest that the wife's comment is ironic, folklorists have contended that folksongs never employ that trope. However, oxymorons (such as the cherry without a stone) are manifest in various traditional songs, many of which, like these ballads, refer to sexual and reproductive love. "The Handsome Cabin Boy" contains at least one oxymoronic concept, that of the pregnant man; impregnation by a woman is another that may be implied. This "impossibility" allows the text to conceive[17] of the possibility of sex between women. Just as other oxymoronic tropes think the (im)possible, in the context of sexuality they think the unthinkable, and enable the impossible (see also Greenhill 1995).

Ballad scholarship has almost completely ignored or silenced the gay and lesbian possibilities in these texts. Gay male allusions, for example, are explained away. A.L. Lloyd invokes a standard denial when he suggests that "the dream that one of their companions might be a girl dressed as a boy is an inevitable fantasy for lonely men in barrack bunk or fo'c'sle hammock" (1967:225). I'm not arguing that this explanation is an impossibility, but instead that alternatives are equally possible. What appears to be – or is depicted as – a same-sex attraction need not be Lloyd's decidedly heterosexual fantasy. For example, a bawdy song verse dating from around World War I explicitly imagines gay male sexual behaviour:

The cabin boy was chipper,
Pernicious little nipper
He stuffed his ass with broken glass
And circumcised the skipper. (Cray 1968: 116–17)[18]

Similarly, historic gay male pornography often employed a standard scenario in which a sailor smuggles his girlfriend on board, and is discovered by the captain having sex with her. The captain then has intercourse first with her, and then with him (Anne Brydon, personal communication).

The work of Dianne Dugaw is an exception to the scholarly avoidance of lesbian or gay possibility. Though her study, the most complete to date of the genre of "female warrior" ballads, spends little time on the topic, she reports that, "the ballads – like all forms that feature the transvestite heroine – enthusiastically exploit the homoerotic implications of the gender disguising. However, this probing of sexual ambiguity is only one aspect of their meaning. Indeed, the preoccupation with homosexual attraction – both for women and for men – that stories of female transvestites almost always feature, brings with it the larger implication that gender-based attraction is a fragile construction – indeed, that gender itself may be a fragile construct" (Dugaw 1989:145). Her lengthy discussion (Ibid., 143–62) admirably departs from much earlier scholarship in focusing specifically on these ballads' rendering of women's experience.

I'm sure I'm not the only woman who has identified strongly with the protagonists of these cross-dressing ballads. Although most narrate in the third rather than – or as well as – the first person, they include, like other broadside ballads, extensive reported speech – quoted as well as unascribed dialogue[19] – which draws the listener into experiencing rather than merely observing the action. Apart from the lure of their romantic and active stories, I was attracted by the women's heroic actions and escape from the constraints of kinship.[20] Indeed, my first analysis of these songs was strongly influenced by those youthful impressions.[21] Thus I initially concluded that women – singers and audiences – in traditional communities might, as I did, have perceived these female protagonists as heroic, and that these women's interest in such songs could stem from their iconoclastic representation of women's role in political economy, in contrast to (male) society's obsession with the exchange of women and control over their reproductive power.[22] In my interpretation these songs portrayed women's own control over their own "repro-ductive use value" (Irigaray 1985:174) – that is, the protagonists choose to marry the man they want, or to continue searching – in a society in which that control is often limited. The art form may be permitting precisely what is publicly denied.

Both my interpretations of these songs assumed a heterosexual identification by female audience or singer. That is, whether singers and audience relate to the woman in the song as one who controls her own reproductive powers, or to her bold and unorthodox behav-iour, these interpretations failed to consider the possibility that the singers, the audiences, and the women protagonists represented in the songs may have another sexual agenda.

However, when I went to test my hypothesis about personal iden-tification, heroism, and marriage choice among contemporary women singers in Newfoundland, I found that they did not share my interpretation.[23] As often occurs in fieldwork, the women I worked with indicated that I was asking the wrong questions, but it took me some time to hear the alternative interpretations they were presenting. I found that relatively few women singers in Newfoundland actually perform these ballads. As songwriters – and I found that many women composed as well as performed songs – they wrote about what might be termed an everyday heroism; more immediate and less symbolic than that of the cross-dressing ballads. Most expressed a preference for realistic, contemporary topics, and many composed songs on such topics which reflected upon women's strengths. Ernes-tine O'Rourke Power of Branch discussed her composition "Tommy's Song," about her own experience of having a son with cerebral palsy, which was often requested when she performed (Power 1989). Of this song, Michelle Myrick, another singer, commented, "That's such a powerful song. It's all about how she felt having a child granted to her, how grateful she was to have a little boy, but the difficulties that they face with his disease, and in the end about how she thanks God for having Tommy to love and … how much joy he's brought to her home. It's a beautiful song, honestly" (Myrick 1989).

Michelle Myrick herself wrote "Voices On the Wind," a reflection on the place where her father and uncle were drowned, and she also sings a version of her cousin's song "Lost Adrift," "about how she felt that day, when they came to tell her that they were gone" (Ibid.). Though shipwrecks and men being lost at sea are traditional song topics, they are not ones which I had hitherto associated with female heroism.

These women's implicit definition of heroism was everyday, con-crete, and realistic; the heroism which attracted me to the cross-dressing ballads was clearly more escapist. Crucially, the reaction of several singers and audiences to my descriptions of the cross-dressing ballads indicated that they assumed that the texts referred to gay and lesbian activities, and they commented that such behaviour – and such songs! – were unheard of in the communities they knew.[24] I eventually took their reactions as a starting point for taking the lesbian and gay implications of these songs seriously.

But Newfoundland women singers were not the only ones to indicate that same sex orientation might be significant in reading cross-dressing ballads. Women's studies students and other feminists with whom I discussed this work were disappointed with my interpretation in which a marriage plot (Aisenberg and Harrington 1988:6–19) appeared as the primary choice.[25] That is, no woman actually chose a career (though "The Soldier Maid" wanted to), or celibacy (except in preference to marrying a man she didn't want), or another woman. The outcome was a decision to marry now or to continue the search for a desirable and/or desired male partner. My focus in that analysis (see Greenhill 1990) on the final outcomes of these cross-dressing ballads, I think, obscured the areas of same sex orientation I discuss here.

But following their ideas, I have tried to explore here some possible interpretations of cross-dressing ballads that do not assume they are about heterosexual women and heterosexual men, but allow them to refer to gay men and lesbians. These songs suggest a great deal about sexualities as they might have been perceived by the songs' creators, recreators, and audiences, both now and in the past. Thus one should not fall into my initial temptation to understand these songs as expressions of heterosexual women's experiences, or even exclusively of women's experiences in general. Indeed, differences between ballads in first and third person do not necessarily correspond with female and male perspectives. As Anita Best suggested (Best 1989), not all cross-dressing ballads necessarily gave a woman's point of view, and this is an important insight.[26]

For women, the story may pertain to heterosexual contemporary life, and thus concern adventure and escape. Or it may refer to traditional life, implicating women's control over their own reproduction. Or it may concern lesbian contemporary and/or traditional life, suggesting that contrary to some community perceptions, "that kind of thing" did then – and does now – happen. None of the readings is more inherently hidden or subtextual. In "The Handsome Cabin Boy" and "The Soldier Maid," cross dressing apparently gives a woman sexual access to another woman. In "Blue Jacket and White Trousers," it allows a woman to discuss having sexual access to another. Again it seems uncoincidental that these three songs sung by women have more "lesbian possibility" (see Ristock, this volume), and three of the four women's songs do not have marriage as their outcomes. Women singers appear to choose cross dressing ballads in which the main female character's independence is stressed.

For men, cross dressing ballads may have different meanings. Given that the quintessential historic context for singing these songs was the all-male environment of the lumberwoods (see also Fowke 1970a), or on board ship, both sexual orientations give possible meanings. Male singers and audience may, as Lloyd suggested, imagine that though they are in an all-male context, female sexuality is near if not actually available. Or the plot could also, as discussed above, be a homoerotic fantasy, which may or may not admit actual homoerotic practice. I haven't had much access to contemporary men's understandings of these songs, and won't speculate further.

Anyone familiar with theatrical traditions of Shakespeare's time, for example, will be aware that men dressing as women was standard stage behaviour (see also Garber 1992). While some works suggest that cross dressing need not indicate same sex orientation (see e.g., Brown and Collier 1989), recent analyses (e.g., Orgel 1989; Straub 1991) suggest that it pertains to more than simply a choice of cloth-ing.[27] Here as elsewhere, context is crucial. As sex, gender and sexu-ality are increasingly disentangled one from another (see e.g., Rubin 1984; Sedgwick 1985; Rivera 1988; Butler 1990), the question of what these songs "mean" becomes at once more and less problematic.

I was unaware of these issues as a young woman attending Mari-posa, and naive about sexual orientations other than my own. Even some twenty years later, when I began to examine these songs, I initially allowed my personal heterosexist bias to prevail over my analysis of them. Many other folklorists' interpretations have done likewise, and have thus obscured our possible understanding of his-toric and contemporary contexts. Let us now help these cross dress-ing ballads, and our understandings of them, out of the closet.

NOTES AND ACKNOWLEDGMENTS

I'd like to express my most sincere appreciation to Anita Best, Michelle Myrick, and Ernestine O'Rourke Power for their insights into songs. I appreciate the alternative readings of this essay suggested by Anne Bry-don, Barbara Rieti, Roger Renwick, Diane Tye, and several women's stud-ies classes at the Universities of Winnipeg and Waterloo. I'm also grateful to Barbara Rieti and Martin Lovelace for their hospitality when I was doing fieldwork in Newfoundland. Some of this research was funded by a University of Waterloo Social Sciences and Humanities Research Council of Canada grant.

1   A reader for the Publications of the American Folklore Society was disturbed by the multiple "I'"s in this piece. She noted the experiential, in which I invoke my personal experience; the scholarly, in which I discuss my own writing; the dialogic, my address to an implicit you, the reader. She found my usage emotional (and thus, apparently, manipulative), and said that it had the effect of discounting my own arguments. Canadian readers may be less uncomfortable with this style of argument which is seen by Americans as an indication of uncertainty (but which is no more so than is the gendered female style of talking which makes an answer into a question, as in "What's your name?" "Pauline?"). I urge readers to note that the experiential, the scholarly, and the dialogic "I" are all – simultaneously – parts of the creator of this essay.

2   The folksong revival of the 1950s and later involved performers and audiences whose links with folk tradition were not in the original communities where such songs were originally performed and heard (see Rosenberg 1993). Similarly, the contemporary "world music" scene involves audiences, and sometimes also performers, who have comparably distant links with the music.

3   Since all quotations from songs are from the same collection, I will subsequently give page numbers only. "N8" refers to the number given this ballad in the G. Malcolm Laws' (1957) typology.

4   Though I have not attempted a statistical survey, being fundamentally unsure that it would prove much particularly useful or telling about anything other than collecting standards, my impression from reading through Atlantic Canadian song collections is that women singers are overrepresented as singers of cross-dressing ballads. That is, one is as likely to find a woman singer for such a song as a male, though women are underrepresented in the collections overall.

5   Sedgwick (1985) argues that such all-male contexts contain implicit elements of homoeroticism.

6   There is no lack of undisciplined readings in this collection, but Ristock's deals with a similar topic – the denial or silencing of non-heterosexual contents, contexts, or readings.

7   Indeed, considerable denial by folklorists of the present reading was evident from members of the audience when I first presented this paper at a joint session of the Folklore Studies Association of Canada and the Canadian Women's Studies Association in 1993. Eve Kosofsky

Sedgwick discusses several of the ways in which scholars suppress or deny homosexual possibility in literature. They are also useful in considering other disciplines:

1. Passionate language of same-sex attraction was extremely common during whatever period is under discussion – and therefore must have been completely meaningless. Or

2. Same-sex genital relations may have been perfectly common during the period under discussion – but since there was no language about them, *they* must have been completely meaningless. Or

3. Attitudes about homosexuality were intolerant back then, unlike now – so people probably didn't do anything. Or

4. Prohibitions against homosexuality didn't exist back then, unlike now – so if people did anything, it was completely meaningless. Or

5. The word "homosexuality" wasn't coined until 1869 – so everyone before then was heterosexual. (Of course, heterosexuality has always existed.) Or

6. The author under discussion is certified or rumored to have had an attachment to someone of the other sex – so their feelings about people of their own sex must have been completely meaningless. Or (under a perhaps somewhat different rule of admissable evidence)

7. There is no actual proof of homosexuality, such a sperm taken from the body of another man or a nude photograph with another woman – so the author may be assumed to have been ardently and exclusively heterosexual. Or (as a last resort)

8. The author or the author's important attachments may very well have been homosexual – but it would be provincial to let so insignificant a fact make any difference at all to our understanding of any serious project of life, writing, or thought. (1990:52–3)

Exceptions include Constance Penley's symbolic feminist reading of fanzines (1992).

8 This series is loosely reminiscent of the kinds of narrative analysis conducted by Propp (1968). Some of these five elements may be emphasized more than others; some may be completely absent; and songs may also include other elements.

9 See Herrmann (1991) for a discussion of occupational cross dressing, theatrical and otherwise.

10 Female song protagonists apparently do not wear men's clothing and retain female work role behaviour. Michael Taft's work on mock weddings (1989 and this volume) suggests that the humour of women dressing as men in rural North American Prairie culture is not as great

as that of men dressing as women because in fact the work and role behaviours expected of women include doing "men's work," but not vice versa.

11 As discussed extensively in Dugaw (1989).

12 Note, however, "one [female] impersonator's statement ... that 'in practice' perhaps some impersonators were straight, but 'in theory' they could not be. 'How can a man perform in female attire and not have something wrong with him?' he asked" (Newton 1972:100). Class often enters the picture. In "The Soldier Maid," a "lady" betrays the (working class) soldier, leading to her public discovery.

13 I'm playing with connotation here. Radicalesbians' use of the term meant "woman identified *with* woman," not "woman identified *by* woman," as in this case. In the form of the cabin boy herself, the two identifications are conflated. See also Rich (1980).

14 It is also important to note that when the opposite "reversal" occurs – a man dresses in women's clothing – the outcome for the male protagonists is negative, usually complete ridicule. In "The Shirt and Apron," for example, also found in Newfoundland (Greenleaf and Mansfield 1933:222–3), a sailor meets a prostitute who steals everything from him, including his clothes. He has to return to the ship wearing her shirt and apron, instead of going home, as he'd planned. In addition, he is humiliated by his peers for wearing women's clothes. See also Renwick's discussion of symbolism and song outcomes in his chapter "The Semiotics of Sexual Liaisons" (1980:54–112).

15 This tellingly suggests work by anthropologists such as Gayle Rubin (1984), which show the linkage of division of labour to assignment of sex role. That is, the cabin boy "labours" as both a female and a male and his/her sex is consequently ambiguous.

16 Roger Renwick (personal communication 1993) comments:

I've never been happy with that literalist interpretation of the "'Twas either you or I" line ... denoting a lesbian relationship between the missus and the girl-boy ... there is nothing in the folklore tradition as a whole to support it – no motifs, no tale types, no patterns, themes, etc. of women lovers ... Unfortunately I've never been able to come up with a convincing explanation; all versions I've seen, British or North American, have the line, and none has any extra textual matter that throws light on the ambiguous meaning. One possibility is that the wife knew from the start that the boy was in fact a maid and pretended she didn't in order to free her from her husband's sexual demands, thus "betraying the girl" by keeping silent, but it is not the nature of broadside songs to be so elliptical; if that were the meaning, there would be a stanza *telling* us that the wife recognised the maid's disguise and decided not to reveal it. Actually, the song is far more popular with folksong students and revival singers than it is with the folk; it was common on broadsides, but [Cecil] Sharp collected only two traditional versions in England, and Peacock's text was only the second one published from North American tradition.

17 Bad pun intended.

18 I appreciate Michael Taft's drawing this text to my attention, and Roger Renwick's sending me a version. Interestingly, the song's headnote indicates "The Good Ship Venus" is also associated with homosocial contexts in the army, university (Cray 1968: 116), and British rugby (Legman 1975: 175). The remaining verses deal with masturbation, sexual torture of both women and men, gang rape, prostitution, and bestiality. Folklorist Martin Lovelace commented on reading this paper that the British Navy has "always been known for 'rum, bum and baccy'" (Barbara Rieti, personal communication). For a historic consideration of homosexuality and piracy, see Burg (1984).

19 Reported speech is "speech within speech, message within message, and at the same time also speech about speech, message about message" (Volosinov 1971:149). Unascribed speech does not indicate the speaker. A version of a cross-dressing ballad from Ontario ("The Banks of the Nile," Clark 1965) is entirely in unascribed dialogue. Each speaker alternates with verses of commentary, in a four-stanza song. It is primarily knowledge of the genre that enables one to understand who is speaking – first the man, then the woman – and the conversation's context.

20 The happy ending is usually that the woman gets the partner of her choice, who is usually *not* the choice of her kin, often because he is of a different class. I was similarly fond as a young woman of songs in which blood kinship connections were undervalued and a lover saves the protagonist from the gallows while her/his family stands spectatorially by. For example, a song called "The Pricklie Bush" was popular in the folk revival circles in which I moved. It was entirely in unascribed speech, and involved a series of dialogues between the individual on the gallows (whose sex I personally used to assign according to that of the performer) and family members who were asked:

[Mother] have you brought me gold?
Silver to pay my fee?
Or have you come to see me hang
On the gallows tree?

The interlocutors' roles were often performed by different people. It was their choice whether to choose "No I've not brought you gold ..." or "Yes I have ..." but most commonly it was the "true love" who did the latter.

21 See Greenhill (1990), a version of which was originally presented at the Heroic Women in Politics, Society, and Religion conference at Carleton University in 1987.

22 For further discussion see, for example, Irigaray (1985) and Rubin (1984).

23 I conducted a very brief period of research there in the summer of 1989, funded by a small SSHRCC grant at the University of Waterloo.

24 This seems unlikely. Folklorists have collected the songs in Newfoundland, and Barbara Rieti (personal communication) reports a term for gay males, "whores' angels" used in Bishop's Cove. Similarly, Sharon Dale Stone and the Women's Survey Group (1990) point out that "bay dykes" – former residents of outport rural Newfoundland communities – comprise a significant proportion of the lesbian population in St John's.

25 Narratives about women are often plotted to make marriage the final outcome, from the fairytale's "And they lived happily ever after" to Jane Eyre's "Reader, I married him." See also Carolyn Heilbrun's (1988) discussion of female narrative plots.

26 Note that A.L. Lloyd's comments, quoted above, simply assume that the point of view in the songs is male.

27 Stephen Orgel concludes that dramatic presentations of love in Shakespeare's plays indicate that "Homosexuality in this culture appears to have been less threatening than heterosexuality, and only in part because it had fewer consequences and was easier to desexualize. The reason always given for the prohibition of women from the stage was that their chastity would thereby be compromised, which is understood to mean that they would become whores. Behind the outrage of public modesty is a real fear of women's sexuality, and more specifically, of its power to evoke men's sexuality" (1989:26).

Men in Women's Clothes: Theatrical Transvestites on the Canadian Prairie

MICHAEL TAFT

In the early seventh century A.D., Archbishop Isidore of Seville complained of actors, whom he called *histriones* – "those men who, dressed in female garb, mimicked the demeanour of loose women" (Tydeman 1978:184–5). Feelings of unease, shock, and fear, as well as the release of laughter, have accompanied theatrical and ritual male transvestism through time and across cultures. I would like to examine a particular modern instance of this behaviour, and what it reveals about social conceptions of the nature of masculinity and femininity and relationships between the sexes.

I shall describe a dramatic tradition which I have been investigating for several years, namely the mock wedding as performed in the Canadian prairie provinces and the northern plains of the United States. Although usually performed in conjunction with the community celebration of a couple's marriage or, more commonly, a milestone anniversary, the mock wedding is part of a larger North American dramatic tradition. Like the Tom Thumb wedding (a children's wedding skit), described by Susan Stewart (1984:117–25), the mock wedding is a dramatic parody of the liturgical wedding ritual. Like the womanless wedding (an adult, all-male wedding skit), described by Jane Woodside (1987), the salient feature of the mock wedding is gender reversal.[1]

Even by Thomas Green's restrictive definition (1978, 1981), this form of theatre is classic folk drama: a scripted, rehearsed masquerade, in which the actors play clearly recognizable roles and have assigned lines, and in which the drama unfolds in a linear fashion through a series of pre-arranged scenes. Most performances are made up of four scenes: the entrance of the *dramatis personae*, who form a tableau of a wedding ceremony; a "Dearly Beloved" speech by the minister or priest; the taking of vows by the bride and groom, usually accompanied by the proddings of the father of the bride and the weeping of the bride's mother; and the pronouncement of marriage, including a ring ceremony, a kiss or two, and the presentation of a bouquet to the honoured couple. The drama might also contain further scenes, such as an elopement, or an objection to the marriage by a former girlfriend of the groom.

The characters are mostly stereotypic: the shotgun-toting father, the weeping mother, the drunken priest or minister, the pregnant bride or girlfriend. The bride and groom might also incorporate certain traits of character or dress from the couple being honoured; thus, they are as much caricatures as stereotypes. The most noticeable feature of the actors is that they are usually cross-dressed; that is, men play the roles of women, while women take on the men's roles. Either a man or a woman might play the part of the minister.

Friends, neighbours and relatives organize the mock wedding and perform it during the wedding reception or anniversary celebration. Somewhat like the shivaree, the mock wedding is disruptive and unexpected, in that the actors interrupt the normal flow of events; somewhat like mumming and Hallowe'en house visits, the drama replaces normal community sociability with antisocial, bawdy behaviour.[2] The mock wedding, in its function as a parody, turns the world upside down, and is a celebration of "nonsense" (see Stewart 1978) as much as anything else.

This drama is rich in symbolism and meaning, both for those in the communities in which it is performed, and for those who study this tradition. My aim here is to examine the presentation, motives, and meanings of the male transvestite actor in mock weddings. What are the circumstances under which men from the traditional agrarian cultures of farming and ranching – who in other contexts display the expected machismo of North American males – dress as women and behave in a decidedly unmanly fashion?[3]

As a starting point it is worth noting that costuming and dress-up behaviour are a part of the ritual life of prairie and plains society, and cross dressing is by no means unusual. Boys entering high school often undergo a form of hazing or initiation which includes dressing as girls and parading down the main street of their community. They are the "possessions" of older students and must, as initiates, perform various acts of humiliation. Hallowe'en is another time when boys and men dress as women, either as part of their house visiting rounds or at masquerades held in local pubs. Parades, benefits, community suppers, dances, sporting events, stag parties, and other such get-togethers might all include some form of cross dressing – some form of transvestite behaviour.

The mock wedding, then, fits into the larger context of community ritual and celebration in which costuming and cross dressing take place. But this particular dramatic parody is undoubtedly the supreme and most graphic example of such behaviour on the prairies, for men not only dress as women, but they also re-enact the wedding ceremony, a ritual which comments most strongly on gender distinctions and expectations.

Discovering why men willingly dress as women in this context is not easy. Reserved, even taciturn, male ranchers and farmers are especially unforthcoming on the subject of cross dressing. Not that they are ashamed of their activities – some take great pride in their roles – but they are not used to articulating their feelings or motivations concerning matters of sexuality, ludic behaviour, or rituals of reversal. Prairie women are more articulate in this respect – they are, after all, the driving force behind most community celebrations[4] – but their views on why men dress as women are not those of men. They are not especially knowledgeable on the partially conscious or unconscious benefits which men gain from dressing as brides, bridesmaids, flower girls, mothers of the bride, and other female characters. For example, Saskatchewan novelist and rancher Sharon Butala wonders why prairie men dress as women at "mock weddings, at Hallowe'en, during Christmas skits and in parades, and at private parties," but she has no answer to this question (1988:273).[5]

The primary motivation for these men may be that they enjoy dressing as women, for they do indeed take great delight and pride in their cross-dressed roles. But this observation only leads to further questions: What lies behind their enjoyment? Wherein lies their pride? If they delight in playing with gender distinctions, what is the source of this pleasure?

When I have asked about motivations, the reason most often given to me is that these men are "good sports." The designation of good sport is a weighty one, and involves a number of positive social attributes: men who are well-established members of the community; men who take part in community affairs; men who have a good instinctual understanding of the male ethos in their society; men who are not extreme in their moral or religious beliefs. The exact dimensions of being a good sport will vary from community to community, but at the heart of this designation is a man who will neither shirk nor fear the responsibilities of community life, a man whose character and personality have created, among his neighbours, certain expectations of cooperation and friendliness. In ritual and ludic contexts, the good sport is one who, in the interest of good fellowship, is willing to endure ridicule, humiliation, and even physical pain at the hands of other community members. Perhaps the good sport is the opposite of the "local character," but it is probably better to see all members of a community on a continuum between the extremes of the good sport and one who is "socially incomplete."[6]

Of course, playing in local skits helps to define the good sport, so that the good sport argument for male theatrical transvestism is a bit circular. Certainly one conscious motivation for a man to dress as a woman in a mock wedding drama is to enhance his reputation as a good sport. But there is more at work here than a matter of social status. This form of male transvestism also has a psycho-social basis – one which is more speculative from an ethnographic viewpoint than are the good sport rationales given by men and women in the community.

In searching out such psycho-social motivations, it is best to re-examine what kind of drama this is. The mock wedding folk drama is, to use William Gruber's terms, non-Aristotelian (1987); it is Platonic, or in more modern terms, it is a Brechtian type of performance, wherein both the actors and the audience are constantly aware of the simultaneity of the actor and the role which the actor is playing. Contrary to the Stanislavkian approach to theatre – with which modern audiences are familiar – wherein the actor and audience lose themselves in the character being played, the mock wedding actor makes use of what Bertolt Brecht called the "alienation effect." Brecht wrote, "At no moment must he [sic, the actor] go so far so to be wholly transformed into the character played. The verdict: 'he didn't act Lear, he was Lear' would be an annihilating blow to him ... his feelings must not at bottom be those of the character, so that the audience's may not at bottom be those of the character either" (1964:193–4).

Parody itself creates an alienation effect, since actors and audience are made constantly aware of both the parody and the thing being parodied; but the mock wedding's transvestism has parallels, as well, with the non-parodic theatre of medieval and early modern Europe, wherein men and boys played all the roles on stage. Many scholars have noted, for example, that Shakespeare's audience incorporated the sexual ambiguity of transvestite actors into their understanding of female characters. In fact, Elizabethan audiences did not appreciate women playing women's roles because of the loss of dramatic ambiguity which this entailed: Cleopatra was understood to be a boy playing Cleopatra, and not a woman playing the role (see Gruber 1985:45–6).

Obviously, most Elizabethan drama demanded more serious performances from its transvestites than the pantomime-like roles of the mock wedding. Yet the parallels between these two dramatic traditions still hold in terms of the expectations of both the audience and the actors; both traditions demand that the masculine and the feminine occupy the same character at the same time on stage. Unlike their counterparts in traditional Javanese drama (see Peacock 1978), for example, prairie men make no attempt to become women. Rather, they play clownish and distorted women. They exaggerate the female physique with over-large breasts and behinds. They mince and wiggle in mockery of femininity. In essence, they tell their audience (and themselves) that they are not playing the roles of women, but playing *with* the roles of women.

At the same time, their women's costumes invariably reveal the "true man" beneath the dress, wig, and mask. In fact, the organizer of the mock wedding often tries to find the biggest, hairiest man to play the part of the bride, thus emphasizing the ambiguous nature of the role. When not mocking the characteristics of women, male transvestites will overtly display their masculinity by swaggering, bulging their muscles, or flipping up their dresses.

What does all this mean? The good sport is one who suffers humiliation gracefully, especially if it is for the good of the community. Likewise, the man who is confident in his masculinity – or who, at least, wishes to portray himself as confident – will not be afraid to dress as a woman. Reversal, as discussed by Mikhaïl Bakhtine (1970:9–27), Victor Turner (1967:93–111) and others, emphasizes the obverse. The more that the male actors mug as women, the more they accentuate their own manliness. They say to the audience: "this is what I'm not – look at what I *really* am." As William Gruber has noted, concerning the "boying" of the Elizabethan Cleopatra: "Sometimes transvestite acting is said to be a means to help an audience focus critically on femininity as an intellectual or social phenomenon; but it would be more accurate here to say the reverse: 'boying' Cleopatra becomes a formula through which masculinity is redefined or even reinvented. Mimesis in this case is less representation than aggressive assimilation" (1985:43).

By taking on femininity and braving humiliation as mock wedding women, good sports accentuate their masculinity and receive the heightened manly status which accompanies such acts of bravery.

There are, however, other motivations lurking in the psychological or psychoanalytic realm, which reveal another facet of this form of theatrical transvestism.

Some might take the Freudian tack that "the human being oscillates all through his [sic] life between heterosexual and homosexual feelings" (Freud 1911:46). In other words, cross dressing allows men to express their female side. But Freud was concerned with "pathological" transvestism, rather than theatrical cross dressing, and while this yin-yang theory of human sexuality has its allure, it doesn't get us very far in understanding the more specific motivations of the farmer dressed as a bride. There is more to this behaviour than meets the Freudian eye.

Transvestism or acting "female" – whether in drama or in ritual – is not so much a mixing of genders as it is a commentary by men upon women. Thus, Gregory Bateson discovered that Iatmul male initiates take on female roles in order to become "contra-suggestible to the female ethos," to become "proud of the male ethos" (1958:133). In describing a male transvestite dancer from India, Peggy Phelan understood this aspect of theatre: "The fetishized 'female' image so perfectly encoded ... works not to bring the female into the spectacle of exchange between spectator and performer but to leave her emphatically outside. In place of the female, a fetishized image is displayed which substitutes for her and makes her actual presence unnecessary" (1988:111). From the male point of view, transvestism disempowers the woman. We are dealing here with what Robert Stoller has called the "phallic woman" (vaginal man?) who adds the woman's potent sexuality to his own power, thus becoming more powerful (1975 1:177).

As Meg Twycross had written concerning transvestism in medieval drama, the reaction of women in the audience was different from that of the men (1983). Likewise, as Bateson has noted from an anthropological perspective (1958), and Sandra Gilbert has shown from a literary perspective (1980), women cross dress for very different reasons from their male counterparts (see also Greenhill, this volume). Stoller, in fact, goes so far as to write that "fetishistic cross-dressing is almost nonexistent in women" (1975, 1:143). However, in the prairie mock wedding, whatever the women understand when men dress as women or when women dress as men – two whole other subjects – the men are certainly expressing themselves to themselves through the drama. In Phelan's words, there is an "exchange between men about women" (1988:111) going on, which not only asserts the power of masculinity but which attempts to lessen the power of femininity.

I can offer no quotations from men I have interviewed which support the psychoanalytical position I have just taken. As I stated earlier, these men do not readily discuss (or are not capable of discussing) their inner motivations. But it is worth pointing out that mock weddings, like all such functions in the prairie community, are usually organized and run by women. As well, the family farm or ranch affords women considerable power, since its operation often necessitates that women do work usually considered the domain of men.[7] The economics of modern prairie life means that many women must take outside jobs to support their husband's farming. At the same time, the men often feel that they are not in control of the agricultural and economic forces which determine whether they prosper or not.

Taken together, these sociological and economic factors work to disempower men while they extend the power and control of women.[8] The male farmer or rancher wishes to see himself as the master of his own destiny: someone whose independence is based on land ownership and freedom from the urban workplace. In reality, he is the servant of government bureaucrats, the commodity exchanges, urban consumerism, and international subsidy wars.[9] Women, however, remain the mistresses of their household, and the controlling forces in childrearing and community activities; as well, their outside jobs have given them a sense of independence which their mothers and grandmothers never felt.[10]

In short, the good sports of the community are under siege. They need every chance they can get to re-assert their power and control. After all, it is the good sport who manifests the proper qualities of being a man. Despite chronic hard times, and his resulting disempowerment, he must remain the model of strong, prairie masculinity. The ludic misrule of the mock wedding will not empower him, but it allows him to comment on the state of his manhood – whether he is an actor or a member of the audience – in a way which is non-threatening and covert, which is acceptable to the community as a whole, and which is psychologically beneficial.

The transvestism described here not only fits within the larger dress-up tradition of prairie society, but is another manifestation of the theatrical transvestism found throughout western culture. As such, it confronts the same issues of cross-gender representation, parody, and power. The gender ambivalence of the mock wedding never fails to evoke shock and laughter from its audience, yet the phenomenon of this form of folk drama is not at all shocking in prairie society perhaps because, according to Garber, transvestism is "normative" in all cultures (1992:353). Wherever it is found, theatrical transvestism acts as a sounding board for commentaries on gender relations.

NOTES AND ACKNOWLEDGMENTS

I would like to thank the Social Sciences and Humanities Research Council of Canada for financing my research.

1 For a more complete description of the mock wedding, see Michael Taft (1989); for an analogous mock wedding tradition in Ontario, see Pauline Greenhill (1988).
2 Shivarees occur on the prairies, although there has been no study of this phenomenon; for shivarees in other parts of Canada, see Greenhill (1989b) and Monica Morrison (1974); on Halloween traditions in Saskatchewan, see Darryl Hunter (1983) and Taft (1994); on mumming see Halpert and Story (1969). Other discussions of cultural disruptions are in Anne Brydon's consideration of the *níðstöng*, Barbara Rieti's of witches, and Janice Ristock's of killer movie dykes.
3 A mirror-image study would explore the women-dressed-as-men in mock weddings. In general, scholars have paid less attention to female-to-male cross dressing than male-to-female transvestism (Garber 1992:44). The former is, however, addressed by Greenhill in this volume.
4 In agrarian, rural North American society, women are often responsible for community celebrations; see Micaela di Leonardo (1987) and Seena Kohl (1976:71) on this point.
5 In an interview, Butala reiterated her incomprehension as to exactly why men dress as women – see Taft (1991).
6 I have taken this term from John Szwed's analysis of the bachelor and hermit Paul E. Hall, a traditional singer-composer in Newfoundland (1970:163). The local character is also mentioned briefly in Tye (this volume). Compare good sports with Garber's discussion of cross dressing among the "power elite" (1992:52–66).
7 For other considerations of women's work in men's domain, see Cynthia Boyd on taxi drivers; for the opposite, see Susan Shantz's article on quilting.
8 See Jean Lipman-Blumen (1973) for a discussion of how gender roles break down during social and economic crises.
9 "Much as [farmers and ranchers] like to emphasize their individualistic competence and pioneering self-help, they are part of the larger network of facilities and institutions of the North American agrarian economy and its political representatives" (Bennett 1969:296).
10 Virginia Fink (1991:19) has shown that younger farm wives are more likely to work off the farm than did women of older generations.

Kiss and Kill: Some Impacts of Cultural Representations of Women's Sexualities

JANICE L. RISTOCK

Popular culture offers few representations of the range of women's sexualities. We are, at best, still presented with stereotypes of women as madonna/whore, good girl/bad girl. Feminist scholarship has responded to this situation over the last twenty years with extensive critical examination of the portrayal of women's sexualities in popular expressions from commercials to soap operas. Essentialist discourse about the nature of women's sexuality as passive, submissive, and frequently masochistic abounds, maintaining, as feminists argue, misogynist misrepresentations about women (as examined in, for example, Vance 1992; MacKinnon 1992; and Segal 1992). Predictably, there are very few representations of lesbian sexuality in North American popular culture, unless the images reinforce heterosexist notions of lesbianism. These images are fraught with demeaning stereotypes of (so-called) "mannish" women who hate men and who are more than likely "radical feminists."[1]

Yet recently mainstream Hollywood films are showing a new range of women's sexualities, at least on the surface.[2] A new trope has been introduced in the nineties: female buddy films. As epitomized by such box office successes as *Thelma and Louise*, *Fried Green Tomatoes*, and *Leaving Normal*, they portray women as (asexually?) bonding with one another and rallying against male violence.[3] Less welcome is the re-emergence of another symbolic figure: the powerful but murderous femme fatale of *Fatal Attraction*, *The Hand that Rocks the Cradle*, and *Basic Instinct*. The twist in *Basic Instinct*, which links it with female buddy films, is that the blonde bombshell is a lesbian. These "psycho femmes" elicit a different response from male characters than their usual urge to dominate over sexy, blonde, female characters. Men in these films are intrigued, often frightened, and always controlled by these dangerously powerful women.

Any feminist examination of these films must point to the continued homophobia and misogyny (not to mention racism as evident in the predominance and centrality of white characters) operating in mainstream Hollywood. Despite their provision of truly leading roles for female actors – a clear step forward – no new messages about women's sexualities are being developed in these narratives. According to Susan Faludi (1991), much of Hollywood's portrayal of women in the eighties conveys a moralistic, heterosexist message: marriage and motherhood are what make "good" women happy. Faludi traces a backlash against independent women which is perhaps best underscored by the ending of *Fatal Attraction*, where the family's restoration depends on the dutiful wife killing the unmarried, adulterous woman.

The necessary analysis of these messages is not always straightforward or easy given the current context of flux in power relations between men and women, and of increased visibility of gays and lesbians. These films' popular reception may thwart the recognition that they can be misogynist while paying lip service to a pro-feminist message, or that gay or lesbian characters may conceal closeted directors or producers threatened with being "outed" by Queer Nation. A recent article on "psychofemmes" in the popular magazine *Mirabella* comments on this shift in sexuality for the nineties:

A couple makes red hot love on the silver screen. Or rather she makes love to him: she's on top moving in urgent rhythm above his blissed-out body, pale hair obscuring her face. Abruptly, his body arches to meet hers as the pulsing background music builds. We know where they're going, the hammerlock intimacy of film has hauled us halfway there already, this is ... climax! You bet: see the ice-pick flashing in her hand as she stabs him again and again as his body jolts and the music explodes and the blood flies all over the place.

Welcome to Hollywood's vision of love in the nineties. There's something out there and its going to get you. Reader, you may be forgiven if you think we're talking about AIDS, but no. Judging by the industry's Psychofemmes output, AIDS only afflicts people in modestly budgeted art films. Back here among the megabucks, what's going to get you is women (Durbin 1992:44).

Reactions to these nineties Hollywood representations are varied and complex. Some women and some gays and lesbians like the characters in these films. They see the female buddies, and even the psychofemmes, as a positive development showing women as sexually aggressive, independent, strong, and capable – forces to be reckoned with. As well, many see the mere inclusion of gay and lesbian characters in mainstream films as a step forward. Others view them as more of the same old song – misogyny and heterosexism – but with a different beat.

I wish to sort out some of these controversies, providing an overview of how women's sexualities are shown in some female buddy films and psychofemme films, and specifically examining messages about lesbian sexuality. My review is not exhaustive; I focus on films that are being written about in popular magazines, and those that have caused debate and controversy in the women's and in gay and lesbian communities. I rely on articles in popular magazines – *The Village Voice*, *Ms.*, *Mirabella*, and *Deneuve* – to capture some of the ways in which these films' discourse of sexuality is being interpreted in other forms of popular culture. This discourse and the films themselves are part of the social backdrop for research that I am currently conducting on abuse in lesbian relationships. I am particularly concerned to explore the impact of cultural representations of women's sexualities on my own struggles to research and document this sensitive topic. This paper, then, is not meant to offer a thorough critique of the films but rather to provide commentary based on my observations of two predominant strands of discourse on lesbian sexuality. I have summarized these as the theme of lesbian invisibility/impossibility in female buddy pictures and the theme of "killer dykes" in psychofemme films.

The *Mirabella* passage quoted above implies that sexual women are seen as secretly harbouring a homicidal streak. This general theme is explicit in psychofemme films and in other sexist works. Yet it may also be looming as a message in female buddy pictures. Three recent examples – *Leaving Normal*, *Fried Green Tomatoes*, and *Thelma and Louise* – suggest that all women have a pathological side; they are either murderers or hysterics. These films on female friendship have a common plot in which women bond in response to male violence.[4]

In *Leaving Normal*, Marianne, a twenty-seven-year-old, white, twice-married, hysterical woman is being brutalized by her current husband. She hits the road, leaving her "normal" life, and eventually meets Darly, a tough, world-weary waitress who, according to one reviewer, "sweeps teary Marianne into her convertible and off on an Alaskan adventure" (Dargis 1992:58).

Similarly, *Fried Green Tomatoes* is a story set in the thirties about two white women, Idgie and Ruth, who open The Whistle Stop Cafe in Alabama and maintain their life together in a time when women were not to live autonomously from men. Life-long friends, they first bond when Idgie – described as a daredevilish tomboy – rescues Ruth from an abusive, physically violent marriage. Murder shows up in this plot when the abusive husband tracks Ruth down and wants to kidnap their son, but he is soon despatched and served up to the investigating officer in a pig barbecue.

Finally, *Thelma and Louise*, the most popular film of the three, is the story of two women on the run for murder. Louise, discovering Thelma being raped in a parking lot, shoots her attacker. We learn that Louise was likely also raped, a partial reason for her anger and ability to kill Thelma's attacker. Together the two travel across the southern states, their friendship intensifying while they run from the police. Unlike the other films which have happily-ever-after endings, Thelma and Louise are last seen driving off the edge of the Grand Canyon. They take the ultimate lovers' leap rather than being arrested by the police.

The messages from this new genre of female buddy films seem contradictory. On the one hand, each shows women responding to male violence, taking control over their lives, and benefitting from the friendship of other women. *Thelma and Louise* particularly has apparently had far-reaching impact on many women's lives. It has been called feminist; there have been presentations about it at women's studies conferences.[5] The characters have become role models, of sorts, for their response to male violence. T-shirts proudly proclaim "graduate of the Thelma and Louise finishing school," a blunt warning to any man who has seen or heard about the film. Yet its critics suggest that the more powerful impact is in the distinctly non-feminist tip-off that women may turn on men and retaliate (Durbin 1992). In other words, the feminist message that Thelma and Louise's responses to men's violence were *justified* because the court system, police, and society have failed women may not be the one intended by the film nor the one perceived by mainstream audiences.

And in fact, the film has been seen as promoting man-hating. Debates about *Thelma and Louise* have appeared in newspapers, radio, and television, and have included many interviews with the film's stars, focused on the question "Haven't you gone too far?" This question reflects male fear: beware of women bonding; they hate men and will retaliate against them. Living independently from men is linked to man-hating, which is in turn equated with lesbianism; two women together is seen not as an affirmation of same-sex love, but merely as a rejection of heterosexuality. These films, then, are evidence of Lindsay Van Gelder's (1992) suggestion that lesbians in our society receive all its generalized fears of what things would be like if women cut off their focus on men.

The lesbian theme is not allowed to surface. Instead, these films present the Hollywood solution to mainstream audiences' fears of sexually free women. Thelma and Louise must die at the end if they are autonomous and resist male control. Or, they commit suicide *because* women loving women is itself, ultimately, self-destructive. Similarly, Idgie and Ruth, and Darly and Marianne, can be happy in their relationships – but they cannot be sexual. The invisibility – or impossibility – of lesbian sexuality in these films may temper male anxieties about not having control over female sexualities. Although it is difficult to determine the filmmakers' – and Hollywood's – intentions, in the novel *Fried Green Tomatoes at the Whistle Stop Cafe* by Fannie Flagg (1987), it is clear that Idgie and Ruth have a sexual relationship.

Leaving Normal might have shown Marianne and Darly as lovers – even the title hinted at this – but instead falls short with a contrived ending disclaiming any lesbian content to their ardent embraces and passionate devotion. Thus the heterosexist and misogynist messages these films convey, despite their portrayal of female friendship, are that lesbians do not (cannot) exist, and that when women love women they are asexual. On those rare occasions when lesbians are depicted, their characters are warped, even malevolent. According to Van Gelder "in the thirty years that the motion picture code has allowed depictions of lesbians at all, most images have involved either homicidal women or their flip side, suicides" (1992:82). A recent example of this continued trend can be seen in the psychofemme film *Basic Instinct*.

Basic Instinct has been written about as a film that deals with changing notions of women's sexuality by showing sexually aggressive women and by explicitly portraying lesbianism. The three central characters are Nick, a San Francisco cop investigating a murder; Catherine, the bisexual women whom Nick becomes involved with; and Catherine's girlfriend Roxy, the "true" lesbian in the film. Although both women are attractive, intelligent, successful, and sexually "exotic", they are also ice-pick wielding Killer Dykes. Needless to say, there has been a great deal of debate about this film and its depiction of women's sexualities. On the one hand, some women like the in-control, sexually assertive characters and see them as a satisfying flip of the old porn cliché about male voyeurism of lesbian sex: in this film the lesbian, not the man, watches. On the other hand, gay and lesbian activists have been boycotting *Basic Instinct* for what they see as its blatant homophobia. Richard Goldstein, in an article for the *Village Voice*, "Base Instinct," discusses Hollywood as a contradictory liberal institution. Many actors, directors, and producers are gay and lesbian, and Hollywood sports red ribbons in support of AIDS, yet at the same time it produces a film about "man-haters with ice-pick dicks ... [who] may actually quiet the anxieties of heterosexuals" (1992:37).[6] Thus, just like the female buddy pictures, *Basic Instinct* reasserts the rightful dominance of men/heterosexuality by showing sexually assertive women/lesbians as homicidal.

Popular culture, including films, sends out contradictory messages and peoples' interpretations of them can vary.[7] Yet what is disturbing to me is the lack of attention to messages that are misogynist and homophobic. Many apologists for Hollywood even deny that these films are anti-female and anti-gay and lesbian. Gossip columnist Liz Smith stated "Nobody's going to leave this film and bash a lesbian because it's not about lesbians or gay life" (according to Goldstein 1992). Yet that is precisely the point – no homophobic film is *about* gays or lesbians.

Ignorance and denial of gay and lesbian experience are common. Research on gay bashing indicates that gays and lesbians, like other minorities, are often popularly presented as preying upon society or aggressively recruiting new members. This in turn is seen as a justi-fication for violence against us (Van Gelder 1992). Further, lesbians have long been typecast as "mannish murderers or dragon ladies" (Faderman 1988). For example, a great deal of media attention to the real life trial of Aileen (Lee) Wuornos, a Florida prostitute accused of murdering five johns has sensationalized her as a lesbian serial killer. A Winnipeg newspaper had this to say about Wuornos: "Detectives found that Aileen had a long criminal record, which included disor-derly conduct, armed robbery and prostitution. She was the constant companion of Tyria, whom she referred to as her wife. Authorities soon found out that the pair were lesbian lovers, who hung around rough tough bars in the Daytona area" (Haines 1992:24). Rather than being interested in why and how a woman who suffered a great deal of abuse throughout her life had taken on a more typically male predatory pattern, the media focused on her sexuality as an "expla-nation" of her actions. Since "real" women do not kill, unless they are saving their children, she had to be constructed as not really being a woman – by implication, "real" females don't love others of the same sex but must be heterosexual – and therefore not truly a female serial killer. Van Gelder's analysis is that "lesbians are [pre-sented as] male-violence wannabes who can only pathetically aspire to the real thing – what might be called the Dildo Theory of Serial Murder" (1992:80).

Thus the recent focus on women's sexualities in films and other popular cultural media reflect what Durbin and others have come to see as heterosexual crisis: "This is a crisis provoked by feminism and augmented by gay liberation, a crisis of power and legitimacy. Who has the power now that it's not all on one side? And what is legitimate now that our notions of bad women and good, normal and deviant, of male and female are crumbling?" (Durbin 1992:48). Though the messages about lesbians and woman may be similar to previous stereotypical discourses (Faderman 1991; Van Gelder 1992), the context surrounding this misogyny and homophobia is shifting under the pressure of increased visibility and power of lesbian and gays.

I have presented a sketch of some recent films and commented on their two predominant themes: the denial of lesbianism; and the view of lesbians as pathological individuals. For me these issues have particular importance given my efforts to research abuse in lesbian relationships. I am struggling with how to present my work to avoid contributing to the discourse on lesbians as deviant and pathological, which is certainly not part of my analysis of abusive relationships. My understanding of abuse in lesbian relationships is congruent with a feminist analysis of violence. The same misuses of power, ownership, and control can exist in lesbian relationships as in heterosexual relationships because of the systemic, institutionalized forms of dominance in our society. Along with a socialization process that teaches us to accept violence as a form of power, ownership, and control, we internalize self-hating messages from the dominant culture; violence against women (and in this case, against lesbians) is rooted in misogyny and heterosexism. Yet this form of abuse also challenges our reliance on a gendered analysis of violence. Given the possibilities for articulation with the dominant public discourse on the pathology and deviance of lesbians, even hearing about my topic may reinforce a negative view of lesbians. The impact of the discourses is ironically double-edged: the topic of lesbian abuse is often met with incredulity, and the effects trivialized.

Testimonies about the real life experiences of lesbians must be used to challenge the themes of lesbian sexuality in the female buddy and killer dyke films that I have reviewed, which parallel and reinforce many misconceptions about lesbian abuse. Some common examples (Minnesota Coalition for Battered Women 1990; Chesley, MacAulay, and Ristock 1992) are:

Misconception: There is not much incidence of lesbian battering.
Fact: Recent research and testimonies of lesbians suggest that violence does exist in some relationships.
Misconception: Offenders are psychopathic or mentally ill; their victims, too, are sick.

Fact: There are no psychiatric characteristics distinguishing lesbians in abusive relationships from lesbians who have never been in abusive relationships.

Misconception: Lesbians are non-violent, passive and caring.

Fact: Lesbians, like all other human beings, are capable of an extensive range of behaviours and feelings.

Misconception: The victim has an investment/payoff in staying in the relationship; she is masochistic.

Fact: The abused partner in a lesbian relationship is subject to unwanted physical, sexual, and emotional abuse.

Misconception: Lesbian battering occurs only in "butch/femme" relationships. The butch is the batterer and the femme the victim.

Fact: Beyond the fact that few lesbians assume explicitly butch/femme roles, the roles themselves do not automatically dictate who has more power or the desire to exercise more control in a relationship.

The misconceptions above reflect common assumptions and stereotypes about lesbians in our society. They also parallel some of the messages in female buddy pictures and psychofemme films. The killer dyke films assert that lesbians are somehow different – sick, psychotic, or masochistic. The female buddy pictures, on the other hand, erase not only lesbianism but also woman-to-woman violence; they show relationships between women as invariably loving, caring, and non-violent as well as asexual. Thus, as a researcher trying to eradicate misconceptions and further our understanding of abusive lesbian relationships, I must reckon with these films, and the social backdrop they provide. In order to go on to represent an accurate picture – with both positive and negative features – of lesbian culture, I always start discussion of my research with a consideration of the misrepresentation of lesbians in popular, homophobic, heterosexist discourses like those of the films.[8]

Because of such ideas, I cannot simply build on previous literature and deal with a particular issue in abusive lesbian relationships (as do others researching abuse in intimate relationships) without having my work misread. My research must identify the ideologies that are part of the homophobic discourse on lesbian sexualities, whether they romanticize or make invisible lesbian relationships (seeing them as nice, asexual pairings) or negatively simplify them as sick and deviant.[9]

Paying attention to the social backdrop is always important if researchers are to understand the complex context of our work, but particularly so when looking at how popular culture represents and misrepresents lesbians. The impact of this ideology is perhaps most felt by lesbians who have been abused. Breaking the silence is very difficult. The issue has only begun to be openly discussed since the early 1980s. Abused lesbians fear that no one will believe them, particularly since lesbian relationships have been presented as utopian by early strains of radical feminism. But there is also fear that reporting the abuse to police, shelter workers, or counsellors may reinforce the view that lesbians are sick or pathological. Further, evidence of violence between lesbians may contribute to the misconception that lesbians are really like men and not real women (as in the reaction to the lesbian serial killer). Many writings that have begun to emerge about lesbians' experiences in abusive relationships highlight the silence and the shame they feel given a heterosexist social context that does not allow them to freely talk about their lives. A poem by the Native American poet Chrystos, "What did he hit you with? The Doctor Said," exemplifies this point:

Shame   Silence
Not he
She
I didn't correct him
Curled into myself like a bound foot.   (1991:17)

Testimonies from responses to open-ended questions in my survey research share similar sentiments: "I became immune to her physical abuse. I only started to pay attention to it when she hit me in the bar in front of people and they acted surprised. I didn't even notice until someone asked me why I was so calm." Or: "She had a thing for baseball bats and pipes ... she broke my thumb, my front tooth and cracked the bat on my back – which still causes me major movement problems and miscellaneous minor jazz ... I think the hardest thing to deal with were comments like 'why don't you just slug her back?', 'why don't you just leave?' If I hit her back, I would lose whatever part of me that kept me sane. It's all I had to hang on to. If I was capable of leaving, I would have." Or:

Her shame in being lesbian was strong and I was sexually, physically and emotionally abused on numerous occasions for being a "proud lesbian" ... The wounds from this relationship went very deep for they were inflicted on my identity, as well as on my sexuality. I'm too embarrassed to relate the impacts of abuse on my sex life, but I can say that I went back to the closet for two years. Although I'm now working my way to being a "proud lesbian," I honestly don't know if I'll ever be able to completely reclaim such a label. (And this is almost eight years after the fact.) I guess I'm saying that the homophobia that one is left having to deal with is one of the most painful and persistent things that I've ever encountered.

Lesbians will only be able to discuss the pain (never mind the joy) in our lives when the constraining dominant discourses that are linked to homophobia are eradicated.

Acknowledging and understanding the existence of abuse in lesbian relationships and raising consciousness about lesbian sexuality requires a paradigm shift, dislodging the dominant heterosexual and misogynist world order. It also requires that we resist seeing heterosexual battering as the normative framework for all abusive intimate relationships.[10] We know comparatively little about the dynamics of abusive lesbian relationships or about the role of women as perpetrators of violence in intimate relationships with partners, children, and elderly relatives.[11] One area of controversy within the lesbian community is the issue of "mutual battering." Many lesbians see this concept as another common misconception that lesbian relationships are always equal partnerships. They stress that there is *always* a perpetrator and a victim. Yet other lesbians have described to me that the dynamics in their abusive relationships felt different, more complex and muddled. Some described having been abused in one relationship and being abusive in the next. Others have felt constrained by the use of dominant feminist analysis of gender inequities, and of power and control as the key components of violent relationships. One woman wrote to me about her different understanding of control:

People say abuse is a matter of control, and that's true. But it isn't control in the sense of her saying "do this" and then I do it. It's much more complicated than that. It's to do with both of you being controlled by her emotional agenda – her lack of control. So always she feels like a victim of her pain and anger. If she isn't in control of herself then she thinks, who is? Who else but her lover? So she has to fight to wrest this control away from you. But you don't have it, so it doesn't work. She feels more and more powerless, less and less in control. At the same time there is, at least the emotional catharsis of being able to let out the anger and pain. Even if it's toward the wrong object, this release, I think becomes addictive to her. Both of you are trapped in the end.

Seen through the lens of a heteronormative analysis of abuse, this description might conjure up an abusive male role and a manipulated female role to form this couple. If we leave gender differences aside as a presumptive critique, though, we see a richly evoked scene not at all central to gendered analyses of abuse but perhaps central to lesbian experience. Being able to see the differences between heterosexual and same-sex dynamics, then, is an important way of dislodging misrepresentations of lesbians. And in this case, it also assists those who want to learn more about lesbian abuse and asymmetries of power in lesbian relationships.

Popular culture often misrepresents lesbians and women in order to preserve the status quo. Some producers and critics would argue that the films I have chosen to review are neutral statements, but I see their messages as indicative of their investment in maintaining the current social context of heterosexism and misogyny. (Similarly, Greenhill's chapter shows how scholars can selectively interpret traditional culture and, in so doing, preserve the heterosexist order.) Heterosexuality is presented as a social system, rather than as one possibility in the range of sexualities; it is defined as the norm and also defined what it means to be woman and lesbian.[12] This system produces popular culture and popular culture reproduces it. And this system needs to be resisted.

But resistance isn't absent entirely from popular culture itself, as in the case of a t-shirt referring to *Basic Instinct* and sold at lesbian events. Its blood red lettering "Catherine was here" surmounts a drawing of an ice pick. Lesbians wearing these t-shirts resist the killer dyke as a pathological character and reclaim her as a powerful image, defying the homophobic intentions of the film. As feminists and lesbians who are committed to changing damaging discourse on women's sexualities it is clear that we must know our culture. We must be vigilant in our analyses of the social context that informs and shapes our work in order to see the texts that too often misrepresent, or even silence, our lives.

NOTES AND ACKNOWLEDGMENTS

I'd like to thank Pauline Greenhill and Diane Tye for their most helpful editorial comments. I'd also like to thank Catherine Taylor for her insightful comments, reactions, and careful editorial work on the numerous drafts of this manuscript. A version of the first part of this chapter appears in Nijole Benokraitis, ed., *Subtle Sexism: Current Practices and Prospects for Change*, Newbury Park: Sage, 1997.

1 By "radical feminist" I refer to the label given to women who do not fit traditional stereotypes of femininity in appearance or behaviour and who are therefore assumed to hate men (see, for example, Barbara

Rieti's quotation from Pat Robertson). This is distinct from women who call themselves radical feminists, who support a strain of feminist thinking that views patriarchy as the primary root of women's oppression.

2 Vivian Labrie also considers popular films as expressions of narrative and social structures.

3 Barbara Rieti's paper on witches also considers symbolic representations of violence against women.

4 More solitary responses to male aggression are discussed by Cynthia Boyd; heterosexual bonding in response to male aggression is one of Vivian Labrie's topics.

5 A recent presentation at the 1992 National Women's Studies Association conference in Austin, Texas, was entitled "Thelma & Louise: Feminist Education Shifts Hollywood's Portrayal of Women."

6 See also Carr and Taubin (1992), and Gilkas (1992).

7 As noted particularly by Anne Brydon, Barbara Rieti, Kay Stone, Vivian Labrie, and Pauline Greenhill.

8 Note that Susan Gordon's approach to a problematic, negative, even evil female figure, as discussed by Kay Stone, similarly does not try to mitigate that woman's actions, but to understand them and their context.

9 See Celia Kitzinger (1987) and Ristock (1991) on ideologies about lesbians.

10 See my article (Ristock 1994) for a discussion of how the legal justice system has responded to lesbian abuse by using heterosexual abuse as the normative framework.

11 See Carlson (1992) for a discussion of the role of women as perpetrators of violence; she argues that gender-related inequalities are not significant in these forms of abuse.

12 See Durocher (1990) for a discussion of the system of heterosexuality.

Help! Me, S/he, and the Boss

VIVIAN LABRIE

When you work for a boss in a job that makes you an intermediary between him/her and the rest of the world, you must understand the goals of both sides. If those goals conflict, you're in for a dilemma: as a helper, whom do you serve, your boss or the others? This insider position is known to many women who work as secretaries or receptionists. It is also familiar to ethnographers when they find themselves in dissonance between academe and the field;[1] and to figures in film and folktale, which I'll discuss here. If you are an ambitious outsider, and find there is no way up for a person like yourself through the prescribed procedure, you might contemplate covert paths. Then if both of you, intermediary insider and ambitious outsider, meet, you might contract an undisciplined alliance, often created through and within the fracturing of personae.

This paper is about such alliances. As part of a book woven by, for, and of undisciplined women, it reflects the necessity for indiscipline when the system has no place for your potentialities. My work is not exclusively gender-centred – although much of the discomfort and stress of the situations I consider is women's – but rather site-centred. However, the site is differentially occupied by women and men; gender associations here are by context, not inherent in nature. In the everyday world as well as in various kinds of narratives, this site is one of transition between a known but outdated setting and a new but untried one; between *here* and *beyond*. I focus on five stories – two folktales and three movies, summarized below – that have struck me as sharing the pattern of transition shown in Figure 1.[2]

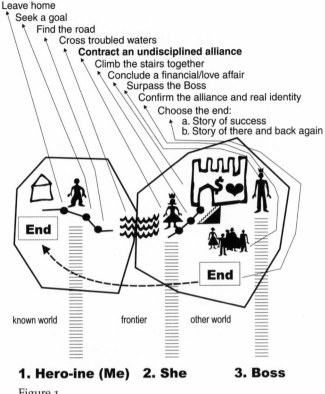

Leave home
  Seek a goal
    Find the road
      Cross troubled waters
        Contract an undisciplined alliance
          Climb the stairs together
            Conclude a financial/love affair
              Surpass the Boss
                Confirm the alliance and real identity
                  Choose the end:
                    a. Story of success
                    b. Story of there and back again

End

known world   frontier   other world

1. Hero-ine (Me)   2. She   3. Boss

Figure 1

The mixing of fictional genres, folktales, and movies is compelled by my feeling that they share a common topology linked somehow to everyday life. Topological analysis, a term I use to describe a form of symbolic investigation which combines levels of character, function, place, and movement, allows me to construct analyses which take structure into account, yet are not confined to any one discrete level. The two tales, "Bonnet Vert, Bonnet Rouge"[3] and "Le Conte de l'Aufrage,"[4] were first linked in my mind as theoretical models when I was researching bureaucratic culture among persons on welfare assistance and civil servants in social welfare agencies. Whereas "Bonnet Vert, Bonnet Rouge" exemplified the home-centred approach to the institution typical of persons outside office life – the agencies' clients – "Le Conte de l'Aufrage" well described the office-centred approach typical of persons experienced with bureaucracy through their education and work – the civil servants (Labrie 1987; 1990).[5] When mapped, though, both showed the same topology, a common

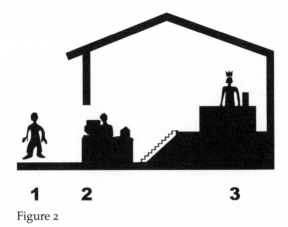

Figure 2

structural arrangement of territories, characters, paths, and functions. During this research I also developed a pictographic model of
bureaucratic situations in order to facilitate interviews (Figure 2). In
this three-person model, the house represents the institutional setting. Person one is the client, the outsider. In an analysis of transitions, s/he is the subject. Person two is the civil servant, the insider
in contact with the outside world, situated in a subordinate, clerical
position within the institution. In a transitional situation, she – this
position tends to be occupied by women – is the agent and functions
in a peer relationship with the outsider. An executive with ruling
power, Person three is Person two's superior within the institution.
S/he functions as a senior, master-of-the-passage for transitions
related to this institution. Though traditionally male, this function is
increasingly occupied by women.

Some time later, two office-centred films I happened to see struck
me as similar to this topology. *The Secret of My Success* was very close
to "Le Conte de l'Aufrage," while *Working Girl* provided a female
heroic alternative to the same plot.[6] Still later, I discovered another
movie, *Trois places pour le 26,* which shared more or less the same
topology in a show business setting.[7] Although each story keeps its
specificity, collectively they can be superimposed over certain *loci*,[8]
providing common denominators as keys to understanding other
levels of signification. First, it is impossible for the outsider (Person
one) to penetrate the macrosystem of the new world without breaking its rules. Second, given this impossibility and abuse of power on
the part of Person three, the new world's senior or ruler, Persons one
and two form an undisciplined alliance which involves a great deal
of dissociative behavior, even to the point of the splitting and/or

doubling of personae. Third, at least one member of the undisciplined pair is, unknowingly, in an incestuous relationship to Person three.[9]

Person two, standing just inside the frontier or reception office, possesses the keys for the other world – the (often bureaucratic) beyond – and has the choice of a disciplined alliance with Person three, the Boss, or an undisciplined alliance with Person one. If she chooses the first, Person two contributes to preserving the established order, maintaining at the same time her own ambiguous, subordinate, and metamorphic position within the system. If the second, she contributes to structural changes, gambling her own position to establish a partnership where she can clarify and augment her identity and autonomy. However metaphorically satisfying it may be, this scenario does not offer an immediate solution for real life problems, but it allows Persons two to name the game in real settings and gain awareness and understanding.

This discussion would be best with the original materials at hand.[10] Less ideally, here are brief outlines. In "Bonnet Vert, Bonnet Rouge,"[11] Bonnet Rouge, a king's son, is unbeaten at marbles. He meets Bonnet Vert along the seashore. They play three games, agreeing that the loser must comply with the winner's wish. Bonnet Rouge wins the first two and asks that some of his father's property be changed to gold. Bonnet Vert wins the third and orders Bonnet Rouge to find him within a year and a day or his head will roll off, and disappears. A servant advises the depressed Bonnet Rouge to go to her mother, who sends him to her older brother, who sends him to his older brother. Here, all the world's birds happen to gather. The last to arrive, an eagle, agrees to fly Bonnet Rouge over the Blue Sea to Bonnet Vert. On the other shore, Bonnet Rouge meets Jarretière Verte, one of Bonnet Vert's three daughters, and with her cooperation, succeeds in all the tasks assigned by Bonnet Vert and wins her hand. The couple runs away. Bonnet Vert follows but is prevented from catching them by the magic objects they throw behind. When Bonnet Rouge returns home, he forgets Jarretière Verte, who finds asylum in a shoemaker's house. They meet again on the day of his wedding to another. Dialogue between a rooster and hen reminds him of his past. On the advice of the assembly, the marriage between Bonnet Rouge and Jarretière Verte is celebrated.

In "Le Conte de l'Aufrage,"[12] a rich man survives a shipwreck but loses everything, including his family. A couple finds his baby on the shore. When the man comes to their house asking for the baby, they say nothing. They take care of the child as their own and give him the best possible education. After graduation, the young man seeks a clerical position but initially fails because he is overqualified. He is eventually hired as lowest clerk by a very rich businessman on the other side of the sea. Rapidly promoted, he becomes first manager and marries the boss's daughter. She persuades them all to visit his foster parents, who recognize her father as the shipwreck survivor and reveal the son's true origins. A priest nonetheless blesses the couple and the son/son-in-law/employee returns to the business as his father/father-in-law/boss's successor.

In *The Secret of My Success*, Brentley, young and ambitious, leaves Kansas and his parents to seek his fortune in New York. After many attempts to find a job, he gets an interview with his uncle Howard, owner of an important consortium, by having the secretary send Howard Brentley's photocopied face. Hired at the lowly position of messenger, he meets a beautiful young executive, Christie, at a fountain. While chauffeuring Howard's wife (his aunt), he is sexually assaulted by her in a swimming pool. Brentley discovers an unoccupied office and installs himself under the name of Carlton Whitfield. Christie, who is having an unsatisfying affair with Howard, the boss, gets progressively involved in a business and love relationship with Brentley/Carlton. During a garden party the multiple couples and identities are revealed. Brentley/Carlton is fired but he, Christie, his aunt, Carlton's secretary, and his messenger friend Melrose counter Howard's merger proposal at a business meeting. The company is saved, Howard is fired, Brentley/Carlton wins, and he and Christie plan to visit his family.

In *Working Girl*, Tess, a young, impetuous, imaginative secretary who does not tolerate sexual harassment is eventually offered a job with Catherine Parker, a young executive to whom she reveals brilliant investment ideas. Catherine breaks her leg on a ski trip and asks Tess to take care of her pending home and office affairs. Tess discovers that the boss has stolen her idea. Furious, on the ferry home she decides to take Catherine's place and conclude the deal herself. In a cocktail lounge, she meets Jack Trainer, Catherine's lover. Tess convinces him to get involved in the deal, and they become lovers. They crash the wedding reception organized for his daughter by their potential client Trask, and Tess tells him about the idea while they dance. Catherine returns, claims the deal, and denounces Tess as her secretary and an impostor. Tess is fired but Jack defends her when Trask arrives. In the elevator, Trask asks Tess to explain how the deal idea occurred to her. When Catherine is unable to answer adequately the same question, he is convinced of Tess's legitimacy. Catherine is fired, Tess and Jack move in together, and Tess gets a executive job from Trask. The movie ends with Tess humanely explaining her expectations to her new secretary.

Trois places pour le 26 stars Yves Montand as himself, coming back to Marseille to do a musical comedy about his own career's beginnings. Marion, a young girl whose father is in prison and whose mother has financial problems, works in a perfume shop but has studied singing and dancing and dreams of a show business career. She wants tickets for Montand's show, scheduled for the 26th. Rehearsals show the young Ivo Livi's involvement with "Maria" (before he adopted the stage name Yves Montand), whom he knew as Mylène, and for whom he now searches. Marion, unable to get tickets, presents herself to Montand as "Roxanne," and explains that her goal in life is (to be like) him. She obtains both the tickets and permission to attend rehearsals. Marion's mother leaves her visiting card at Montand's hotel. Rehearsals emphasize the port setting of Ivo Livi's becoming Montand, and of Maria/Mylène's marriage to a rich ship owner. The show's female player must quit because she is pregnant, and Marion/Roxanne gets the job. At the hotel, Montand arranges a rendezvous with the card owner/Marion's mother/Maria/Mylène. Marion, rehearsing the roles of various women with whom Montand has had affairs, gets closer to him. Marion/Roxanne (who is, on stage, Maria/Mylène and also Monroe/Piaf/Signoret) is in bed with Montand the morning after the first show; he reads the newspapers' very positive reviews of their performances. During breakfast, Montand alludes to Mylène, whom he still loves, and her taste for rose jam,[13] which shows Marion/Roxanne that Mylène is her mother. At the train station, Marion/Roxanne steps back and presents her mother to her father. They embrace. The film ends with the title which means "three tickets for the 26th."

The structure of these stories can be seen in Figure 3. Each story involves a Person one (Bonnet Rouge, the young man, Brentley, Tess, and Marion[14]). Only Bonnet Rouge does not have an alter ego (the young man as clerk, Brentley as Carlton, Tess as an executive, and Marion as Roxanne). These alter ego figures also serve as Person two mediators, but there are also separate Persons two, who ally themselves with Person one (Jarretière Verte with Bonnet Rouge, the businessman's daughter with the young man, Christie and also the boss's wife with Brentley, Jack with Tess, and Montand with Marion). Note that in three cases (the young man and his half sister, Brentley and his aunt, and Marion and her father) these relationships are incestuous. Arguably there are also closeness problems when Brentley sleeps with his uncle/boss's lover Christie, or Tess with her boss's

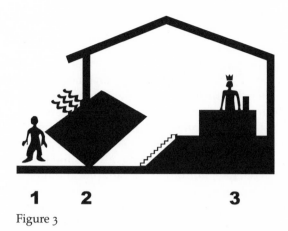

1   2   3

Figure 3

lover Jack.[15] Finally, there are Person three characters (Bonnet Vert, the employer/father, Howard the uncle, Catherine [but also Trask], and Montand). Once again, there are direct familial relationships between Person one and Person three in three of the stories.

Each story involves three locations. First is the known world, the original home of Person one (Bonnet Rouge's father's kingdom, the foster parents' house, the parents' house in Kansas, the working class New York neighbourhood, Marseille) which does not allow her/him to succeed. The world beyond, containing what Person one seeks (Bonnet Vert, an appropriate job [in three cases], and stardom), also takes various forms (Bonnet Vert's kingdom, the businessman's company, New York's business world [in two cases], and show business). In between the two is a frontier which is usually marked by water (the Blue Sea, the sea, a water fountain, a swimming pool, New York harbour, a ferry crossing, and the wings of the theatre).

The itinerary each Person one follows differs in form, but each leaves home to seek a goal, finds the road, then crosses troubled waters – metaphorical (Brentley photocopying his face, or Tess presenting her idea to her new boss) or literal (Bonnet Rouge crossing the Blue Sea, or Brentley being sexually assaulted by his aunt – his boss's wife – in a pool). Person one then contracts an undisciplined alliance with a Person two with whom s/he climbs the metaphorical stairs of success (accomplishing a series of progressively more difficult yet more rewarding tasks, going from promotion to promotion, planning a controversial project or a difficult deal, going on stage), and with whom s/he has an affair involving both emotional and material reward. Person one's success is clear when s/he moves from junior to senior, and her/his alliance with Person two, along with

her/his true identity, is confirmed. At the end, Person one is integrated into the new world or, in Bonnet Rouge's case, reintegrated
into the old.

In the resulting narrative ecosystems, elements are not isolated;
they influence each other in a dynamic of places with their rules,
persons with their life histories, and events with their causal chains.
These links form a topology – the represented lifespace's configuration with its boundaries, paths, and elements. The complex building
mechanisms of each tale or film may pertain to very different levels.
For example, water – the seaside setting, always the site of transition
– usually has a concrete, figurative, topographical dimension. On the
other hand, unknowingly having an incestuous relationship refers to
an intangible order of psychology and social convention. Both kinds
of elements seem equally salient topologically; each is a common
denominator to all the stories.

The unfolding of each story, highly complex and metaphorical, also
shows commonalities. In this two-world universe, the hero-ine-s (Person one) pass a threshold of overqualification with respect to what is
available for them in their place of origin. Despite peers' warnings,
they cross a frontier into a location beyond the culture and knowledge
of their own world, where things are more difficult for them. In this
qualitative jump, they give a part of themselves and put their identity
at stake. When Brentley gives the secretary the photocopy of his own
face, or when Bonnet Rouge cuts off a piece of his own buttock to
feed the bird who is transporting him over the sea, they offer fragmented versions of the self/body to gain access to the new world.

There, the hero-ine-s exhibit competence and ambition: "No, I
want to reach the summit by myself,"[16] Brentley answers when his
aunt says she will make sure her husband gives him a more worthy
job. Yet talent alone is insufficient, and the hero-ine-s conclude that
they will never reach their goals if they follow the rules. "When
you're nothing you cannot become a lot more than that," says
Montand's partner. Therefore, our hero-ine-s cheat, pretend to be
somebody else, and take *"l'habit qui fait le moine,"*[17] be it Jarretière
Verte's garter, an executive office, clothes borrowed from a superior
or donned in the elevator, or a stage name. Breaking the rules fright-
ens more timid peers. "This can't turn out well. Either you're caught
and then you're fired, or you're not, and then you become one of
them, a suit. In both cases you lose," says Melrose to Brentley.
"Sometimes I sing in my underwear at home. That does not make
me Madonna," says Tess's friend.

Through this doubling process, the hero-ine finds an ally in an
experienced peer from the other world and involves her/him in his/
her cheating. The attachment becomes mutual, but originates with

the hero-ine. As soon as the pair is formed, horizontal mobility (changing places) becomes vertical mobility (ascent within the new setting). This change in the dynamic of the story is well marked, by the use of staircases and elevators in the films, and flight in "Bonnet Vert, Bonnet Rouge." Growing difficulties are met covertly and subversively, eluding the authority's control, and often outside regular institutional time, space, and methods. Carlton and Christie work after office hours; Tess and Jack intrude upon Trask's daughter's wedding; Bonnet Rouge and Jarretière Verte use her magic instead of a pierced bucket to empty a lake. Night plays an important role as a time of waking and work.

The hero-ine's life conditions progressively improve: the authority is enchanted by the apparent results, and confers status and privileges. At the same time, tension and risk grow for the insider half of the pair as this person or alias is torn between her institutional allegiance and her new alliance. Any error may be mortal. This is literally true for Jarretière Verte, who helps Bonnet Rouge by transforming herself into a ladder, but because of his carelessness is reconstituted with a visibly crooked finger which she must hide from her father.

Just when love and success become available, a meeting with witnesses to both the old and new identities uncovers the construction and it falls. The young man goes with his family-in-law to visit his parents; Catherine reappears; the rose jam brings Mylène/Mother into the conversation. A period of demotion follows for the hero-ine and leads to a moment-of-truth experience for the allied person who questions the affiliation and feels deceived. However, an explanation brings renewed confidence in the hero-ine, and from then on, the ally will use experience and influence to save her/his partner.

The next step involves a test of strength between the duo and the authority, based on merit instead of identity. This time the authority loses and the duo wins; the two juniors, Persons one and two, free themselves of dependence on the senior Person three and establish themselves either by succeeding him ("Le Conte de l'Aufrage," *The Secret of My Success*) or by leaving his/her sphere of influence ("Bonnet Vert, Bonnet Rouge," *Working Girl*). This new start is securely grounded, public, and confirmed by peers. The ending's location also signifies. Either the new team establishes itself within the new world – a story of success – ("Le Conte de l'Aufrage," *The Secret of My Success, Working Girl, Trois places pour le 26*); or returns to the first world – the allied person undertaking the change of worlds ("Bonnet Vert, Bonnet Rouge").

The topology of these stories pertains to several alternative dynamics: individual (everything is me, every aspect is part of me); interpersonal (we share the roles among us); psychosocial (we take roles and functions in accordance with who and what we are); ritual (here are ways of coping with periods of separation, marginalization, and aggregation in a situation of transition); institutional (here is the procedure, official and officious); and so on. This multiplicity contains no contradiction: current thought on signification accepts polysemy and open meanings.

The topology reflects the bureaucratic cultural context shared by "Le Conte de l'Aufrage," *The Secret of My Success*, and *Working Girl*. Hilaire Benoit, who was over seventy when we collected "Le Conte de l'Aufrage" in 1976, had learned it in his own youth from a much older tale teller; it originates at least from the beginning of this century. It describes the office culture of this period: employees are exclusively male, the company is an extension of the family, and the head office is the family residence. It is to this real site of power that the employer's wife and daughter introduce the hero, once he has made it at the shop.

In the two movies, the historical transition is complete; women not only occupy secretarial and receptionist positions but are also intermediary executives. Thus the *hero (Person one)–adversary's daughter (Person two)–adversary (Person three)* triad of "Bonnet Vert, Bonnet Rouge," is transposed into the corporate triad of *hero-ine (Person one)– boss's subordinate (Person two)–boss (Person three)* of bureaucratic culture (Figure 2) (Labrie 1987; 1990). Person two, often a woman, acting simultaneously as helper for Person one and as buffer for Person three, is exposed to high stress, notably concerning her identity and allegiance. To whom should go her loyalty and duty, the client or the boss? And who is she, a person or a function?

The narrative topology names aspects of these tensions; Person two owes a double allegiance. As part of an institution, she lives within a world to whose rules she conforms, while at the same time she is directed to receive clients to whose demands she is requested to respond. This situation puts her in hot water when the two ethics contradict. The topology shows that her response can be disciplined or undisciplined. For instance, his uncle's secretary both blocks and listens to Brentley. Facing his unusual demand, she subverts the rule and sends the photocopy of his face to her superior, giving Brentley access. Tess, on the other hand, is positioned as a secretary, but aspires to higher things. Thus she is at the same time Person one and Person two, just as Catherine is at the same time Person two and Person three. Not a quiet surbordinate at the beginning, Tess becomes even more undisciplined on discovering her superior has stolen her idea; she then leads Jack, her Person two, to indiscipline in his turn.

Actually, indiscipline is the key to success in all the stories. The young man in "Le Conte de l'Aufrage" dares to engage in a conversation with the boss despite the reigning convention of silence.[18] Changing appearance is necessary for the outsider attempting to penetrate the inside: Brentley exchanges his uniform for a jacket; Tess cuts her hair. Person one's dissociative behaviour belongs to the liminal (marginal) phase of a rite of passage, which often features ritual dissolution of the identity, along with exterior signs of that transformation.[19]

For Person two, instability of personae is in addition associated with the difficulty of reconciling *self* and *function*. In many traditional tales, the hero's helper, a "transitional partner" (Houde 1991:271-4),[20] often metamorphoses. As a Person two, Jarretière Verte's form is highly volatile: sometimes a carbon copy among her sisters, sometimes a duck, sometimes a woman, sometimes bones in a cauldron, sometimes a ladder, and so on, she is pressured to malleability as she accompanies her Person one. Bonnet Rouge, in contrast, remains a "stable composite" through the changing conditions imposed on him. Similarly, while Brentley, Tess, and Marion remain relatively themselves, their Person two doubles (Carlton, Catherine, Roxanne) pass through constant transformations. Roxanne, for example, assumes a wide variety of roles in the production.

The Person two's dilemma resembles that of the civil servant, who must reconcile contradictory roles. If s/he privileges person, s/he stops playing an employee; if s/he privileges function, s/he feels like nobody. Between these two is an ambiguous and quite often painful zone, where it remains doubtful whether the body links to appearance – thus becoming a *corps-sans-âme*[21] – or to the self – thus appearing naked. The choice is clear when Brentley/Carlton's new secretary enters his office as he is changing: "I am Jane, your new secretary." – "I am, as far as I can say, nude."

In folktales, the metamorphosed person is often under an enchantment from which she can be delivered only by the person she is helping, but is constrained from asking. These stories accomplish the change through partnership; by establishing an affective link between peers or by the served recognising the server as a person. The tales also show that despite all the privileges attached to her/his function, the Person two institutional partner is subject to hidden, harmful control by the authority, which provides the motivation to risk an association with a newcomer.

The relational situations of the institutionally junior Persons two (Jarretière Verte, the employer's daughter, Brentley/Carlton, Christie, Tess, and Marion/Roxanne) engage them in a family secret, a taboo form of violence. The relationship can be with Person three (Jarretière Verte is closely checked and regularly undressed by her father; Christie sleeps with her boss) or Person one (the young man and the employer's daughter who discover only when married that they are half-brother and sister). For those who are Persons one and two simultaneously, familial and corporate incest also occurs, but usually complicating self and function. Brentley/Carlton is more or less raped by the wife of his uncle/employer; Tess sleeps with her superior's lover; and Roxanne/Marion sleeps with her father (who is both Person two and three to her). The literal incest is not consciously intentional; the institutional incest is blatant. However, when the story is resolved, the central characters are delivered from this victimization – juniors pair off with juniors and seniors with seniors – and this gain rewards the risk they underwent. In fact, the institution as a whole profits from this clarification.

These stories show that bureaucratic space is not beyond our mythical projections, and that it does not express only rational constructions. Even in this "real world" location, there are a metaphoric castle, king/father/boss, and troubled waters. Its relationships and personae reflect certain fundamental human dramas and allow new ethical perspectives. What then is the appropriate level of understanding? In real life there are consequences when a perfectly adequate process at one level is transposed to another register. For example, the dissociative behavior necessary in Brentley's doubling into Carlton and Marion's into Roxanne might match the psychiatric standard (Kluft 1987:367) for diagnosing multiple personality disorder (MPD),[22] but at another level, it could be considered suitable metaphoric thinking. The distinction depends on whether the many personalities occur as disturbances of identity and memory within a unique individual in the real-life space and time, or as strategies of a mind seeking solutions through some dramatization. In one case the result is disorder and disruption of a person's quality of life; in the other, the outcomes – at least in the stories – prove creative.[23]

The stories take place in a secondary polysemic world derived, perhaps through artistic representation, from reality, but suitable to reappropriations on a number of levels. Unfortunately, topologies as configurations, in and of themselves, do not provide clues as to which level – therapeutic, expressive, metaphorical, and so on – applies. Dissociative behavior and incest co-occur in five topologically similar stories, as they do in the psychiatric literature on MPD.[24] In some stories, characters' dissociative/incestuous behaviour matches the intrafamilial level but is transported into the corporate world, opening the question of institutional incest. Confusion may also reign in real life between family and business, paternalism and bureaucracy, and domestic/familial mechanisms transposed to the world of commerce. These narratives about the bureaucratic space reflect back to family space. Their expression of dominant links between a dissociative junior and an incestuous senior at least invites us to reflect on the cultural-symbolic organization of these connections, as well as on their possible real life parallels and settings.[25]

As the *junior female (Person two)–senior male (Person three)* pattern still remains typical of real life bureaucratic settings, Person two's dilemma can also be seen as a feminist issue.[26] Most people are aware of situations where sexual demands on women were or are preconditions to their promotion. While incest is certainly seen as abuse when imposed by seniors on juniors within the family, these stories suggest that sexual intimacy between senior male and junior female members of the same institution, a symbolic incest, is equally disruptive.[27]

These five stories outline some risks for women placed in a Person two helper position: of helping junior men into senior positions without changing the male-specific aspect of the Person three function; of allowing the institutional dynamic to modify Person three positions into Person two positions when women get these jobs; of being entrapped in family-like, patriarchal, institutional bonds; of being placed under a great deal of dissociative pressure.[28] They also provide an opportunity to open a debate about indiscipline as an answer to – as well as simply a result of – structural violence. The knowledge associated with a Person two position is as least as strategic as it is stressful; she speaks both the inside and the outside languages, and, although uncomfortable, her borderline situation gives her the possibility of translation in either direction. As an intermediary between the makers of rules and their subjects, Person two retains the real balance of power – when she becomes aware of it – and thus, in life as well as in art, she can become a major agent of social change – once she decides to make use of her position.

NOTES AND ACKNOWLEDGMENTS

I really should have written this paper in French, which is my ordinary mode of expression, but have decided to be undisciplined in order to be read by the other contributors and the mainly anglophone audience of this book. This has meant lots of trouble for Laurel Doucette, Pauline Greenhill, Diane Tye, Kay Stone, and some others, who offered lengthy and very useful comments and even rewrote some passages in order to make my English version readable! Thank you all.

1 As discussed extensively by the authors in the first section, but particularly Doucette, Tye, and St. Peter.

2 The narrative stages outlined here are descriptive rather than categorical.

3 Archives de Folklore de l'Université Laval, Collection Bouthillier-Labrie, numéro 1338. Aarne-Thompson tale type 313 (*The Magic Flight*).

4 A bureaucratic tale of unknown origin, Archives de Folklore de l'Université Laval, Collection Bouthillier-Labrie, numéro 1219.

5 This research was funded by the Social Sciences and Humanities Research Council of Canada and focused on the relationships between "Les gens, les papiers et les institutions" (see Labrie 1987; 1989).

6 *The Secret of My Success* is a 1987 Herbert Ross film, featuring Michael J. Fox; *Working Girl*, directed by Mike Nichols, came out in 1988 starring Melanie Griffith, Sigourney Weaver, Harrison Ford (and New York again).

7 This 1988 musical was written and directed by Jacques Demy.

8 This is the Latin term used by rhetoricians to refer to common places used for the process of memorization.

9 Though these last two observations were made independently, without recourse to sources other than the narratives, they proved consistent with recent findings (Kluft 1987:363–73, Ross et al. 1989:413–18) on multiple personality disorder (MPD), showing antecedents of childhood physical and sexual abuse – which is, of course, an abuse of power by authority figures – among MPD patients. Thanks to Pauline Greenhill for pointing out this direction to me.

10 The tales can be accessed through the Archives de Folklore de l'Université Laval, Division des Archives, Cité Universitaire, Ste-Foy, QC, G1K 7P4, and the movies through a video outlet.

11 This version was recorded from Hilaire Benoit, Tracadie, NB, in 1976.

12 This version was also collected from Hilaire Benoit in 1976. Although he mentioned having learned it from a traditional tale teller, it probably has a literary origin.

13 "To discover the truth" is metaphorically expressed in French as "découvrir le pot aux roses."

14 There is an additional Person one in *Trois places pour le 26*, in the form of Ivo Livi, becoming Montand, but we will not address him here for the sake of clarity.

15 The incestuous relationship in "Bonnet Vert, Bonnet Rouge" takes a more symbolic form when Bonnet Vert carefully checks his daughter's body.

16 I viewed *The Secret of My Success* and *Working Girl* in French, so the translated excerpts here may differ slightly from the original movie dialogue.

17 Literally, the robe which makes the monk; the appearance that confers identity.

18 Similarly, Melrose chastises Brentley for saying hello to the executives when initiating him (a Person two job) to the messenger run:

> *Melrose*: No, I told you, not with suits. You never fraternize with suits unless they fraternize first.
>
> *Brentley*: This is stupid. They are persons. I am a person. Why not say hello?
>
> *Melrose*: They're not persons, they're suits. We're mail. No fraternization.

Various feminist thinkers have asserted that women often find themselves, individually and collectively, silenced.

19 As established by Van Gennep for example in *The Rites of Passage* ([1909] 1975).

20 This is the vocabulary of adult development. Houde (1991:272) cites a definition given by Wadner (1987:14) which seems quite appropriate: "les individus ou objets qui, consciemment ou inconsciemment, desservent des fonctions d'empathie et de soutien à l'intérieur d'une relation étroite de type symbiotique dont le degré d'intimité varie et où il y a partage des aspects du self. Leur première condition est d'aider la personne du mitan à accomplir les tâches majeures de développement."

21 This is the French terminology for characters whose soul is separated from the body as in Aarne-Thompson tale type 302.

22 A. The existence within the individual of two or more distinct personalities, each of which is dominant at a particular time; B. The personality that is dominant at any particular time determines the individual's behaviour; C. Each individual personality is complex and integrated with its own unique behaviour patterns and social relationships (American Psychiatric Association 1980).

23 In fact, therapeutic interview techniques directed towards the different MPD personae must recognize that "All of these can be thought of as the use of metaphoric thinking with a non-MPD patient. It can reference thought processes or ego states rather than full personalities" (Braun 1989:315).

24 Given Susan Gordon's use of traditional tales in therapeutic contexts, described by Kay Stone (this volume), perhaps these narratives could be employed in working with MPD patients. Such stories also have obvious implications and linkages in dealing with issues of workplace sexual harassment (see also Cynthia Boyd's discussion of personal experience narratives as tactics) and family violence.

25 Interestingly enough, the integration sought as a result of MPD treatment is presented in a businesslike manner in Kluft (1987:370): "While

integration is desirable, pragmatism must prevail ... It seems to me that after treatment you want a functional unit, be it a corporation, a partnership, or a one-owner business ... A negociated 'detente' may be the best result achievable at the time."

26 In fact, this is part of the problem faced by the female taxi drivers Boyd discusses.

27 In the therapeutic context between male doctor and female patient, it is seen "at the same time as an abuse of power and professional incest" (Frenette 1992). In this statement published in a daily newspaper, Frenette, a psychologist and psychotherapist who is also author of *Abus de pouvoir, récit d'une intimité sexuelle thérapeute-cliente*, documents the treatment given to a complaint made to the Corporation des psychologues du Québec. At the time of writing this paper, Augustin Roy, president of la Corporation des médecins du Québec, was reproached by l'Office des professions du Québec for unethical public statements about sexual harassment complaints made to his corporation.

28 Incidentally MPD "has a reported 9:1 predominance of females among its victims" (Kluft 1987:364). However, it remains unclear whether this proportion reflects the actual population or the reportage.

PART THREE

Women Transform Their Lives and Traditions

Undisciplined Women began by looking at how the gender of collectors and representers of traditional and popular culture affected their work and the academic field of folklore. The book continued with a close look at various constructions of women and men in sociocultural texts. In this section writers turn to looking at women's own creations. While neither the first section's women collectors and representers nor the second section's images of women represents a single point of view, this third section clearly shows the variety of ways in which women creatively deal with their everyday lives. And while resistance is implicit in the very acts of collecting and representing culture for some of the women discussed in the first section, and is equally suggested by some of the women characters presented in the previous section, resistance is perhaps most obvious in the traditions discussed in this section. By examining the range of women's folklore, these papers reflect the extent and variability of women's traditional and popular cultural creations.

"Woman" is a complex, changing category. Contrary to patriarchal and feminist reductionism alike, women themselves cannot be essentialised. As Geraldine Finn writes, "*as women* we share a position in the social and political hierarchy organized by and for male dominance, we do not [all] share a position in, or experience of, other hierarchies of privilege and power, founded on and for other orders of difference, like race, religion, class, age and sexual orientations" (1993:323). If one understands that the category "woman" designates a "place" in society, a position of subordination to which all women are assigned and which all women therefore must negotiate (Ibid., 326), then clearly women's cultural creations cannot successfully, or without significant misrepresentation, be limited – not even by the notion that they are distinctively or specially female. The papers here resist classification according to conventional notions of women's culture and prohibit its characterization in universal terms, instead suggesting some of the specificities, densities, textures, and laminations of women's thought.

All the authors indicate that the concept of the "private" – usually the home – as women's domain, and the "public" – nearly everything else – as men's is problematic. Recognizing the fact that folklore and women have been seen as irrelevant to, or at least judiciously absent from, public culture does not require people to accept this evaluation uncritically. Feminists have of course been challenging both the actual and the symbolic confinement of women to the private sphere and the home. At the same time as they assert the necessity of giving women access to public domains, such as that of wage labour (see for example Cynthia Boyd's paper on women taxi drivers), feminists also indicate that men's effects on, and patriarchy's damage to, the private realm are more pervasive than people might sometimes expect or hope. The binary opposition of public/private is thus not without some explanatory power. It can be used to show how the unequal distribution of roles and responsibilities alienates men from their children, and even from their own emotions. At the same time, it helps to explore how women's experience is confined and restricted, and to argue the necessity of moving beyond these limitations.

However, several papers show that women's entry into the conventionally defined public sphere does not necessarily mitigate patriarchy's control over their lives. The appearance of a woman in a public place does not invariably threaten patriarchy or guarantee any fundamental change in women's status. Too often women's presence is not welcomed; sometimes it is barely tolerated. For example, as religion and society student Pamela Klassen shows, Agatha Schmidt's preaching is not an expression of feminist principles but of her sense of duty and responsibility to God and to the Mennonite community. She is highly concerned with what religious authorities, and men in general, think, although opposition has not stopped her from preaching. Freelance researcher Cynthia Boyd's paper shows the ongoing difficulties women encounter in the non-traditional work context of taxi driving. These drivers' narratives about sexual harassment from men – family and friends as well as colleagues and customers – help them to cope with their difficult situation, and to develop tactics for resistance. But despite these stories' considerable transformational potential, they may make it possible for women to endure unsatisfactory work conditions rather than change them.

Genres like clothing and creative textile forms like quilting are associated in many ways with women's traditional domestic domain, but they are in fact equally linked with men and the public sphere. Laval ethnologist Jocelyne Mathieu points out that while women may make at least some of their clothes at home, they may also produce and exchange them in and for the market. And no matter where it is produced, clothing is clearly required in most "public" even more than in some "private" spaces. The public/private distinction, and its associations with women and men, and with handwork and economic redistribution, further blurs in art historian Susan Shantz's paper. Frances Mateychuk's quilts are displayed as well as marketed publicly, while her husband quilts within the private confines of their home. Frances seeks a broad audience by displaying her quilts in the front yard, and by advertising and selling them at her friend Zonia's house. "Domestic" space moves into the realm of exchange and the marketplace, and its role as a "private" sanctuary or retreat for those who live there is diminished.

Researcher and subject may employ profoundly different notions of what is public and what is private. As Shantz shows, Frances' husband not only quilts but is proud of his creativity and handiwork. Initially, Peter was reluctant to have the author, who was from outside his community, discover the extent of his involvement in quilting, though his local friends were quite aware of it. Shantz expected the very opposite; that he would allow an outsider to have this knowledge but might keep it from his own community. The concept of public space here subdivides and fragments as much as does the private.

Folklorist Marie-Annick Desplanques discusses how Newfoundland women socialize and work in their homes. Although such spaces are circularly defined – locations where women gather with other women are private because only women gather there; and women gather there because they are private places where only women gather – they cannot avoid being intruded upon by manifestly public concerns. Desplanques shows that the post office, the shops, and the school not only provide topics for conversation but also structure the times when women can get together.

Whatever places women employ for performance or presentation, they often choose different folkloric texts and genres than men, and deploy their material in varying ways. Though folklorists have argued that some genres, such as the recitation, monologue, or toast (see Goldstein 1976) are quintessentially male, while others, like the "kernel story" (see Kalcik 1975) are basically female, such simple dichotomies fail to reflect actual use (see Greenhill 1984).

Literary scholar Robin McGrath demonstrates how women's personal, individual concerns for self-expression can be expressed publicly in both oral and written forms. Men and women are their readers and hearers. Her work, along with sociologist Gail Grant's and Pamela Klassen's, shows that women who perform "men's" genres in locations dominated by men must preserve a delicate and creative balancing of social expectation with action if they wish to maintain ties with their communities. That so many manage, despite considerable and overt opposition, to go ahead and perform miraculous acts of healing (Grant's work), preach in public (Klassen's), and write their autobiographies (McGrath's), shows that women are not merely victims of a male-defined, deterministic society. They resist its strictures.

By effecting change, these women show its possibility. They do so in part by using genres and texts which have been performed by men to make comments on the value of women's culture. Folklorist and storyteller Kay Stone's work suggests that women and men may experience and remember folktales differently (1993b). But she also indicates that women are no more the slaves of received texts than they are of biology and physiology. Storytellers Marvyne Jenoff and Susan Gordon manipulate the meanings, if not the actual words, of the traditional tales they tell. That women and men both participate, however selectively, in each other's traditions as well as in each other's domains argues for the unruly – undisciplined – character of the categories of male/female, public/private.

Desplanques suggests that women's collaborative work becomes a social outlet for women and an opportunity to exchange news and reinforce personal links. The circulation of narratives from one woman to another expresses and reinforces their network of family and friends, as evidenced also by the taxi drivers Boyd discusses. While many traditions reinforce women's links to each other, they also illuminate women's relationships to men. For example, though women dominate the religious healing Gail Grant discusses – both as givers and as receivers – men are involved in various significant capacities. Men – as harassers, relatives, and fellow workers – are a predominant topic of the taxi drivers' narratives considered by Boyd. McGrath shows that some Inuit women's autobiographies are symbolically sanctioned by fathers.

These papers all argue for the malleability of conventional notions of public and private, but also of male and female. As researchers gather evidence from a broader range of women's traditional and popular culture, the discursive contingencies of women's folklore may extend beyond its simply being composed, made, or presented by a woman. Indeed, in this section's articles, women-centredness means recognizing, valuing, and locating women, and presenting the world from their point of view. To be women-centred does not require one to focus exclusively upon women and their products.

In giving voices to women themselves, their creations, and their communications, these papers not only remedy the exclusion of women's culture within folklore and Canadian studies, they also highlight the irony inherent in such an exclusion. These (inter)disciplines are centrally concerned with identity, and construction of self and community, yet they ignore some of the most distinctive locations for such action. Canadians should attend to folkloric materials precisely because they are exchanged, communicated, and recreated. Traditional and popular cultural forms are dynamic rather than static. Hence they help people to understand one another, to articulate expectations and boundaries in their groups, and to develop personal, family, and community identities. Relegating all folklore to the simple and frivolous is like suggesting that all women's activities occur in the private sphere; it obfuscates central issues.

As in the previous sections, the individuality of the writers is evident in the papers. Shantz's is the most clearly experimental, with a sometimes parallel, sometimes contrary dialogue between Shantz herself and quilter Frances Mateychuk. But in their contents, too, the writers' indiscipline and personal resistance is evident. Shantz, Mathieu, and Desplanques test and critique conventional ideas of women as they operate in conventionally-female domains and genres. Stone discusses how the public presentation of such traditions and genres can change ideas about women's natures and experiences. The women discussed by Klassen, Grant, Boyd, and McGrath use narratives as forms of resistance. Their work demonstrates only a few of the ways that women use folklore to help make their own places, as well as to compose and tell their own stories even in the face of cultural proscriptions. McGrath's study of Inuit women's autobiography, a genre which could be considered simply an expression of adherence to patriarchal and colonialist imperatives, de-codes (see Radner 1993) these narratives' implicitly feminist messages. This is but one example in this section of how, through traditional and popular culture, women find methods and opportunities to express individuality and voice their own as well as their group's concerns. The creative results, from sermons to clothes to stories to quilts to academic papers, contain relevant messages for women that often not only circumvent the taboos, but critique their existence. In compelling and truthful yet poetic ways, undisciplined women transform their lives, as well as their traditions.

Frances Mateychuk's Quilts: Mapping a Place

SUSAN SHANTZ

In the following article segments of text in the voice of Frances Mateychuk are interwoven with my own voice.[1] Correspondence between the two is not always sequential nor even present; this is deliberate, as I want Frances' voice to speak parallel to my own, rather than be subordinated to the author-itative voice of the writer. My representation of her experience thus becomes closer, I hope, to the open-endedness of lived experience. While it is difficult to minimize the scholar's voice-over, it is a necessary task if ethnography is truly to become empathic dual-tracking where I, the inquirer, consciously bring my own interests and assumptions into conversation with the persons or materials with which I am engaged.[2]

The quilts of Frances Mateychuk came to my attention when I stopped at a farmhouse in rural Saskatchewan in response to a hand-lettered sign announcing "QUILTS 4 SALE." This farm, which appeared to be Ukrainian (a large whitewashed stone near the road bore red and black flowers painted in imitation cross-stitch design)[3] was on a main highway one hour east of Saskatoon. The woman who answered my knock, Zonia Pidlisny, was in the midst of making bread and cabbage rolls. When I expressed interest in seeing her quilts, she took me upstairs to a small spare room where a metal bed was loaded with folded quilts. All were brightly coloured and made of fortrel fabric.[4] Most, the woman explained, were made by her friend, Frances Mateychuk, also Ukrainian, who lived several miles off the main highway on a gravel road.

Figure 1. The Mateychuk farm near Saskatoon.

I'm bored in winter and you can't crochet that much and you can't embroider that much ... Are you going to be pushing dust all the time in the house? No! As soon as our work starts holding up in the fall I start to quilt. November. October. When it first snows. We have no other chores in winter, we have just straight grain ... When it's very cold I don't like being out; it's scary. It doesn't matter how good the vehicle is, they freeze when it's cold.

I took several photographs that day of both women's quilts, but it was Frances' I returned to track down the following summer. I found the Mateychuk bungalow, set back from the gravel sideroad on its quarter section (160 acres) of prairie, atop a rise of dry, mown grass (Figure 1). Small red outbuildings, as well as farm implements, dotted the slope in front of the house. But for a straight windbreak of trees behind the house, the site was bare and unlandscaped. Functional, I thought, and revealing nothing of the colour and energy I'd seen in the quilt tops. What I remembered of Frances' quilts was the bold contrast of bright and dark fabrics in most of her pieced tops, and the occasional unexpected colour combination (a border of checked red, blue and yellow surrounded the subtler mauves, browns and white of the central motifs in a Butterfly quilt). The use of fortrel I remembered with alternating repulsion and fascination; it was a fabric I had used to sew clothes for myself two decades ago but which I now found distasteful enough to initially prevent me from buying one of Frances' quilts, despite the appeal of their colours and patterns.

I was not unfamiliar with quilts, having grown up in a Mennonite[5] community where they were made in homes and churches, exchanged as gifts at weddings and births, donated to charities, and passed between generations. I had made several quilts myself and had recently written the text for a book that included, among others, quilts by four generations of women in my family.[6] I remembered few made of fortrel though, as it was the "fancy" quilts, with their fine, even stitching, that these women discussed and displayed in their families and church communities. Informally, from my mother and aunts, I had learned the values of traditional quiltmaking.[7]

What fortrel quilts I could vaguely remember in the Mennonite community were "everyday" ones, composed of large squares of fabric pieced together and tied with yarn through a thick batt to a backing, rather than quilted with thread. These were called "comforters," as they lacked the surface stitching that is, technically, quilting. They were used to add extra warmth in the winter on a bed that was covered with a better everyday quilt, or were donated to charities and overseas relief projects. In the hierarchy of Mennonite quilts, fortrel quilts – comforters – were at the bottom of the pile.

Zonia said she made this spring a quilt from cottons for her cousin or somebody. And she said, "Never again from cottons! I'll stick to my fortrels!" I know some people prefer cotton, but I don't see why. See what makes a difference. With fortrel it doesn't show if you stretch it a bit. Some people, they don't match the corners too carefully, and it shows! I try to do the best I can. And I think these colours [in fortrel] are so much prettier than the cotton ones. Cottons don't give the brightness, you know. And I don't think they would last as long. What's the use of making a quilt and putting it in the cupboard? No use!

Frances Mateychuck's quilts differed from both the fancy and everyday quilts with which I was familiar. Many of her patterns – Double Wedding Ring, Grandmother's Flower Garden, and Log Cabin – involved complex cutting and piecing; Mennonite women used them to make fancy quilts. They took more time and care to construct than the simple, tied fortrel comforters that I recalled. And Frances always quilted, rather than tied, the pieced top to the backing fabric. My attempt to place Frances' quilts into my framework was frustrated further when I examined the backs of her quilts. Frances chose to finish these colourful, bold tops with printed bed sheets that were often marred with the flaws that had designated them "seconds" when she had bought them. The stitching joining this bottom sheet to the pieced top was large and uneven, a factor necessitated, to some extent, by the thickness of fortrel which prevents fine hand sewing. This limitation, I suspected, could explain why fortrel had never become popular among the Mennonite quilters I knew, who valued very fine stitches (as many as fifteen to twenty per inch, in comparison to Frances' three to four per inch) even more than overall design.

When I queried Frances as to whether some of her quilts were fancier than others, or of more importance to her, she responded emphatically, "No! They're all equal. All my quilts are equal. I cherish all of my work." She was aware that some quilters valued fine stitching and that the use of lighter-weight materials would allow her to do more delicate work. However, she expressed no interest in changing to cotton or cotton/polyester fabric, even when I suggested that it might help her quilts to sell.

If I get going I'll start to quilt at eight in the morning, seven in the morning 'til two, three in the morning. I plan in bed my colours! Once I sat 'til three o'clock in the morning trying to figure out this pattern [Attic Fans]. There was a pattern in a book but it did not show how to put it together. Just the picture, and it wasn't very good. So I sat there and my husband says, "Leave it, throw it out and that's that!" In the morning I had it set on the table when he came down.

It's against my religion to sit idle, I tell my husband!

Since learning to quilt thirteen years ago, Frances has made over eighty quilts, all of fortrel; she has no children to whom she can pass them on, so at least forty have been given away to friends and a few to relatives (a niece and her two children). When I first met her, Frances had placed some of her quilts on consignment in a local craft store and had others for sale at Zonia's house on the highway, but she had sold only one. Despite the fact that her quilts seldom sell and she can recover little of the money that she invests in them, Frances continues to produce between five and ten quilts each year.

I was intrigued by this level of creative production. Frances' fortrel quilts reminded me of the diverse forms that quilts can take; they represent a development in quiltmaking that has been given little attention. For socioeconomic and geographic reasons, Frances and her quilts exist at the margins of North American artistic culture, and because they conform to neither traditional nor contemporary, avant-garde standards of quiltmaking, they are marginal even within the subculture of quilters.[8] Yet, rather than representing the decline of quilts from some "authentic" model, Frances' quilts are evidence of a distinct response to the requirements of her time and place and the realities of quiltmaking itself.

I'll sell a quilt for anywheres from a hundred to three hundred dollars. Depending on the pattern, how difficult it is. And I think that's very, very reasonable! Think of all the hours! Really – five hundred hours! It doesn't pay. Just to keep on buying stuff. 'Cause the material costs lots – the backing sheets, the polyester filler, threads – around fifty dollars for a quilt. It costs quite a bit!

How do I support my quilting? From the farm. We have two more quarter sections. But what can you do with grain just two dollars a bushel now?

Frances obtains all the fortrel she uses for piecing her quilt tops free from friends or for minimal cost at second-hand stores and garage sales. While there is currently no shortage of fortrel, for, as Frances notes, "it will last *forever*," she has nearly depleted her own supply (until the clothes she currently wears are relegated to the scrap box) and that of her immediate neighbours. Frances will now travel several hundred miles to pick up boxes of fortrel collected for her by friends who live at some distance. She knows of local quilters who buy new fabric for their quilts and might spend as much as $300 on materials alone, an expense she considers high as well as unnecessary.

Less popular as a material for clothing since the ecological 1980s when natural fibres (cotton, linen, silk, wool) became fashionable, fortrel is still the fabric of choice for those who value practicality over fashion. Among many middle-class, urban people, fortrel now carries the stigma of being out-of-date, non-organic and lower class; its durability and cheap availability in second-hand stores makes it a necessary choice of those with less income. It is seen as tacky, gaudy, and in bad taste – judgments implying that more genuine materials exist elsewhere.

Collectors overlook quilts made of synthetics, positing an authenticity of the past when quilts were made of cotton or wool.[9] Yet historic quilts, like their contemporaries in polyester, simply reflect the availability of fabrics at any given time. The strong hues of Frances' quilts are determined to a large extent by the colours fashionable in the 1960s and 1970s when fortrel fabric was at its height of popularity. Some of Frances' quilts look psychedelic, like the loud, print fabrics of that era (Figure 2).

This is what will sell [Frances points to a "multi-colour" quilt like the one she sold]. This kind of colours – all kinds of colours – matches everything. Quilter's Guild in Saskatoon were telling me that. I'm using scraps that's left over. I don't make a plan. I sew up a row, unless there's two colours too close together, kind of spread them out. You wouldn't want two blacks together ... well ... [holding a completed strip of dark squares against the edge of an incomplete quilt] ... maybe nobody would notice it. If I

Figure 2. A "multi-colour" quilt made entirely of fortrel belts
sewn by Frances into a pattern of her own invention.

*haven't got enough, like in here – for one colour I had to put two colours.
Nobody sees it!*

Even before fortrel was "hard to come by," Frances made use of all
her scraps. In addition to what she calls her "more complicated"
pieced tops (those which make use of quilt patterns obtained from
books or friends), Frances invents "multi-colour" quilts (her term),
specifically to use up the scraps created from cutting out the larger
shapes needed for the pattern-based quilts. The multi-colours consist
of squares or triangles as small as one inch and might be randomly
joined or follow a simple pinwheel or nine-patch pattern of larger
squares. Looking at one, Frances commented, "I really like this one! It's
kind of cluttered and kind of … gets your eyes!" Like most traditional
quilters, her aesthetic is more intuitive than conscious or articulated.

The multi-colours use up the leftover pieces of what was already
scrap fabric, and are priced lower than her "more complicated" quilts.
"The tinier pieces, I don't care … Well sure it takes time, but I don't
throw out pieces." Her pricing reveals that her enjoyment of the
visual effect is subordinated to the value she attaches to the harder-

Figure 3. A Puff quilt composed of over one thousand pockets of fabric, individually filled with polyester.

to-get, large scraps of fabric needed for a more colour-coordinated quilt which might also require more wasteful curved pieces. The extreme thriftiness of the geometric, multi-colour quilts contributes to their lower price. "If you can iron it you can probably use it too," Frances quoted her husband as saying; he is in fact the one who rips open the seams of the old fortrel clothes and irons the pieces flat. Frances has made one quilt entirely of fortrel belts that her husband opened, flattened and cut into shorter lengths ready for her to sew (Figure 2).

Zonia made a Puff quilt in red and black – is that ever beautiful! She made it for her cousin. The lady supplied the materials – she had a red sheet she didn't like. And it's satin! Is it ever beautiful! Red and black and it looked gorgeous!

A Puff quilt is a little square ... you get to pleat as you sew [demonstrating] ... three sides, and you leave one side open and you fill it [with polyester batting]. Last winter we never quilted one because we were doing for our neighbour Puff quilts. Nine Puff quilts. Plus I made some tops. But I never quilted any. A Puff quilt isn't hard like a quilt – the more stitching there is the harder the quilt. A Puff quilt cuddles up around you when you sleep (Figure 3).

Figure 4. An old suitcase, which once served her husband's uncle as a briefcase, now stores Frances' quilting patterns and magazines.

Frances' scrap-bag quilts, composed of hundreds of pieces and organized into many centres, are ideal maps for the social networks they serve to mark. The actual fabric of Frances' quilts may have been [clothing] worn by herself, neighbours, friends, or relatives. She collects patterns for quilts on trips, and from friends who quilt, copied out of their magazines and taken home. Frances stores these items in boxes, closets, an old suitcase ("it was Pete's uncle's, when he was secretary for the church; he took this suitcase around with him"; Figure 4). When she is planning a quilt, magazines and fabric scraps spill across the busy medallions of the basement carpet. Rec room, dining room, living room, all become sites of production. Frances' work as a quilter is nomadic; it does not require its own space but a multitude of spaces. Scholars of women's art have seen in quilts a non-hierarchic assemblage of fragments and suggested a parallel between this and the quality of women's time which, if not oriented toward a career but to a traditional domestic setting, is often fragmented and multi-directional (Dewhurst et al. 1979: 127).

Virginia Woolf suggested that women's art resembles a diary, a desk, a tote-bag (Blau 1985:279). Frances' quilts begin in similar spaces and become, when completed, a record in recycled cloth of the lives of people both known and unknown to her. In a small photo album, Frances keeps pictures of some of the quilts she has given away. There are pictures as well of many of the women she "got started on quilting." Other photos show Frances and her husband and neighbours quilting in their living room; the men, unlike their wives, have their faces turned away from the camera.[10]

The sheer volume of quilts that Frances has made and given away points to their function as more than utilitarian objects. While quilts literally keep people warm, they are layered as well with social and symbolic warmth. Emotional warmth is embodied in the completed quilt, so that it becomes difficult to commodify – to translate the worth of the hand-made object into dollars and cents. Like other products and work associated with women, they have a substantial aspect of "gift labour"; for example, the preaching discussed by Pamela Klassen (this volume) and the healing work considered by Gail Grant (this volume) is also unremunerated. Women are supposed to labour out of love for their families and communities.

Lewis Hyde observes that many traditionally "female" professions in our culture (child care, social work, nursing) "contain a greater admixture of gift labour" than male professions (banking, law, engineering), and do not pay as well (1983:106). The gender inequality in these professions is in part due to the non-quantifiable, emotional, "gift" portion of the labour. Hyde argues for the necessity of gift labour – for keeping aspects of life out of the marketplace, where commodity exchange engenders no corresponding social bond between people – but points out what feminists have long recognized; these labours must become human, not just female, tasks (1983:107). The feeling bond established by gifts can amplify the tension between individualism and community which is particularly acute in our culture, because gifts carry elements of obligation as well as spontaneity. Gifts push us toward community, whether we are eager or reluctant for it.

These are all I gave away [pointing to photos in her album]. Two of these [Diamond Log Cabin] ... I gave this one away [Cornflower], it's gone for a wedding present, two years ago. This one went to Edmonton [Star and Tumbling Blocks]. This one ... I don't even know who has it! ... This one went to Ontario ... I gave this to the neighbour. This one her daughter got ...

Her, I gave maybe six to her. But she knits. I don't knit so she does knitting. This one my niece got, and her two children [got one each]. That's my hairdresser! She cuts my hair all the time so she has to get something! I can't remember who all I gave to! I gave too many away! Some relatives ... but friends are first!

The differences between Frances' and my perceptions and expectations of community became increasingly apparent as my interaction with the Mateychuks entered a second summer. Initially, Frances' comments indicated that she saw me as a prospective buyer, or at least a writer who might bring attention to her work in her community.[11] Since my research activity would not repay her in this manner, I wanted to thank her in practical ways for the hours of time she gave me: I brought her fortrel from Saskatoon second-hand stores, and duplicates of the photographs I took of her quilts; and when my mother and sister were visiting, we went to see Frances' quilts and I was glad when they purchased three of them, leaving Frances with $500. These payments, I felt, helped balance my debt, as *time*, to me, is the most valuable asset, and one I have too little of.

For Frances, however, these exchanges pulled me further into her social network of friends. She would call when her garden was producing too many vegetables, expecting me to drop everything and come to collect my gift. That I had a career, even in the summer, was incomprehensible to her. Once, when I was too busy to make the hour drive (that I knew would include an hour-long visit as well), she was clearly disappointed, but then called in the evening, announcing herself with the question, "What size bag you want for the peas? Two cups or four cups?" Rather than seeing them go to waste, she'd picked, podded, blanched, and frozen the peas for me to pick up later. When I protested her excessive generosity, she dismissed me: "Well, what are friends for, eh?"

The boundary of the group which thinks of itself as one body sharing, if not blood, similar values and lifestyle, usually determines the limit of gift exchange. The gift itself might even function to define and establish this community – Frances' quilts that are given away outline a network of people who, more than likely, share her tastes and values. Although I had not personally acquired a quilt, my family's purchases, and my enjoyment of gathering wild berries with the Mateychuks, pulled me part way into this shared value system. But I did not entirely fit. To Frances, I seemed inexplicably preoccupied with things less important than harvesting food and visiting friends.

An item used in gift exchange with friends can become a commodity when it is exchanged with strangers. Thus my family, like the man travelling from Saskatoon to Winnipeg who stopped at Zonia's farmhouse and bought one of Frances' quilts for his wife, paid the requisite $100 or $200. Because my position is ambiguous, I too exchanged money for a quilt when I finally decided I would like one.

I believe there was a lady inquired ... She's opening a craft store in Saskatoon. She inquired of my sister if I wanted to put quilts in ... I said definitely! Well, I don't use all of them and I enjoy doing it. When I started I wasn't thinking of selling them. I didn't think I'd ever make so many.

And a lady from British Columbia, she appraised this one [Golden Wed-ding Ring] and she said $600. She said her husband bought one for her and he paid $1500. But she said it's not half as nice ... I didn't ask [if it was made of fortrel].

Quilting, a very labour-intensive process, allows its practitioners to meet the needs of their (personal and community) strong work ethic. Yet the fact that it is gift labour – work outside the volatile commodity-exchange system to which the Mateychuks' summer farm work is especially vulnerable in the 1990s – makes quilting leisure activity in their minds, rather than real work. Victor Turner notes that leisure is largely an urban phenomenon where it comple-ments and rewards work. He adds, however, that in rural communi-ties where agriculture has been industrialized (as it was on the prairies in the prosperous 1960s and 1970s), leisure, with its aspects of freedom from ordinary structure and freedom to enter symbolic worlds of diversion and play, has entered as a pleasurable counter-point to a rationalized economy (1977:41–2).

Modern leisure activities, taking place between periods of norma-tive structural behaviour, contain the possibility of experimentation with forms and ideas as well as with social relationships. Hence Frances can spend long hours each winter puzzling over new com-binations of colour and design to make vivid objects that are osten-sibly practical, but more indulgent and pleasurable than most of her other domestic duties. Men can quilt in a leisure time (winter) and space (the home) as they could not if quilting took place in the time and space of their "real work," when they would feel constrained by conventional gender expectations.[12]

Turner identifies the human need for both structure and antistruc-ture as essential for social and psychological well-being, though ill-provided-for in modern culture (1977:46–7). Quilting, a leisure activ-ity that results in a concrete, visible object embodying something of the maker's personality, provides Peter, as well as Frances, with a seasonal break from the routine of his larger, structured existence.

I crochet. And I cross-stitch [from kits]. I like it, but too expensive. And hard on my eyes. For such a small picture and it costs so much to make! When crochet was out for a while, I gave everything away ... I guess I just got tired of it. Then I see all of a sudden everybody putting crochet pieces. So again I went back to crochet! When I want to see something on TV, I can't quilt. So I crochet.

Quilting used to be a tradition years back and then it died off and then it started ... I'd say in the last ten years it started really again, strong. Years back there was no magazines, I don't think so. They used to only make blocks. Actually I never, never saw a quilted quilt until ... I bet you it was about fifteen years ago, north of Prud'homme, at Smiths. A German family, they'd been making them years back.

The volume of quilts that Frances has produced in thirteen years, and the fact that many of them are tops, and thus not yet taken to their final state of completion, suggests that for Frances much of the pleasure lies in the process of piecing rather than in the end product. The use of fortrel is part of this pleasure as she prefers its colours, its durability and the fact that it is easier to sew. When I suggested to Frances that she might be forced to make quilts from cottons if her supply of fortrel dries up, she exclaimed forcefully, "Not in my life-time!" The use of cotton would, for Frances, introduce a degree of anxiety that would reduce, if not end, the pleasure of the activity.[13] Anxiety was present for Frances in the first quilt she made, Jacob's Ladder, of which she is now critical, recalling with a groan, "It was hard! I didn't have the colours. I was just learning to do something." Yet as she gained confidence in quilting, she sought more and more difficult patterns, admitting that she preferred quilting to crochet or embroidery because "it's more challenging."

Yet the rewards Frances receives from quilting are intrinsic rather than extrinsic; her products require an investment of money that is considerable for her, and they seldom sell. That this is less important than her enjoyment of the task is hinted at in the quality of timeless-ness she described as being part of her winter quilting schedule, when she might work a twenty-hour day without complaint. While she explains this as part of her work ethic and response to boredom, these factors cannot alone account for her level of involvement. Frances hints at something of the pleasure she derives from quilting when she explains how she plans her quilts ("That's why I don't sleep at night. I lay in bed and plan my colours.") or works out a challenging pattern ("I sat 'til three o'clock in the morning trying to figure it out."), or when she describes how she would feel if she could no longer quilt ("I'd go haywire!").

Frances relives the enjoyment of the original experience several times each summer as she takes her quilts out of storage to air them on the washline in the front yard. Here, the beauty of her work, as well as the scale and volume of it, unfolds before her, and is strik-ingly visible from the road, adding unexpected vibrancy to the plain farmyard (Figure 1). What was hitherto confined to basement, bed-rooms and chests, moves into a more public space. Looking through her photo album at miniature reproductions of the quilts she has given away, Frances is reminded of the scope of her social commu-nity through time as well as space: her quilts have gone to Alberta, Saskatchewan, Manitoba, and Ontario. These portable objects help minimize the geographic isolation of a rural community which has declined and shifted toward urban centres in recent years.

These are the neighbours who came down and showed me how to quilt thirteen years ago [pointing to a photograph in her album]. That was very nice of them to come out and show me. We had a great time! She likes her drinks! "Pour me a man-size one," she says to my husband!

This one [pointing to another picture], I got her started on quilting. This one too.

How many quilts did I give away? I forget ... But I get a lot of people started on quilting. In the neighbourhood. And farther. They come and I show them.

If I couldn't quilt? God! – I'd go haywire! I love to do it!

The completed quilts, having assembled into themselves materials and ideas from neighbours and more distant friends, radiate out from the Mateychuks' farmhouse, connecting it to other sites. Places, Edward Relph notes, are often distinguished by their quality of "insideness" and are "centres of special importance and meaning" (1976:21–2). Frances' quilts *are* such places, composed of cloth fragments given to her by many people, and the extensive labour of her quiltmaking process. Her gift labour has transformed the fragments so that the finished quilts go out from what is, to others, the peripheral location of her home on a sideroad in rural Saskatchewan, to the various geographic sites that are also places by virtue of the friendships that link them to her farm.

Frances' quilts are traditional objects made of a contemporary fabric that afford her a legacy of permanence, since fortrel "will last forever!"[14] While others might see her location and her choice of material as marginal and of little significance, Frances has few doubts as to the appropriateness of her choices. When discussing her quilts, it is the community of friends[15] who have been involved in her quiltmaking process that she mentions most frequently. To these friends she has given most of her quilts, thereby identifying, while also reinforcing, the boundaries of her social group and actively mitigating the distance of its members.

NOTES

1 The texts of Frances Mateychuk are based on transcriptions of audio- and videotaped interviews I conducted during the summers of 1991 and 1992; I have retained her speech patterns but edited them into thematic units.

2 The concept of dual-tracking, as described by Michael Fischer, stresses the importance of ethnographic listening and experimental writing in

which the author's voice is muted and made marginal to the voice of the other (1986:198–201).

3 This design and colour scheme is unique to Poltava, a central region of the Ukraine. As I was aware of the large Ukrainian population in and around Saskatoon, the stone painted with this pattern immediately signalled "Ukrainian" to me.

4 Fortrel is one of numerous trade names for the synthetic polyester fabrics developed during the 1940s. They became popular for use in clothing in the 1960s and 1970s due to their easy care (they could be machine-washed, needed no ironing, and did not wrinkle) and durability. (Trade names were often substituted for the generic name, polyester, in popular usage.) Frances Mateychuk uses "fortrel" to refer to all the *heavy*weight polyesters with which she makes her pieced quilt tops. "Polyester," technically the generic name, is Frances' term for a *light*weight, crepe polyester which she uses exclusively in making Puff quilts. I will retain Frances' usages and meanings throughout this article.

5 Pamela Klassen's paper, this volume, discusses another aspect of Mennonite culture through her examination of one woman's preaching.

6 I had been commissioned to write the text for *Quilts of Waterloo County: A Sampling* (Shantz and Kaethler 1990) by Marjorie Kaethler, a Mennonite woman who had selected the quilts and was herself an avid quilter. In it I attempted to introduce something of the contexts and meanings quilts have for their makers and users. I provided "genealogies" of quilts (an idea suggested to me by Pauline Greenhill) to clarify the paths they took as they were passed along the generational lines of inheritance so important within the Mennonite community.

7 In her study of traditional quilting groups in southern Indiana, Mary Stevens found these same values to be widespread; large quilting stitches and the use of synthetic and/or mixed fabrics were disdained (1989:16).

8 Frances' fortrel quilts fail to meet either the collector's notions of what constitutes a traditional quilt or current ideas of authenticity promoted by quilt marketing networks. Frances' aesthetic is indigenous and local, not a nostalgic allusion to an ideal type. Quilting publications, workshops, and classes in the 1980s were aimed at middle-class women with some leisure and money, and fed on the nostalgia in popular home decorating for "country" designs. One popular quilter, Jinny Beyer, published books that promoted the use of traditional pieced patterns with special border-print fabrics she designed and copyrighted. Beyer argued that quilts were never really scrap-bag projects and promoted the use of new, 100% cotton, print fabric – only

rarely did she use solid colours (1980). Frances was not aware of this quilt aesthetic, which is antithetical to her own, and when I pointed out facsimiles of these designs in her quilting magazines, she was uninterested. Beyer also encourages quilters to sew the entire quilt by hand (1979), a proposition Frances found ludicrous: "*Who's* going to stitch by hand! I'd be there *forever!*"

9 This belief in an authenticity of the past is popular evidence of anthropology's salvage paradigm, which James Clifford critiques, while also noting its continuing prevalence in many ethnographic and travel accounts that see historical changes in material culture as destructive (1989). See also Doucette (this volume).

10 In an interesting reversal of conventional gendered roles, which suggest that quilting is a female activity, Frances' husband Peter has, in recent years, begun to quilt. First he quilted with the husbands of the women who come to finish the quilts in their living room; later he began to prepare the fabric for Frances by ripping the seams, ironing them flat, and then cutting out the shapes she has marked with a pen. Last winter, he sewed about one-quarter of the twenty thousand Puff squares needed for the nineteen quilts they made for a neighbour. A few years ago, he made a pieced quilt, a simple Maple Leaf pattern in maroon, navy, and black-and-white check fortrel that Frances had selected (colours closer to typical men's clothing than any of her other quilts). When I mentioned to Peter that I had seen his quilt, he flushed and said lamely, "I don't care that much. There's nothing to do in winter ..." Like the men who turned away from the camera in the quilting photograph, Peter was embarrassed to be portrayed to an outsider as a man who does a task so stereotypically feminine. Despite the fact that it relieves his boredom in winter, quilting is represented by both of the Mateychuks as Frances' work. The farm is Peter's.

11 Frances initially thought I was writing for the *Western Producer*, a rural newspaper popular in all three prairie provinces which includes a biweekly supplement, *Western People*, featuring human interest stories. Although it was not my original intention to write a popular article, I would like to do this as one more way to repay Frances for her time.

12 The intermingling of, and conflicts between, gender and work expectations when women enter the conventionally male occupation of taxi driving are discussed by Cynthia Boyd (this volume).

13 Frances' speed in quiltmaking seems a natural extension of her quickness in speech and movement; she jokes that her friends tell her she talks too quickly. When I showed my mother and aunts unedited video footage of Frances and her quilts, they gasped, in good humour, "Lady, slow down!"

14 The eternal function of quilts – as objects by which to be remembered
   – is discussed by Stevens who suggests that, for older quiltmakers,
   this is a quilt's most important role (1989:263).
15 See also Marie-Annick Desplanques' discussion (this volume) of how
   friends maintain group ties through another traditional medium, talk.

Continuité ou rupture : des signes vestimentaires sur la situation des femmes (Québec, vingtième siècle)

JOCELYNE MATHIEU

L'histoire des femmes tente d'expliquer leurs conditions de vie particulières en fonction des grands mouvements sociaux et selon les différentes époques. Elle rend compte de la place que les filles, les épouses et les mères tiennent officiellement dans la société, des rôles qu'on leur attribue et de leur démarche d'affirmation. Mais qu'en est-il de leur image quotidienne et de leur pouvoir sur la continuité ou la rupture des traditions ?[1] Elles apprennent et elles enseignent; elles conservent et elles transmettent; elles créent et elles inspirent. En fait, leur vie quotidienne de femme, d'épouse et de mère les incite à donner un rythme plus ou moins accéléré à la banalité du quotidien.[2] Selon les personnes et les contextes, les femmes freinent le progrès en promouvant la tradition ou le stimulent en bousculant les habitudes.

Sans s'orienter vers l'histoire des femmes proprement dite, force est de reconnaître que l'étude du costume nous en rapproche. Il faut se rappeler l'étymologie commune des termes *costume* et *coutume*, qui renvoient l'un et l'autre à la manière d'être, à l'apparence extérieure, qui traduisent l'état de la personne et sa situation dans la société : « Être en costume, c'est au fond exposer la coutume. »[3] L'anthropologie du vêtement, selon Yves Delaporte,[4] tient compte de divers aspects, tant matériels que sociaux-culturels, qui doivent être mis en rapport pour une interprétation juste du costume. La tradition, ce qui persiste au fil des générations, et la mode, ce qui change périodiquement, s'affrontent inévitablement et ce dans la plupart des cultures.[5] Depuis le dix-neuvième siècle, le phénomène de la mode s'associe largement à la condition féminine; costume, apparence codée[6] et mode, manière de paraître, offrent des indices intéressants sur la condition des femmes et sur leur situation sociale. L'étude du costume peut donc contribuer de manière pertinente à une meilleure connaissance des femmes par l'analyse de leur apparence et de leurs pratiques vestimentaires.[7]

UNE ENQUÊTE DANS LA RÉGION DE CHARLEVOIX : PRÉSENTATION DU TERRAIN[8]

Située à une centaine de kilomètres au nord de la ville de Québec (figure 1), cette région, du nom du jésuite François-Xavier de Charlevoix, considéré comme le premier historien de la Nouvelle-France, se caractérise par son relief montagneux, son activité agricole, la présence du fleuve Saint-Laurent, qui mène à l'entrée du golfe, et ses paysages enchanteurs. La région de Charlevoix couvre un territoire accidenté de 6 000 km². La majestueuse chaîne de montagnes des Laurentides se jette en cascades dans les eaux salées du fleuve. Ce contexte géographique favorise des activités économiques telles que l'agriculture, le cabotage et la coupe du bois. Dans un tel contexte, la population apparaît non seulement très attachée à sa région, mais aussi quelque peu refermée sur elle-même.

Dès le dix-neuvième siècle, Charlevoix devient un lieu de villégiature très important, ce qui a pour effet de modifier peu à peu son profil.[9] Par l'entremise des propriétaires du domaine seigneurial, d'origine écossaise, cette région reçoit des visiteurs de marque dans les manoirs, où l'hébergement s'organise. Région considérée comme traditionnelle et relativement autosuffisante, Charlevoix porte donc une autre sorte de tradition, celle d'accueillir des touristes, surtout américains et européens; dès lors, les influences extérieures modifient quelque peu son visage et introduisent des modes et des façons de faire qui émergent subtilement.

Au moment de l'enquête, la population charlevoisienne s'élevait à 32 000 habitants vivant de la forêt, de l'agriculture et du tourisme. Les informatrices interrogées dans le cadre du projet proviennent des différents milieux et des deux classes d'âge identifiées plus haut (voir note 7). Au total, pour cette enquête précise, dix-sept femmes ont répondu aux questions, soit deux agricultrices, quatre commerçantes, deux professionnelles, cinq travailleuses non spécialisées (ménagères et autres) et quatre travailleuses spécialisées dans le domaine de la mode (couturières, chapelières, …).

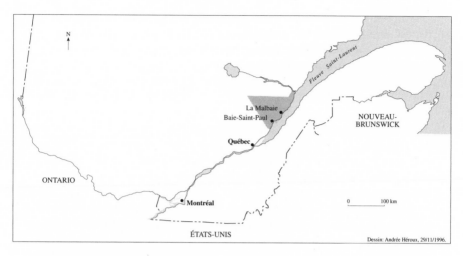

Figure 1. La région de Charlevoix

La région de Charlevoix avait déjà retenu l'attention, entre autres, de Madeleine Doyon qui s'est intéressée à la régionalisation de l'habillement. À la suite d'enquêtes entreprises en 1944, elle publie deux articles dans la collection des Archives de folklore, dont un sur le costume de Charlevoix (1947), et dessine des cartes postales dont elle diffuse la série intitulée «Costumes populaires».[10] Cette recherche et cette diffusion reposaient sur une problématique régionaliste.[11] Mais qu'en est-il vraiment de la place de la tradition et en quoi peut-on reconnaître des signes de mode? Voilà le nouveau questionnement qui a retenu notre attention.

DES VALEURS QUI S'AFFRONTENT

L'enquête a confirmé ce que nous soupçonnions: le milieu social d'appartenance conditionne les réactions impulsées par une éducation traditionaliste et par un environnement perméable aux nouveautés. Cette observation, malgré sa prime évidence, s'appuie sur le discours des informateurs qui apportent des nuances intéressantes quant au rapport entre les valeurs inculquées depuis leur enfance et la pression sociale qui s'exerce sur les individus au fur et à mesure des changements de situation qu'ils connaissent au cours de leur vie. Ainsi, certaines personnes, plus spécialement des femmes, adapteront leur comportement aux prescriptions véhiculées dans les médias et agiront par conséquent sur leur entourage du moment.[12]

L'on peut prétendre que l'aisance financière favorise la consommation de biens à la mode; pourtant ce n'est pas un facteur infaillible. Dans un milieu rural comme celui de Charlevoix, l'aisance matérielle que peut procurer, par exemple, la tenue d'un magasin général, n'est pas garante de changements de comportements liés, entre autres, à l'apparence physique. L'esprit conservateur qui caractérise la famille se trouvant dans cette situation a plutôt eu raison des modes proposées, et cela jusqu'aux années 1960. Nous avions déjà perçu ce phénomène dans le cadre d'une étude portant sur les intérieurs domestiques, alors que l'accumulation de richesses avait d'abord pour objet un patrimoine à transmettre, de préférence à des biens éphémères et apparents.[13]

Bien sûr, dignité oblige. Les épouses de professionnels, comme les épouses de médecins ou d'avocats, se révèlent des modèles sociaux par leur attitude et leur façon d'assumer leur rang. Empreintes des conventions qui leur sont imposées, elles affichent un style que l'on qualifie de classique au sens, agréé par le dictionnaire, de «faisant autorité» et «qui mérite d'être imité». Ces dames s'habillent donc de costumes-tailleurs, de toilettes sobres et élégantes par leur simplicité et leur harmonie, en somme, sans aucune extravagance. Leurs fantaisies se résument à quelques adaptations graduelles des lignes de leurs vêtements, en accord avec l'évolution générale des silhouettes. L'ingéniosité de certaines d'entre elles les amènera à imiter l'allure urbaine, synonyme de modernité. Ainsi en est-il de cette ménagère de l'Île aux Coudres, mariée à un médecin et qui, durant les années 1950, roulait des feuilles de papier journal pour former un cercle rigide qu'elle fixait au bas de son jupon en taffetas, en s'inspirant des modèles proposés par le couturier français Christian Dior, qui avait remis à l'honneur l'amplitude des jupes. Elle suggérait ainsi l'adoption d'une mode diffusée alors dans les catalogues commerciaux.

L'importance de ces catalogues est primordiale. Les plus connus, les catalogues des magasins Eaton, Simpson's et Dupuis, ont inspiré nombre d'informatrices, de tous les milieux. Plusieurs ont dessiné des patrons à partir des modèles présentés ou ont modifié certains de leurs vêtements dans un esprit de mise à jour. De plus, ces catalogues ont bien sûr favorisé l'achat de prêt-à-porter, particulièrement en région, où le magasinage ne s'est vraiment intégré au genre de vie qu'avec l'arrivée, à partir des années 1960, des centres commerciaux. L'abandon graduel de la confection domestique a ainsi marqué l'avènement de la modernité dans la vie quotidienne. Un certain décalage caractérise donc les expressions de mode en milieu rural car, il faut bien le reconnaître, les modes passent d'abord par la ville où l'accès plus facile et la variété d'interprétation plus grande, voire presque illimitée, exorcisent les marginalités soudaines et passagères.

Signe d'une certaine désobéissance aux règles établies par la majorité, ces marginalités vont à l'encontre des principes de sobriété et d'économie qui caractérisent les sociétés traditionnelles occidentales. Ne pas paraître son âge et exprimer une ambiguïté quant à son sexe ou à son statut social posent un problème de communication aux collectivités, qui ne savent plus qui elles comptent dans leurs rangs. Le savoir-vivre transmis dans la famille, puis à l'école, impose la modestie et condamne le gaspillage. C'est ce que nous ont révélé unanimement nos informateurs.

Certains événements offrent l'occasion d'affirmer l'adhésion à ces principes, en l'occurrence les offices du dimanche, les visites officielles, dans la parenté, chez des amis ou des connaissances, les noces et les funérailles. Dans ces moments, l'assimilation des codes est particulièrement jaugée par les collatéraux. L'expression individuelle des goûts et des idées est davantage tolérée lors des sorties de divertissement hors des cadres coutumiers, particulièrement dans le cas de la jeunesse. La liberté associée à cette période de la vie nourrit la quête de modernité. C'est l'affrontement, jugé normal, des générations, des anciens et des jouvenceaux.

Un vêtement a particulièrement marqué le changement d'apparence et annoncé le bouleversement des mentalités : le pantalon. Il va sans dire que ce pantalon, déjà revendiqué par les hommes qui s'y sont identifiés et y ont accroché leur pouvoir, traduit la révolution des mœurs qui ouvre la voie, non sans effort, à une certaine égalité des sexes. La silhouette féminine change donc; elle emprunte le longiligne et la commodité du pantalon pour affirmer un autre statut qui permet d'accéder à l'autorité, à l'autonomie et à l'indépendance, au confort dans la liberté de mouvement, au quotidien, pour le sport ou la détente.

Dans les milieux que nous avons étudiés de plus près, les réseaux de parenté ont joué un rôle catalyseur. L'influence des tantes se dégage de plusieurs entrevues auprès de nos informatrices. Célibataires, actives sur le marché du travail ou domiciliées aux États-Unis, elles ont apporté lors de leurs visites les nouveautés américaines ou même européennes qui passaient par chez nos voisins du sud. Plusieurs, affichant leur émancipation, ont ainsi procuré à leurs nièces l'occasion de les imiter et de se convertir à un autre style de vie. Ces tantes ne faisaient alors que renforcer les messages émis par les nombreux touristes qui transformaient le paysage humain des Charlevoisiennes.

Les considérations qui se sont révélées dans les discours recueillis au sujet de la mode nous ramènent à certains aspects abordés par Roland Barthes dans son *Système de la mode* (1967).[14] La « production du sens », soumise à ce qu'il a appelé une « liberté surveillée », correspond à l'interprétation des informatrices de ce qui leur était permis ou défendu. Celles-ci livrent alors comme message que les vêtements qu'elles ont portés concrétisaient à la fois leur propre perception de la mode diffusée, par l'écrit comme par l'image, et la perception des autres membres de la collectivité à laquelle elles appartenaient, qui sanctionnent ou réfutent le rôle social qu'elles affichent.

L'analyse des discours recueillis en enquête a tout de même fait ressortir que, d'une génération à l'autre, il y a des indices qui démontrent soit une persistance, soit une remise en question des valeurs. Cela se perçoit dans le costume quant au choix des éléments qui le composent et à la façon de les porter, de même qu'à leur fabrication et à leur transmission.

LA TRANSFORMATION DE L'IMAGE QUOTIDIENNE : LE COSTUME DES ADULTES

En dehors des rites de passage, comment s'exprime l'importance de la tradition? Quelle place occupe la mode? À l'âge adulte, deux types de vêtements composent la garde-robe : ceux de la semaine, pour le travail, et ceux du dimanche et des fêtes. Notre enquête mettant davantage en évidence les pratiques des années 1920 à 1970, d'autres types de vêtements, reliés aux activités de loisirs, aux sports et à la détente, n'y figurent pas, puisqu'ils ne font pas encore partie de la garde-robe courante de la majorité de nos informateurs. Il serait sûrement intéressant d'analyser le costume dans cette autre perspective d'organisation du temps et des activités qui marquera l'âge d'or du prêt-à-porter, ce qui ne faisait pas partie de notre problématique initiale.

La génération des 60 ans et plus a appris de façon générale à faire des différences, à distinguer le rare du commun, le fin du grossier, le spécial de l'ordinaire. La vie traditionnelle était pondérée dans le temps, dans l'espace et par rapport aux circonstances. Entre autres, le dimanche tranchait sur la semaine, les sorties imposaient leurs exigences, les occasions se démarquaient chacune par leur décorum. Tout semblait prédéterminé : chacun devait garder sa place, jouer son rôle. L'âge, le sexe, l'occupation, l'origine définissaient des profils en marquant des limites.

Presque toutes les femmes de cette génération savaient coudre. Elles l'avaient appris à l'école des religieuses et s'étaient exercées sous l'œil attentif de la mère ou de la grand-mère. D'abord souvent pour elles-mêmes, puis pour leurs enfants et parfois pour leurs frères, leurs sœurs ou leurs maris, elles cousent, pour suivre l'ordre des choses, par nécessité ou par simple esprit d'économie. À la couture s'ajoutent d'autres techniques comme le tissage, la broderie ou la dentelle. Même lorsqu'elles bénéficient de meilleurs moyens financiers, plusieurs femmes de cette génération continuent à exercer les talents qui les valorisent. Avec le temps, cependant, elles ajustent leurs valeurs à celle de la collectivité, passant graduellement d'une société traditionnelle à une société de consommation.

Dans les familles charlevoisiennes, la mère faisait tout, confectionnant les vêtements de semaine ou quelques toilettes spéciales. Généralement, celle qui faisait tout répondait à la nécessité et celle qui ne cousait que des pièces spéciales exprimait surtout son goût du particulier et de l'original. Savoir coudre, tisser, broder n'était pas qu'affaire de sous. La compétence de bien vêtir la famille, en tout temps et pour tous les âges, caractérisait le profil de la femme modèle. Partie intégrante de l'éducation des filles, l'apprentissage du fait-main était normal. La fierté liée au savoir-faire prévalait souvent sur l'esprit d'épargne.

Bien que les changements de l'économie aient joué un rôle important dans le choix des activités des femmes, l'évolution du statut social exerça une influence encore plus grande. La transformation progressive du profil féminin, du modèle traditionnel en milieu domestique au modèle plus moderne de celle qui travaille à l'extérieur du foyer, a incité les femmes à délaisser des pratiques valorisées au sein de la famille et de l'environnement immédiat au profit du système de consommation envahissant. Alors que la couture avait fait partie de la vie quotidienne des femmes âgées de plus de 60 ans au moment de l'enquête, elle devient de plus en plus facultative dans le cas des femmes plus jeunes. La confection domestique est réduite graduellement à l'ordinaire par rapport aux achats plus spectaculaires. Les catalogues de grands magasins (Eaton, Simpson's, Dupuis) ont pris la place de la ménagère, en fournissant des vêtements de travail à prix abordable et la montée des boutiques spécialisées a catalysé les goûts plus dispendieux.

Cette accessibilité des grands marchés dont les produits pénètrent dans tous les foyers du Québec estompe plusieurs différences entre les classes. Le fait-main devient pendant une période – depuis la Deuxième Guerre mondiale jusqu'aux années 1970 – un palliatif pour les personnes à revenus plus modestes. Le prêt-à-porter, pour sa part, apparaît comme la marque d'un certain « standing » et ce, malgré une sensible nostalgie de la couture, dont plusieurs ont gardé le goût. Il faut noter que l'esprit d'économie, inculqué aux femmes dès leur jeune âge, demeure perceptible dans la façon d'acheter les vêtements. On les choisit « classiques » pour suivre une mode durable. Seules quelques fantaisies attestent de la créativité du moment et permettent une expression personnalisée : dentelle et broderies peuvent alors y retrouver leur place.

La mode dite classique, c'est-à-dire sobre et sans excès dans la coupe, le tissu ou le décor, offre une autre garantie : elle permet de s'habiller modestement et d'avoir l'air digne. Ainsi, même en adoptant des vêtements proposés on répète un modèle traditionnel. Plusieurs informatrices l'ont signalé : leurs filles ne portent plus les mêmes vêtements, mais les mêmes principes de lignes et d'agencement régissent toujours leur habillement.

L'augmentation des biens de consommation a, par corrélation, dévalorisé tout le phénomène de la récupération. On ne conserve plus les vêtements usagés, ni pour les donner à l'intérieur de la famille, ni pour les transformer ou en faire de plus petits pour les enfants, encore moins pour fabriquer des pièces d'art domestique ou d'artisanat. Seul le comptoir communautaire, anonyme, en bénéficie.

Durant les années 1950 et 1960, après les privations dues à la crise économique et à la guerre, on essaie d'oublier les tapis crochetés, les nappes brodées et la courtepointe, souvent symboles de vie difficile. Et puis, c'est anti-moderne. Les prix du marché étant abordables, on ne voit plus l'avantage de coudre des vêtements d'enfants dans ceux des grands : cela demande trop de travail et renvoie à un système économique d'autosuffisance qui ne prévaut plus que dans certains milieux considérés comme plus défavorisés en raison de leur éloignement et de leurs occupations de subsistance. La fabrication domestique gêne. Les Charlevoisiens qui côtoient les villégiateurs sont de plus touchés par leurs modes. Il faudra attendre les années 1970 pour voir réapparaître toute la production du fait-main. Mais l'esprit avait déjà bien changé.

UN FAIBLE INTÉRÊT
POUR LES TRADITIONS ?
L'EXEMPLE DU TROUSSEAU DE BAPTÊME

On reconnaît habituellement le costume de baptême comme un des ensembles vestimentaires les plus traditionnels parce qu'il est relié à un rite de passage initial. La recherche nous apprend que son

Figure 2

importance est pourtant relative. Seulement la moitié des personnes interrogées savent ce qu'est devenu le trousseau. L'aspect précieux de l'ensemble n'est donc pas évident et le phénomène de transmission perd son caractère traditionnel. Treize personnes connaissaient l'origine de leur trousseau : six trousseaux ont été achetés par la jeune mère, quatre confectionnés par cette dernière et trois fabriqués par la grand-mère. Après avoir servi quelques fois, au fil des besoins dans la parenté, les pièces du trousseau sont dispersées puis disparaissent à cause de l'usure ou, souvent, par manque d'intérêt.

L'évolution des mœurs et des pratiques religieuses a fait en sorte que le baptême est de moins en moins administré aux plus jeunes générations. De plus, les bébés étant généralement baptisés à un âge plus avancé, ils sont plus gros, lors de leur baptême, que les bébés d'autrefois; c'est pourquoi plusieurs n'ont pu revêtir le trousseau familial. Dix informatrices âgées de plus de 60 ans avaient maintenu la tradition, contre seulement quatre de la classe d'âge précédente. Parmi les plus jeunes, ce sont les femmes issues de familles où l'on cousait, tissait ou faisait le commerce des tissus qui ont perpétué cette tradition. C'est encore dans de tels milieux que l'on peut observer une fragile continuité.

La fabrication domestique du trousseau de baptême était l'apanage d'une femme très proche, le plus souvent de la parenté, une grand-mère ou une tante, par exemple; d'ailleurs, le trousseau était souvent un présent de circonstance. La plupart des trousseaux contemporains sont en soie ou en lainage de couleur naturelle. Ils se composent encore de cinq pièces principales : un bonnet, un jupon, une robe, un manteau à collerette et un châle, sans compter les pattes (figure 2). L'ensemble est souvent brodé, orné de dentelles ou de points de nid d'abeille, ce qui rehausse sa valeur et met en évidence les habiletés des artisanes. À l'instar de la robe de mariée, plus la robe est longue et traînante, plus le cérémonial apparaît insistant.

Après la Deuxième Guerre mondiale, l'habitude d'acheter le trousseau se répand : l'aisance financière s'accroît, on ne valorise plus le travail manuel – surtout en milieu domestique – et le goût pour le « fait par soi-même. » La période du « baby-boom » favorise le fait que chaque petite famille possède son propre trousseau de baptême, qu'elle ne transmettra pas nécessairement à la génération qui procréera plus tard dans un cadre socio-religieux renouvelé et laïcisé. Dans ce contexte, l'enquête révèle que seulement sept trousseaux ont été conservés et que huit ont été déclarés perdus. Les collections muséales, les boutiques d'antiquaires et même les marchés aux puces ont hérité de plusieurs de ces biens familiaux abandonnés et cela même si certaines parties manquent, le châle ou le jupon par exemple, les deux pièces les mieux conservées étant la robe et le bonnet.

Si le trousseau traditionnel se caractérisait entre autres par sa fabrication domestique, on peut déjà affirmer que cet ensemble vestimentaire ne témoigne plus de l'habileté et de l'intérêt des femmes de 40 à 60 ans qui se laisseront tenter par les articles mis en valeur dans le commerce (pyjama pour les garçons et robe de toilette pour les filles). Quand les femmes se désintéressent des traditions, celles-ci risquent de disparaître ou subissent des modifications majeures, selon les choix de ces femmes face à la modernité. On pourrait démontrer le même phénomène avec le costume de mariée et l'habillement de deuil. Les prescriptions sociales, de moins en moins contraignantes, laissent s'exprimer les humeurs individuelles. Cela fait partie de la libération, ou du moins de son apparence.

UNE DYNAMIQUE ENTRE LA TRADITION ET L'INNOVATION

Autrefois nécessité et signe de bonne éducation, le savoir-faire des filles et des femmes est devenu loisir. L'école et la famille ne sont plus complices pour former des « ménagères dépareillées », puisque le contexte ne s'y prête plus. Jusqu'aux années 1960, les jeunes filles étaient surtout formées dans les écoles normales et ménagères;[15] elles devaient y acquérir toutes les techniques essentielles pour répondre aux exigences familiales. Depuis, ces écoles sont disparues et les filles ont accédé à une formation professionnelle qui ne met plus nécessairement en valeur leur rôle traditionnel.

L'enquête nous apprend qu'il faut nuancer notre perception des deux genres de vie. D'une part, dans un contexte traditionnel d'auto-suffisance relative, on ne cousait pas que par nécessité; d'autre part, dans un contexte de consommation, on revient à la couture par éco-nomie, mais aussi pour exprimer son originalité. Dans les deux cas, même s'il y a nécessité, l'imagination tient une place importante. L'économie oriente toujours les choix mais, bien qu'importante, elle n'est pas la seule variable contextuelle.

Les filles apprenaient à se distinguer dans une société tradition-nelle où leurs qualités d'âme devaient transparaître et se traduire par une allure digne, de la modestie, de la finesse et du savoir-faire, en somme par un savoir-être traditionnel. Après la Deuxième Guerre mondiale, quelques révolutions s'étaient opérées : un marché du tra-vail de plus en plus ouvert, une mode se voulant de plus en plus libératrice du corps[16] et une économie de consommation envahis-sante. Il devient moins nécessaire de savoir faire puisqu'on peut tout acheter, mais la satisfaction d'ajouter quelque chose de particulier demeure.

Le costume trahit l'histoire des femmes, leur place dans la société et le rôle qu'on leur attribue. Par leur habillement et leurs manières d'être, les femmes révèlent non seulement leur degré de liberté, mais aussi l'état d'esprit de la société dans laquelle elles évoluent.

L'image de la Québécoise traditionnelle, attachée au passé et à ses valeurs, n'est plus évidente. Cette femme, gardienne de la famille et du foyer, apparaît de plus en plus comme une création des pouvoirs politiques et religieux, inquiets devant l'explosion d'une société moderne et post-moderne. Bien sûr, bon nombre de femmes ont été soumises à ces pouvoirs et ont occupé le rang qu'on leur assignait, mais la profondeur de leur engagement laisse sceptique. L'étude du costume nous a entre autres révélé que l'intérêt pour la perpétuation d'un modèle traditionnel largement diffusé est beaucoup moindre que ce que la littérature et le cinéma nous ont laissé croire. La Québécoise serait-elle rebelle?

NOTES

1 On a abordé l'histoire des femmes de diverses façons; avec le recul, les spécialistes reconnaissent l'apport intéressant de l'histoire orale. À ce sujet, Denyse Baillargeon a récemment publié une synthèse historiographique (1993). Notons l'étude de Denise Lemieux et Lucie Mercier (1989) et celui d'Alison Prentice et al. (1988). Il ne faut évidemment pas oublier l'ouvrage magistral dirigé par Georges Duby et Michelle Perrot (1991).

2 Voir le texte de Marie Annick Desplanques, à propos de l'organisation du quotidien des femmes à Cape St George (Terre-Neuve).

3 Jean Cuisenier résume ainsi le rapport direct entre ces deux termes et leur signification dans l'introduction de l'imposant catalogue d'exposition *Costume, coutume* publié lors du cinquantenaire du Musée national des arts et traditions populaires, à Paris (1987). Plusieurs autres auteurs ont tenu un langage semblable, comme par exemple Yvonne Deslandres (1976), et, plus récemment, Maguelonne Toussaint-Samat (1990). Je me permets de rappeler aussi l'article que j'avais publié dans le numéro spécial de la revue *Canadian Folklore canadien* portant sur le costume (Mathieu 1988).

4 Yves Delaporte collabore à un groupe de travail du Musée de l'Homme à Paris. À deux reprises (1979 et 1984), les chercheurs de cette équipe ont publié des actes de colloque faisant état de travaux sur l'anthropologie du vêtement.

5 Denise Pop (1984), Tatiana Benfoughal (1984), et Nina Abramtchik et Éliane Dorst (1984) ont entre autres traité particulièrement de ce sujet. Pour sa part, André Leroi-Gourhan avait déjà affirmé que «tous les peuples, pour peu qu'on les ait suivis pendant un demi-siècle, accusent des variations considérables... Le vêtement est donc en perpétuelle transformation» ([1945] 1973:199–200).

6 Si J.C. Flügel publie dès 1930 *Psychology of clothes*, ce n'est qu'à la fin des années 1960 que Roland Barthes s'attaque au *Système de la mode* (1967). L'étude du costume a alors été influencée par la sémiologie. Depuis, plusieurs chercheurs se sont inspirés de ce type d'analyse pour essayer d'expliquer le phénomène vestimentaire. L'étude de l'apparence, comme système de codes, en a par la suite préoccupé

plus d'un. Notons entre autres les ouvrages de Marylène Delbourg-Delphis (1981), de Philippe Perrot (1984), et de Marie-Thérèse Duflos-Priot (1987).

7 À titre d'exemple, nous présenterons ici quelques résultats d'une recherche effectuée dans le cadre d'un projet subventionné par le C.R.S.H., «L'influence de la mode sur le costume québécois». Pour répondre aux objectifs qui sont d'étudier le rapport entre la tradition et la modernité, nous avons interrogé des hommes et des femmes sur leur perception du costume, sur la place de la tradition et sur le rôle de la mode. Deux générations (40–60 ans et plus de 60 ans) livrent leur position face à cette dynamique mode-tradition, en milieu rural et urbain.

8 Pour illustrer ce propos, nous ferons état d'une enquête effectuée dans le cadre du projet mentionné plus haut, dans la région de Charlevoix, au Québec, durant l'été 1991. Cette enquête a été réalisée par Christiane Noël, que je remercie.

9 Philippe Dubé l'a démontré dans son ouvrage *Deux cents ans de villégiature dans Charlevoix* (1986).

10 Pierre Lessard présente les quatre cartes illustrant des costumes de la Beauce et de Charlevoix, dans «Costume populaire sur cartes postales» (1988).

11 La problématique du régionalisme a fait l'objet d'un séminaire dont les travaux ont été publiés dans *La région culturelle: problématique interdisciplinaire* (Harvey 1994). Dans mon article qui portait sur «La région: un terrain ou un concept? Approche ethnologique» (1994:97–110), j'ai discuté de la notion de région et de l'utilisation qu'on en a faite au fil des ans et des recherches.

12 J'ai déjà abordé les facteurs d'influence des comportements, concernant entre autres la notion de perméabilité, dans mon article intitulé «Au sujet des rapports entre le costume traditionnel et la mode. Le cas du costume canadien» (1988).

13 L'étude comparative que j'ai déjà menée sur «Les intérieurs domestiques comparés Perche-Québec, XVIIe-XVIIIe siècles» soulève entre autres cette question. À l'instar de James F. Deetz (1978), j'ai observé que selon les milieux de vie qui conditionnent les mentalités, la richesse, très relative, n'est pas nécessairement apparente, compte tenu des valeurs du groupe.

14 Particulièrement p. 14, 1.2 Le vêtement réel, p. 32, 2.3 Classes commutatives: le vêtement et la mode, et p. 168, 11, Le système, 1 Le sens, liberté surveillée.

15 Voir l'ouvrage de Nicole Thivierge (1982).

16 Suzanne Marchand a présenté un mémoire de maîtrise intitulé: «Le culte du corps ou le culte de l'âme: mode féminine et société québécoise au cours de la période 1920–1939» (1989). Ce mémoire fait ressortir la

quête de libération du corps alliée à celle du rôle social. Si les contraintes physiques s'amenuisent dans l'allure vestimentaire, la « nouvelle liberté » ouvre la voie à un autre type d'exigences envers les femmes, celui, plus subtil, de la construction d'un modèle empreint de modernisme. Suzanne Marchand poursuit son doctorat sur les représentations collectives du corps féminin et du corps masculin (Québec 1920–1990).

Miracle Lore and
Metamorphoses

GAIL PATON GRANT

This study addresses the ongoing production and reproduction of "miracle lore" – traditional narratives and beliefs – by the communicants of a religious healing group, the International Order of St Luke the Healer (OSL),[1] in a small Ontario city a decade ago. The viability of this folk therapy is maintained by female healers who constantly replenish their lore by incorporating personal experience narratives validating the legends of healing – which in turn shape the experiences of bodily change.

The lay members of this Order were predominantly white,[2] middle-class, middle-aged full-time wives and mothers, who supported the teachings and structure of the traditional, patriarchal Church. I incorporate both their voices and my own readings into this interpretation.[3] The male Archdeacon's role was quite separate from that of the female lay members; he maintained proper Anglican decorum and lay subordination. This priestly-laity distinction was concretely established and represented by the healing activities; only the priest was privileged to anoint with oil and proffer the Eucharist. A female physician acted as gatekeeper,[4] mediating between sacred and secular therapies. Thus, healing activities were gendered.

The OSL was founded by American Episcopalians in 1948.[5] Unlike most such ministries, it rejects neither mainline religion nor mainline medicine. Its healing activities are undertaken within mainstream denominations (Anglican, Lutheran, United) in conjunction with allopathic (conventional) medical practices. The ministry has one stated fundamental purpose: to revitalize the charism of healing within the Christian Church. Thus, OSL members are different from charismatics or neo-pentecostals, who seek the blessing of all of the gifts of the spirit described in I Corinthians 12.[6] This distinction, however, was often blurred in practice. For example, OSL healers sometimes practised glossolalia or "tongue prayer," though the Archdeacon officially disapproved of and discouraged this behaviour. The women's covert continuation of tongue prayer demonstrates both their resistance to formal constraints and their sense of ownership of their healing practices.[7]

Folk or faith healing is most apt to be employed when a condition reveals the limits of allopathic medical knowledge and/or is recalcitrant to conventional ("scientific") therapies. But OSL members perceive religious therapy and biomedical treatment as complementary rather than contradictory. Practitioners of scientific medicine are God's agents; thus, biomedical care is sought when needed. Though necessary, it is not sufficient; spiritual healing is their initial and ongoing form of therapy, and members express both sacramental and bioscientific phenomena in religious idioms. Subjective healing is primary in their religious discourse, in contrast to the objective curing emphasised in medical discourse.

The OSL meets monthly for a formal healing service, but members are firmly convinced that ongoing faith and divine presence are essential. Healing and prayers are offered daily for supplicants who have requested them for themselves or others. Spiritual healing is mandated by James 5:13–16, which begins "Is any among you suffering? Let him[8] pray," and continues: "Is any among you sick? Let him call for the elders of the church, and let them pray over him, anointing him with oil in the name of the Lord; and the prayer of faithful will save the sick man, and the Lord will raise him up; and if he has committed sins, he will be forgiven. Therefore confess your sins to one another, that you may be healed. The prayer of a righteous man has great power in its effects." OSL members adhere to this charter. For the most part, healing is undertaken in conjunction with the Eucharist – communion. Prayers and the laying on of hands are offered by priests and full members of the OSL. The majority of those who act as healers are women (about 80 per cent of the group with which I did my fieldwork); the typical imbalance of women over men seeking and practising religious healing obtains here.

As in any medical system, a most important dimension of this therapy is *conviction*. The power of belief and positive expectations to influence treatment success has been extensively documented. "Faith ... may be healing in itself" (Frank 1974:137).[9] Bioscientific practitioners attribute the psychological and physiological effects of spiritual healing to the production of endorphins – endogenous neu-rochemicals which generate tranquillity, euphoria, and analgesia (pain relief) – rather than to divine intervention. Most are also con-vinced that their allopathic remedies will work regardless of the patient's belief in them. OSL members' belief in Christian healing, however – the firmly held belief that God heals and that the laying on of hands and the prayers of the righteous do indeed have great effects – cannot be divorced from the convictions that underlie their rituals, which are strengthened and sustained by the legends which evoke the experienced metamorphoses.

The miracle lore members of the OSL produce and, most impor-tantly, disseminate underlies and validates this healing modality's efficacy. The stories generate, enhance, and strengthen the expectant trust that adherents-petitioners bring to the healing ritual; they pro-vide the rationale for conversion; and, finally, they sustain and rein-force a convert's conviction. "To have a conversion experience is nothing much. The real thing is to be able to keep on taking it seri-ously: to retain a sense of its plausibility" (Berger and Luckmann 1967:168). Miracle lore plays a central and critical role in generating and maintaining belief, sustaining plausibility, and thereby perpetu-ating, justifying, and legitimizing spiritual therapy. The gospel of Mark (9:23) reminds the members that "all things are possible to him who believes." Thus, the secular psychosomatic model – that convic-tion mediates between a sufferer's subjective experiences of illness and of healing efficacy – is assimilated and subsumed to the religious model – that one *can* or *will* be healed by human petition and touch, confirmed and endorsed by God. This endorsement is essential for therapeutic success.

The act of healing itself, conventionally sequestered within the eucharist at the Healing Love Conference – and thus within space designated "sacred" – is the ritualized expression of belief, the enact-ment of conviction. Here the focus on religious healing transforms the conventional eucharist service into a ritual of affliction or cura-tive rite (cf. Turner 1969). Participants are in a state of liminality, that ambiguous "betwixt and between" which, at its most effective, its most potent, is characterized by *communitas*, the somewhat mystical *esprit de corps* which transcends mundane human intercourse (includ-ing everyday communion) and creates a sense of almost palpable community and well-being. The social component of spiritual heal-ing is the experience of "total, unmediated relationships" that cele-brates both uniqueness and connectedness (Turner 1974:274), and marks the participants' personal and joint encounter with the sacred. The recurring experience of *communitas* may have profound healing properties. These are understood by OSL members as self-help with God's help, and validate their medicoreligious epistemology that assures them that God heals.

The healing rite is a symbolic enactment of the "healing love" which is the OSL's root paradigm or motif. The monthly homily often concerned the release of love through remission, confession, and forgiveness of sin. OSL activities are suffused with the conviction and experience of love's healing properties, reflecting what is often seen as a distinctively female focus on the power of affect and relationships, on nurturance and caring. This all-encompassing love is consciously expressed in practitioners' words and actions. These women both revere and sanctify as divine love the traditional female virtues of nurturance and selflessness.[10] Their expression of profound caring enhances the experience of *communitas*.

The efficacy of this healing modality depends largely on the miracle lore. The curative rite itself is a source of narrative material, but stories are created and disseminated by the women who act as healers. They give voice and substance to the healing lore by transforming personal experience narratives into legends of miracles. This documentary healing lore is continuously expanded, adjusted, and conveyed to OSL members and potential members. It recounts *specific* experiences of illness and affliction, but these accounts are soon converted into generic, universal stories and thus become *modes* of healing. One woman insisted:

I've seen healings. They're not figments of the imagination, they're all recorded medically. My daughter has multiple sclerosis [a chronic, debilitating condition characterized by remissions and exacerbations] and God has healed her with each recurrence for the past ten years. My sister had two brain tumours and she has survived for twenty-seven years because there were prayers all across the United States for her. My sister-in-law had terminal cancer of the breast and that was thirty-two years ago, she is still alive through prayer. My first husband was dead for one and one-half hours and the Lord told me what to do [left unexplained] and he revived and lived six more months. He had had a fantastic experience with the Lord. God told me it was for real when he died later and there was peace in the room. I've seen healings.

Another stated: "I saw one girl healed of migraines just like that!" [snap of fingers]. Through their narratives, the members' experiences are forwarded as circumstantial evidence, both confirming and enlarging the corpus of legends.

The female members of the osl are its linchpins. The central actors in the healing rite, they propagate the miracle lore. Although they have little formal control over the International osl's medicoreligious bureaucracy, they feel empowered by their involvement in healing within their chapters. The osl chapter I worked with was initiated through the women's efforts and is perpetuated through their healing and narrating. Yet the women (including the female physician) deny personal power. Avowing human impotence, they refer to themselves as channels, conduits, or instruments of divine healing: "We don't do the healing, it's the Spirit who uses us, we are a channel"; "It's God's work, we're only pawns, willing pawns"; "It comes from God, God can heal anyone ... and he can let it happen through the laying on of hands." Just as the osl women attributed healing to divine agency, so women preachers define themselves as "the mouthpiece of God" (Lawless 1988a:93) or "handmaidens of the Lord" (Lawless 1988b). Like osl members, they may deny agency by demurring, "I just think it was God doing through me" (see Klassen, this volume).

Miracle lore is unfalsifiable. Failure – an apparent lack of response to therapy – need not be interpreted as therapeutic ineffectiveness. It could result from human fallibility, either technical (improper ministration or administration), cognitive (lack of conviction and/or faulty understanding), or moral (unchristian conduct which indicates the need for profession of faith or conversion by the petitioner before healing can be experienced). These explanations demonstrate the safety clauses vital for sustaining an alternative belief system in the face of a dominant ideology.

Supplicants generally approached the osl for healing in crisis situations; if their needs were satisfied, they might become committed members (a typical mode of recruitment). Among the osl membership, religion was the primary mode for negotiating everyday life as well as for crisis management; they related to the world by framing human experience within a superhuman context. As Rieti (in this book) has observed, "supernatural" belief can provide an explanation for adversity, and magical behaviour a course of action.

Lore was transmitted and enlarged through ritual expressions of affirmation or "sharing": witnessing, giving testimony, or praising God for favours (miracles) received. Sharing functions to symbolically express, reinforce, and validate conviction: all experiences are interpreted from the perspective of *belief*, informed by doctrine, but re-framed and articulated with real-life experience. Sharing takes place both *ad hoc* and during the fellowship meetings which follow the monthly healing rite. In fact, the title of the monthly journal of the Order is *Sharing*, and it provides the model for discourse among the members. The faithful endow superficially inconsequential events with religious significance and attribute or link apparently natural phenomena to the supernatural. The mundane is sanctified, the homely events of everyday life are miraculously adjusted by God through the prayers *of* the faithful *for* the faithful. God's personal concern and care were ritualistically proclaimed during the Fellowship period: "I fell on the ice the other day and sprained my wrist badly. It was starting to improve but tonight, during the healing service, I took off my bandage and – praise the Lord! – my wrist is healed!" "One of our members called to say she had been bedridden with her arthritis for several days. She had asked for our prayers and she said that she could feel the warmth of God's love and the strength of our prayers every night. Yesterday, she was up and visited her grandchildren." Sharing was the predominant mode of discourse among the faithful at the annual Healing Love Conference I attended. These conferences served as forums for the inception and transmission of healing lore as precedents for validating future miracles. The personal experiences narrated at a healing conference were reworked, recreated, repeated, embellished – *shared* – throughout the year. These activities legitimized and enhanced both the worth and efficacy of healing activities; as Matthew (10:8) commissioned the faithful, "Heal the sick, raise the dead, cleanse lepers, cast out demons."

This conference lasted from Friday evening until Sunday noon. Ten healing stations were available in a large gymnasium on Friday evening and a number of more private healing rooms were scattered throughout the site. The following miracles occurred and were shared with me, even though I was only marginally involved: a stroke victim experienced extraordinary improvement; a terminally ill individual improved remarkably (observed at the Morning Watch communion); a supplicant's vision improved; another was cured of glaucoma; a mentally challenged participant had enhanced mental capacity (reported by parent); a petitioner experienced the living presence of Jesus as she was anointed with oil – his voice, the touch of his robe. Most dramatically, a young woman was exorcised of the demons which possessed her, her cries and blasphemies gradually quieted through the power of fervent prayer. This exorcism was the most talked-about event at the entire conference, and the two seminars on deliverance given by a Jesuit priest were filled to overflowing. The once-possessed, now-cured, wan young woman herself spoke that evening to a hushed gathering of the evil that had been excised – proof indeed of the power of prayer and touch!

This exorcism demonstrated the source and power of sharing in the substance and diffusion of miracle lore. While not necessarily common,[11] this dramatic incident was important because it so clearly stirred the participants. Since the young woman had ties to the OSL chapter with which I was associated as a fieldworker, I was able to closely observe the miracle lore's generation and transmission. One woman breathlessly described the event to me:

I was there, I was involved. It was the most amazing thing. I never had anything happen to me like that before ... I've seen healings and I've seen some rather odd things, but ... this was, was *evil*, it was *satanic*. I was in the auditorium that morning ... I don't remember getting up from that chair and walking to the door, but all of a sudden, I was *there*, at the door. I can only say that either I got up so fast that I wasn't aware of it or that *the Holy Spirit picked me up out of my chair and set me by the door* so I would be there to intercept this girl who was walking toward me and crying ... she was alone ... And I said, "You look very upset. Can I help?" and she ... sort of shook her head. And I said, "Come into the washroom and you can pull yourself together" ... and she started crying all the harder ... I was in charge of the prayer room ... so I said, "Come with me and we'll go over to the prayer room and we can sit and talk there." ... [At the prayer room] she sort of pulled herself together and we talked a little bit and she said, "I'll be all right now." [Informant starts to leave, after advising "Cary" that someone else is available to talk to her.] All of a sudden, I heard this terrible, terrible crying. It wasn't just crying, it was almost like a roaring noise she was making and I ... ran back in. As I moved toward Cary, I could sense that there was a *darkness*, a *blackness* around her ... I could sense spirits. Cary was practically screaming and she kept saying, "They won't let me go. They won't let me go." Then she'd say, "Oh, go away and leave me alone." Then, in another voice altogether, "Get away from me! Leave me alone! Get away from me!" The others in the room were bewildered. I took her head in my hands and ... I can never tell you why I did it, but I ... called out on Jesus and I said, "In the name of Jesus Christ, *let this girl go. Leave her. Let her alone, get away from her. In Jesus' name.*" I kept repeating, "Jesus, Jesus." And the poor girl, she just kept screaming. I said, "Get Ruth [the physician member] ... get a priest, get a minister." The [priest-physician who came in] said, "Cary, do you believe in Jesus Christ?" "Yes, I do." "She'll be all right." [A team of four then "worked on" Cary.] For two hours, we stood outside the door and prayed ... at one time, she was out on the floor, writhing on the floor. Toward the end of the two hours, it was the most *amazing* thing, *you could almost feel the atmosphere clearing and lifting*. It was just as if the sun was coming out. And we wound up, we were praising the Lord, we were all in tears, we were crying ... she was standing with her hands up and I knew everything would be all right ... It was a frightening thing, I was scared out of my mind. But I know that it wasn't me, *I was just the instrument the Spirit was using* ... the Spirit needed someone there and he ... put me beside the door so I could take her to the prayer room and brought Dr B. and Al Reimers [from the religious television program "100 Huntley Street"] right on cue. It's amazing how the Lord works ... that was my first really close encounter with anything satanic like that.

The exorcism was an "experience-near" event (cf. Geertz 1973) on several levels: it both substantiated the belief in human vulnerability to pernicious evil *and* validated the belief in human access to divine power and protection. Thus, it was obvious material for sharing and for the creation of miracle lore. Throughout the following year the exorcism was often employed as a charter for mobilizing the faithful as members were kept up to date on Cary's progress. The deliverance concretely established that good is always more powerful than evil.

Similarly, the curing of a young person's cystic fibrosis (an allegedly incurable condition, transmitted genetically) entered into the group's miracle lore. The cure apparently took place at the Healing Love Conference and was shared sometime later with one of the chapter's members. This healing became the exemplar for discourse about miraculous physical cures for both the faithful and for potential new adherents; it was frequently referred to as preparations were made the following year for the annual conference, and it heightened anticipation of new healings.

These events demonstrate the key aspect of how OSL members envision illness and treatment, a characteristically female, non-reductionistic framework which foregrounds the *non*-logical nature and course of human suffering (cf. Saltzman 1987). The OSL healers minister to the petitioners as they nurture their children, with no assurance of a linear relationship between their effort and its effects. The women accept the paradoxes, inconsistencies, and anomalies inherent within bodily responses to human-superhuman ministrations and they incorporate these paradoxes into their medicoreligious model. When a supplicant or adherent is *in extremis*, for example, "soaking prayer" (twenty-four-hour prayers untiringly offered in relays by groups of women) may be instituted. These prayers *are* answered but, as the physician member explained, dissolving the contradiction between healing and death, "God makes his own universes and stands on them. Healing takes place in the emotions and in the spirit, maybe not in the physical ... even death can be a healing, a taking-up and a glorious journey."

For OSL members, there *is* no contradiction between religious and biomedical healing modalities, between the physical and spiritual. They are simply documentations of the various ways of dealing with illness provided by God. Healing (or outcome), rather than diagnosis, is emphasized. As the physician member noted: "God wants people to be well and we can substantiate this from the Bible. God built in healing, it has been built in to our system. God's plan is in Genesis 1:31 where he says that everything he made was excellent indeed. There are human medicines ... and there are medicines of the Spirit ... Sickness is a battleground between good and evil ... Scripture says to use every means you can ... we must not renounce what God has given us as crutches. Doctors and nurses are God's people, on his team, they are there to bring God's people back to holiness."

Clearly, holiness and wholeness are conjoined here. Another member stated: "God uses doctors as instruments of his healing." Created originally to appease the Church, the strict Cartesian separation of mind (or soul) and body is not salient to the OSL model of overcoming affliction. Mind, soul, and body are inextricably connected, and mending the breach between God and self mends the mind, soul, *and* body; indeed, healing the breach between suprahuman and human heals the breach between self and others. Spiritual healing is effective on all levels of being.

"God moves in mysterious ways." No problem there; that is a commonplace, everyday fact of existence, part of the background assumptions of the members. The devout members of the OSL *accept* that bodily events are or reflect psychological and spiritual events, that one's spiritual condition is manifest in one's physical and/or psychological state. Spiritual phenomena *are* psychobiological phenomena. This spiritual component in religious healing lore fosters changes in the body and mind just as the technological component in allopathic healing lore alters the body and mind.

When I was a very young woman, I nursed in the hospital that housed the first "cobalt bomb" in North America for cancer treatment. This new therapy's potency was rapidly enshrined in medical folklore. Patients from all over the continent travelled to London (Ontario) to have their suffering and disease processes halted. Not unlike the hopeful supplicants for the miracles potentially available at the famous healing grottoes in Lourdes, France, and Ste Anne de Beaupré or St Joseph's, Quebec, many of these patients were far too ill to be travelling. But their faces reflected the hope that our "bomb" had catalyzed. *Some* of these people – some, for *ever* so briefly – felt better. They were not cured, but healed.

Miracle lore evokes metamorphoses.

NOTES

1 Jesus Christ's disciple Luke is typically characterised as "the beloved physician."

2 While this is not necessarily true of all chapters, the Order's Episcopalian roots would suggest a predominance of white members.

3 I see the position of these women within the Order as replicating their social position: as they selflessly undertook caring and sharing, their waning or vanished physiological reproductive powers were transmuted into a symbolic reproduction of health and God's blessings for the petitioners.

4 As Vivian Labrie's paper (this volume) shows, female gatekeepers are figures in both narrative and everyday life.

5 A full account of the history of the Order of St Luke may be found in Grant (1981).

6 The gifts or charisms are: word of wisdom and word of knowledge, and gifts of faith, healing, miracles, discernment, prophecy, tongues, and interpretation of tongues.

7 Several women mentioned that their husbands, too, disapproved of their charismatic practices. The charismatic adaptation which swept through the mainstream (particularly ritualistic) denominations in the seventies was a manifest critique of the Church. This suggests that there was a contradiction between the women's professions of faith in the traditional Church and the small resistances in their religious practices.

8 The original male-biased language in the King James version of the Bible has not been changed for this paper.

9 Freud observed that "expectation colored by hope and faith is an effective force with which we have to reckon ... in *all* our attempts at treatment and cure" (Freud 1953:289). Similarly, current investigations of psychoneuroimmunology emphasize the potency of belief (Cunningham 1992; Lyon 1993).

10 Lawless (1988a) has observed that female Oneness Pentecostal preachers were metaphorical, if not actual, "mothers" and the Holy Mother, Mary, of course remains a potent source of healing within Roman Catholicism.

11 Although a Roman Catholic priest involved in the ministry of deliverance (Guelph, Ontario) apparently was kept very busy indeed during the period of my fieldwork (1979–1981) and more than one-half of the people attending the conference attended the seminars on deliverance. Evil is very real to the members of the OSL.

"Just Like One of the Boys": Tactics of Women Taxi Drivers

CYNTHIA BOYD

Living for five years in a cold part of Atlantic Canada without a car, I've hailed taxis weekly, if not daily. Almost immediately, my curiosity got the best of me and I began to ask drivers about their cars and their jobs. During the summer of 1990 the local newspaper described an incident in which a female driver was assaulted by a male passenger (*Evening Telegram*, St John's, 5 May: 6). It occurred to me that women taxi drivers must have to be particularly cautious on the job. Although I had not planned to study their occupational folklife, the fact that such a small number of women were employed by taxi companies led me to do just that.

I selected three from one company, Boulevards' Taxi, to interview: Judy, Sue, and Nancy.[1] I spoke to women drivers from other companies, but these three provided the most valuable and candid information about their occupation and lives. They are in many ways very different from one another. At the time I conducted this research, Sue was thirty-eight years old, recently divorced, with three daughters, aged fifteen, eleven, and three, residing with her. She was self-conscious about her blonde, petite appearance, which sometimes hindered her in a male-dominated occupation. She had been a taxi driver on and off for three years; one year part-time with Boulevards'. Judy was thirty-one years old, married, with two children. Her bubbly personality and "take no shit" attitude were striking. She was the most outgoing taxi driver I knew, and her vivaciousness toward her job, clients, fellow workers, and family are clear in her comments. She had been driving for four years both full- and part-time with Boulevards' Taxi. Judy's best friend and co-worker, Nancy, was the youngest driver I met. At twenty-two, she was single. Although outwardly shy, she vividly, articulately, and intelligently expressed her experience in a manner belying her one year of full-time work with Boulevards'.

Every occupation is comprised of techniques, customs, and expressive behaviours characteristic of its everyday context. Folklorist Robert McCarl calls this complex set "the canon of work technique" (1986:71–2). Much is expressed, taught, and constituted in verbal forms from anecdotes and stories to simple information; understanding the lore is crucial to understanding the occupation, as well as how workers feel about it. In the first part of this paper, I will present the canon of work technique of the three women at Boulevards' Taxi. In the second, I will focus primarily on the tactics they employ on a daily basis, as well as on the ones they devise to avoid unwanted sexual comments and sexual harassment.[2]

A taxi driver needs to know the operation and mechanics of a car, understand the geography of the city and its outskirts, remember key locations such as important buildings, and possess adequate social skills to deal with the public. But in addition to these, there are the underlying rules – "dos and don'ts" – and inner workings of the occupation that can be learned only from other drivers. As McCarl states, "in spite of what new workers think they know, there are traditional ways of doing things in the workplace which workers themselves create, evaluate, and protect" (Ibid., 72). Furthermore, he indicates that occupational groups use expressions, terms, names, jokes, and narratives that make up the "verbal arts" which describe elements peculiar to the working environment (Ibid., 76).

A new driver must rely on fellow drivers, dispatchers, and sometimes passengers for information. Because of intense competition between drivers, as well as between companies, they may not disclose to one another hints about the occupation itself or about taxi jobs or runs. New drivers ask the dispatcher[3] for rates, directions, and costs for specific jobs, but they often fail to receive help, as the dispatcher can be responsible for as many as ninety cars on any given day.

Boulevards' Taxi drivers are not above frequently taking jobs from one another. Some augment the number of runs they receive in a day by "stealing jobs" or by "being fed." Stealing a job can be done when Driver A hears the dispatcher give out an address to Driver B. Driver A will try to get there before Driver B. As Judy indicated, "there is an underlying rule (at Boulevards') that if no one is parked at the dispatched location then anyone who gets there is entitled to the job."

Being fed is the dispensing of favours or jobs by dispatchers to certain drivers, usually because of a special relationship. Women taxi drivers who were sexually involved with the male dispatchers were regularly given more lucrative jobs. A typical reaction by one woman driver to another who had been more successful during her shift was: "Yeah, well you're being fed, you're fucking the dispatcher." A dispatcher may also feed an extra job to a family member. As Judy described, drivers saw this as a much more acceptable reason for feeding, because "you got to take care of family ... One dispatcher would do a lot for his brother-in-law where he'd call him on the mike saying: 'Dan call Kate.' In other words, call me, I've got a job for ya ... a better one than the other driver is getting."

The dispatcher might also feed particular drivers who were having a slow day or needed a little extra for their children. This type of feeding was not given to everyone in need, but only to a driver whom the dispatcher especially liked. Judy indicated that she got along well with most of the dispatchers and that she "gets fed herself a little bit ... There is a difference in the feeding going on ... So if you need money, he'll slip you a job, and you might buy him lunch. You scratch my back, I'll scratch yours sort of thing."

Sue, Judy, and Nancy each had their own form of introduction for passengers who entered their car. They usually started with casual questions like "How are you today?" and "What about this lousy weather we're having?" They had to learn to "read the customer," and with practice, perceive her/his personality and disposition quickly. Drivers must rely on themselves to discover which passengers are likely to be pleasant and amiable, and which unpredictable and threatening. According to Judy, some customers are extremely quiet and others talk pleasantly, and then there are those who "are just so far out in left field they don't know the war is over." Judy commented, "as soon as they open the door and sit their ass on the seat, I say, 'Hi, how are ya?' If they clam up after saying 'I'm fine' or whatever, then I drives 'em, that's it."

Initially the type of customer defines most jobs or runs. For example, the driver usually opens the door for older people and assists them with baggage. And, as Judy explains, "If you've got an older person, you're not going to take off from a dead run and do sixty in two seconds flat ... I mean let's face it, granny's in the backseat going AHHHH!! But if some young dude gets in, you don't give a shit, you walk on it a little bit."

One type of run is the "water-haul," which occurs when the person who called for a taxi does not appear at the dispatched location. For instance, Judy once picked up a woman, who, upon entering her car, "scrunched down" in the backseat. Judy asked, "Where you going?" and the woman replied, "Around the corner, but I don't want my neighbours to see me." Judy suggested, "I mean Missus gave me four dollars, she was only going around the corner and that was alright by me. But I could have put it in reverse, backed out around the corner and said 'I haven't got nobody.'" Under these circumstances, Judy could claim the job as a water-haul.

Where all taxi drivers share certain expressions, knowledge, and techniques inherent to the job, the women need to create and maintain additional techniques. They must develop tactics which enable them to deal specifically with unwanted sexual comments and harassment. According to local media, women taxi drivers faced a greater amount of risk in the occupation because of instances – however isolated – of assault and robbery (*Evening Telegram*, St John's, 5 May 1990:6). Although male drivers told me very little about confrontations such as assault, robbery, or sexual harassment, there was every possibility that it happened to them as well. Mr Justice Riche implied as much when he commented "taxi drivers have to be protected and female taxi drivers cannot and should not be considered easy prey" (Ibid.).

I asked Judy, Nancy, and Sue what tactics they employed to handle such threatening situations. My direct questioning did not reveal much, but in their narratives of personal experience I could recognize tactics being used to avoid confrontations.[4] The women did not define any confrontations as sexual harassment, even when the label seemed appropriate. They considered them part of the territory of the job, although their narratives reveal that they did not sit back and take it.[5] In many cases, they coped through rather aggressive tactics.

Nancy told about one experience. On her first night shift, she received a call from the dispatcher to pick up a passenger. The man was intoxicated, but he had fifty dollars, wanted to go for a ride, and did not care where. Nancy headed "down Kenmount Road ... figured I'd take him downtown, cruise around down there ... closer to everybody else too so if we got into trouble I had everybody around me." Nancy's tactic was to "stick close to where the cars are." She also mentioned that she always had her mike next to her or in her hand, especially with a passenger whom she suspected could cause her trouble.

When the man started to use vulgar language and remove his clothes, Nancy "keyed her mike" for assistance: a third tactic. When another taxi arrived to assist her, Nancy pulled her cab to the side of the road. The other driver hauled the passenger out of her car and

took him to the police, but Nancy did not press charges. She indicated that she just wanted to get away from there and go home.

This experience was important to Nancy because she witnessed
first hand the "night-time male" – a term she coined – a type she
must know and deal with on occasion. Retelling this "cautionary
tale" (Santino 1978:198) to Judy as well as to me, Nancy was able to
share her experience and provide insight on how to handle such
situations.

Sue also has a story of an afternoon when she had to use similar
tactics. Although no harm came to her, she had to ward off harassment and a possible sexual assault:

One incident where I had one guy and I knew he wanted to go into the
Goulds [a small town] and he said his house was right on down this gravel
road. Now, I was not going down any road that doesn't look like there were
any houses. "Sorry pal, I don't go any further than this." And you got to let
them know you're in charge here. And that did happen to me. I started to
go down the road and ah, suddenly, the little thing in the middle of your
seat? He took that and he put it up. I sort of grabbed the mike and it went
up in my hand right? And I just put the car in park. "Now," I said, "the
door's there, if you don't get out, I will."

Sue, like Nancy, did not press charges; instead she chose to take
control of the situation in her own way. Sue insists that such confrontations are simply an unfortunate part of the job.

In *Georgie Porgie: Sexual Harassment in Everyday Life*, Sue Wise and
Liz Stanley describe how "the various behaviours that make up 'sexual harassment' are usually called by many different names so that
women's common response to a common problem is masked"
(1987:72). Further, they note that all these "behaviours are linked by
the way they represent an unwanted and unsought intrusion by men
into women's feelings, thoughts, behaviours, space, time, energies,
and bodies" (Ibid., 71). With this definition in mind, it was fascinating to discover that the women I spoke to had numerous complaints
not only about male passengers, but also about how their male co-
workers treated them on the job as well as how the men in their
personal lives treated them off the job.

As well as encountering threatening situations, women taxi drivers
encounter additional pressures from family and friends who do not
understand why they have chosen this occupation. The women drivers do not always have tactics to deal with these forms of harassment.
Though Sue's friends thought she had "guts" to drive a taxi, and Judy's

children were proud to tell their friends that their mom drove a cab, most reactions were negative. The women responded to my questions about family and friends' reactions with emotional narratives describing false accusations by, and near break-ups with, spouses or boyfriends. Judy, Nancy, and Sue complained bitterly that they were not treated fairly by men – male co-workers or other men in their lives.

Judy revealed that she and her husband were having serious marital problems, in part because she drove a taxi for Boulevards': "It wasn't to the point that I was getting all this attention from the rest of the drivers but ... When somebody looks at you and says, "God, your hair looks great today, what'd you do with it?" it builds you up. And I loved taxiing ... every chance I got I was out on the road ... where, he, my husband, figured I was out on the road with them ... my clan, the b'ys, my friends ... somebody's showing me a bit of attention and he doesn't like the idea."

Not only did Judy's husband become irritated because she enjoyed her job, but he became jealous when she made a lot of money on the job. Judy described one customer, a well-dressed, sixty-two-year-old man who decided to celebrate his birthday by visiting every bar in town by taxi. "We went everywhere so that he could go in and have a drink, leave after fifteen minutes, and every time this happened, he'd throw me a twenty-dollar bill." At one point, Judy realized this job would make her late to pick up her children from school, so she called her husband (who was working for a mini-bus service) and asked him to pick them up. This was three o'clock and she already had $250. Her husband did not believe her, and ridiculed her. When she finally arrived home, her husband said that there was no way she could have made $250. Judy replied: "'No, I didn't get $250, I got $400!' – well, his jaw dropped." Judy's husband not only disapproves of her job because he believes she does it for male attention, but also when she does her job well, he is jealous of her accomplishments.

As mentioned earlier, Sue had been working with Boulevards' for one year. At the previous cab stand that she worked, she was not able to do night shifts because of her young children, but when she began driving for Boulevards' she asked to work the night shift (11 P.M. – 5 A.M.). Her boss refused her request, stating; "Sue ... you work till 11 P.M., I don't want you to work after that." When she persisted by giving examples of other female drivers who worked nights, he replied: "There's a difference between you and Nancy ... you're dainty; Nancy can handle herself really well."

In discussing taxi driving with a small group of male drivers of another cab company, one large man indicated that his boss would not be able to sleep nights knowing that Mary (the only female driver with their company) was on the road. I asked him to define the type of woman who would be allowed to drive cabs at night. He chuckled as he stated: "Well, she'd have to be about 300 pounds." To which another male driver added: "Yeah, and as saucy as a bastard." These same male drivers indicated that they continually make fun of Mary because she is the only female driver.[6] Tauntings such as "Woman driver!" when she backs up the car at the cab stand to "Hey, Mary, why don't you take out the garbage … this is women's work!" indicate that her male colleagues do not respect her as equal and competent.

As indicated by Sue's boss, and by these other male taxi drivers, men do not feel comfortable having women drive at night, particularly women who they perceive as attractive, small, and quiet. Sue's boss wanted to protect her from any possible victimization she might encounter at night on the job; however, his rationale for not offering her a night shift discriminated against her on the basis of her appearance and personality, not on the basis of her driving skills or capability of handling herself in a problematic situation.

Much of the attention the women drivers did receive from male drivers was in the form of sexual harassment on the job. Apparently, male drivers were continually placing bets on which female driver they would "get" to sleep with them.[7] The women stated that they either avoided, humoured, or dismissed as ignorant the men who harassed them on the job. Sue discussed this issue at length; she felt that there must be something "written across her forehead" that made the men treat her the way they did. She thought that if they could just "ask her out for a coffee without the sexual part that would be okay."

On one occasion, Sue described a "wake-up call" she received for her early morning shift. She had asked the dispatcher to call her. Unfortunately, one of the drivers heard her request so he called her himself, at 3:40 A.M.:

Derek: "Sue? You awake?"
Sue: "Yeah … I've been awake now for about ten minutes."
Derek: "Yeah, well, how would you like to have your pussy licked at this morning?"

Sue was furious with him for using such vulgarity, but when she asked him why he treated her like this, he insisted that she loved to be talked to in this manner. Despite her strong belief that Derek had absolutely no right to speak to her like this, she felt that he, like her other male co-workers, perceived that they had the right, as men. They worked with her every day and therefore they felt that they had more right than a stranger to make rude comments and unwanted sexual advances. When I asked Sue why she did not complain to her boss, she indicated that she was afraid she would only be laughed at.

Marlene Kadar indicates that "sexual harassment is one of the levers those in power use to control those who are not" (1983:337). While the woman taxi driver completes the task at hand as well as, and often better than, her male co-worker, she is not considered his equal.[8] That the women drivers do not discuss their feelings of mistreatment and inequality as workers with each other is detrimental to their ability to change their circumstances. Further, the women drivers believe that unwanted sexual advances and comments are an inherent part of the territory. Sadly, the women, once harassed, are not likely to press charges or make formal complaints because they believe that they will be ridiculed, and are afraid they will lose their jobs. Perhaps this is yet another technique, though somewhat disguised, in which workers test each other for their ability to take abuse. In some cases, the women just want to be accepted by the men as taxi drivers, nothing more, nothing less; however, the division between women and men in this occupation is especially wide even though female drivers like Sue indicate that all they really want is "to be just like one of the boys."

If sexual harassment were their only salient experiences as taxi drivers, Sue, Judy, and Nancy would not express such positive feelings toward their work. In this job they have an opportunity to be in a position of power and knowledge, and to use their many skills to their personal and monetary advantage. Taxi driving enhances their confidence. Providers of excellent service, they are personable, friendly, informed drivers who care for the public. As Judy suggested, they are ambassadors of the city: "I'm the first person that this guy meets when he gets off the plane and into my car, headed for the hotel." While they may be verbally abused by men at work and at home, generally everyday encounters with clients are rewarding, often engaging experiences. Within the context of each encounter, the driver is listening, observing, participating, and learning another's culture, life, or circumstances.

Boulevards' women drivers enjoy their work. Judy says that taxi driving gets in your blood, a sentiment that she says the women drivers feel but the male drivers do not: "With us it's totally different … I do it because I love it, I enjoy it … but with most of these guys, they've been at it for so long … and in the taxi business it gets in your blood. You could quit five million times in a week, but it will always be with you. Sometimes you feel like washing your hands clean of it, but no matter how many times you think you're never going back at it again ... before you know it ... you're behind the wheel."

NOTES

1 To maintain confidentiality, I have given pseudonyms to both the taxi companies and their drivers. Unless otherwise indicated, Sue's, Nancy's, and Judy's comments are direct quotations. Words or phrases like "being fed" are the exact ones they used to refer to specific aspects of their job. Sue was interviewed in her home on 10 October 1990; Judy and Nancy were both interviewed in Judy's home on 18 October 1990. All recorded material has been deposited in MUNFLA.

2 I use the word "tactic" based on the actual problematic situations in which the women drivers found themselves on the job. Further discussion of narratives which reflect upon workplace problems is found in Vivian Labrie's paper. Originally, this essay was entitled "Just One of the Boys: The Tactics and Strategies of Women Taxi Drivers." Following the advice of another contributor to this collection, I decided that the women drivers here did not apply strategies, but instead tried to manœuvre around difficulties with male passengers, male co-workers, and other men in their lives as "tactfully" as they could. The tactics themselves do not signify that the women felt in control of the situation at all. Unfortunately it is, again, the men who wield power.

3 Although no reasons were given why most dispatchers were men, the women I interviewed indicated that the pressure and stress of that position was more than they wanted to deal with.

4 Marie-Annick Desplanques, in her discussion of women's talk, similarly shows women using personal experience narratives in their coping techniques.

5 Similarly, the articles by Pamela Klassen, Gail Grant, and Robin McGrath show women who, directly or indirectly, counter the stereotype of women as simply the passive victims of their own lives and experiences.

6 On 16 October 1990, I interviewed four men in this company, which I call Jerry's. Between the ages of twenty-five and sixty, they had been employed as taxi drivers for two to ten years.

7 The women taxi drivers told me that their male colleagues were known to brag that they had sex with many female passengers. As a result of a male taxi driver raping a female passenger, a London, England, cab company has been established that employs and serves women only (*Evening Telegram*, St John's, 21 February 1992, Lifestyles: 1).

8 Many women taxi drivers indicated that their bosses considered them highly dependable and reliable employees. One taxi stand operator maintained that women drivers were safer and tended to be less likely to damage the stand's cars. Accidents lead to increased insurance costs, an important consideration for an operator since most vehicles are owned by the cab company.

Circumventing the Taboos:
Inuit Women's Autobiographies

ROBIN McGRATH

There are a number of reasons why autobiography is one of the first forms of written literature to emerge in a newly literate society. First, one of the most obvious subjects for a new writer to attempt is that which he or she knows best – the self; second, the contact that promotes literacy constitutes a major disruptive force in the lives of pre-literate people, and autobiographies seem to thrive during times of political, technological, or environmental upheaval; and finally, autobiography has a pre-determined chronological structure, a limited subject matter, and generally requires little research or invention, but at the same time it is flexible enough to accommodate the inclusion of oral songs and stories, religious or spiritual speculation, political opinion, or history.

In Canada, literacy among aboriginal people was promoted primarily by Christian missionaries. The ability to read and write was necessary for Bible study, so missionaries provided paper, and natives were encouraged to write out their life stories to practice these newly acquired reading and writing skills. Keeping diaries was also encouraged as a way of ensuring that the Sabbath was identified and observed as a day of prayer and reflection, and these diaries frequently took on the form of autobiographies or were later used in their composition. In more recent years anthropologists in native Indian and Inuit communities have supported the writing and dissemination of native autobiography in isolated areas.

Like many newly literate people, Canadian Inuit tend to favour the autobiography as a vehicle for their observations, opinions and experiences (see McGrath 1984). Of 783 works published by Inuit prior to 1981, more than one quarter can be identified as being primarily reminiscent or autobiographical. However, if you divide these works according to the sex of the writer, a peculiar imbalance emerges; although both Inuit men and women write literature of all types, Inuit women write only half as many autobiographies as men.

A close look at the works reveals several interesting points. First, unlike Inuit men who tend to pattern their autobiographies upon already established narrative structures borrowed from the epic tradition, Inuit women do not use myths and legends to structure their autobiographies. Second, in Inuit culture it is taboo for women to draw attention to themselves as mature adults, so they either confine their autobiographical writings to memories of pre-adolescence, or wait until they are approaching old age to write about themselves. Third, Inuit women who wish to discuss their lives often fictionalize them and, in contrast to the male writers, use autobiographical form to structure stories rather than the other way around, thus circumventing the taboo.[1]

Inuit men writing about themselves frequently use some or all of the elements of the narratives of the two major epic heroes, Kaujjarjuk and Kiviok. Ben Cockney's *I, Nuligak*, translated and edited by Maurice Metayer (1972), follows the predictable linear sequence of birth, life, and old age leading to death, with a regular internal pattern of seasons shaping the sub-sections, but the legendary structures that shape the work as a whole are evident to anyone familiar with the Kaujjarjuk myth, and it is this that gives the book an artistic integrity that goes beyond that of the factual chronicle. In Peter Pitseolak's *People From Our Side* (1975), the details about his life echo the story of Kiviok. The episodic structure of the work mirrors the circular journey pattern of the Kiviok myth, just as the linear structure of *I, Nuligak* follows the linear pattern of Kaujjarjuk.

Not all autobiographies by Inuit men display such close connections to the epics of the oral tradition as these two, but similar patterns can be found in a more fragmentary form in "The Story of John Ayaruaq" (Ayaruaq 1969), Anthony Thrasher's *Thrasher: Skid Row Eskimo* (1976), Armand Tagoona's *Shadows* (1975), Bernard Irqugaqtuq's "The Autobiography of a Pelly Bay Eskimo" (1977–1979), *The Recollections of Levi Iqalujjuaq* (1988) and the work of Norman Eekoomiak (1980). Taken together, these works give a diverse and well-rounded picture of life as it has been experienced by Canadian Inuit men in this century. Nuligak and Ayaruaq were successful, elderly hunters, Thrasher and Eekoomiak were relatively young and wrote from prison cells, Tagoona was a highly regarded Anglican minister,

Peter Pitseolak was an artist and photographer. Their works deal with all aspects and phases of their lives, and include discussions of their personal relationships with their parents and wives.

Works by Inuit woman, however, seem to be almost entirely childhood memoirs, and even those women who have achieved fairly high status within the newly formed settlements have not written about themselves in the way men have. According to Inuit women, it is proper to recall the "learning years," to show themselves as children or young girls who make mistakes and accept correction, but it is improper to boast or attract attention as adults. For women to draw attention to themselves overtly is to invite ridicule.[2]

In traditional times, Inuit girls were conditioned to appear shy, even if they weren't that way by nature. A hunting-gathering society generally divides work along gender lines, and Inuit have a strong sense of what is appropriate behaviour for each sex. Leah Nutaraq, recalling how as a child she danced for the whaling captains who came into Cumberland Sound, explained that on such occasions, "It was a time to be shy, but I hadn't learned that" (Eber 1971:9). Cape Dorset artist Kenojuak, who in the 1960s was awarded an Order of Canada and was internationally acclaimed as an artist, describes in her autobiography how reluctant she was to make drawings for the printshop because it was "men who made drawings," and she insisted that her "role as a mother and an Inuit woman always took precedence over this new work" (Blodgett 1985:20). Elder Joan Attuat, a famous hunter even in her old age, once said that her knowledge of certain historic events was limited because, "when I was small I used to be sent away when the adults were discussing because I was always talking too much" (Eber 1971:133).

When Pitseolak Ashoona dared to publish her oral biography, *Pitseolak: Pictures Out Of My Life* (Eber 1971), it apparently triggered an avalanche of disapproval from other Cape Dorset residents. According to editor Dorothy Eber, the author was accused of adding several years onto her age and of self-aggrandizement. Comments in the community were highly critical and personal. Some of the remarks were directed against her claim that her husband was an excellent provider: "Pitseolak's husband never was rich – he never had eight dogs," and "Pitseolak's husband's igloos – you couldn't even *get into* her husband's igloos." Other comments were directed more towards the artist herself: "The standards of housekeeping in *that* family were never very high" (Eber 1977:126,128).

Both categories of comment indirectly attack Pitseolak's decision as a young, impoverished widow to support herself and her children by drawing pictures for sale to the co-operative, which until then had been a male preserve. Her published claim that she once caught a goose bare-handed sparked a major controversy among Baffin elders; Etidlui and his son Udjualuk went out on the tundra to try it, just to prove it was impossible, and the widow Echaluk, herself once a hunter with her own team, declared that if Pitseolak ever caught a goose, it was a very small goose. Pitseolak amended her story to say that she had not caught one goose, but had, in fact, caught two. One critic told Eber that "she should have said she didn't know about these things when she was questioned" (Eber 1977:128). It is impossible now to say if Pitseolak Ashoona really did catch a goose, or two geese, but it does seem clear that her decision to "put herself forward" was not a popular one.

The result of the cultural taboo against women discussing their adult lives has meant that Inuit women tend to write complete auto-biographies only when they are very old; other autobiographies come to an abrupt end when the authors have brought us as far as their maturity. This is not to say that the latter works are inferior, but one does get the feeling that a great deal has been left unsaid and there are not the tight structural connections found in male autobi-ographies.

One of the problems with trying to read Inuit autobiographies is that the patterns of narrative that are specific to the culture are invis-ible to us. We can see, as Susanna Egan (1984) suggests, background patterns such as journey, confession, and conversion, and we can see the foreground of dates, places, and events, but the middle ground that we see male writers developing from legends such as those of Kiviok and Kaujjarjuk is almost entirely overlooked because we are unfamiliar with the bulk of Inuit folklore. It could well be that Inuit women use patterns of narrative that are not as easily recognized, or that are unknown outside the culture because the majority of non-Inuit who recorded Inuit oral literature were male missionaries and male anthropologists who had no interest in or access to the female domain.[3]

The earliest autobiographical work by an Inuk to be published in Canada was Lydia Campbell's *Sketches of Labrador Life* (1980), first printed in the St John's *Evening Telegram* in 1894. Mrs Campbell, a mixed blood "Livyere," a Labrador settler, was given an exercise book by the Rev. Arthur C. Waghorne when she was seventy-five years old. Rev. Waghorne begged her to write some account of Labra-dor life and ways, and on Christmas day, in 1893, after walking four miles through waist-high snow drifts to check her rabbit snares in thirty-degree-below-zero weather, the old woman sat down to comply with his request. She recorded how she killed her first deer when she was a young woman, and noted that no other people lived near her and her husband but her only surviving child and his motherless children: "none near us but them and our dear children's graves. We can see their headstones at a distance over on the cranberry banks, so pretty it looks in the fall when we come home from our summer quarters" (1980:2). In later entries, Mrs. Campbell recalls her "silliness" in her younger years, a common theme in the autobiographies by Inuit women (Ibid., 18).

Lydia Campbell's daughter, Margaret Baikie, was a mere seventy-three when she began work on the manuscript (n.d.) for *Labrador Memories*. The work, which was not published for sixty years, deals primarily with her Inuit grandmother and her own childhood. There are only very brief references to her husband, a Scotsman who courted her by sending her three dresses, some silk handkerchiefs, and a concertina. He seems to have been a shy man, and Mrs Baikie seems shy of writing about him. One of the longest comments we get about Thomas describes his grave, although she is quite emotional when discussing her children. It interesting that despite her mother's example, she waited until her husband died before she began work on her autobiography.

Another Labrador woman of mixed blood produced the first book-length autobiography, *Land of the Good Shadows: The Life Story of Anauta an Eskimo Woman* (Washburne 1940), published in 1940 by Lizzie Ford Blackmore, of Ford Harbour, and Heloise Chandler Washburne, an American woman she met in the United States. At least twice widowed and three times married, Anauta seemed to have a penchant for wandering, and after travelling all along the Arctic coast and the southern shore of Newfoundland with her various husbands, she moved to the States where, like Pauline Johnson and Grey Owl, she made her living as an exotic on the lecture circuit. Dressed in caribou clothing, she gave inspirational talks to church groups. Two more books followed, *Wild Like the Foxes* (Blackmore 1956) and *Children of the Blizzard* (Washburne 1960), but they tell us little about Anauta's adult life. They focus, instead, on the lives of her parents and on her childhood in Labrador.

Elizabeth Goudie, Lydia Campbell's great-grand niece, wrote her autobiography in 1963, and for ten years it circulated in manuscript form before being published under the title *Woman of Labrador* (1973). Whether it was because Mrs Goudie was held in very high regard within the Labrador community, or because she was only one-quarter Inuit, or because of her advanced age, she managed to break free of the pattern of childhood and adolescent memoirs. She was obviously devoted to her husband, Jim, and she describes many happy trips they took together, but she does not hesitate to describe the severe poverty they endured as a young married couple with numerous small children, and tells of how difficult it was for Jim to approach her father for help. His death is described in sad detail, but she assures the reader that even as a widow she was quite capable of supporting herself by keeping a boarding house. She concludes her chapter on her husband's death with this paragraph: "We worked side by side those forty-two years together, and it was pretty rough sometimes. We respected each other and when he was taken from me I didn't feel too bad. Life is meant to be that way. I think a person has nothing to regret when they are happy and we were very happy, so I am quite content now. There is always something to think about" (Goudie 1973:148). Although a few older women, like Mrs Goudie, managed to break with tradition, the majority of autobiographies by younger Inuit woman are like Alice French's book about growing up in the Mackenzie Delta. *My Name is Masak* (1977) takes us only up to the point when the author left school at fourteen. The book describes her years in All Saints Residence, but there is no hint of the abuse that has been reported by other Natives who lived in the Anglican hostel at the same time. As a child, Masak was very much under the influence of her grandmother, who insisted she learn traditional Inuit skills, and the work is a lovely lyrical memoir of childhood. The book ends when she leaves the residence: "It was sad to say goodbye to my friends but at the same time I felt a great sense of relief, like a prisoner whose sentence was finally over. When the door closed behind me and my father, I felt like a bird flying home to the vast open tundra" (French 1977:105).

It is possible that Alice French, who was only seven years old when she entered the hostel, did not suffer from the interracial feuding, the chronic lack of food, the beatings and sexual abuse reported by other girls and boys in the residence, but surely she must have seen some of it. We hear nothing about the death of her first husband, only that she is married to a Mountie and lives in Manitoba. One of Alice French's contemporaries, when asked what she thought of *My Name is Masak*, replied "It's a nice book, but it's too bad she didn't tell the whole truth. I guess some things are too painful to remember." In a published autobiography, some things may just be too public, perhaps. Good little Inuit girls don't make scenes or complain openly about mistreatment.

Minnie Freeman's *Life Among the Qallunaat* (1978) is another autobiography which ends just as the author is reaching maturity. This is not to suggest that Mrs Freeman's book is less than honest; it is in many ways a ruthless indictment of white culture, but like *Masak* it limits its mandate. There is a strong sense of the anger, bitterness, and isolation experienced by young Inuit in residential schools and in the south, and Freeman is direct in her description of the sexual harassment native girls suffered at the hands of white teachers and employers, but all her criticism is directed outward, away from her own culture.

Heather Henderson, in her paper on *Life Among the Qallunaat*, sees Freeman's position as a translator, rather than her gender, as central to an understanding of the book. As a translator, Freeman "is expected to be a transparent medium of others' messages and ideas" (Henderson 1988:62), so her passivity and her refusal or failure to assert herself in accordance with Inuit tradition is appropriate. The stress of maintaining such passivity when the consequences for her people are so disastrous eventually pushes Freeman into a radical re-examination of her conformity. Henderson says, "the writing of an autobiography marks the point at which she finds her own voice: it is necessarily an act of egotism and self-assertion" (Ibid.).

One should note, however, that when Freeman records her initial successful acts of resistance towards the demands of others, the examples she gives relate to her white female peers, not towards white men or towards her own people. We are told of more radical changes in her behaviour and speech that occur after her adolescence, but we are given few examples. The work becomes an abstract essay, disconnected from the foreground of dates, places, events, and people that we usually associate with biography or autobiography. Freeman does not say she is writing fiction, like Ruby Slipperjack and other Amerindian woman autobiographers, but she does not "name names," or even give enough information for a knowledgable reader to identify the events or people to which she alludes.

That these writers avoid speaking about themselves as mature women does not mean that the subject is untouched in the books and articles written by Inuit women about themselves. The autobiography by the Cape Dorset artist Kenojuak (Blodgett 1985) is a good example of a work that exhibits the inherent tensions in an Inuit woman's attempt to explain her strength or fame without boasting. In the 1950s, Canadian Inuit were brutally poor, suffering from a decline in the fur market, the decimation of the caribou herds, and the ravages of tuberculosis. Aside from family allowance, which was hardly a secure income when children kept dying, the art industry provided the only regular trickle of cash into Inuit communities. Kenojuak was, like the Labrador women, devoted to her husband, despite the fact that during the first weeks of their arranged marriage she threw rocks at him whenever he approached her. However, she was the one who earned the cash in the family, and while her status as a provider must have been considerable, she was obviously uncomfortable with it.

On two occasions when Kenojuak earned large sums of money, from a film and from a government commission, the money was invested in a boat and a kicker so that her husband, Johnniebo, could achieve some independence as a hunter and escape the dominance of the camp bosses. Kenojuak stresses that even after they moved permanently into the settlement, "Johnniebo did not forsake the traditional ways, and hunted to provide for his family" (Blodgett 1985:23). Johnniebo was himself a noted artist and whenever possible Kenojuak worked and exhibited with him, but he did not have the international recognition Kenojuak commanded.

Most of Kenojuak's autobiography concerns itself with family matters but one can see elements of the "escape from death" theme that established the male writers Nuligak, Ayaruaq, and others as having special status within the Inuit community. By facing death and being, in effect, born again, the individual is singled out as different. Often the survivor would take on a new name, or if female, might have herself tattooed to indicate restoration of order to her life. Kenojuak's escape from death took place in a southern sanatorium and it marked a radical change in her approach to life. In 1952, Kenojuak was brought south and hospitalized for tuberculosis. While she was away, both her young children died. The blow was dreadful. "Suffering unbearable pain over this loss," she said, "I never wanted to bear children again" (Ibid., 18). The news caused a critical relapse and Kenojuak was moved to a ward for the terminally ill. While she lay dangerously sick, she had a profound dream in which her dead father appeared and forbade her to join him until her mother had done so. She says, "At that moment, I nearly lost my soul. I believe that owing to my father's intervention, my life was saved" (Ibid.). Kenojuak lost seven of her first nine natural and adopted children; the next five all survived, in part because of the improved circumstances Kenojuak's income from her artwork provided for them.

Many reminiscences by female artists and leaders record a miraculous recovery or escape from death as a turning point in their lives, and in many cases it would appear that the father – who is the only person with more authority over an Inuit woman than her husband – has given permission for that woman to put herself forward. For instance, Marion Tuu'luk, a prominent Inuk from Baker Lake, records (1977) how during a starvation time her father strangled himself with a rope; the next day, his disembodied voice led her to a cache of meat that saved the entire camp. Tuu'luk, under the direction of her dead father, was able to assert her leadership despite her youth and her sex.

Kenojuak's dream of her father could be said to have had the same result as Marion Tuu'luk's. The dream contains contradictory elements, as many dreams do. This is how Kenojuak describes it: "I saw an enormous structure with many entrances. My children, along with other children and adults, were inside. I recognized a friend's sister who had died in the hospital. In another area stood a group of agitated people. My father, in a magnificent white robe, was seated atop a ladder. A large accordion hung suspended over his head. I struggled to touch him, but he refused to allow this. He said that I could not go to him until Seelaki [Kenojuak's mother] had done so" (Blodgett 1985:18). Kenojuak's father's insistence that she survive both her illness and her grief over her children's death, and his appearance in the garb of the non-Inuit, must have greatly influenced her decision to accept the paper and pencils proffered by the white man and take up "men's work" when the Dorset workshop ran out of sewing materials.

Where Inuit women have not been given overt or tacit permission to draw attention to themselves in print, they find other ways around the taboo and disguise their stories as fiction. Years before writing *Life Among the Qaalunaat*, Minnie Freeman wrote a play, *Survival in the South*, whose young protagonist was a translator by the name of Minnie. In the prologue, the narrator, a part originally read by the author, tells us that she was brought up to listen and obey her elders and "not to give advice until I have reached that stage where I am considered to have gained wisdom" (Freeman 1980:102). Minnie assimilates on the surface, getting her hair cut like the white girls and so on, but underneath she retains her Inuit values and abides by the wishes of her grandparents, becoming only "white" enough to survive in the south. The fictionalized version of Freeman's life gives greater insight into her state of mind than her much longer autobiography.

Leah Idlout's memoir, *C.D. Howe* (D'Argencourt 1977), is named for the hospital ship that took her south to a sanatorium as a young girl. White foster parents wished to adopt her, but Idlout eventually returned to Pond Inlet where she found re-entry into the culture difficult. *C.D. Howe* tells us a lot about Idlout, but one of her earlier works tells us more. *The Little Arctic Tern, the Big Polar Bear* (Idlout 1980) is a beast fable about a bird who allows her egg to be hatched by a polar bear; the result is a bear-bird who does not know who its mother is and who is eventually exhibited as a freak in a Florida circus. Idlout's version of the story differs from Dr Seuss's *Horton*

Hatches an Egg, upon which it is based, in some subtle but important ways; the mother tern's migratory instinct is seen as irresistible, while Seuss's mother bird just wants to go to Florida to lie on the beach; the tern deeply regrets leaving her egg and is grieved, rather than annoyed, when it chooses to go with the foster parents. The mother tern's resignation to her loss is terribly sad, and there is pathos in the song the bear-bird sings:

> Again, again, it's going to snow.
> And how do we know it's going to snow?
> Because it always snowed before. (Ibid., 39)

The taboo against autobiography is evident even in stories by very young girls. One fairy tale by a teenager from Iqaluit, entitled "The Magic Pens and Pencils," describes how the magic pencil was punished for kissing the magic pen, and ran to hide down by the pipeline while her parents went off to Apex to drink beer and fight. One cannot help noticing that the male figure is an indelible pen while the female is an erasable pencil. Inuit women do not find it as easy to be personal or intimate on the printed pages as male writers do, but the steps they take to circumvent the problems produce intriguing literature, so perhaps it is turned to advantage in some ways. Once we can decode the fiction and pull the embedded meaning out of the stories non-Native readers may be closer to understanding what the lives of Inuit women are really like.

Leah Arnaujaq, at the end of her autobiographical essay, "In the Days of the Whalers," writes, "I did not think I could ever tell stories like this and it was difficult to put all of it in writing" (Arnaujaq 1986:20), but she did do it, and each day more and more Inuit women are putting their thoughts in writing, breaking taboos and speaking up for themselves. Mary Carpenter, who is currently writing her autobiography, has included in the draft manuscript a poem about her mother's failure to communicate directly with her. Carpenter's mother was hospitalized for a long time and the child used to go and stand in the street outside the hospital, hoping to catch a glimpse of her in the windows above. The reality takes on a metaphorical meaning when Carpenter writes:

> I knew you loved me
> But I did not understand
> Why you were behind that clouded pane
> And all I could see was your waving hand... (1990).

Inuit women write to us from behind a window that is clouded by the restrictions on speaking directly of self, but they are communicating. What was a means of circumventing a taboo has become an art form in itself.

NOTES

1 Similar circumventions by undisciplined women are clear in Agatha Janzen's disclaimers about preaching, discussed by Pamela Klassen; and in a rather different mode, in the storytellers' refigurings of traditional narratives discussed by Kay Stone.
2 Clearly, this is not exclusive to Inuit tradition, as several papers in this section indicate.
3 This pattern should be all too familiar to readers who have looked at the first section of this book.

Making Time for Talk: Women's Informal Gatherings In Cape St George, Newfoundland

MARIE-ANNICK DESPLANQUES

Women's patterns of socialization, their friendships, and their modes of informal leisure gathering – a hitherto underrated topic (Green et al. 1990) – have recently attracted the attention of social scientists (O'Connor 1992). Work on women's friendships and leisure time suggest that women need to identify with each other as a gendered group (Gullestad 1984). Women's friendship groups and their dynamics can provide a catharsis from which a sense of identity emerges. As elsewhere, married women and single mothers in Cape St George, Newfoundland, feel a need to socialize with their peers. Their concepts of leisure and their access to it are intrinsically linked to the availability and manipulation of time. Unlike men in the same community, whose occupations are circumscribed by external, relatively predictable activities and environments, women's lives are defined in terms of their relationships and responsibilities to others. The traditional social context specifically allocates time for men's leisure activities, while women must secure their own. Women's roles as wives, mothers, and householders are so demanding that they must actively create opportunities to meet with other women. Two such kinds of informal social gatherings are both regular and significant in Cape St George. One takes place after collecting mail; the other centres around sewing in someone's house.

It is generally agreed that women in Euro North American society must "squeeze in" time to get together and enjoy each other's company (Wimbush 1986). Edward T. Hall's (1983) analysis of gender and time organization attempts to propose a plausible model. Men,

Hall says, use time monochronically, they do one thing at a time, and work through organized schedules. Women use and conceptualize time polychronically – they are capable of handling several matters concurrently, and are in fact expected to do so – and schedule their time informally. But such rigid distinctions don't fit the women in Cape St George. I will argue that they use both polychronic and monochronic time, yet their scheduling remains essentially informal. The ethnographic examples given in this essay demonstrate that Hall's model is not systematically applicable because of the complexity of the various contexts in which women operate.

In the following discussion I emphasize the processes which allow women's informal gatherings to take place. Time manipulation delineates this process, and allows for the synchronization of women's lives which is essential to the continuum that establishes their gatherings as tradition.

I collected the material discussed here during three summers (1985–1987). My fieldwork and subsequent analysis were essentially emic[1] and followed feminist principles; I sought to understand the women's own definitions of experience with regard to the contexts I studied. Conversations during informal social gatherings showed no pretentious or competitive elements. Instead, they were based on cooperation between the members of the group on the one hand, and between the group and myself – the researcher – on the other.[2] I focus here on the gatherings' value as contexts for communication; that is, on the relevance of socializing as a conduit for transmitting knowledge and information within the informally established group. Hence, I will emphasize process rather than content.

Women's informal social gatherings in Cape St George clearly have "private" dimensions. The groups are small and participants are socially and emotionally close to each other. Women choose gender-exclusive social events; the fact that only women are there is not dictated by the domestic settings where interaction takes place. Rather, groups of women initiate regular meetings, which become a much-anticipated part of their lifestyle. Conversation, then, aesthetically conveys values which clearly indicate the negotiation of participants' power and control over their own lives and those of others.[3]

Like most Newfoundland outports, Cape St George has been severely affected by the gradual decline which led to the moratorium on the fishery. Deprived of its economic mainstay, the area sustains the highest unemployment rate on the island, averaging around seventy per cent of the population. For married women and single mothers in Cape St George, access to most facilities available in urban settings is practically nonexistent. There is no public transportation other than the school bus, and no services such as banks, shopping malls, and hospitals. In this environment the demands on women householders are high. Some responsibilities tie a woman to her home, while other activities are performed outside it. Of the latter, shopping, for example, requires planning. The local convenience store stocks just about everything, but in limited quantities and at very high prices, so most women do their main shopping in Stephenville, forty miles away. They usually go to "town" once every two weeks, upon receiving their husband's unemployment or welfare cheque, which supposedly comes every fortnight through the post, but is notoriously unreliable. Shopping trips often coincide with women's further – "public" – responsibilities, such as meetings with children's schoolteachers, nurses, or other authorities. Women give priority to the shopping trip over other appointments, which can usually be postponed by phone.

Shopping trips are not occasions for women to get together. Shoppers must take the 8:30 morning bus; most get back around lunch time, unless they have other town duties such as hospital appointments, in which case they must take the 5:00 evening bus back home. Because of the aforementioned irregularity of the post, trips to Stephenville cannot be planned and thus do not facilitate small group socializing. Yet such outings are opportunities for the chance acquisition of items of news or gossip which may later be circulated during informal gatherings.

The daily late-morning walk to the post office to collect the mail, is, when the weather is fine, a much enjoyed social stroll. Picking up the mail almost inevitably affords the opportunity for informal social gatherings for one of the groups of married women I was friendly with, and whom I interviewed. In fact, the mail collection serves as cognitive[4] scheduling for their morning activities. Thus, women ensure that their housework, laundry, and lunch-making will be complete by the time the mail officer's car is spotted on its way back from the post office, so that they can spare an hour or so for a chat on their way back home.

After-the-post-office gatherings are usually short. Their primary purpose is to allow women to mix socially and exchange news. As I've suggested, women carefully save time to be allocated to this kind of gathering. Their time is, however, bounded by responsibilities to children: by their return from school for their lunch break – which depends on the distance and the happenings between school and home – or by the amount of time an elder daughter or babysitter can take care of them.

After-the-post-office gatherings, at the time of my fieldwork, would take place at my host's house, convenient because of its location next to the post office. My host, whom I will call Julie, would daily anticipate her friends' visit. Except for her youngest son, all male members of the household would have left for work or other outdoor activity. Julie would sometimes send her teenage daughter on her way also. However, she would periodically be required to participate in housework, as her mother considered the work essential to her life skills education, often on laundry day (usually Monday) and on floor-washing day (Thursday or Friday).

Most women in the community do their laundry on Mondays, another indicator of women's synchronised organisation of time. After-the-post-office gatherings were rare on Mondays because laundry was an all-day chore. But on days when women could be expected to gather, we would engage beforehand in what seemed to me a crash course in housework, although for Julie it was a series of routine tasks. Breakfast would be over by 9:30. The dishes remained on the table until the youngest child was washed, dressed, and set in a corner of the living room with his toys. Then Julie would clear the breakfast table, wash the dishes, clean the counter and stove, and sweep the floor. This done, she would make the beds and put the clothes away. Finally, she would clean the bathroom, vacuum the living room, and dust the furniture.

We would then sit down for a well-deserved cup of tea. Julie would have hers in her rocking chair by the wood stove, facing the window. She could then see passers-by and wait for her friends to drop in. Julie could tell from the way they were dressed, the pace they walked, or the company they were with whether they would drop in and approximately how long they would stay. If a woman was dressed very casually, she had probably interrupted her chores to go to the post office and would not have time to drop by on her way back. The same conclusion would apply to a friend who walked quickly. On the other hand, if the passer-by was taking her time and looked slightly better dressed, it was more likely that she would drop in. Similarly, if two of Julie's friends were walking up together and glanced at the house or signalled, they would surely visit for the best part of an hour. Three or four friends would usually drop in on their way back from the post office. The women would sit at the kitchen table with a cup of tea and a few cigarettes and chat until each returned to her own house for lunch.

These morning gatherings are breaks between different sets of household activities. They occur between breakfast and lunch, although they do not occupy all the time between the two meals. The content of conversation and narratives[5] is affected by the limited time available. The women share news, comments, or talk triggered by the activity on the road, monitor the comings and goings of passers-by, and discuss economic and matrimonial life. For instance, the group would make guesses as to who was getting a cheque, or why and how often someone would go to the post office, or where else they might be headed. Or the women might comment on local community politics relating to this or that passer-by.

They would also converse about the mail itself, discussing its contents or the slow pace of the postal system. When discussing incoming mail – usually welfare cheques – talk would centre on economic difficulties and unemployment. Women would then compare each other's situations, and usually would finally agree that they were "all in the same boat."

That would be the time when they would share narratives of their marriages and talk about men. Julie's friend Jeanne would take advantage of the gatherings to have a cigarette, for her husband did not allow her to smoke. The tone of conversation was then tenser than usual, and participants expressed a lot of complaints. I often heard women say they were "glad to get away from the men and the kids." After-the-post-office gatherings are a prime opportunity for women in this group to reflect on and discuss their status as women in the community.

The same group of women also gathers to work on collective or individual projects. Like their mothers and grandmothers, who would gather at a spinning wheel owner's home, women still perform textile work in groups. Now they get together at the home of Jeanne, a sewing machine owner. Like after-the-post-office gatherings, these events are collective, gender-exclusive, interactive, and organized around time.

In this case, however, interaction revolves around work. Thus, the content of conversation and the flow of speech differ. Unlike after-the-post-office gatherings, which are casual chats and happen *if* there is time, "work-oriented" gatherings are scheduled in advance and happen *when* all participants involved have time. These events are planned, usually over the phone two or three days in advance, and take place during an evening after supper, when five or six women can participate.

On such an evening, before going to Jeanne's, Julie would gather her needles and thread and whatever clothing or other textiles needed repair. She would also select old clothing items to be presented as gifts or swapped with other participants. As she chose each piece, she would comment on its origin or its price and the reason it was not worn any more.

The gathering itself would follow a certain timetable which, although not strictly defined, would be equally distributed between collective interaction and tasks, and individual access to the sewing machine. Initially all participants would swap clothes, as everyone "happened" to have brought a few "extra things" which would "suit" other participants or their families. The exchange served as an informal market, and would last approximately half an hour or until the major project was in place.

On these evenings, women would occupy the entire social space of the house: the kitchen and living room. Tables and seats were taken up by clothing and sewing apparatus. The sewing machine was set up on its own table, and only a corner of the kitchen table was available for cups and ashtrays. Two or three women would sit at the kitchen table hemming or doing preliminary work with material before bringing it to the machine. While working, they would compare patterns, order from catalogues, or recount shopping trips. At the same time, they would discuss children's education, teenage behaviour, and community politics.

Other women would be in the living room by the sewing machine, preparing a major piece of work such as a curtain. Because of the noise of the machine, which was operated by its owner, those next to it could not talk very much. The women would take turns as the ones in the kitchen would bring in their work to the machine and replace those readying the curtain. Only when Jeanne took a break from the machine did they all sit together at the table.

Such work-related gatherings would last three or four hours. During them, a major piece of work would be completed and other minor repairs done. Everyone involved would cooperate and benefit from each other's contribution. Cooperation was effective at several levels: those of the work itself, of clothes-swapping, and most importantly of conversational exchanges whose involved nature required a significant input of energy.

Topics revolved around issues of direct relevance to participants' lives: their commitments, their relationships, their children, and their perspectives on their role and status as female members of their families and community. Because there was more time than during the morning, personal matters would be more prominent. Women would, by way of personal experience narratives, constructively seek and offer support to each other on issues that included child molestation, rape, and psychological violence, all of which would affect women in the group to a certain extent.

The primary reason many women expressed for getting together was "to get away from the men and the kids"; that is, to escape their expected traditional role and step into another sphere where they could experiment with a different sense of security and power. To achieve this, however, they had to make time and/or find opportunities which would allow them to spend that time together.

Women in Cape St George have a common understanding of the value of time, and their informal gatherings are communicative events in which interaction is a priority. Work, including all their responsibilities, functions as a frame of reference. They use time polychronically when they undertake many tasks in the same time frame. They also use time monochronically when one purpose or one task is attributed to one time frame, as in sewing events. Notions of the availability and manipulation of time determine the form and content of each type of gathering.

Thus, Hall's attribution of time use distinctions to gender differences does not strictly apply to Cape St George women. After the post office gatherings are monochronic because they are strictly scheduled, and their sole purpose is conversation. But this scheduling is not measured by a clock, but rather by the more informal and cognitive notion of the time between the mail delivery and the children's lunch. Monochronic because they focus around a notion of schedule, they are nevertheless quite informally organised.[6] The sewing gatherings also have monochronic, formal dimensions in terms of their scheduling. Yet they are polychronic because their happening depends on women's availability, and because they fulfil more than one purpose: they are for work, but also for conversation.

Understanding power and control over time from a woman's perspective is essential to understanding women's social and communicative traditions. Part of shared experience for women in Cape St George is negotiating leisure time in their daily life while also coping with work routines and environments. They preserve their right to networks of communication and friendship that are essential to their identity as women (and probably also to their sanity!). Elucidating, describing, and analysing aspects of women's lives shows not only what is significant to social and cultural dynamics, but also, most importantly, what is useful and meaningful to the women themselves.

NOTES AND ACKNOWLEDGMENTS

The field research for this essay was done for my doctoral dissertation (Desplanques 1991). I would like to thank the Institute for Social and Economic Research of Memorial University of Newfoundland for funding part of this research, and Dr Roberta Buchanan, dept of English, Memorial University of Newfoundland, for her initial editorial comments.

1 Emic refers to an ethnographic approach seeking to understand the subjects' own definitions of experience, rather than aiming to develop an
outsider's viewpoint.

2 For more information on issues related to women and fieldwork see
Peggy Golde (1970) on women fieldworkers and Debora Kodish (1987)
on women informants.

3 Folklorists and anthropologists have observed similar social gatherings,
mostly in passing or as related to other aspects of traditional life (e.g.,
Wright 1981; Abu-Lughod 1985; Carpenter 1985; Davis 1983).

4 Cognitive here refers to cultural knowledge, and to how rules are
learned and used to organise behaviour (Spradley 1972:5).

5 Consideration of more formal oral genres in this volume include Stone
(on storytelling) and Klassen (on preaching). Talk at healing conferences
(Grant) and cab driver's conversational narratives (Boyd) are more
informal.

6 There have been a number of studies of women as householders which
have considered time as an important factor in the organisation of their
lives (Luxton 1980; Bourne 1985; Luxton and Rosenberg 1986). Many,
however, do not focus on such leisure activities as the ones described
above, other than by reference to the past and nineteenth century society (Davis 1983; Bennett 1989; Murray 1979). Studies in occupational
folklore which consider time manipulation for breaks and rests as
means to cope with the work environment have dealt mainly with
male-dominated or wage-labour contexts (McCarl 1976; Nickerson 1974;
Santino 1983).

Speaking Out in God's Name: A Mennonite Woman Preaching[1]

PAMELA E. KLASSEN

Traditionally, Mennonite women in North America have been forbidden to preach and denied ordination in the church, meaning they cannot speak from the pulpit or officiate at rituals such as communion, baptism, and weddings.[2] Though women are becoming increasingly active as ordained ministers and lay pastors, pockets of strongly ingrained resistance to women preachers endure (Nyce 1983:iii; Franz 1991:B1). While younger Mennonite women can rely on their education for irrefutable qualifications as preachers,[3] older Mennonite women must often tap other sources to authorize their right to speak from the pulpit.

In this article I present the experience of Agatha Janzen,[4] who, despite resistance from both men and women, established herself as a lay preacher. Maintaining her tenuous role as a preacher demands that Agatha have arguments capable of convincing her congregation and, more importantly, herself, that she is worthy to speak. This older woman's negotiation of patriarchal structures in her church shows some of the complex strategies women employ to challenge tradition, while struggling to remain part of their communities.[5]

A member of a predominantly Russian Mennonite General Conference church,[6] Agatha was born in 1922 in the Soviet Union. She emigrated to Canada in 1947 after fleeing from the Ukraine through the chaos of World War II. A homemaker, wife, mother, and grandmother, Agatha is also an herbalist, quilter, amateur historian, and artist, as well as a lay preacher.

The Mennonite church Agatha attends is unique, in that two services are organized every Sunday morning, the earlier one in English and the later one in German. Older people who emigrated from the Soviet Union in the 1920s and 1940s, including Agatha, attend the German service and have a say in how services are conducted and who speaks. Despite the objections of some to women preaching, the team which asks people from the congregation to preach, made up of church members and a middle-aged, progressive, male pastor, has asked Agatha to speak five times. Only one other woman has preached in the German services, making Agatha's role as lay preacher somewhat exceptional in her congregation.

Agatha's reasons for preaching are articulated in concert with her faith in God the Father, Jesus the Son, and the power of the Holy Spirit.[7] In trying to establish herself as a competent preacher, Agatha employs three main strategies that invoke and/or reinterpret male authority: she calls on family precedent set by her father who was also a preacher; she resists conventional interpretations of Biblical text dictating women's silence (especially 1 Corinthians 14), reread-ing the Bible to find justification for her desire to speak; and she disavows any assertions of her ability to preach, claiming instead that she is being fully obedient to God's will.[8] Agatha thus situates herself firmly in the Christian tradition, while challenging some of its Mennonite manifestations.

Despite objections to her preaching from men and women in the church, Agatha has taken on the mantle of her father's vocation. Agatha's father, who died when she was nine, figures prominently in her own self-definition both because she is proud of his vocation as a preacher and because she suffered a great deal in the atheistic Soviet Union as a result of being a "preacher's kid." Agatha tenta-tively claims an ancestral connection to preaching the Gospel, saying that perhaps she is carrying on the aspirations of her father by speak-ing in church.

A careful and diligent reader of the Bible (in three languages: Ger-man, Russian, and English), Agatha contextualizes the writings of Paul, combing through the text to form her own interpretation:

PK: Do you look at the Bible historically, and say well, Paul would have said this because he was living at this time, that was his culture, or do you think that you have to think of it as the word of God and you can't –

AJ: I think the – what your question is[9] – like there are groups of Mennonites, especially these ones that have come from Russia, ladies who wouldn't go anywhere without a kerchief on, or certain clothes on. And they think of Paul saying that a woman has to cover her head. But he wouldn't have said – yeah and he also said that the man wasn't supposed to cover his head. And he didn't say that to Jews. Had he said that to Jews they would have really been angry at him, because the Jews think differently. A man will cover his head when he goes to pray. So, if he would tell a Jew to uncover his head when he goes to pray, that wouldn't work.

So, Paul had to tell these people who didn't come from the Jews, had come from the heathen, because this was their custom. And if the woman had her hair open and uncovered and so on, then she would be a cheap woman or a street woman. That's how they are themselves. So he didn't want them to look like someone from the street. But that doesn't mean that we can't have our heads bared now. Or hair cut and so on. It's just because that was the time.

Of course Paul was still a little bit under the influence that prevailed at the time that woman was below man, but Jesus actually didn't treat women that way. There were lots of women that followed him and looked after him and did all kinds of good things and he sent them out, and some of them had preached.

Agatha pulls from the text a Jesus who would support her as a preacher. She states that Paul was affected by the patriarchal climate of the time but that Jesus was free of such influences. She maintains her attachment to Jesus and her tradition, while abjuring interpretations that would forbid the fulfillment of her commitment to Christianity – a commitment demanding that she preach.

In accepting the request to preach, Agatha denies that she is especially gifted or deserving of praise because of her efforts. She says instead that God is speaking through her.[10] Her voice utters his words, her body is a channel for his message. She does not claim the right to speak based on theological training or a captivating preaching style. She says she relinquishes herself in the delivery of God's message, transforming a potentially controversial act of speech into an act of obedience:[11]

AJ: When I feel there is still someone who objects to it, I wonder if I should be up there on the pulpit. And I resisted it for a long time. But then I wondered, am I listening to the people around me when I resist, or does God want me to be out there? And it came to me that I think I should be obedient here too. If I have something to say, then I should get up there and say it. And I did it a few times. I prayed to God not to bring what I want to say, but I prayed for him to use me, and to sort of speak through me. And I think he did ...

PK: What did it feel like when you were preaching. Did you feel like you were doing something rebellious?

AJ: No. I had prayed to God to speak through me, and not to let me say my own things. And I want the honour to all be his, not mine. And that's how I feel about it. If people come up to me and say, that was a good sermon, I feel very uncomfortable. I wish they wouldn't say that because it wasn't my – I just think it was God doing through me.

Agatha refers to obedience to convince both herself and the congregation that she is not undermining the structure of the church.[12] Despite the possibility that presenting herself as a channel for God's word could be seen as an even more audacious act than speaking with her own voice, Agatha confidently states her obedience to legitimate her preaching.

Agatha encountered objections to her preaching from older men in her congregation, who conveyed them through her husband. These men assured him that it was not *Agatha* as a preacher they were opposed to, it was a *woman* as a preacher. Agatha agrees that men are the ideal preachers; women's bodies are unsuitable behind the pulpit. By wearing make-up and fancy clothing women "arouse men," says Agatha, and keep them from concentrating on the sermon. "A man in a nice suit looks much better up there," she says. Given the choice, she would rather see a man preaching. But she does not feel that she has such a choice:

AJ: And if there were enough men willing to fill the pulpit and do the jobs, I would gladly step back, let them do the preaching. But sometimes I see some lay person on the pulpit and I think, "Well, I wish he wasn't there." Not that – I don't know, maybe I'm sometimes too critical too. But I have never volunteered any preaching. As a matter of fact I was asked a few times before I said yes I would. And I even had a feeling that my husband wasn't very thrilled about it. But after I had done it once he never said anything critical about it.

Not content with the ability of some lay men to convey the gospel, Agatha puts aside her prejudices about women behind the pulpit and takes the step from Bible study leader (a role she is more comfortable in) to preacher. Agatha does not want her preaching to be taken as a critique of the patriarchal structure of the church. At times she asserts she is merely filling a void.[13] Just as when Mennonite women in the Soviet Union took the roles of sermon readers when there were no men around during the German occupation of World War II, so Agatha feels it necessary to fill the lacuna she sees in her church.

The Sunday I went to one of Agatha's sermons the church seemed more sparsely attended than previous Sundays I had been there. Agatha wore a grey skirt and jacket with a blouse that covered her neck well. She sat on the stiff, high-backed chairs behind the pulpit together with the worship leader while she waited for her turn to speak. She told the congregation of how Jesus is the only door through which one can pass to heaven. This is the message that Agatha wants to sound louder than the effect of her body behind the pulpit: people must be more "secure in their beliefs," they must be convinced of their salvation.

Parallel to her idea that men make ideal preachers, Agatha feels that men should be in charge of the family. When directly comparing the church to the family, however, Agatha grants women equality in churchwork which she feels they should not have as wives:

PK: What do you think about women preaching?
AJ: I've done that too. I've preached. I don't think we can – before God there is no man or woman, they're all the same, before him. In the family it's different. Just like any institution needs someone at the head, that sort of oversees the whole thing, so the family does too. And the man should actually be able to oversee the family. He's not always able to and too bad when he isn't. And we see all kinds of problems in families. But in church work, I think women should have a chance to preach. I had my own doubts about it, especially since I knew that many old men wouldn't like a woman on the pulpit. And I hate the thought of someone not coming to church because I'm at the pulpit. I wouldn't want that. But I think that will disappear.

When Agatha preaches in church, she is secure in her status as a wife. Agatha feels she does not, by example or intent, pose a threat to gender arrangements in the family, though those opposed to her preaching may feel otherwise. When preaching, Agatha tries to efface her womanly attributes as much as possible, but speaks firm in the conviction that she does not challenge her community in her family life. Elaine Lawless found a similar dynamic in Pentecostal churches: "An unmarried woman, rejecting the life of wife and mother, would pose a serious threat to the equilibrium of a fundamentalist congregation. A woman preacher's own maternal experience becomes weighted and must be foregrounded in order to minimize the threat that her position 'in front of' the church is a rejection of her 'natural' role as wife and mother" (1988b:149). As a wife and mother, Agatha allows herself more freedom of speech in church than do women with less conventional marital status (Klassen 1994:116).

In calling on God to use her as a conduit, Agatha enacts the opposite of what Susan Sered calls the "domestication of religion."[14] When Agatha's religious life takes on public form she *depersonalizes* it. She wants to detach her preaching from all personal attributes –

the way she speaks, her body, and her gender. She wears neutral colours and modest styles, and speaks in a serious tone with little smiling. Her detachment, however, is implicitly buttressed by her role as wife and mother.

While she justifies preaching with reference to obedience, Agatha feels no need to legitimate her pastoral role when she visits patients in the hospital. There she plays a nurturing, maternal role, one consonant with her identity as a woman. Nor does she defend her leadership of the Bible study in her quilting group, where she takes on a public speaking role, reading the Bible and giving a short exegesis. Her audience in the quilting group is women, so there is no resistance to her as a speaker, and no need for legitimation. When her step into the public eye involves addressing an audience which includes men *and* assuming a position of prestige and power in the church as a preacher, however, she fashions a defense. Agatha feels compelled to prove her right to speak to herself and her congregation, while trying to remain non-threatening.[15]

When I first met Agatha, she seemed to be living a traditional life. She had married a widower and had raised a family. She did not have a professional occupation, she seemed comfortable as a Mennonite, and she spoke reverently about her faith. I guessed that she would not have stories to tell that were critical of the church, and that there would be great dissonance between her attitudes and my own.

Over the course of our conversations, however, I realized that all I had surmised was mistaken. Agatha, by virtue of her determination to preach, fell into an implicitly critical stance towards traditional elements in her church. Recognizing how different her attitudes were from what I had expected was a profoundly humbling process. I realized that despite my enthusiasm for hearing women tell their own stories, I had been quickly lured by easy stereotypes (cf. Mbilinyi 1989). Younger women must realise the complexities of older women's lives, the limitations on their choices, and their very real fears, commitments, and passions.

Though Agatha may be conventionally pious and supportive of women's submission in the family, she also holds that women have the right to speak God's word, a most auspicious task. That she must speak in an environment of resistance causes her pain, sleepless nights, and self-doubt. Agatha's transformation of defiance into obedience which she asserts in her own legitimation of her preaching does not completely solve the problem of being a woman speaking from a man's place. Even in concert with other strategies of resistance such as calling on her father's precedent and avidly studying the Bible, Agatha remains concerned about the moral ambiguity inherent in her adoption of a public role behind the pulpit. She manœuvres through both her own doubts and the objections of others by rooting herself in wider networks of nurture, both personal and pastoral, from which she gathers the moral authority to speak out, a few times a year, in God's name.

NOTES

1 This article is a revised version of parts of chapter four of my book *Going By the Moon and the Stars: Stories of Two Russian Mennonite Women* (Klassen 1994).

2 One exception was Ann Jemima Allebach, ordained in a General Conference Mennonite church in Philadelphia in 1911 (Juhnke 1986:17). Not until 1980 was another woman ordained. The Mennonite Church (distinct from the General Conference church) first ordained women in 1978 (Peters 1990:934). Ordination, however, does not guarantee that a woman becomes pastor of a church. For more on women's ordination in Ontario see Epp and Epp (1986:235, 237).

3 This is not to say that younger Mennonite women do not encounter resistance or difficulties when preaching. Cf. Epp (1987:104) and Good (1988).

4 Not her real name.

5 This article is based on fieldwork carried out in Southern Ontario between June 1991 and April 1992 (see Klassen 1994). Quotations are from videotaped interviews.

6 Russian Mennonites came to North America in three waves: the 1870s, 1920s, and post–World War II. Russian Mennonites have different traditions and dialects from Swiss Mennonites, who emigrated to North America in earlier waves. General Conference churches are considered a liberal branch of Mennonites in North America. For a brief history of Mennonites paying particular attention to women, see Epp and Epp (1986).

7 I refer to God in the masculine because this is the language Agatha uses.

8 I do not mean to imply that Agatha's strategies are all calculated choices. (In contrast, the storytellers discussed by Kay Stone in this volume reflectively and consciously choose narrative methods and forms). Agatha works with the stuff of her life to make sense of her position, but she also works strategically.

9 I had not mentioned women in the Bible prior to this point in the conversation. While Agatha was keyed into my concerns about gender, I

think she turned the conversation to preaching at this point because it is a prominent topic for her. After reading this note she added, "Because I was still going through intense battles within me at the time. I still am sometimes."

10 Claiming to speak in God's name is a practice found more in charismatic strains of the Mennonite church than in General Conference churches. More research into sermon styles within different churches is necessary before patterns can be firmly identified. For my purposes what is important about Agatha's claim that God works through her is that it is stated in reaction to people's resistance to her speaking. On God speaking through the faithful, also see Gail Grant's article in this volume.

11 Both Agatha's link to her father and her relinquishing of self for God is paralleled by what Robin McGrath finds in some Inuit women's autobiographies (in this volume): women write when "the father – who is the only person with more authority over an Inuit woman than her husband – has given permission for that woman to put herself forward."

12 Agatha's espousal of obedience is mirrored by many Christian women claiming to speak God's word, including Margery Kempe, a fifteenth-century mystic (Butler-Bowdon 1954:287), Sister Connie, a twentieth-century Pentecostal preacher (Lawless 1988a:85), and Ruth Brunk Stoltzfus, a twentieth-century Mennonite preacher (Rich 1983:224).

13 Sister Alma, a Pentecostal preacher, echoes this defence, "If you men will do what God wants you to do, we women won't have to!" (Lawless 1988b:42).

14 The domestication of religion occurs when people (especially women) bring the symbols, rituals, and myths of their formal religion into their domestic life, weaving the formal tradition into their personal concerns and relationships (Sered 1988:516).

15 The public/private split has rendered women's activites in the Mennonite church invisible, since the public realm has been equated with spheres dominated by men. Quilting groups and women's Mission Circles are just as public as sanctuaries and Conference board meetings. The difference lies in the absence of men and in the lesser power and influence of decision-making in women's groups. Epp (1987) begins to remedy this false dichotomy.

Difficult Women in Folktales:
Two Women, Two Stories

KAY STONE, WITH
MARVYNE JENOFF AND
SUSAN GORDON

As I child I had a guilty fascination with the undisciplined women in the folktale books I inevitably received each Christmas. I secretly approved of their deliberate belligerence, but I also noted that justice prevailed. I wondered if it was possible to be undisciplined without suffering the gruesome fates of Cinderella's stepsisters or the wicked women in "Hansel and Gretel" and "Snow White." Many years later, while interviewing girls and women for my dissertation on women in folktales (Stone 1975a), I found that others admitted to a similar fascination with the "bad" characters. Their unexpected reactions compelled me to expand my notions of folktale women and to break away from a simplistic good woman/bad woman approach.

While I worked on my dissertation in the early 1970s, professional storytelling was in the process of bursting into full bloom as a performance art after several decades of quiet activity in libraries and schools. My continuing interest in women and folktales eventually led me to a curiosity about this "new" telling of old tales, and I began a formal examination of the phenomenon. In previous articles I have described professional storytellers in general (Stone 1984 and 1986), surveyed stories favoured by a sampling of tellers in North America (Stone 1993a), and examined "Frau Trude" in detail, along with its development through several years of oral performance (Stone 1993b).

I have been motivated by others who have studied individual artists and their personal connections with their stories.[1] Although I am not suggesting that urban professional performers are a part of a "pure" oral tradition of the sort usually investigated by folklorists, I see that a parallel tradition has come into being through the popularization of folktales over the past few centuries. While the current storytelling revival is popularly believed to have begun in this century, it actually started with the publication of a handful of French folktales rewritten by Charles Perrault in the late 1600s (see Perrault 1969), and leapt into prominence with the Grimm editions little more than a century later (see Grimm 1987).

These two collections were widely translated, spreading the tales far beyond their original time and place. They have been taken even further by Walt Disney's films, one (*Snow White and the Seven Dwarfs*) based on Grimms' German stories and three (*Cinderella*, *Sleeping Beauty*, and *Beauty and the Beast*) on earlier French tales. Disney films have played a significant role in the popularization of folktales, reinterpreting the material already rewritten by the Grimms and Perrault.

Contemporary storytellers in North America have continued the reworking of popularized folktales in their oral and written work. When I began to survey professional tellers who favoured traditional collections as sources, two who responded sent examples of their own interpretations of Grimm tales. I was excited to see that each featured decidedly undisciplined women – the unnaturally cruel mothers in "Snow White" and "The Juniper Tree."[2]

Marvyne Jenoff is a Toronto storymaker whose transformed "Snow White" (see Appendix) has shifted between oral and written composition in the years she has struggled with it. She has been working on a collection of traditional fables and folktales, finding them a challenging contrast to her more autobiographical poetry and prose. I have heard her present some of the darker Grimm tales at Toronto storytelling festivals in the 1980s, and have read several of her original compositions based on folktales and fables. Susan Gordon is a folklorist, oral performer, and workshop leader who lives in rural Maryland. She has devoted several years to a handful of traditional tales, including "The Juniper Tree," telling and retelling them in a variety of contexts.

Gordon and Jenoff use disparate means to accomplish similar objectives: Jenoff reinterprets the text through her own direct interaction with the story; Gordon does so indirectly, through subtle changes and by involving the audience in the interpretation.[3] Jenoff completely remotivates the wicked queen in "Snow White," while Gordon stays close to the printed text but finds extra-narrative ways of challenging stereotypes in "The Juniper Tree."

My interest in their reinterpretations resulted in this paper, originally given at the International Society for Folk-Narrative Research in Budapest in 1989. The conference's topic, "Storytelling in Contemporary

Society," inspired papers on a wide sampling of genres: from traditional oral tales to urban legends, jokes, and family stories. Four in particular were directly relevant to my interest in the conscious artistic reworking of folktales, and influence my essay here; I will describe them briefly.

The first reflected on the communication of folktales in the next millennium. Giovanni Bronzini believed folktales would continue to be an important expressive art, largely due to their archetypal nature, which allows them to function "as a catalogue of the destinies a man or a woman might have" (Bronzini 1989:5). However, he observed that the continuing fragmentation of everyday life, and increasing literacy, would favour writing and electronic reproductions over oral narration as the medium of creation (Ibid., 1). Jenoff's and Gordon's artistic efforts show that folktales still have the potential to express the deeper values of human existence – and, furthermore, to confront these values, not only to mirror them.

Each teller also offers a challenge to the assumption that oral performance will cease to be important. Even Jenoff, whose rethinking of "Snow White" is accomplished mainly through rewriting, has experimented with retelling this and other traditionally inspired folktales. Gordon relies almost entirely on oral performance. A second conference paper focused directly on the oral nature of modern professional performances – in this case the "revival" of storytelling in France since the late 1960s (Gorog-Karady 1989).

Veronika Gorog-Karady noted that many urban tellers, who rely primarily on printed sources, reinterpret the tales. To achieve new relevance for their listeners, some employ theatrical methods that take them away from the "original" story, while others remain close to it. But no matter what means they used, Gorog-Karady regarded their artistic efforts as a renewal of "one of the most democratic forms of aesthetic awareness," noting that tellers and listeners take part in an "intimate complicity" that goes beyond the more usual dichotomy of performer/audience (Ibid., 3). In interactive performances, a story's significance lies beyond the words of the spoken text. Susan Gordon, particularly, negotiates with her listeners each time she retells "The Juniper Tree"; their responses expand the sense of the story even though her "text" may not change significantly from one telling to the next.

A third presentation challenged narrow notions of storytelling as an old traditional art by placing the stories of Perrault and the Grimms firmly in the "modern age" and emphasizing the history of literary exchanges between oral and written tales (Voigt 1989). Vilmos Voigt noted that popular folktales have survived not only in printed collection and electronic reproduction, but also in parodies, satires, jokes, and commercial advertisements. Seen in this light, the stories of Jenoff and Gordon are part of a long literary tradition in which "folk" tales continue to evolve in form and meaning as methods of communication.

Considerations of "folk" and "non-folk" and oral vs written expressions did not at all concern a fourth participant, Donald Ward (1989). Instead, he emphasized the broader concept of *homo narrans*, human beings evolving as natural story makers, capable of reflecting on reality and transforming it through both personal and traditional tales. He observed that active story making begins with "idionarration," an internal process that occurs when we are alone with our own thoughts: "These moments of solitary reflection are, I suggest, a vital element in the processes that ultimately lead to social change. It is in these moments that narrative structures that later enter into the dynamic between the individual and his [or her] society have their genesis" (Ibid., 6). He cites personal stories told to one of his graduate students by abused and homeless women who reworked their lives by rethinking their stories. Jenoff and Gordon also use this process; through their stories they express the private thoughts developed in solitude and later performed in public. Each woman is conscious of the potential social impact of her idionarrated stories of undisciplined women.

MARVYNE JENOFF

Jenoff was already a published poet when she began to take an interest in telling stories. In preparing to work on "Snow White," she searched through all English versions she could find; she chose to use the earliest text because it was so completely different from the well-known version (which was further adapted and popularized by the Disney film).[4]

In this story, the mother wishes for a lovely child but later regrets this as Snow White matures. She takes the girl out to the woods to pick flowers and abandons her there, not knowing that the girl eventually finds her way to the helpful dwarfs. After consulting her mirror and finding Snow White still alive, she tries to destroy her (disguised as a peddlar, not a hag) using the familiar motifs of the poisoned comb, strangling bodice, and fatal apple. Snow White's father, not the prince, finds and removes her coffin, orders his royal physicians to revive her by tying her body to ropes connected to the four corners of the room. After her resurrection the prince appears and the story proceeds (as in the later editions) with the cruel queen attending the wedding and dancing to her death in red hot iron shoes (from David and David 1964:303–15).

The fact that the natural mother retains her central place in this variant, instead of dying at the beginning, gave Jenoff more scope for a positive transformation. She also uses the father's expanded active role in the story to develop his character more negatively. She begins her story with a dream, rejecting the stark red and white imagery of blood and snow in favour of a contrast of human-made and natural worlds: "One winter morning the Queen was embroidering the scene outside her window. The King was looking beyond her at the steel city in the distance. Their sad eyes met, and the Queen pricked her finger. That night the Queen dreamed of colours, of her own red blood against the black wood window frame. She dreamed of a daughter." (Jenoff 1993:1).[5]

Jenoff continues her subtle transformation by giving the father a more overbearing role. He bans all mirrors in order to keep his wife young when he abandons her to go off to war. Without the mirror, the motif of vanity disappears; the queen does not become jealous of her maturing daughter. Thus they develop a loving relationship rather than a deadly enmity.

Snow White's curiosity about the world, encouraged by her mother, leads her away from home and into the steel city that, for Jenoff, replaces the Grimm texts' threatening forest. The girl is found by the seven dwarfs, misguided urbanites who turn her into a fashion model. Her mother incessantly searches for her and finally rescues her from the impersonal steel city and the foolish dwarfs, who are interested only in image and facade; she returns home where her mother gradually reintroduces her to a more natural life in which birds sing, the seasons pass, and love between human beings can develop.

Jenoff's involvement with the story is with the mother, who becomes the central character in this text. This shifting of the tale's focus from the daughter to the mother fundamentally alters the balance of the story; if the mother's character is positive, then the threatening forces must be found elsewhere – in Jenoff's tale, the overbearing father and the materialistic, opportunistic dwarfs. However, these antagonists are not portrayed as evil figures, or even as consciously destructive. Evil is expressed through the anonymous steel city and its inhuman technology that creates the pretentious world of fashion modelling – and also the helicopters that carry men off to war.

Jenoff's personal identification with the characters gives this text its vibrancy. She implies her own involvement when she describes how stories develop for her: "In a story (I am 'doing' Snow White and Cinderella) I have to consider all the characters and their relations to one another and what happens, and I'm bound firmly and complicatedly to the text" (letter, 2 March 1989). Jenoff employs both a shift of viewpoint (from daughter to mother) and the introduction of a contemporary setting to transform her story. Her emphasis on character rather than action or motivation underscores the message she wishes to express: that sinister forces unfold when we forget our personal connections to other living things.

Jenoff's approach takes this well-known tale in very different directions that reconstruct instead of rejecting an old genre. By re-figuring the "bad" mother as helper rather than destroyer, Jenoff offers a transformed text that speaks specifically to those for whom "steel cities" are not only dehumanizing but dangerous. More specifically, she challenges the woman-against-woman conflict found in many popular and popularized folktales – daughters threatened by mothers and stepmothers, "bad" fairies, elder sisters, and false brides. In this way, Jenoff moves deliberately in undisciplined directions, focusing on relationships between women that lead to freedom rather than competition and control.

SUSAN GORDON

I first heard Susan Gordon at a week-long storytelling retreat in 1982, when she was working on "The Maiden Without Hands."[6] This Grimm tale, along with "The Juniper Tree" has been a central story in Gordon's workshops and performances for more than a decade. "Maiden" deals with violence against women while "Juniper" centres on violence *by a woman*. Because she considers "Maiden" so eloquently elsewhere (Gordon 1993) I will not treat it here. However, her reasons for choosing to work on "Juniper Tree" apply to "Maiden" as well: "I initially came to the story seeing it as a depiction of great depravity and evil, which it is. But I think that the process [of story-telling] is one of balance, that guilt and self-hate alone will not allow one to really achieve personhood" (letter 2 May 1989:2).[7]

The story "of great depravity and evil" begins gently, with the familiar motif of parents longing for a child. As in "Snow White" the mother cuts her finger, sees blood on the snow, and wishes for a child "as red as blood and as white as snow." A boy is born, the woman dies, and the man finds a new wife with her own daughter. Motivated by jealousy she entices her young stepson to put his head in a chest to find an apple and then plunges the lid down, decapitating him and putting the blame on her own innocent daughter. She cooks the boy in a stew and serves it to her husband when he returns home, claiming that the boy has gone to visit a relative. After the grisly meal (eaten only by the unknowing father), the grieving sister carefully gathers the bones and plants them all under a juniper tree, in which the boy is reborn as a vengeful bird. The singing bird kills his stepmother by dropping a mill wheel on her, rewards his father and sister with gifts, and regains his original human form (from Grimm 1987:186–95).

Unlike Jenoff, Gordon stays with the Grimm text so faithfully that she reproduces the sounds described: the chest closing on the boy's neck, the turning mill wheel, the twenty millers cutting a new millstone, and, most importantly, the singing of the bird. She makes no alterations in the plot, no changes in character, no shifts of the point of view. Instead of transforming this mother into a nurturing woman – as Jenoff did for the character in "Snow White," Gordon tries to illuminate how the story struggles with evil in ways relevant to modern listeners. "Maybe a real confrontation with this story pulls a person up short and makes them realize the level of human depravity, but I think a real integration of the evil aspects and the good aspects in us only takes place over time" (letter, 2 May 1989:1).

Because she remains so close to the text, Gordon finds it problematic in terms of contemporary expression. In particular, she has come to find some of the story's most gruesome parts almost ridiculous: "I must say that when I went to tell the story for you on tape parts of it did seem harder to tell without laughing, basically the parts that are the most horrifying, the cutting off of the boy's head, the setting of his head on his body and its knocking off by his sister. While I know full well the horror of them, they seemed almost ludicrous and slapstick" (Ibid., 2).

Gordon does not merely recite the story but manages instead to subtly extend it through her creative involvement while remaining faithful to the Grimm text. She narrates in her own words rather than reciting by rote from the printed text, which gives her the opportunity to suggest delicate shadings of character. She also emphasizes the song with which the bird serenades the other story characters, giving this grisly tale a more lyrical tone. Most important, she engages the audience directly by asking them to reflect on their own interpretations of its meaning.

Since her telling is so faithful to the Grimm text, the smallest deviations are significant. The sister is even more pathetic in her guilty weeping for her murdered brother, and also in her exuberance when she receives the red shoes dropped by the golden bird. The father's insensitivity is expressed by his brusque demands for his dinner and his sharp words expressing his greed: "All of this is for *me*. None of you may have any of this." In the Grimm text, his words are softer and more ironic when he says, "Give me some more! I'm not going to share this with you. Somehow I feel as if it were all mine" (Grimm 1987:89).

The stepmother is portrayed more tragically. She alone understands the true meaning of the bird's song and goes out to meet her fate, saying mournfully, "Then I will go out and see what the bird has for me" (transcription:8). Gordon makes her own compassionate identification more explicit when she states how she came to understand the story as "unrelentingly patriarchal both in its depiction of the woman as solely responsible and in the solution to kill only her" (letter, 2 May 1989:1); that is, because of its failure to implicate the father in the tragedy. Because she makes only minor modifications to the Grimm text, these might easily go unnoticed without her additional comments – particularly her insistence that each of the characters is responsible for the outcome: "It was when I finally had her [the mother] and didn't diminish her, just let her be who she was, that I then began to – the story began to de-focus off of just her and began to move to look at the other characters. A very simple thing to notice is, *where is the father*?" (Ibid.).

Gordon finds her own storytelling voice in the bird's song, which had to be exactly right before she could tell the story. "I worked for a long time trying to learn the song, which I felt was so important to the story" (Ibid.). Since the bird is the teller of the boy's tale, Gordon, as singer of the bird's song, is bound by her identification with son rather than mother. The bird unrelentingly punishes the murderous mother, but rewards the devouring father, making it all the more difficult for Gordon to resolve her own doubts in her retelling.

She solves this in part by dividing audiences into small groups and having them retell the story from other viewpoints. They are asked to portray the mother as sympathetically as they can, and to reconsider the daughter and father as accomplices in the crime rather than as innocent bystanders. Gordon's performances are for very specific audiences whose interests she is aware of in advance.[8] Audience context thus has a direct effect on the increased understanding of the story as it comes back to her from their responses: "In therapeutic, educational, and religious settings the story is chosen with care to the occasion, with some knowledge of the people I'm telling it to and the desire to tell them a story that is, in some way, their story, which will provide them the opportunity to reflect on their own lives" (Ibid.). She modestly feels that such audience responses, rather than her own retellings, have helped to encourage a more compassionate perception of the tale's murderous mother.[9] Gordon allows listeners to interact more directly with the story through their own reinterpretations.

Stories like "Snow White" and "Juniper Tree" retain a great deal of transformative power because they function both literally and figuratively. This is certainly the case for those who listen to Gordon's performances and have themselves experienced the reality of childhood abuse. When real violence is treated at a distance in a seemingly unrealistic folktale, both teller and listeners create their own space for making personal connections.[10] These tales can also function as an emotional release from the stresses of ordinary day-to-day parenting, or from childhood fantasies and fears of abuse and abandonment. I say this as a child who was convinced my "cruel" parents couldn't possibly be my "true" parents, and as a mother with distressing dreams of losing two children in natural disasters. It is my sense that story makers like Gordon and Jenoff succeed because they understand the archetypal nature of the material they choose to work with. In their stories, literal and figurative come together; actual and imaginative worlds meet and interact, as they have for centuries.

Jenoff and Gordon have consciously chosen old stories with the intention of finding new meaning for them, seeing in them the "catalogue of the destinies a man or a woman might have" (Bronzini 1989:2) discussed earlier. Both women have been lead into their stories through personal connections – idionarration – rather than intellectual explications (Ward 1989). In their differing ways, these two women reconstruct "old" stories for today, and allow them to function as both reflections of lived reality *and* as means of transforming it.

Several essays in this anthology focus on this flexibility of interpretation that allows us to see other perspectives. Janice Ristock's treatment of differing responses to "killer dyke" films and Barbara Rieti's comments on witch beliefs in Newfoundland, among others, challenge us to avoid narrow responses to negative characterizations. While Janice Ristock's essay deals with negative portrayals of destructive women in popular films rather than folktales, I find these two formulations – Ristock's and Jenoff's – connected by common concerns; they attempt to explore the positive within the negative and thus to reclaim rather than reject "undisciplined women." The dreadful mothers in "Snow White" and "The Juniper Tree" are not cardboard characters with no possibility of three-dimensionality; they reveal at least the possibility of alternative destinies. As a fellow contributor to *Undisciplined Women* observed, such stories remain relevant because they do not flinch from the stark realities of human existence: "Embedding difficult issues in the artifice of the folktale allows the narrator to raise and address the issues in an acceptable context."

Jenoff and Gordon identify themselves directly with their stories instead of taking a more objective, critical outsider's stance. They parallel the individual creativity of the Hungarian peasant narrators described by Linda Dégh: "The personal text not only shows the narrator's ability to formulate a story from available plot episodes, but also his or her way of making the world of fantasy palpable by connecting it with the world of everyday reality: the told story also mirrors the narrator's specific conceptualization of the world and its affairs: his [or her] cultural and personal meanings" (Dégh 1990:48).

For Jenoff and Gordon, the "cultural and personal meanings" centre on figures of powerful women who – in the Grimm variants – are incapable of using their strength for creative purposes. The tellers' "idionarrative" comments in personal letters reveal that they are aware both of their own involvement, and of the transformational potential of traditional tales in contemporary life. Gordon in particular uses her storytelling – not only in this particular text – to encourage listeners to tell their own difficult stories and to reflect on their own lives. She concludes her own article on the Grimm tale of "The Maiden Without Hands" in these moving words: "I hope that you [the reader] will hold "The Maiden" against the fabric of your experience, as I held the Grimms' tale against mine, and note where the story informs your life, and where your life informs the story, and create it anew" (Gordon 1993:285).

In their personal struggles with these stories, holding them against the fabric of their own experiences, Jenoff and Gordon attempt to transform stereotype to archetype. It is in this way that old stories are continually kept alive and accessible to a world of new possibilities – through disciplined indiscipline.

APPENDIX   SNOW   WHITE: A   REFLECTION
Copyright Marvyne Jenoff, 1993

The King and Queen were sad because they had no child. The King was also annoyed because the Queen's beauty was marred by her sadness.

One winter morning the Queen was embroidering the scene outside her window. The King was looking beyond her at the steel city in the distance. Their sad eyes met, and the Queen pricked her finger.

That night the Queen dreamed of colours, her own red blood against the black wood windowframe. She dreamed of a daughter, named Snow White, for winter. Yet she was searching for her daughter, birds searching with her, through an endless summer. Waking, the Queen told it all to the King.

The King thought a daughter would be a good start. From that time he was always at the Queen's elbow as she embroidered garments for the child growing inside her. In time the child was born. Everyone was prepared to love her. Their love was reflected in her face, and they saw her as beautiful.

When Snow White was still a child the King went reluctantly to war. He ordered the soldiers to start out on foot and then prepared his helicopter. On the eve of his departure he had a dream that made him sit up. He was searching for his wife and child but kept finding only a harsh woman who spoke in rhymes to her evil-looking mirror. To prevent this dream from becoming prophetic, he issued an edict banning all mirrors from the kingdom, in deference to the seriousness of the war. To foil the rest of the dream, to keep his wife and child waiting for him exactly as they were, he banned the years as well and the seasons with them, so that no one would die or age or even grow. No sooner was the edict signed than the earth shuddered to a stop on its path, spun out of control – dark, light, dark, light – then settled into a succession of long summer days.

With no mirrors the Queen looked to her child for confirmation of her own beauty. But she soon realized that in her husband's absence she no longer had to be preoccupied with her appearance. She did as she pleased. She involved herself in every detail of caring for her child. She bathed her, dressed her, taught her to spin, weave, embroider, and read. They made up games and rhymes. And when the Queen realized that under her husband's edict no harm would come to her complexion, they spent time outdoors. Snow White loved the mingled summer fragrances. She ran after the birds, imitating their calls. She learned and loved every detail of her mother through the endless summer.

At the same time Snow White was curious about what lay outside the castle. The gate was often unattended now with the men at war. One day as Snow White was looking through the gate she saw a small, misshapen man, a dwarf, walking along, swinging his arms and singing to himself. Snow White hardly remembered men. She wriggled out between the bars. Imitating his jaunty walk, she followed him into the city. When she saw she had lost her way she stopped him and asked for help.

The dwarf had no idea what to do with a young girl in an ermine robe and a diamond tiara alone in the city. He took her to the penthouse where he lived with his six brothers. It was easier to think with the seven of them together.

At first the dwarfs were shy. But Snow White described her life in the castle. She told them how she happened to wander off and how much she missed her mother. The dwarfs were charmed to a man, and determined to help her. Being sophisticated city dwarfs they would do better than return her to her archaic existence. They would show her the modern world, the better world. Not being quite part of the world in the way they wished, they were very aware of trends.

This was a time when women, with only each other to look at, dressed as wildly as they wished. But in order to admire themselves, they had to catch their reflection in a windowpane when the sun was at just the right angle. The alternative was to become a fashion model and see themselves in magazines and on TV. The dwarfs would turn Snow White into a model with the advantage of a young start. They went out every day to get assignments for her. The left her in the penthouse, forbade her to work, denied her food, put her under sun lamps, and told her to let no one in. They didn't want her to wrinkle her skin by smiling or speaking.

Snow White appreciated their kindness. To please them she did nothing but gaze at her own image on commercials and in the photos they had pinned up on the walls. Birds came to teach her: the owl, the dove, the dodo, the raven, and the Canada goose. But Snow White was absorbed in her task and didn't see them. The birds couldn't even make themselves heard through the sealed double glass of the penthouse windows. Thus, still and silent, Snow White spent her days. But at night in her dreams were birds frantic with messages, and her mother dancing with supplicating motions. Come home, my child, she seemed to say, Come home.

One day as the Queen was out looking for her daughter, she noticed some birds on the ground, pacing around a magazine. On the colourful cover was a picture of Snow White, thin, smiling in an unfamiliar way. A breeze tore the cover loose and carried it, into the city. The Queen followed its fluttering path through the streets to the right building. As the cover flew upward and disappeared, she entered the building and found Snow White, more or less safe, in the penthouse.

The Queen had brought a sash which she had woven herself of silk and cotton in the colours of the fields. When she wrapped the sash around her daughter's waist, Snow White fell into a swoon of pleasure. As a model she was normally dressed in vinyl, hard leather, or metal, and couldn't remember ever wearing anything so soft or being touched so gently. The Queen was pleased she had made some headway. Before the dwarfs could find her there, she returned to the castle.

When the dwarfs revived Snow White she was sparkling and wistful, and they warned her sternly that she must absolutely let no one in. For, fervently and secretly, the dwarfs hoped to find out what it meant to be a husband and to marry Snow White themselves. Snow White tried to obey them out of respect. But at night as she slept there was the feel of grass in her hands and the scent of her own skin in the sun. During the day she began to dance a little, and speak as if to the flowers in the castle garden. She longed for the relief of light softened by green.

When the Queen returned, she brought a wooden comb which she had carved and polished by herself. Snow White's hair had been bleached, coloured, permed, straightened, gelled, blown dry, and shaved, but never combed with wood, and never gently. When the Queen began to comb her daughter's hair, Snow White once again fell into a swoon. When the dwarfs revived her this time she was so animated that her simplest movements held them fascinated. They repeated their warning more strongly. Angrily. Why would she want a visitor? Did they not provide well for her? Were they not all fine fellows, the best of company? Once again Snow White determined to obey. In her sleep there were the dwarfs, much larger, arms folded to block the dreams that nevertheless shone through.

The Queen brought an apple, which she had picked herself on the castle grounds. At first Snow White didn't remember what an apple was for. The dwarfs kept her on liquids. They would have fed her intravenously if they hadn't been concerned about visible bruises. At her mother's urging she bit into the apple. As soon as she tasted it she fell into a swoon. This time the dwarfs could do nothing for her. This was the third time, and dwarfs in folktales knew the power of the number three. They laid her out on her bed in what they hoped was a comfortable position.

Snow White neither woke nor even stirred in her sleep. But as loyal supporters of the King's edict, the dwarfs never once believed she was dead. They dreamed the sky was a great mirror seeking beauty. And so they built a coffin-like structure out of a special kind of glass to display and protect her at the same time. Gently they arranged Snow White inside it and carried her up to the roof. And they thought perhaps it was just as well for this to happen now. For the trend was that women were getting bored with modelling. They no longer had to think about keeping their figures, and without exercise they became despondent. When they had the spirit to want anything, rather than mirror substitutes they wanted change, they wanted seasons, even years. And they wanted their men home.

Motionless in the coffin Snow White craved her mother's gifts, her embrace, her fragrance. She dreamed of the dwarfs chasing birds and missing them. When she dreamed of her father there was only a crowned helicopter in the distance and people bowing to it. The seven dwarfs kept watch. They brought the TV up to the roof and there they stayed. Once more birds came to teach her: the owl, the dove, the dodo, the raven, and the Canada goose. But the dwarfs had designed the glass for their own purpose, and once again the birds couldn't reach her. There they were, all on the roof of the penthouse, when the King returned from the war.

From his helicopter the King caught sight of Snow White looking exactly as he remembered her. He congratulated himself on his foresight. His immediate concern was to cure her and take her home to the Queen, thereby restoring the life he had left. And so, scattering the birds and the dwarfs, he brought down the helicopter on the penthouse roof.

The King had once travelled with poets, then with philosophers, then with jesters. With him now in the helicopter were physicians, who were happy to have a change after the sights of war. They were very interested in curing Snow White and finding out what she would say, for she was one of those rare people who had experienced both the ancient and the modern world. They removed her from the coffin and lay her down on a bed in the castle. They researched modern cures, but hers was not a modern affliction. They researched ancient cures, and agreed on the one where string was wound around the afflicted person and then fastened to the four corners of the room. But it took them forever to find enough string, the kind that had already been used to wrap three packages, for no one saved string any more. The King, fancying himself a scientist, joined the physicians in their search. And the kingdom might have had to wait forever for its seasons, if not for the innocent intervention of the Queen's heart.

The Queen was happy to have her daughter back in any state. Every day she bathed her, rubbing scents and lotions into her body. She dressed her in different kinds of cloth so the variety of sensations would tempt her to wake. Soon Snow White had only to feel one of her mother's sashes around her and she would begin to stir with pleasure. Then, intoxicated by her own movement she would sit up, then walk a little. Soon she was running and dancing in the fields. Every day the Queen combed her daughter's hair and it grew long. Snow White learned to twist it and pin it into graceful shapes. This was when she would reflect. Mother and daughter picked apples and Snow White ate them, apples of every colour. With her throat so sensuously opened, Snow White began to sing and speak.

They read from the ancient books they found in the castle. They spun, wove, and embroidered. During these full and endless days the birds were at last able to reach Snow White and teach her what they knew. The owl, wisdom and folly. The dove, peace and war. The dodo, pride and humility. The raven, stories. The Canada goose, recovery from being an endangered species.

Then the Queen, ban or no ban, decided to teach her daughter one last thing. One afternoon as they were embroidering, the Queen taught Snow White to prick her finger. At that moment there was a shudder beneath them as, sped on by the pent-up years, the earth spun forward on its path, the seasons hot and cold as they flashed by. The child, soothing her bleeding finger in her mouth, grew taller. She became a girl, then a woman. Love for her mother, the lessons of the birds, all she knew surged through her changing body.

The Queen gazed at the woman, her daughter. Beyond her through the window was the Prince, black hair, red lips. The last of the Queen's dream was falling into place. She embraced her daughter and discreetly left the room.

The Prince had been looking for a bride. Not finding her in the city he searched further, even to the far side of the castle. There he felt the ground shudder and the earth begin to turn. At last he would experience the seasons he had heard about. Exhilarated by the motion, he was drawn to the castle window.

Being a Prince he had been exposed to only the finest of popular culture and had never seen a woman as old as himself. As he looked in the window he recognized at once what had been missing from his life. You must be Snow White, he said. He touched her hair. The smell of blood was in the air, and the chill of winter. What new worlds were these, inviting him?

He touched her hair again, and she touched his. And, as everyone knows, they began to live happily ever after.

NOTES AND ACKNOWLEDGMENTS

It has been a pleasantly challenging task to revise this paper for an anthology that is truly collaborative. My essay has been much improved and strengthened by helpful comments from other contributors to this volume, and I thank them for their suggestions.

1 See, for example, Mark Azadovskii's classic monograph (1974) on Siberian narrator Natal'ia Osipovna Vinokurova.

2 "Snow White" is number 53 in the Grimm collection and type number 709 in the Aarne-Thompson (1910) folktale index. "Juniper Tree" is number 47 in Grimm and 720 in Aarne-Thompson. Note that these women's indiscipline is expressed differently from the metamorphoses of the undisciplined women in Vivian Labrie's paper.

3 Gorog-Karady's (1989) observation above on the "democratic" nature of orally performed stories is certainly relevant here.

4 Wilhelm Grimm revised "Snow White" more than most others in the collection; it changes noticeably from earliest to latest editions. The earliest known text of the story is in an unpublished manuscript sent by the Grimms to Clemens Brentano in 1810. An English translation of this text and the 1812 variant, which changes the story further, can be found in David and David (1964:303–15).

5 Marvyne Jenoff initially sent me the full text of her 1989 version of "Snow White: A Reflection." After reading the first draft of this article, "Two Women, Two Stories," she was inspired to revise her story. It is reprinted in the Appendix with her enthusiastic permission. All references here are to the 1993 version.

6 The intensive workshop for professional storytellers was offered at the Eugene O'Neil Theater Center in August, 1982, lead by professional performer Laura Simms. Each of the seventeen participants spent the week working on a single story of their own choosing. Susan Gordon's adventures with her story are detailed in a lengthy article (Gordon 1993).

7 Susan Gordon sent me both a cassette tape and two letters discussing her reactions as a storyteller. I will indicate when page numbers refer to the letters or to the transcript.

8 I was part of the audience at the 1989 American Folklore Society meeting, during which Gordon used this method of expanding the story. It was an effective means of seeing alternate "readings" of the text.

9 In her view of her role as teller rather than creator, Gordon resembles Agatha, the Mennonite preacher in Pamela Klassen's essay here. Both women attempt to remain inside the boundaries: Gordon within the Grimm text and Agatha within her church. Klassen's observation on Agatha speaking in God's voice rather than her own "as an even more audacious act" can be seen in Gordon's storytelling as well. The story is not hers – she is only the speaker of the words.

10 I was surprised by the responses of a group of thirteen-year-old girls I interviewed in 1974 in a Winnipeg working class neighbourhood; after totally rejecting "fairy tales" as unrealistic romantic stories, they insisted that the stories were also "real" in their representation of various forms of family violence.

Editors' Concluding Statement

We hope you have enjoyed meeting a great variety of undisciplined women in this collection. From Catherine Jolicœur to Jean Heffernan to Anne Cameron; from the witch to the *fjallkona* to the female sailor to the killer dyke; and from Frances Mateychuk to Judy, Sue, and Nancy, to Pitseolak Ashoona, Lydia Campbell, Margaret Baikie, Elizabeth Goudie, Minnie Freeman, Kenojuak, and Leah Idlout, to Agatha Janzen, to Marvyne Jenoff and Susan Gordon, the women into whose lives we have had a brief view show their indiscipline in a variety of modes. So do the many authors who have contributed, who do not speak with a unified voice, but who are commited to maintaining a community of undisciplined women inside and outside the boundaries of academe. Those who study culture and society often see folkloric forms as mirrors for a group's ideology. But traditional and popular culture does not simply reflect. It is also a chosen expression of individuals' ideas which actively and dialogically creates and recreates social configurations. As the papers in *Undisciplined Women* show, there is no single viewpoint which adequately expresses every individual's ideas. Folklore counters stereotypes and prejudices as often as it creates and reinforces them. Heterosexism, classism, and racism, for example, are as often absent from traditional and popular culture as they are present in its texts. Indiscipline is as common as discipline.

Though we have clearly focused here upon folklore's place in the reification and reinforcement of ideas about female identity, traditions also construct male identity. LeBlanc's and Taft's papers, for example, are concerned with gender in more extensive terms rather than focusing specifically upon women. They indicate that symbolic and culturally produced male gendered identities have the same quality of arbitrariness and malleability as do those of women. Similarly, as discussed in the introduction to the second section, multiple sexual orientations imply unfixed gender identities. The female sailor bold and the good sport show that male and female identities alike can be found in a variety of orientations, genders, and sexes. Together the papers challenge the very notion of a specific and invariant identity for any group – or gender, class, ethnicity, sexual orientation, and so on. Indeed, Greenhill, Taft, and Labrie elaborate on the gendered construction of symbols as well as on how symbols evoke gendered ideas which explain, locate, and work through women's and men's experiences.

Many academic studies have looked at the implications of gendered identities as they are expressed in literature and the fine arts but, particularly in Canada, they have attended insufficiently to non-elite forms. It is possible that a greater variety of representations of sexual orientation and other ideas and practices which challenge patriarchy and hegemony make their way into traditional and popular forms because they avoid the institutional hegemonic control that is constantly maintained over, and thus pervasively reflected in, so many other forms, including elite and mass culture. Thus, many disciplinary as well as interdisciplinary – or undisciplined – perspectives can benefit from taking testimony and evidence from folklore as its point of departure. While Greenhill's and Ristock's works, which dislocate gender from heterosexuality, suggest possible direction, clearly more work is needed.

Canadian folklorists looking at Canadian society are both selves and others. They are selves in the sense that they participate in the ongoing (re)creation of Canada, yet they are others in the sense that no one can fundamentally and completely represent any group. Even more obviously, some authors are men looking at women; some belong to a different ethnic, religious, class (etc.) group than their subjects'; and some are non-Canadian-born looking at Canadian-born. This range of viewpoints – and the contributors' sensitivities to them – is pivotal. Many writers make a point of stressing their personal locations. The research presented here begs many questions about the extent to which anyone really can understand, let alone explain, their own identity. To account for the identity of another is, of course, at least equally difficult.

Similarly, though most of the examples contributors consider are from Canada, they can't be determined as exclusively Canadian.

Traditional and popular culture forms cross and permeate borders. Ristock shows, for example, that Hollywood's images affect our traditional and popular expressions, as well as our ideas of selves and others. But all forms of traditional and popular culture are essentially multinational and multicultural; wherever they may originate, they eventually find a distinctive manifestation in the expression and communication of an individual or group who personally embodies an almost endless series of associations – by class, gender, ethnicity, religion, race, linguistic group, family, and so on.

As women's folklore becomes a more central field of study, we will surely learn more of genres and cultural groups not conventionally considered by folklorists. But we should not expect a unified vision of women's folklore in Canada to emerge. Women's folklore does not exist in isolation from other cultural groupings to which women belong. As the final section particularly demonstrates, the idea of one women's folklore shared by all members of the sex – heterosexual or lesbian, in the north or south of Canada, labouring in or outside the home, working, bourgeois, or élite class – is problematic. Even the aim for an ideal universal women's culture may be unrealistic. As St. Peter's essay shows, women do not always share common interests or political locations.

Gathering, representing, and analysing women's culture will not be universally perceived as a positive step. Resistance will come not only from hegemonic and patriarchal locations, but also from groups who may legitimately expect to control and effect the communication of their culture to others – and to members of their own groups. Anne Cameron's relationship to aboriginal culture as examined by St. Peter is only one example of the possible conflicts. Anyone who studies this material must constantly struggle to balance accuracy with ethics, and human dynamics with scholarly representation. How successful we may be, as St. Peter's example shows, does not depend simply upon goodwill, political commitment, or even a sense of accountability. No matter how hard one tries to be completely ethical and responsible, and to anticipate every possible problem, perfection is impossible. But scholars must at the very least ask the right questions, as St. Peter does, because such action allows their work to approach nearer the ideal.

Similarly, papers such as Tye's offer less hierarchical alternatives for approaching texts and people. Scholars need to be open to the possibility that new perspectives and information may lead to profoundly different conclusions. As St. Peter's and Greenhill's articles assert, allegiance to one's own first idea(s) is unproductive, even unwise. Academic and patriarchal fixations with objectivity, truth, and correctness fail to recognize the contingency of their manifestations. Here feminist theory has a great deal to contribute to folklore theory in general. A commitment to understanding and (re)presenting cultural truths must be given higher priority than what Fowke calls "adher[ence] to the gospel as set forth by the currently anointed prophets" (this volume). But such a commitment is necessarily undisciplined.

The relations between aspects of women's lives, and of their lives to collecting and representation, are implicated. For example, Mathieu's study suggests that what people preserve from their entire wardrobes of clothing is connected with gendered values. Though some women treasure christening robes and wedding dresses, few men invest their emotions equally in their clothing, or reserve it for specific rituals. Materials which are valued give a particular and special view of peoples' lives.

The processes of critique, recovery, reconstruction, and analysis continue. As woman-centred research comes to characterize more folkloristic collecting and evaluation, and as case studies of women from all parts of Canada and from a greater variety of sociocultural groups expand the literature, we will develop a better understanding of how traditional culture represents women as well as of how women shape and reshape folklore. New insights promise to aid the appreciation of aspects of folklore – genres, texts, contexts, performers, audiences, and so on – which have been relatively undervalued. More importantly, further study can develop understandings of women's conventional roles and the kinds of power they may entail, but also show how women contest, rework, and manipulate convention.

The contributors' own lives, especially those of women who have been marginalized by the academy, are central to their understandings of others' positions. The fact that contributors have drawn on their own personal experience and fieldwork, primarily with anglophone women in eastern Canada, should not suggest that women in native, francophone, non-white, or other cultures lack vibrant and fascinating traditions which could exemplify female folklore. Anglophone eastern women have dominated the study of traditional and popular culture because of historic patterns of centralization and marginalization that accrue power in certain contexts to particular groups. Contributors draw from the materials they know best. We hope not only that the face of academic folklore will soon include a more pluralistic representation of the Canadian population as coming generations of Canadian women realise how much remains to be gathered and analysed, but also that Canadian universities begin to recognize the value of a variety of perspectives. Canadian folklore research must be extended into previously unexplored areas, and Canadian folklorists must reflect a variety of identities if we are better to understand ourselves, our cultures, and our creativity.

In closing we return to the issues and questions raised and addressed throughout this volume concerning the linkages between women and their folklore in Canada. As the undisciplined women in this book rethink women's culture, we also confront existing notions of tradition. As we newly evaluate who women are and what their culture is, we correspondingly challenge definitions of folklore. And these new concepts will help to revolutionize concepts of Canada.

Undisciplined Women underlines the importance of resistance. There is inspiration in these studies, which show that though women are variously restricted by religion, taboo, and social expectation, they nevertheless manage to do what they want and take what they need. Such contradictions need to be sustained and empowered, not transcended. As we better understand how women have always sought power, we learn how they have sometimes achieved it. Traditional knowledge can assist in social change, by affording women a stronger voice in developing their own destinies.

References

Aarne, Antti, and Stith Thompson. 1910. *The Types of the Folk-Tale*. Folklore Fellows Communications vol. 184. Helsinki: Suomalainen Tiedeakatemia, Academia Scientiarum Fennica.

Abbott, O.J. 1951. *Irish and British Songs from the Ottawa Valley*. Folkways 4051.

Abramtchik, Nina, et Éliane Dorst. 1984. Du costume "traditionnel" au costume dit "à la mode" (Biélorussie occidentale, région Pruzana). *Vêtement et sociétés 2. L'ethnographie* 80(92–94): 107–13.

Abu-Lughod, Lila. 1985. A Community of Secrets: The Separate World of Bedouin Women. *Signs* 10:637–57.

Adams, Timothy Dow. 1992. Painting above Paint: Telling Li(v)es in Emily Carr's Literary Self-Portraits. *Journal of Canadian Studies* 27(2): 37–48.

Aisenberg, Nadya, and Mona Harrington. 1988. *Women of Academe: Outsiders in the Sacred Grove*. Amherst: University of Massachusetts Press.

Akenson, Don. 1990. *At Face Value: The Life and Times of Eliza McCormack/John White*. Montreal: McGill-Queen's University Press.

American Psychiatric Association. 1980. DSM-III. *Diagnostic and Statistical Manual of Mental Disorders*. Washington, D.C.: American Psychiatric Association.

Arbeau, Thoinot. 1967. *Orchesography*. Translated by Mary Stewart Evans. New York: Dover Publications.

Armstrong, Jeannette. 1985. Writing from a Native Woman's Perspective. In *In the Feminine*, ed. Ann Dybikowski, Victoria Freeman, Daphne Marlatt, Barbara Pulling, and Betsy Warland, 55–7. Edmonton: Longspoon Press.

– 1991. Death Mummer, in *Breath Tracks*, p. 31. Stratford, ON: Williams-Wallace/Theytus Books.

Arnaujaq, Leah. 1986. In the Days of the Whalers. *Recollections of Inuit Elders.* ICI Autobiography Series 2, January.

Arsenault, Georges. 1982. *Courir la Chandeleur.* Moncton: Éditions d'Acadie.

Atwood, Margaret. 1972. *Survival.* Toronto: Anansi.

Ayaruaq, John. 1969. The Story of John Ayaruaq. *North* 16(2): 1–5.

Azadovskii, Mark. 1974. *A Siberian Tale Teller.* Austin: University of Texas Press.

Babcock, Barbara. 1987. Taking Liberties, Writing from the Margins, and Doing It with a Difference. *Journal of American Folklore* 100:390–411.

Baikie, Margaret. n.d. *Labrador Memories: Reflections at Mulligan.* Labrador: Them Days.

Bailey, John. 1992. Tales of the Evil Eye: Witchcraft and Superstitions. *Weston Mercury* 6 March (Rpt. in part from an issue of 9 June 1967).

Baillargeon, Denyse. 1993. Histoire orale et histoire des femmes: itinéraires et points de rencontre. *Temps et mémoire de femmes. Recherches féministes* 6(1): 53–68.

Bakhtine, Mikhaïl. 1970. *L'œuvre de François Rabelais et la culture populaire au Moyen Âge et sous la Renaissance.* Translated by Andrée Robel. Paris: Gallimard.

Bannerji, Himani. 1991. But Who Speaks for Us? Experience and Agency in Conventional Feminist Paradigms. In *Unsettling Relations: The University as a Site of Feminist Struggles,* ed. Himani Bannerji, Linda Carty, Kari Dehli, Susan Heald, Kate McKenna, 67–108. Toronto: Women's Press.

Bard, Marjorie Brooke. 1988. Domestic Abuse and the Homeless Woman: Paradigms in Personal Narrative for Organizational Strategists and Community Planners. PH.D. dissertation, University of California at Los Angeles.

Barstow, Anne Llewellyn. 1994. *Witchcraze: A New History of the European Witch Hunts.* San Francisco: Pandora.

Barthes, Roland. 1967. *Le système de la mode.* Paris: Seuil.

Bascom, William. 1965. The Four Functions of Folklore. In *The Study of Folklore,* ed. Alan Dundes, 279–98. Englewood Cliffs, NJ: Prentice-Hall.

Bateson, Gregory. 1958. *Naven: A Survey of the Problems Suggested by a Composite Picture of the Culture of a New Guinea Tribe Drawn from Three Points of View.* Stanford: Stanford University Press.

Belenky, Mary Field, Blythe McVicker Clinchy, Nancy Rule Goldberger, and Jill Mattuck Tarule. 1986. *Women's Ways of Knowing. The Development of Self, Voice, and Mind.* New York: Basic Books.

Benfoughal, Tatiana. 1984. Traditions, innovations, mode: l'exemple des bijoux de l'Aurès. *Vêtements et sociétés 2. L'ethnographie* 80(92–94): 75–84.

Bennett, John W. 1969. *Northern Plainsmen: Adaptive Strategy and Agrarian Life.* Chicago: Aldine.

Bennett, Margaret. 1989. *The Last Stronghold: Scottish Gaelic Traditions in Newfoundland.* St John's: Breakwater.

Berger, Peter, and Thomas Luckmann. [1966] 1967. *The Social Construction of Reality.* New York: Doubleday.

Best, Anita. 1989. Interview with Pauline Greenhill. Carbonear, NF, 30 July (PG89–40).

Beyer, Jinny. 1979. *Patchwork Patterns.* Virginia: EPM Publications.

– 1980. *The Quilter's Album of Blocks and Borders.* Virginia: EPM Publications.

Björnsdóttir, Inga Dóra. 1992. Nationalism, Gender and the Contemporary Icelandic Women's Movement. PH.D. dissertation, University of California at Santa Barbara.

Blackmore, Anauta (Ford). 1956. *Wild Like the Foxes: The True Story of An Eskimo Girl.* New York: J. Day Co.

Blau, Rachel. 1985. For the Etruscans. In *The New Feminist Criticism,* ed. Elaine Showalter, 271–91. New York: Pantheon.

Blodgett, Jean. 1985. *Kenojuak.* Toronto: Firefly Books.

Boon, James. 1982. *Other Tribes, Other Scribes.* Cambridge: Cambridge University Press.

Bourne, Paula, ed. 1985. *Women's Paid and Unpaid Work: Historical and Contemporary Perspectives.* Toronto: New Hogtown Press.

Bowerbank, Sylvia, and Delores Nawagesic Wawia. 1994. Literature and Criticism by Native and Metis Women in Canada: Review Essay. FS/*Feminist Studies* 20(3): 565–82.

Boxer, Marilyn J. 1982. For and About Women: The Theory and Practice of Women's Studies in the United States. In *Feminist Theory: A Critique of Ideology,* ed. Nannerl Keohane, Michelle Z. Rosaldo and Barbara C. Gelpi, 237–71. Chicago: University of Chicago Press.

Brandon, Tom. 1963. *Tom Brandon of Peterborough, Ontario.* Folk Legacy FSC-10.

Braun, Bennett G. 1989. Psychotherapy of the Survivor of Incest with a Dissociative Disorder. *Psychiatric Clinics of North America* 12(2): 307–24.

Brecht, Bertolt. 1964. *Brecht on Theatre: The Development of an Aesthetic,* ed. and translated by John Willett. New York: Hill and Wang.

Bronzini, Giovanni Battista. 1989. From the Grimms to Calvino: Folk-tales in the Year Two Thousand. Paper presented at the 9th Congress of the International Society for Folk Narrative Research. Budapest, 10–17 June.

Brown, George W., and Lynda Collier. 1989. Transvestites' Women Revisited: A Nonpatient Sample. *Archives of Sexual Behavior* 18(1): 73.

Brunvand, Jan Harold. 1974. *Norwegian Settlers in Alberta.* Mercury Series, vol. 8. Ottawa: Canadian Centre for Folk Culture Studies.

– 1986. *The Mexican Pet: More "New" Urban Legends and Some Old Favorites.* New York: W.W. Norton.

Brydon, Anne. 1990. Returning to the Present: Icelandic Identity and the Festival. *Icelandic Canadian Magazine* 48(2): 13–19.

– 1991. Celebrating Ethnicity: The Icelanders of Manitoba. *Scandinavian-Canadian Studies* 4:1–14.

Burg, Barry Richard. 1984. *Sodomy and the Pirate Tradition: English Sea Rovers in the Seventeenth-Century Caribbean.* New York: New York University Press.

Butala, Sharon. 1988. *Luna.* Saskatoon: Fifth House.

Butler, Judith. 1990. *Gender Trouble: Feminism and the Subversion of Identity.* New York: Routledge.

Butler-Bowden, W. 1954 *The Book of Margery Kempe.* London: Oxford.

Cameron, Anne. 1978. *Dreamspeaker.* Toronto: Clarke, Irwin and Company, Ltd. [Published under the name Cam Hubert.]

– 1981. *Daughters of Copper Woman.* Vancouver: Press Gang.

Campbell, Lydia. 1980. *Sketches of Labrador Life.* Labrador: Them Days.

Carlson, Bonnie E. 1992. Questioning the Party Line on Family Violence. *Affilia* 7(2): 94–110.

Carpenter, Carole H. 1979. *Many Voices: A Study of Folklore Activities in Canada and Their Role in Canadian Culture.* Mercury Series, vol. 26. Ottawa: Canadian Centre for Folk Culture Studies.

– 1985. Tales Women Tell: The Functions of Birth Experience Narratives. *Canadian Folklore canadien* 7:21–34.

Carpenter, Mary. 1990. Ada Gruben-Carpenter, A Cherished Mother. Unpublished poem.

Carr, C., and Taubin, A. 1992. Ice Pick Envy. *The Village Voice (New York)* 22–28 April:35.

Carroll, William K., Linda Christiansen-Ruffman, Raymond F. Currie, and Deborah Harrison, eds. 1992. *Fragile Truths: Twenty-Five Years of Sociology and Anthropology in Canada.* Ottawa: Carleton University Press.

Cartwright, Christine. 1980. Johnny Faa and Black Jack Davy: Cultural Values and Change in Scots and American Balladry. *Journal of American Folklore* 93:397–416.

Chancellerie de l'Archevêché. 1973. *Mandements, lettres pastorales et circulaires des évêques du Québec.* 19 vols. Québec: Chancellerie de l'Archevêché.

Châtelaine. 1983. La croqueuse de légendes. *Châtelaine* 24:8:24.

Chesley, Laurie C., Donna MacAulay, and Janice L. Ristock. 1992. *Abuse in Lesbian Relationships: A Handbook of Information and Resources.* Toronto: Toronto Counselling Centre for Lesbians and Gays.

Chiasson, Anselme, and Daniel Boudreau. 1943. *Chansons d'Acadie, 1re série.* Montreal: La Réparation.

– 1945. *Chansons d'Acadie, 2e série.* Montreal: La Réparation.

– 1972. *Chansons d'Acadie, 4e série.* Montreal: Éditions des Aboiteaux.

– 1977. *Chansons d'Acadie, 3e série.* Montreal: Éditions des Aboiteaux.

– 1979. *Chansons d'Acadie, 5e série.* Montreal: Éditions des Aboiteaux.

– 1983. *Chansons d'Acadie, 6e série.* Cheticamp, NS: Les Trois Pignons.

– 1985. *Chansons d'Acadie, 7e série.* Cheticamp, NS: Les Trois Pignons.

Christiansen, Reidar Th. 1958. *The Migratory Legends: A Proposed List of Types with a Systematic Catalogue of the Norwegian Variants.* Folklore Fellows

Communications, vol. 175. Helsinki: Suomalainen Tiedeakatemia Academia Scientiarum Fennica.

Chrystos. 1991. *Dream On.* Vancouver: Press Gang Publishers.

Clark, LaRena. 1965. *A Canadian Garland.* Topic 12T140.

Clifford, James. 1989. The Others: Beyond the "Salvage" Paradigm. In *Third Text: Third World Perspectives on Contemporary Art and Culture* 6:73–79.

Clifford, James, and George Marcus, eds. 1986. *Writing Culture.* Berkeley: University of California Press.

Cohn, Norman. 1975. *Europe's Inner Demons: An Enquiry Inspired by the Great Witch-Hunt.* New York: Basic Books.

Cray, Ed. 1968. *The Erotic Muse.* New York: Oak Publications.

Creighton, Helen. 1967. W. Roy Mackenzie, Pioneer. *Canadian Folk Music Society Newsletter* 2:15–22.

– 1968. *Bluenose Magic: Popular Beliefs and Superstitions in Nova Scotia.* Toronto: McGraw-Hill Ryerson.

Cuisenier, Jean 1987. *Costume, coutume.* Paris: Éditions de la réunion des musées nationaux.

Cunningham, Alastair J. 1992. *The Healing Journey.* Toronto: Key Porter Books.

D'Argencourt, Leah Idlout. 1977. C.D. Howe. *Inuit Today* 6(5): 30–45; 6(6): 46–51, 89; 6(8): 26–31; 6(9): 16–23, 55; 6(10): 22–9.

Dargis, Manohia. 1992. Film Reviews of *Leaving Normal, Highway 61* and *Cold Moon. The Village Voice (New York)* 22–28 April: 58.

David, Alfred, and Mary Elizabeth David. 1964. *The Frog King and Other Tales of the Brothers Grimm.* New York: Signet Classics, New American Library of World Literature.

Davis, Dona Lee. 1983. *Blood and Nerves: An Ethnographic Focus on Menopause.* St John's, NF: Institute of Social and Economic Research.

Deane, Seamus. 1990. Introduction. In *Nationalism, Colonialism, and Literature,* ed. Terry Eagleton, Fredric Jameson, and Edward W. Said, 3–19. Minneapolis: University of Minnesota Press.

Deetz, James. 1978. A Cognitive Historical Model for American Material Culture, 1620–1835. In *Historical Archaeology: A Guide to Substantive and Theoretical Contributions,* ed. L. Schuyler. 284–86. New York: Baywood Publishing.

Dégh, Linda. 1975. *People in the Tobacco Belt: Four Lives.* Mercury Series, vol. 13. Ottawa: Canadian Centre for Folk Culture Studies.

– 1990. How Storytellers Interpret the Snakeprince Tale. In *The Telling of Stories: Approaches to a Traditional Craft,* ed. Morten Nojgaard et al., 47–62. Odense, Denmark: Odense University Press.

Delaporte, Yves. 1979. Pour une anthropologie du vêtement. *Vêtement et sociétés 1.* Actes des journées de rencontre des 2 et 3 mars 1979. Paris: Musée de l'Homme.

– 1984. Perspectives méthodologiques et théoriques dans l'étude du vêtement. *Vêtement et sociétés 2. L'ethnographie* 80(92–94): 33–57.

Delbourg-Delphis, Marylène. 1981. *Le chic et le look. Histoire de la mode féminine et des mœurs de 1850 à nos jours.* Paris: Hachette.

Deslandres, Yvonne. 1976. *Le costume image de l'homme.* Paris: Albin Michel.

Desplanques, Marie-Annick. 1991. Women, Folklore and Communication: Informal Social Gatherings in a Franco-Newfoundland Context. PH.D. dissertation, Memorial University of Newfoundland.

Dewhurst, C. Kurt, Betty MacDowell and Marsha MacDowell. 1979. *Artists in Aprons: Folk Art by American Women.* New York: E.P. Dutton.

Dick and Fitzgerald Handbook. 1878. *Dick's Quadrille Call-Book and Ball-Room Prompter.* Danbury, CT: Behrens Publishing Company.

di Leonardo, Micaela. 1987. The Female World of Cards and Holidays: Women, Families and the Work of Kinship. *Signs* 12:440–53.

Dorson, Richard H. 1976. *Folklore and Fakelore: Essays toward a Discipline of Folklore Studies.* Cambridge: Harvard University Press.

Doucette, Laurel. 1985. The Emergence of New Expressive Skills in Retirement and Later Life in Contemporary Newfoundland. PH.D. dissertation, Memorial University of Newfoundland.

– 1993. Voices Not Our Own. *Canadian Folklore canadien* 15(2): 119–37.

Doyon, Madeleine. 1947. Le costume traditionnel féminin, documents de Charlevoix. *Les Archives de folklore*, no. 2, Montréal: Éditions Fides:183–9.

Dubé, Philippe. 1986. *Deux cents ans de villégiature dans Charlevoix.* Québec: Presses de l'Université Laval.

Duby, Georges et Michelle Perrot (dir.). 1991. *Histoire des femmes en Occident.* Paris: Plon.

Duflos-Priot, Marie-Thérèse. 1987. *L'apparence et son bon usage dans la vie quotidienne et la presse magazine.* Paris: Université de Nantes, CNRS (Les Cahiers L.E.R.S.C.O.).

Dugaw, Dianne. 1989. *Warrior Women and Popular Balladry, 1650–1850.* Cambridge: Cambridge University Press.

Dundes, Alan. 1961. Brown County Superstitions. *Midwest Folklore* 11:25–56.

– 1964. *The Morphology of North Indian Folktales.* Folklore Fellows Communications, vol. 195. Helsinki: Suomalainen Tiedeakatemia, Academia Scientiarum Fennica.

Dunlop, Allan. 1988. George Patterson: A Pioneer Oral Historian. In *Work, Ethnicity, and Oral History*, ed. James H. Morrison and Dorothy E. Moore. Issues in Ethnicity and Multiculturalism Series, no. 1. Halifax: International Education Centre.

Dupont, Jean-Claude. 1972. *Le monde fantastique de la Beauce québécoise.* Ottawa: Canadian Centre for Folk Culture Studies.

Durbin, Karen. 1992. Psychofemmes. *Mirabella.* June:44–48.

Durocher, Constance. 1990. Heterosexuality: Sexuality or Social System. *Resources for Feminist Research* 19(3–4): 13–17.

Durova, Nadezhda. 1988. *The Cavalry Maiden: Journals of a Female Russian Officer in the Napoleonic Wars*. Bloomington: Indiana University Press.

Eber, Dorothy, ed. 1971. *Pitseolak: Pictures Out of My Life*. Toronto: Collaborative Books with Oxford University Press.

– 1977. Eskimo Tales. *Natural History*. October:126–9.

Eekoomiak, Norman. 1980. *An Arctic Childhood*. Oakville, ON: Chimo Publishing.

Egan, Susanna. 1984. *Patterns of Experience in Autobiography*. Chapel Hill: University of North Carolina Press.

Epp, Frank, and Marlene Epp. 1986. The Diverse Roles of Ontario Mennonite Women. In *Looking into my Sister's Eyes*, ed. Jean Burnet, 223–42. Toronto: Multicultural History Society of Ontario.

Epp, Marlene. 1987. Women in Canadian Mennonite History: Uncovering the Underside. *Journal of Mennonite Studies* 5:90–107.

Faderman, Lillian. 1991. *Odd Girls and Twilight Lovers: A History of Lesbian Life in Twentieth Century America*. New York: Columbia University Press.

Faludi, Susan. 1991. *Backlash: The Undeclared War Against American Women*. New York: Crown Publishers.

Farnham, Christie, ed. 1987. *The Impact of Feminist Research in the Academy*. Bloomington: Indiana University Press.

Fauset, Arthur Huff. 1931. *Folklore from Nova Scotia*. Memoir Series 24. New York: American Folklore Society.

Fink, Virginia S. 1991. What Work Is Real? Changing Roles of Farm and Ranch Wives in South-Eastern Ohio. *Journal of Rural Studies* 7:17–22.

Finn, Geraldine, ed. 1993. *Limited Edition: Voices of Women, Voices of Feminism*. Halifax: Fernwood Publishing.

Fischer, Michael M. J. 1986. Ethnicity and the Post-Modern Arts of Memory. In *Writing Culture: The Poetics and Politics of Ethnography*, ed. James Clifford and George E. Marcus, 194–233. Berkeley: University of California Press.

Flagg, Fannie. 1987. *Fried Green Tomatoes at the Whistle Stop Cafe*. New York: McGraw-Hill Book Company.

Flugel, John Carl. [1930] 1982. *Le rêveur nu, de la parure vestimentaire*. Paris: Aubier-Montaigne. (Original: *Psychology of clothes*, London: Institute of Psychoanalysis.)

Fodor, Iris G. 1989. Agoraphobia. *Women's Studies Encyclopedia*. vol. 1, ed. Helen Tierney, 19–20. New York: Greenwood Press.

Fowke, Edith. 1950. *Folk Songs of Ontario*. Folkways 4005.

– 1961. *Lumbering Songs from the Ontario Shanties*. Folkways 4052.

– 1962. *Ontario Ballads and Folksongs*. Prestige/International 25014.

– 1963. A Few Notes on Bawdy Ballads in Print, Record, and Tradition. *Sing and String* 2(2): 3–9.

– 1964a. *Songs of the Great Lakes*. Folkways 4018.

- 1964b. "The Red River Valley" Re-Examined. *Western Folklore* 23: 163–72; reprinted in *Alberta Historical Review* 13 (Winter 1965): 20–5.
- 1965. *Traditional Singers and Songs from Ontario.* Hatboro, PA: Folklore Associates.
- 1966. A Sampling of Bawdy Ballads from Ontario. In *Folklore and Society: Essays in Honor of Benjamin A. Botkin,* ed. Bruce Jackson, 45–61. Hatboro, PA: Folklore Associates.
- 1969. *Sally Go Round the Sun.* Toronto: McClelland & Stewart.
- 1970a. *Lumbering Songs from the Northern Woods.* Austin: University of Texas Press; reprinted Toronto: NC Press, 1985.
- 1970b. *Sally Go Round the Sun.* Record. McClelland & Stewart.
- 1973. *The Penguin Book of Canadian Folk Songs.* Markham: Penguin Canada; reprinted 1985.
- 1975. *Far Canadian Fields: Companion to the Penguin Book of Canadian Folk Songs.* Leader Lee 4057, 1975.
- 1976. *Folklore of Canada.* Toronto: McClelland & Stewart.
- 1977. *Ring Around the Moon.* Toronto: McClelland & Stewart; reprinted Toronto: NC Press, 1987.
- 1979a. In Defence of Paul Bunyan. *New York Folklore* 5:43–51.
- 1979b. *Folktales of French Canada.* Toronto: NC Press.
- 1981. *Sea Songs and Ballads from Nineteenth-Century Nova Scotia.* New York: Folklorica Press.
- 1986. *Tales Told in Canada.* Toronto: Doubleday Canada.
- 1988a. Irish Folk Songs in Canada. In *The Untold Story: The Irish in Canada,* ed. Robert O'Driscoll and Lorna Reynolds, 699–710. Toronto: Celtic Arts of Canada.
- 1988b. *Red Rover, Red Rover: Children's Games Played in Canada.* Toronto: Doubleday Canada.
- 1989. Filk Songs as Modern Folksongs. *Canadian Folklore canadien* 23(2): 85–94.
- 1994a. *A Family Heritage: The Story and Songs of LaRena Clark.* Calgary: University of Calgary Press.
- 1994b. *Legends Told in Canada.* Toronto: Royal Ontario Museum.
Fowke, Edith, and Carole H. Carpenter. 1981. *A Bibliography of Canadian Folklore in English.* Toronto: University of Toronto Press.
- 1985. *Explorations in Canadian Folklore.* Toronto: McClelland & Stewart.
Fowke, Edith, and Joe Glazer. 1965. *Songs of Work and Freedom.* Chicago: Roosevelt University; reprinted 1973 as *Songs of Work and Protest.* New York: Dover.
Fowke, Edith, and Richard Johnston. 1954. *Folk Songs of Canada.* Waterloo: Waterloo Music.
- 1957. *Folk Songs of Quebec.* Waterloo: Waterloo Music.

Fowke, Edith, and Alan Mills. 1960a. *Canada's Story in Song*. 2 records. Folkways 3000.

– 1960b. *Canada's Story in Song*. Toronto: Gage; revised 1984 as *Singing Our History*. Toronto: Doubleday Canada.

Fox, Jennifer. 1987. The Creator Gods: Romantic Nationalism and the En-Genderment of Women in Folklore. *Journal of American Folklore* 100:563–72.

Frank, David. 1993. Review of *Coal in Our Blood*, by Judith Hoegg Ryan. *New Maritimes* 11(6)(July/August): 27–28.

Frank, Jerome D. 1974. *Persuasion and Healing*. New York: Schocken Books.

Franz, Margaret. 1991. Acceptance comes slowly for women in ministry. *Mennonite Reporter* 21(2)(January 21): B1–B3.

Fraser, Frances. 1990 [1959,1968]. *The Bear Who Stole the Chinook*. Vancouver: Douglas & McIntyre.

Freeman, Minnie Aodla. 1978. *Life Among the Qallunaat*. Edmonton: Hurtig Publishers.

– 1980. Survival in the South. In *Paper Stays Put; A Collection of Inuit Writing*, ed. Robin Gedalof, 101–12. Edmonton: Hurtig Publishers.

French, Alice. 1977. *My Name is Masak*. Winnipeg: Peguis Publications.

Frenette, Lyse. 1992. L'intimité sexuelle en thérapie est un abus de pouvoir. *Le Soleil* 14 mai:A15.

Freud, Sigmund. 1911. Psycho-Analytic Notes on an Autobiographical Account of a Case of Paranoia (Dementia Paranoides). In *The Standard Edition of the Complete Psychological Works of Sigmund Freud*, Vol. VII, ed. and translated by James Strachey, 3–82. London: Hogarth Press.

– 1926. Inhibitions, Symptoms and Anxiety. In *The Standard Edition of the Complete Psychological Works of Sigmund Freud*, Vol. XX, ed. and translated by James Strachey, 75–175. London: Hogarth Press.

– 1953. *The Standard Edition of the Complete Psychological Works of Sigmund Freud*, Vol. VII, ed. and translated by James Strachey. London: Hogarth Press.

Garber, Marjorie. 1992. *Vested Interests: Cross-Dressing and Cultural Anxiety*. New York: Routledge.

Geertz, Clifford. 1973. *The Interpretation of Cultures*. New York: Basic Books.

– 1980. Blurred Genres: The Refiguration of Social Thought. *American Scholar* 49:165–79.

Georges, Robert A., ed. 1991. Taking Stock: Current Problems and Future Prospects in American Folklore Studies. *Western Folklore* 50(1): 1–126.

Gilbert, Sandra M. 1980. Costumes of the Mind: Transvestism as Metaphor in Modern Literature. *Critical Inquiry* 7:391–417.

Gilbert, Sandra M., and Susan Gubar. 1985. *A Classroom Guide to Accompany the Norton Anthology of Literature by Women: The Tradition in English*. New York: W.W. Norton.

Gilkas, Olga. 1992. Basic Instinct. *Deneuve: Lesbian Magazine* 2:26.

Godard, Barbara Thompson. 1985. *Talking about Ourselves: the Literary Productions of Native Women of Canada*. Ottawa: Canadian Research Institute for the Advancement of Women/Institut canadien de recherches sur les femmes.

Golde, Peggy. 1970. *Women in the Field: Anthropological Experiences*. Chicago: Aldine.

Goldstein, Kenneth S. 1976. Monologue Performance in Great Britain. *Southern Folklore Quarterly* 40:7–29.

Goldstein, Richard. 1992. Base Instinct. *The Village Voice (New York)*. 8–14 April:37–41.

Good, Martha Smith. 1988. Women in Ministry in the Mennonite Conference of Ontario and Quebec: Uncovering their Experiences. D.Min. dissertation, St Michael's College and University of Toronto.

Gordon, Susan. 1991. Invitation and Decision: Storytelling in a Residential Treatment Center for Adolescents. Master's thesis, Antioch.

– 1993. The Powers of the Handless Maiden. In *Feminist Messages: Coding In Women's Folk Culture*, ed. Joan Radner, 252–88. Urbana: University of Illinois Press.

Gorog-Karady, Veronika. 1989. The New Professional Storyteller in France. Paper presented at the 9th Congress of the International Society for Folk Narrative Research, Budapest, 10–17 June.

Goudie, Elizabeth. 1973. *Woman of Labrador*. Toronto: Peter Martin Associates.

Grant, M. Gail. 1981. Healing By Conviction: Charismatic Adjunctive Therapy. M.A. thesis, York University.

Green, E., S. Hebron, and D. Woodward. 1990. *Women's Leisure, What Leisure?* London, Macmillan.

Green, Thomas A. 1978. Toward a Definition of Folk Drama. *Journal of American Folklore* 91:843–50.

– 1981. Introduction. *Journal of American Folklore* 94:421–32.

Greenhill, Pauline. 1984. The Family Album: A Newfoundland Women's Recitation. *Canadian Folklore canadien* 6:39–62.

– 1988. Folk Drama in Anglo-Canada and the Mock Wedding: Transaction, Performance, and Meaning. *Canadian Drama/L'Art dramatique canadien* 14:169–205.

– 1989a. *True Poetry: Traditional and Popular Verse in Ontario*. Montreal: McGill-Queen's University Press.

– 1989b. Welcome and Unwelcome Visitors: Shivarees and the Political Economy of Rural-Urban Interactions in Southern Ontario. *Journal of Ritual Studies* 3(1):45–67.

– 1990. The Female Warrior, Sailor, Highwayman, and Other Heroic Women in Anglo-Canadian Folksong. *Past and Present* [University of Waterloo] February: 9–12.

– 1992. A Good Start: A Graffiti Interpretation of the Montreal Massacre. *Atlantis* 17(2): 107–18.

– 1995. "Neither a Man nor a Maid": Sexualities and Gendered Meanings in Cross-Dressing Ballads. *Journal of American Folklore* 108:156–77.

Greenhill, Pauline, with Kjerstin Baldwin, Michelle Blais, Angela Brooks, and Kristen Rosbak. 1993. 25 GOOD REASONS WHY BEER IS BETTER THAN WOMEN and Other Qualities of the Female: Gender and the Non-Seriousness of Jokes. *Canadian Folklore canadien* 15(2): 51–67.

Greenhill, Pauline, and Diane Tye. 1993. Women and Traditional Culture. In *Changing Patterns: Women in Canada*, ed. Sandra Burt, Lorraine Code, and Lindsay Dorney, 309–29. Toronto: McClelland & Stewart.

– 1994. Critiques from the Margin: Interdisciplinary Perspectives on Folklore Studies in Canada. In *Canada: Theoretical Discourse*, ed. Terry Goldie et al., 167–85. Montreal: Association for Canadian Studies.

Greenleaf, Elisabeth Bristol and Grace Yarrow Mansfield. 1933. *Ballads and Sea Songs of Newfoundland*. Cambridge: Harvard University Press.

Grimm, Jacob and Wilhelm. 1987. *The Complete Tales of the Brothers Grimm*. Translated by Jack Zipes. New York: Bantam Books.

Gruber, William E. 1985. The Actor in the Script: Affective Strategies in Shakespeare's Anthony and Cleopatra. *Comparative Drama* 19:30–48.

– 1987. "Non-Aristotelian" Theater: Brecht's and Plato's Theories of Artistic Imitation. *Comparative Drama* 21:199–213.

Guilcher, Jean-Michel. 1969. *La contredanse et les renouvellements de la danse française*. Paris: Mouton.

Gullestad, M. 1984. *Kitchen Table Society*. Oslo: Universitets Forlaget.

Gunew, Sneja. 1991. Margins: Acting Like a (Foreign) Woman. *Hecate* 17(1): 31–5.

Haines, Max. 1992. Only Female Serial Killer in the U.S. *The Winnipeg Sun*. 24 May:24.

Hall, Edward T. 1983. *The Dance of Life*. New York: Anchor.

Halpert, Herbert and George M. Story. 1969. *Christmas Mumming in Newfoundland*. Toronto: University of Toronto Press.

Hanna, Judith Lynne. 1988. *Dance, Sex and Gender: Signs of Identity, Dominance, Defiance, and Desire*. Chicago: University of Chicago Press.

Harding, Susan. 1975. Women and Words in a Spanish Village. In *Toward an Anthropology of Women*, ed. Rayna R. Reiter, 283–308. New York: Monthly Review.

Harvey, Fernand. 1994. *La région culturelle: problématique interdisciplinaire*. Québec: CEFAN–Université Laval et IQRC.

Heffernan, Bill. 1992. Interview with Diane Tye. Springhill, NS, 6 October.

Heffernan, Jean. nd. Heffernan Family. Public Archives of Nova Scotia MG 100 vol 162#39.

Heffernan, W.E. 1906. *Warblings of the Wildwood*. Springhill: Jones Publishing Company.

Heilbrun, Carolyn G. 1988. *Writing a Woman's Life*. New York: Norton.

Henderson, M. Carole. 1973. Folklore Scholarship and the Sociopolitical Milieu in Canada. *Journal of the Folklore Institute* 10:97–107.

Henderson, Heather. 1988. North And South: Autobiography and the Problems of Translation. In *Reflections: Autobiography and Canadian Literature*, ed. K.P. Stich, 61–8. Ottawa: University of Ottawa Press.

Herrmann, Anne. 1991. "Passing" Women, Performing Men. *Michigan Quarterly Review* 30:60–71.

Hobsbawm, Eric. 1990. *Nations and Nationalism Since 1780: Programme, Myth, Reality*. Cambridge: Cambridge University Press.

Hollis, Susan Tower, Linda Pershing, and M. Jane Young. 1994. *Feminist Theory and the Study of Folklore*. Urbana and Chicago: University of Illinois Press.

hooks, bell. 1988. *Talking Back. thinking feminist thinking black*. Toronto: Between the Lines.

Houde, Renée. 1991. *Les temps de la vie : Le développement psychosocial de l'adulte selon la perspective du cycle de vie*. Montréal: Gaëtan Morin.

Hufford, David J. 1982. *The Terror That Comes in the Night: An Experience-Centered Study of Supernatural Assault Traditions*. Philadelphia: University of Pennsylvania Press.

Hunter, Darryl M. 1983. No "Malice in Wonderland": Conservation and Change in the Three Hallowe'ens of Ann Mesko. *Culture & Tradition* 7:37–53.

Hyde, Lewis. 1983. *The Gift: Imagination and the Erotic Life of Property*. New York: Vintage Books.

Idlout, Leah. 1980. The Little Arctic Tern, The Big Polar Bear. In *Paper Stays Put; A Collection of Inuit Writing*, ed. Robin Gedalof, 20–6. Edmonton: Hurtig Publishers.

Inglis, Gordon. 1982. In Bed with the Elephant: Anthropology in Anglophone Canada. *Ethnos* 47:82–102.

Iqalujjuaq, Levi. 1988. *Recollections of Levi Iqalujjuaq: The Life of a Baffin Island Hunter*. ICI Autobiography Series 3, March.

Irigaray, Luce. 1985. *This Sex Which Is Not One*. Translated by Catherine Porter. Ithaca: Cornell University Press.

Irqugaqtuk, Bernard. 1977–1979. The Autobiography of a Pelly Bay Eskimo. *Eskimo* n.s. 14:22–25; 15:14–18; 16:7–10.

Ives, Burl. 1948. *The Wayfaring Stranger*. New York and Toronto: McGraw-Hill Book Company.

Ives, Edward D. 1978. *Joe Scott: The Woodsman-Songmaker*. Urbana: University of Illinois Press.

Jenoff, Marvyne. 1993. Snow White: A Reflection. Unpublished ms.

– 1995. The Emperor's Body. Victoria: Ekstasis Editions.

Jolicœur, Catherine. 1965. Le vaisseau fantôme. Légende étiologique. PH.D. Thèse, Université Laval.

– 1970. Le vaisseau fantôme. Légende étiologique. Les Archives de Folklore, no. 11. Québec: Presses de l'Université Laval.

– 1978. Notes et questions. Bulletin de l'Association canadienne pour les études du folklore 2, 2–3:37.

– 1979. Le petit Poucet à l'école. Bulletin de l'Association canadienne pour les études du folklore 2, 4:22–3.

– 1981. Les plus belles légendes acadiennes. Montréal: Éditions Stanké.

Jonas, Gerald. 1992. Dancing: The Pleasure, Power, and Art of Movement. New York: Harry N. Abrams.

Jones, Michael Owen. 1972. Why Faith Healing? Mercury Series, vol. 3. Ottawa: Canadian Centre for Folk Culture Studies.

Juhnke, Jim. 1986. The Role of Women in the Mennonite Transition from Traditionalism to Denominationalism. Mennonite Life 41(3): 17–20.

Kadar, Marlene. 1983. Sexual Harassment as a Form of Social Control. In Public and Private: Gender and Society, ed. Eva Gamarnikow, 337–46. London: Heinemann.

Kalcik, Susan. 1975. "…Like Ann's gynecologist or the time I was almost raped": Personal Narratives in Women's Rap Groups. Journal of American Folklore 88:3–11.

Kane, Alice. 1983. Songs and Sayings of an Ulster Childhood, ed. Edith Fowke. Toronto: McClelland & Stewart.

Kaplan, Ron. 1981. Old Tales of Sorcery Remembered: Conversations with Marie Deveau, Marguerite Gallant, J.J. and Denise Deveau, and J.J. Chiasson. Cape Breton's Magazine 30:1–18.

Karkeek, Paul Q. 1882. A Budget of Witch Stories. Report and Transactions of the Devonshire Association 14:387–94.

Katz, Ruth. 1983. The Egalitarian Waltz. In What is Dance? ed. Roger Copeland and Marshall Cohen. Oxford: Oxford University Press.

Kealiinohomoku, Joann. 1972. Dance Culture as a Microcosm of Holistic Culture. In CORD Research Annual VI, New Dimensions in Dance Research: Anthropology and Dance, ed. Tamara Comstock, 99–106. New York: CORD.

Kempe, Margery. 1954. The Book of Margery Kempe. London: Oxford University Press.

Kirshenblatt-Gimblett, Barbara. 1975. A Parable in Context. In Folklore: Performance and Communication, ed. Dan Ben Amos and Kenneth S. Goldstein. The Hague: Mouton.

Kitzinger, Celia. 1987. The Social Construction of Lesbianism. London: Sage Publications.

Klassen, Pamela E. 1994. Going by the Moon and the Stars: Stories of Two Russian Mennonite Women. Waterloo, ON: Wilfrid Laurier University Press.

Kluft, Richard. 1987. An Update on Multiple Personality Disorder. *Hospital and Community Psychiatry* 38(4): 363–73.

Kodish, Debora. 1980. Moving Towards the Everyday: Some Thoughts on Gossip and Visiting as Secular Procession. *Folklore Papers of the University Folklore Association* 9. Austin: Centre for International Studies in Folklore and Ethnomusicology, University of Texas.

– 1987. Absent Gender, Silent Encounter. *Journal of American Folklore* 100:573–78.

Kohl, Seena B. 1976. *Working Together: Women and Family in Southwestern Saskatchewan*. Toronto: Holt, Rinehart and Winston.

Kors, Alan C. and Edward Peters. [1972] 1992. *Witchcraft in Europe 1100–1700: A Documentary History.* Philadelphia: University of Pennsylvania Press.

Kristjanson, Wilhelm. 1965. *The Icelandic People in Manitoba: A Manitoba Saga.* Winnipeg: Wallingford Press.

Kuhn, Thomas. 1970. *The Structure of Scientific Revolutions.* Chicago: University of Chicago Press.

Laba, Martin and Peter Narváez, ed. 1986. *Media Sense.* Bowling Green: Bowling Green University Popular Press.

Labrie, Vivian. 1987. *Ti-Jean, ses papiers et l'institution. Tryptique sur la culture paperassière des assisté-e-s sociaux et des fonctionnaires de l'aide sociale.* Québec: limited edition by the author.

– 1989. L'histoire n'est pas sans faim, euh! fin. Note sur la conclusion des contes. Paper presented at the Annual Meeting of the Folklore Studies Association of Canada/Association canadienne d'ethnologie et de folklore, Québec.

– 1990. D'une histoire de galère à une rêverie mathématique: réflexion sur le lien entre la vie et les contes. In *D'un conte … à l'autre : la variabilité dans la littérature orale,* ed. Véronika Görög-Karady, 439–60. Paris: CNRS.

– In press. Topologie, contes et écologie humaine et sociale : des convergences épistémologiques. *Canadian Folklore Canadien.*

Lamphere, Louise. 1987. Feminism and Anthropology: The Struggle to Reshape Our Thinking about Gender. In *The Impact of Feminist Research in the Academy,* ed. Christie Farnham, 11–23. Bloomington: Indiana University Press.

Lawless, Elaine J. 1988a. *Handmaidens of the Lord: Pentecostal Women Preachers and Traditional Religion.* Philadelphia: University of Pennsylvania Press.

– 1988b. *God's Peculiar People: Women's Voices and Folk Tradition in a Pentecostal Church.* Lexington: The University Press of Kentucky.

Laws, G. Malcolm. 1957. *American Balladry from British Broadsides.* Philadelphia: American Folklore Society.

Layton, Gwen. 1992. Conversation with Diane Tye. Springhill, NS, 1 October.

Le Blanc, Arthur. 1954. La Chandeleur chez les Acadiens de l'île du Cap-Breton. Master's thesis, Université Laval.

Le Blanc, Barbara. 1986. To Dance or Not To Dance: The Case of Church and Group Social Control in Cheticamp. Master's thesis, Université Laval.

Le Blanc, Barbara, and Laura Sadowsky. 1985. Collection 1310. Archives de Folklore. Université Laval.

Legman, G. 1975. *Rationale of the Dirty Joke: An Analysis of Sexual Humor.* Second series. New York: Bell Publishing Company.

Lemieux. 1821. *Traité contre les danses et les mauvaises chansons...* Lyon: Rusand.

Lemieux, Denise, et Lucie Mercier. 1989. Les femmes au tournant du siècle, 1880–1940: âges de la vie, maternité et quotidien. Québec: Institut québécois de recherche sur la culture.

Lemieux, Thérèse et Gemma Caron. 1981. *Silhouettes acadiennes.* s.l., p. 220–4.

Leroi-Gourhan, André. [1945] 1973. *Évolution et techniques. Milieu et technique.* Paris: Albin Michel.

Lessard, Pierre. 1988. Costume populaire sur cartes postales. *Cap-aux-Diamants* 4(2): 70–1.

Lewis, Diane. 1973. Anthropology and Colonialism. *Current Anthropology* 14:581–602.

Lipman-Blumen, Jean. 1973. Role of De-Differentiation as a System Response to Crisis. *Sociological Inquiry* 43(1): 105–29.

Littler, Mary Willa. 1992. Interview with Diane Tye. Dartmouth, NS, 7 October.

Lloyd, A.L. 1967. *Folk Song in England.* New York: International.

Longfellow, Henry Wadsworth. [1847] 1952. *Evangeline: A Tale of Acadia.* Halifax: Nimbus.

Luxton, Meg. 1980. *More than a Labour of Love.* Toronto: Women's Press.

Luxton, Meg, and Harriet Rosenberg. 1986. *Through the Kitchen Window: The Politics of Home and Family.* Toronto: Garamond Press.

Lyon, Margot L. 1993. Psychoneuroimmunology: The Problem of the Situatedness of Illness and the Conceptualization of Healing. *Culture, Medicine and Psychiatry* 17(1): 77–97.

Macfarlane, Alan. 1970. *Witchcraft in Tudor and Stuart England: A Regional and Comparative Study.* London: Routledge and Kegan Paul.

Mackenzie, W. Roy. 1919. *The Quest of the Ballad.* Princeton: Princeton University Press.

MacKinnon, Catherine A. 1982. Feminism, Marxism, Method, and the State: An Agenda for Theory. In *Feminist Theory: A Critique of Ideology,* ed. Nannerl Keohane, Michelle Z. Rosaldo, and Barbara C. Gelpi, 1–30. Chicago: University of Chicago Press.

– 1992. Sexuality. In *Knowing Women: Feminism and Knowledge,* ed. Helen Crowley and Susan Himmelweit. Cambridge, MA: Polity Press.

Maracle, Lee. 1989. Moving Over. *Trivia* 14 (Spring): 9–12.

– 1992a. *Sojourner's Truth.* Vancouver: Press Gang Publishers.

– 1992b. A Question of Voice. *The Vancouver Sun.* 6 June: D8–9.

– 1993. *Ravensong*. Vancouver: Press Gang Publishers.

– 1996. *I Am a Woman: A Native Perspective on Sociology and Feminism*. Vancouver: Press Gang Publishers.

March, Hy. Colley. 1900. Dorset Folklore. *Folk-Lore* 11:107–12.

Marchand, Suzanne. 1989. Le culte du corps ou le culte de l'âme: mode féminine et société québécoise au cours de la période 1920–1939. Mémoire de maîtrise, Université Laval.

Marie-Ursule, Sœur. 1951. Civilisation traditionnelle des Lavalois. Les Archives de Folklore, no. 5–6. Québec: Presses de l'Université Laval.

Marlatt, Daphne. 1992. Lecture, University of Victoria, July 28.

Mathieu, Jocelyne. 1988. Au sujet des rapports entre le costume traditionnel et la mode. Le cas du costume canadien. *Canadian Folklore canadien* 10 (1–2): 35–52.

– 1994. La région: un terrain ou un concept? Approche ethnologique. In *La région culturelle: problématique interdisciplinaire*, ed. Fernand Harvey, 97–110. Québec: CEFAN–Université Laval et IQRC.

Matthews, Ralph. 1983. *The Creation of Regional Dependency*. Toronto: University of Toronto Press.

Mbilinyi, Marjorie. 1989. "I'd Have Been a Man": Politics and the Labor Process in Producing Personal Narratives. In *Interpreting Women's Lives*, ed. Personal Narratives Group, 204–27. Bloomington: Indiana University Press.

McAlpine. 1898. *McAlpine's Gazetteer and Guide: Maritime Provinces and Newfoundland*. Halifax: A & W Mackinlay.

McCarl, Robert S. Jr. 1976. Smokejumper Initiation: Ritualized Communication in a Modern Occupation. *Journal of American Folklore* 89:49–66.

– 1986. Occupational Folklore. In *Folk Groups and Folklore Genres: An Introduction*, ed. Elliott Oring, 71–89. Logan: Utah State University Press.

McFeat, Tom. 1980. *Three Hundred Years of Anthropology in Canada*. Occasional Papers in Anthropology no. 7. Halifax: Department of Anthropology, St Mary's University.

McGrane, Bernard. 1989. *Beyond Anthropology: Society and the Other*. New York: Columbia University Press.

McGrath, Robin. 1984. *Canadian Inuit Literature: The Development of a Tradition*. Ottawa: National Museums of Canada.

McKay, Ian. 1994. *The Quest of the Folk: Antimodernism and Cultural Selection in Twentieth-Century Nova Scotia*. Montreal and Kingston: McGill-Queen's University Press.

McKay, Ian, and Joy Mannette. 1988. Studying Work and Gender Historically. In *Work, Ethnicity, and Oral History*, ed. James H. Morrison and Dorothy E. Moore. Issues in Ethnicity and Multiculturalism Series, no. 1, 89–93. Halifax, NS: International Education Centre.

McNaughton, Janet. 1982. A Study of the CPR-Sponsored Quebec Folk Song And Handicraft Festivals, 1927–1930. Master's thesis, Memorial University of Newfoundland.

– 1985. French-Canadian Nationalism and the Beginnings of Folklore Studies in Quebec. *Canadian Folklore canadien* 7(1–2): 129–47.

Metayer, Maurice, ed. 1972. *I, Nuligak*. Toronto: Peter Martin Associates.

Minnesota Coalition for Battered Women. 1990. *Confronting Lesbian Battering: A Manual for the Battered Women's Movement*. St Paul, MN.

Moore, Henrietta L. 1988. *Feminism and Anthropology*. Cambridge, MA: Polity Press.

Morrison, Monica. 1974. Wedding Night Pranks in Western New Brunswick. *Southern Folklore Quarterly* 38:285–97.

Murray, Hilda Chaulk. 1979. *More than 50%*. St John's, NF: Breakwater.

Myrick, Michelle. 1989. Interview with Pauline Greenhill. St John's, NF, 1 August. PG89-44–46.

Narváez, Peter. 1992. Folkloristics, Cultural Studies and Popular Culture. *Canadian Folklore canadien* 14(1): 15–30.

Narváez, Peter, and Martin Laba, eds. 1986. *Media Sense: The Folklore–Popular Culture Continuum*. Bowling Green, OH: Bowling Green State University Press.

Newton, Esther. 1972. *Mother Camp: Female Impersonators in America*. Englewood Cliffs, NJ: Prentice-Hall.

Nickerson, Bruce E. 1974. Is There a Folk in the Factory? *Journal of American Folklore* 87:133–39.

Noel, Jan. 1991. New France: les femmes favorisées. In *Rethinking Canada: The Promise of Women's History*, ed. Veronica Strong-Boag and Anita Clair Fellman, 28–51. Toronto: Longman, Copp Clark Pitman.

Nyce, Dorothy Yoder, ed. 1983. *Weaving Wisdom: Sermons by Mennonite Women*. South Bend, IN: Womensage.

O'Connor, Pat. 1992. *Friendships between Women: A Critical Review*. New York: Harvester Wheatsheaf.

Orgel, Stephen. 1989. Nobody's Perfect: Or Why Did the English Stage Take Boys for Women? *The South Atlantic Quarterly* 88:7–30.

Oring, Elliott. 1986. *Folk Groups and Folklore Genres: An Introduction*. Logan: Utah State University Press.

Paine, Robert. 1967. What is Gossip About? An Alternative Hypothesis. *Man* 2: 278–85.

Pandian, Jacob. 1985. *Anthropology and the Western Tradition: Toward an Authentic Anthropology*. Prospect Heights, IL: Waveland Press.

Peacock, James L. 1978. Symbolic Reversal and Social History: Transvestites and Clowns of Java. In *The Reversible World: Symbolic Inversion in Art and Society*, ed. Barbara A. Babcock, 209–24. Ithaca: Cornell University Press.

Peacock, Kenneth. 1965. *Songs of the Newfoundland Outports* (3 volumes). Bulletin No. 197, Anthropological Series No. 65. Ottawa: National Museum of Canada.

Penley, Constance. 1992. Feminism, Psychoanalysis, and the Study of Popular Culture. In *Cultural Studies*, ed. Lawrence Grossberg, Cary Nelson, and Paula A. Treichler, 479–500. New York: Routledge.

Perrault, Charles. 1969. *Perrault's Fairy Tales*. Translated by A.E. Johnson. New York: Dover Publications.

Perreault, Jeanne and Sylvia Vance, eds. 1990. *Writing the Circle: Native Women of Western Canada*. Edmonton: NeWest.

Perrot, Philippe. 1984. *Le travail des apparences ou les transformations du corps féminin XVIIIe-XIXe siècles*. Paris: Seuil.

Peters, Marilyn G. 1990. Mennonite Women: North America. *Mennonite Encyclopedia* 5:933–4.

Phelan, Peggy. 1988. Feminist Theory, Poststructuralism, and Performance. *The Drama Review* 32(1): 107–27.

Pitseolak, Peter, with Dorothy Eber. 1975. *People From Our Side*. Edmonton: Hurtig Publishers.

Planetta, Elizabeth Catherine Beaton. 1981. Sorcery Beliefs and Oral Tradition in Cheticamp, Cape Breton. Master's thesis, Memorial University of Newfoundland.

Pocius, Gerald. 1976. "The First Day that I Thought of It Since I Was Wed": Role Expectations and Singer Staus in a Newfoundland Outport. *Western Folklore* 35:109–22.

– 1991. *A Place to Belong: Community Order and Everyday Space in Calvert, Newfoundland*. Montreal: McGill-Queen's University Press.

Pop, Denise. 1984. Évolution vestimentaire et mode, l'exemple roumain. *Vêtement et sociétés 2. L'ethnographie* 80 (92–94): 61–73.

Power, Ernestine O'Rourke. 1989. Interview with Pauline Greenhill. Branch, Newfoundland, 1 August. PG98–49.

Prentice, Alison, et al., ed. 1988. *Canadian Women: A History*. Toronto: Harcourt Brace Jovanovitch.

Propp, V. 1968. *Morphology of the Folktale*. Translated by Laurence Scott. Austin: University of Texas Press.

Radicalesbians. 1971. The Woman-Identified Woman. Reprinted in *Liberation Now!* ed. Deborah Babcox and Madeline Belkin, 287–93. New York: Dell.

Radner, Joan Newlon, ed. 1993. *Feminist Messages: Coding in Women's Folk Culture*. Urbana: University of Chicago Press.

Radner, Joan N., and Susan S. Lanser. 1993. Strategies of Coding in Women's Cultures. In *Feminist Messages: Coding in Women's Folk Culture*, ed. Joan Newlon Radner, 1–29. Urbana: University of Chicago Press.

Relph, Edward. 1976. *Place and Placelessness*. London: Pion Ltd.

Renwick, Roger deV. 1980. *English Folk Poetry: Structure and Meaning*. Philadelphia: University of Pennsylvania Press.

Rice, Richard M. 1971. Mothers, Daughters and Grand-daughters: An Examination of the Matrilateral Bias and Related Variables in Jews and Icelanders in Canada. Master's thesis, University of Manitoba.

Rich, Adrienne. 1980. Compulsory Heterosexuality and Lesbian Existence. *Signs* 5:631–90.

Rich, Elaine Sommers. 1983. *Mennonite Women*. Kitchener: Herald.

Rieti, Barbara. 1995. Guns and Bottles: Newfoundland Counterwitchcraft Tactics as Assertions of Masculinity. In *Folklore Interpreted: Essays in Honor of Alan Dundes*, eds. Regina Bendix and Rosemary Lévy Zumwalt. New York: Garland.

Ristock, Janice L. 1991. Beyond Ideologies: Understanding Abuse in Lesbian Relationships. *Canadian Woman Studies* 12:74–81.

– 1994. "And Justice for All?" ... The Social Context of Legal Responses to Abuse in Lesbian Relationships. *Canadian Journal of Women and the Law* 7(2): 415–30.

Ritchie, Jean. 1955. *The Singing Family of the Cumberlands*. New York: Oxford University Press.

Rivera, Margo. 1988. Am I a Boy or a Girl? Multiple Personality as a Window on Gender Differences. *Resources for Feminist Research/Documentation sur la recherche féministe* 17(2): 41–6.

Robertson, Marion. 1991. *The Chestnut Pipe. Folklore of Shelburne County.* Halifax: Nimbus.

Rosenberg, Neil V. 1987. The Springhill Mine Disaster Songs. Paper presented to the Folklore Studies Association of Canada, McMaster University, Hamilton, Ontario, May 30.

– 1988. Ethnicity and Class: Black Country Music in the Maritimes. *Journal of Canadian Studies* 23:138–57.

– 1993. *Transforming Traditions*. Urbana: University of Illinois Press.

Ross, Colin A. et al. 1989. Multiple Personality Disorder: An Analysis of 236 Cases. *Canadian Journal of Psychiatry* 34:413–18.

Roy, Carmen. 1958, 1960. Letters to Helen Creighton. 5 April 1960; 18 Sept. 1958. Creighton Correspondence. PANS MG 1 Vol 2817 #86.

Rubin, Gayle. 1984. Thinking Sex: Notes for a Radical Theory of the Politics of Sexuality. In *Pleasure and Danger: Exploring Female Sexuality*, ed. Carole S. Vance, 267–319. Boston: Routledge.

Rustige, Rona. 1988. *Tyendinaga Tales*. Montreal: McGill-Queen's University Press.

Rutherford, Edward Arthur. 1973. Newfoundland Log Book. *The Newfoundland Quarterly* 70:21–6.

Sachs, Pamela. 1993. Literature and Women's Studies. In *Limited Edition: Voices of Women, Voices of Feminism*, ed. Geraldine Finn. Halifax: Fernwood Publishing.

St. Peter, Christine. 1989. "Woman's Truth" and the Native Tradition: Anne Cameron's *Daughters of Copper Woman*. FS/*Feminist Studies* 15:499–524.

Saltzman, Rachelle H. 1987. Folklore, Feminism, and the Folk: Whose Lore Is It? *Journal of American Folklore* 100: 548–62.

Santino, Jack. 1978. Characteristics of Occupational Narratives. In *Working Americans: Contemporary Approaches to Occupational Folklife*, ed. Robert H. Byington, 199–212. Washington, D.C.: Smithsonian Institution Press.

- 1983. Miles of Smiles, Years of Struggle: The Negotiation of Black Occupational Identity Through Personal Experience Narrative. *Journal of American Folklore* 96:393–412.

Sedgwick, Eve Kosofsky. 1985. *Between Men: English Literature and Male Homosocial Desire.* New York: Columbia University Press.

- 1990. *Epistemology of the Closet.* Berkeley: University of California Press.

Segal, Lynne. 1992. Sexual Uncertainty or Why the Clitoris Is Not Enough. In *Knowing Women: Feminism and Knowledge,* ed. Helen Crowley and Susan Himmelweit, 117–32. Cambridge, MA: Polity Press.

Sered, Susan. 1988. The Domestication of Religion: The Spiritual Guardianship of Elderly Jewish Women. *Man n.s.* 23(3): 506–21.

Shantz, Susan and Marjorie Kaethler. 1990. *Quilts of Waterloo County: A Sampling.* Waterloo, ON: Marjorie Kaethler.

Simpson, Isabel. 1992. Interview with Diane Tye. Springhill, NS, 29 October.

Simundsson, Elva. 1989. *Fjallkonas* of Íslendingadagurinn 1924–1989. Winnipeg: Icelandic National League.

Small, L.D. 1975. "Traditional Expressions in a Newfoundland Community: Genre Change and Functional Variability." *Lore and Language* 2(3)(July): 15–18.

Spacks. Patricia Meyer. 1982. In Praise of Gossip. *Hudson Review* 35: 19–38.

Spender, Dale, ed. 1981. *Men's Studies Modified: The Impact of Feminism on the Academic Disciplines.* New York: Pergamon Press.

Spradley, James. 1972. *Culture and Cognition: Rules Maps and Plans.* San Francisco: Chandler.

Springhill Heritage Group. 1993. *Recollections of a Nova Scotia Town. Writings about Springhill by Jean Heffernan.* Sackville, NB: Tribune Press.

Statistics Canada. 1981. *Census of Canada,* vol. 2 – Provincial Series, *Population – Geographic Distributions – Nova Scotia* 93–903. Ottawa: Statistics Canada.

Stekert, Ellen. 1988. Autobiography of a Woman Folklorist. *Journal of American Folklore* 100:579–85.

Stevens, Mary L. 1989. Women's Work: Traditional Quiltmakers of Southern Indiana. PH.D. dissertation, Indiana University.

Stewart, Susan. 1984. *On Longing: Narratives of the Miniature, the Gigantic, the Souvenir, the Collection.* Baltimore: Johns Hopkins University Press.

- 1978. *Nonsense: Aspects of Intertextuality in Folklore and Literature.* Baltimore: Johns Hopkins University Press.

Stocking, George W. Jr., ed. 1984. *Functionalism Historicized: Essays on British Social Anthropology, 1885–1945.* Madison: University of Wisconsin Press.

- ed. 1989. *Romantic Motives: Essays on Anthropological Sensibility.* Madison: University of Wisconsin Press.

Stoller, Robert. 1975. *Sex and Gender.* New York: J. Aronson.

Stone, Kay. 1975a. *Romantic Heroines in Anglo-American Folk and Popular Literature.* PH.D. dissertation, Indiana University.

– 1975b. Things Walt Disney Never Told Us. *Journal of American Folklore* 88:42–50.
– 1984. To Ease the Heart: Traditional Storytelling. *National Storytelling Journal* (Winter): 1–3.
– 1986. Oral Narration in Contemporary North America. *Fairy Tales and Society: Illusion, Allusion and Paradigm*, ed. Ruth Bottigheimer, 13–31. Philadelphia: University of Pennsylvania Press.
– 1988. Three Transformations of Snow White. *The Brothers Grimm and the Folktale*, ed. James McGlathery, 52–65. Urbana: University of Illinois Press.
– 1993a. Once Upon A Time Today. In *The Reception of the Grimms' Fairy Tales*, ed. Donald Haase, 250–69. Detroit: Wayne State University Press.
– 1993b. Burning Brightly: New Light on an Old Tale. In *Feminist Messages: Coding In Women's Folk Culture*, ed. Joan Radner, 289–305. Urbana: University of Illinois Press.
Stone, Sharon Dale, and the Women's Survey Group. 1990. Lesbian Life in a Small Centre: The Case of St John's. In *Lesbians in Canada*, ed. Sharon Dale Stone, 94–105. Toronto: Between the Lines.
Straub, Kristina. 1991. The Guilty Pleasures of Female Theatrical Cross-Dressing and the Autobiography of Charlotte Charke. In *Body Guards: The Cultural Politics of Gender Ambiguity*, ed. Julia Epstein and Kristina Straub, 142–66. New York: Routledge.
Szwed, John. 1966. Gossip, Drinking and Social Control: Consensus and Communication in a Newfoundland Parish. *Ethnology* 5:434–41.
– 1970. Paul E. Hall: A Newfoundland Song-Maker and His Community of Song. In *Folksongs and Their Makers*, eds. Henry Glassie, Edward D. Ives and John F. Szwed, 147–69. Bowling Green, OH: Bowling Green University Popular Press.
Taft, Michael. 1994. Adult Halloween Celebrations on the Canadian Prairie. In *Halloween and Other Festivals of Death and Life*, ed. Jack Santino, 152–69. Knoxville: University of Tennessee Press.
– 1991. Tape-recorded interview with Sharon Butala, Eastend, Saskatchewan, September 13.
– 1989. Folk Drama on the Great Plains: The Mock Wedding in Canada and the United States. *North Dakota History* 56(4): 16–23.
– 1983. *Discovering Saskatchewan Folklore*. Edmonton: NeWest.
Tagoona, Armand. 1975. *Shadows*. Toronto: Oberon Press.
Tallman, Richard S. 1979. Folklore Research in Atlantic Canada: An Overview. *Acadiensis* 8(2): 118–30.
Thivierge, Nicole. 1982. *Écoles ménagères et instituts familiaux : un modèle féminin traditionnel*. Québec: Institut québécois de recherche sur la culture (IQRC).
Thomas, Keith. 1971. *Religion and the Decline of Magic: Studies in Popular Beliefs in Sixteenth and Seventeenth Century England*. Harmondsworth: Penguin.

Thrasher, Anthony Apakark. 1976. *Thrasher: Skid Row Eskimo*. Toronto: Griffin House.

Tipps, Dean C. 1973. Modernization Theory and the Comparative Study of Societies: A Critical Perspective. *Comparative Studies in Society and History* 15:199–226.

Tomm, Winnie. 1992. Knowing Ourselves as Women. In *Anatomy of Gender*, ed. Dawn H. Currie and Valerie Raoul, 209–21. Ottawa: Carleton University Press.

Tongue, R.L. 1963. Some Notes on Modern Somerset Witch-Lore. *Folklore* 74:321–5.

Toussaint-Samat, Maguelonne. 1990. *Histoire technique et morale du vêtement*. Paris: Bordas.

Trigger, Bruce G. 1988. A Present of Their Past? Anthropologists, Native People, and Their Heritage. *Culture* 8(1): 71–9.

Trinh Minh-Ha. 1991. *When the Moon Waxes Red: Representation, Gender and Cultural Politics*. London: Routledge.

Turner, Victor. 1967. *The Forest of Symbols: Aspects of Ndembu Ritual*. Ithaca: Cornell University Press.

– 1969. *The Ritual Process: Structure and Anti-Structure*. Ithaca: Cornell University Press.

– 1974. *Dramas, Fields and Metaphors*. Ithaca: Cornell University Press.

– 1977. Variations on a Theme of Liminality. In *Secular Ritual*, ed. Sally Moore and Barbara Myerhoff, 36–52. Assen/Amsterdam: Van Gorcum.

Tuu'luk, Marion, with Susan Tagoona. 1977. A Story of Starvation. *Inuit Today* 6(9): 26–31.

Twycross, Meg. 1983. "Transvestism" in the Mystery Plays. *Medieval English Theatre* 5:123–80.

Tydeman, William. 1978. *The Theatre in the Middle Ages: Western European Stage Conditions, c. 800–1516*. Cambridge: Cambridge University Press.

Tye, Diane. 1987. Aspects of the Local Character Phenomenon in a Nova Scotian Community. *Canadian Folklore canadien* 9:99–111.

Þór, Jónas. 1989. *Íslendingadagurinn 1890–1989: Saga Íslendingadagsins: An Illustrated History*. Gimli, Manitoba: Icelandic Festival of Manitoba.

Van Gelder, Lindsay. 1992. Attack of the Killer Lesbians. *Ms. Magazine* 2:80–82.

Van Gennep, Arnold, [1909] 1975. *The Rites of Passage*. Chicago: University of Chicago Press.

Vance, Carol. 1992. Social Construction Theory: Problems in the History of Sexuality. In *Knowing Women: Feminism and Knowledge*, ed. Helen Crowley and Susan Himmelweit. Cambridge, MA: Polity Press.

Voigt, Vilmos. 1989. Modern Story-telling – Stricto Sensu. Paper presented at the 9th Congress of the International Society for Folk Narrative Research. Budapest, 10–17 June.

Volosinov, V.N. 1971. Reported Speech. In *Readings in Russian Poetics: Formalist and Structuralist Views*, ed. Ladislav Matejka and Krystyna Pomorska, 149–75. Cambridge: MIT Press.

Voyer, Simonne. 1986. *La danse traditionnelle dans l'est du Canada: Quadrilles et cotillons*. Québec: Les Presses de l'Université Laval.

Ward, Donald. 1989. Idionarrating and Social Change. Paper presented at the 9th Congress of the International Society for Folk Narrative Research. Budapest, 10–17 June.

Warshaver, Gerald. 1991. On Postmodern Folklore. *Western Folklore* 50(3): 219–29.

Washburne, Heloise Chandler. 1960. *Children of the Blizzard by Heloise Washburne and Anauta* (pseud.). London: D. Dobson.

– 1940. *Land of the Good Shadows: The Life Story of Anauta an Eskimo Woman*. New York: John Day.

Weedon, Chris. 1987. *Feminist Practice and Poststructuralist Theory*. London: Basil Blackwell.

Whisnant, David E. 1983. *All That Is Native and Fine: The Politics of Culture in an American Region*. Chapel Hill: University of North Carolina Press.

Wickwire, Wendy. 1993. Women in Ethnography: The Research of James A. Teit. *Ethnohistory* 40:539–62.

Wilgus, D.K. 1973. The Text is the Thing. *Journal of American Folklore* 85:72.

Willis, William S., Jr. 1972. Skeletons in the Anthropological Closet. In *Reinventing Anthropology*, ed. Dell Hymes, 121–52. New York: Random House.

Wimbush, E. 1986. *Women's Leisure and Well-Being: Final Report*. Edinburgh: Centre for Leisure Research, Dunfermline College of Education.

Wise, Sue and Liz Stanley. 1987. *Georgie Porgie: Sexual Harassment in Everyday Life*. London: Pandora.

Wolf, Eric. 1982. *Europe and the People Without History*. Berkeley: University of California Press.

Woodside, Jane Xenia Harris. 1987. The Womanless Wedding: An American Folk Drama. Master's thesis, University of North Carolina.

Workman, Mark E. 1989. Folklore in the Wilderness: Folklore and Postmodernism. *Midwestern Folklore* 15:5–14.

Wright, Susan. 1981. Place and Face of Women in Doshman Ziari, Iran. In *Women and Space: Ground Rules and Social Maps*, ed. Shirley Ardener, 136–156. London: Oxford University Press.

Young, Katharine, ed. 1993. *Bodylore*. Knoxville: University of Tennessee Press.

Zimmerman, Bonnie. 1993. Perverse Reading: The Lesbian Appropriation of Literature. In *Sexual Practice, Textual Theory: Lesbian Cultural Criticism*, ed. Susan J. Wolfe and Julia Penelope, 135–49. Cambridge, MA: Blackwell.

Contributors

CYNTHIA BOYD is a self-employed writer and researcher in St John's, Newfoundland, currently researching a Newfoundland gardener and his garden diary.

ANNE BRYDON focuses her research on the social production of perception, discourse, and knowledge as they relate to attitudes toward modernity, nature, nationalism, and gender. This focus has led to investigations of whale hunting, cottage development, ethnic festivals, visual art, architecture, film, travel writing, and fashion consumerism. Despite their apparent diversity, these analyses share a concern with the ways in which self and collective identities are constructed and represented. In fieldwork carried out in Iceland and North America, she traces current debates over environmentalism, nationalism, and consumerism and how they affect perceptions of nature, history, and self. Brydon teaches symbolic anthropology at the University of Western Ontario in London, Canada.

MARIE-ANNICK DESPLANQUES is currently the research coordinator for Folklore and Ethnology at University College Cork where she has set up the Folklore and Ethnology archive and is involved in an urban ethnography project. She received a Ph.D. in folklore from Memorial University of Newfoundland for her research on French Newfoundland women's communicative traditions and was subsequently awarded a postdoctoral fellowship from the Institute for Social and Economic Research in St John's for an Irish/Newfoundland comparative study of contemporary women traditional musicians.

Since obtaining her doctorate in folklore studies at Memorial University of Newfoundland, LAUREL DOUCETTE has been teaching courses in women's studies and in the sociology and anthropology of aging in St John's.

EDITH FOWKE (1913–1996) was probably Canada's best-known folklorist. Her own perspective of her life and career is the subject of her contribution to this volume.

GAIL PATON GRANT was originally a nurse (and social worker). She returned to school while raising her family. While pursuing degrees in anthropology and sociology, she retained her interest in medical matters. Since completing her Ph.D. (University of Waterloo 1988), she has been teaching at the University of Guelph. Her primary focus is the lives of women (including the experience of abuse), the gendering process (including the "myths" of proper womanhood), and medical sociology/anthropology.

PAULINE GREENHILL taught Canadian studies before moving to her current position in women's studies and anthropology at the University of Winnipeg. She is currently working on the definitive biography of Ottoline Willwood, sister of the unjustifiably more famous Otto.

PAMELA E. KLASSEN is a doctoral candidate in Religion and Society at Drew University, and assistant professor in the Department for the Study of Religion at the University of Toronto. She is the author of *Going by the Moon and the Stars: Stories of Two Russian Mennonite Women* (Wilfred Laurier University Press, 1994), and several articles. Her current research focuses on religion and women's experiences of home birth in contemporary North America.

RONALD LABELLE est le responsable des archives de folklore au Centre d'études acadiennes de l'Université de Moncton depuis 1979. Il a aussi été directeur de ce centre de 1988 à 1992. En 1986, il a obtenu le prix France-Acadie pour son volume intitulé *Au Village-du-Bois – Mémoires d'une communauté acadienne*. Il a publié de nombreux travaux ayant trait au folklore et à l'histoire orale en Acadie. Son ouvrage le plus récent s'appelle *The Acadians of Chezzetcook*.

Since 1975, VIVIAN LABRIE has pursued research work on folktales, literacy, bureaucracy, and the dynamics of transitions both in fiction and reality, most of the time as an independent scholar. She is also engaged in the Quebec social change grassroots movement as an animator, thus maintaining a vital link between theory and praxis. Much to her astonishment and pleasure, folktales have constantly provided sound and often the best theoretical explanations and strategic advice available about the ecology of everyday life.

Ethnologist DR BARBARA LE BLANC teaches for the Department of Education at Université Sainte-Anne in Nova Scotia. She has written a number of articles on Acadian culture and a children's book, *L'Acadie en fête*. An upcoming book, *All Join Hands: Traditional Acadian Dances of the Cheticamp Region / Tous ensemble: Les danses traditionnelles de la région de Chéticamp*, prepared in collaboration with Laura Sadowsky, examines the traditional dances of an Acadian area of Nova Scotia. In addition to her academic duties she is president of the Acadian Federation of Nova Scotia and of the Folklore Studies Association of Canada.

JOCELYNE MATHIEU est professeure titulaire en ethnologie des francophones en Amérique du Nord à l'Université Laval. Elle se spécialise en la vie domestique et quotidienne, costume et textiles, manières d'habiter, et méthodologie d'enquête orale de terrain.

ROBIN MCGRATH is a writer living in Beachy Cove, Newfoundland. Her most recent books are a collection of short fiction, *Trouble and Desire* (Killick Press, 1995) and *A Heritage Guide to Portugal Cove-St. Philip's* (Oceanside Press, 1996). Her essay "Cats and Dogs: On Being a Jew in Newfoundland" received the 1996 Newfoundland and Labrador Arts and Letters award for non-fiction. She was the 1996–97 Halbert Chair for Canadian Studies at the Hebrew University of Jerusalem.

BARBARA RIETI has an M.A. in Folklore from the University of California at Berkeley and a Ph.D. in Folklore from Memorial University of Newfoundland. Her book, *Strange Terrain: The Fairy World in Newfoundland*, was awarded the Raymond Klibansky Book Prize for 1993 by the Canadian Federation for the Humanities. She is presently writing a study of Newfoundland witch tradition based on archival sources and field research.

JANICE RISTOCK is associate professor and coordinator of women's studies at the University of Manitoba. She is the co-author, with Joan Pennell, of *Community Research as Empowerment: Feminist Links, Postmodern Interruptions* 1996, Oxford University Press. She has a co-edited volume (with Catherine Taylor) forthcoming from the University of Toronto Press, entitled *Sexualities and Social Action: Inside the Academy and Out*. She continues to do anti-heterosexist work with lesbian and feminist groups.

CHRISTINE ST. PETER is associate professor and chair of the Department of Women's Studies at the University of Victoria. She has taught and published in the areas of women's literature, women's life writing, feminist theory and research methods, and reproductive technologies. She is presently completing a book on contemporary Irish women's fiction, and is co-editor, with Marilyn Porter, of *Atlantis: A Women's Studies Journal*.

SUSAN SHANTZ has previously written about visual culture in *Quilts of Waterloo County: A Sampling* (1989) and *The Stations of the Cross: A Calculated Trap?* (1991). She is also a practicing artist and exhibits her work regularly across Canada and internationally. She holds graduate degrees in Visual Art (M.F.A., York University) and Religion and Culture (M.A., Wilfrid Laurier University) and is currently Associate Professor of studio art at the University of Saskatchewan.

Folklorist and storyteller KAY STONE is professor of folklore in the English department at the University of Winnipeg. She has written numerous articles on women in folktales and on contemporary storytelling. She is currently working on two books, the first on professional storytellers and their tales and the second on dreams, folktales, and life experience stories.

MICHAEL TAFT is the sound and image librarian and director of the Southern Folklife Collection at University of North Carolina, Chapel Hill. He holds a doctorate in folklore from Memorial University of Newfoundland and a masters in library studies from University of Alberta. He has spent many years investigating Canadian folklore, especially in the prairie provinces, and has authored or co-authored a dozen books on various aspects of folklore and oral history.

DIANE TYE is an assistant professor in the Department of Folklore at Memorial University of Newfoundland. Her recent research explores aspects of women's traditional expression in the maritime provinces.

Index